9 01
H27s

70734

DATE DUE			

STUDIES IN

MEDIAEVAL CULTURE

STUDIES IN
MEDIAEVAL CULTURE

BY

CHARLES HOMER HASKINS

FREDERICK UNGAR PUBLISHING CO.

NEW YORK

Library of Congress Catalog Card Number 58-7726

Second Printing, 1965

Reprinted from the first edition, 1929

PRINTED IN THE UNITED STATES OF AMERICA

PREFACE

SO far as these studies in mediaeval culture have a common theme, it is the illustration of mediaeval civilization through the Latin literature of the times. The first three chapters deal with the mediaeval student, as seen in his letters, in sermons and *exempla*, and in the Latin manuals of deportment and conversation prepared for his guidance. The next chapter sketches the channels through which ideas and information spread in the Middle Ages. Chapter V treats of the Latin literature of sport and games, Chapter VI of the impression which the Emperor Frederick II and his court made upon his Latin contemporaries. Science is then touched in a Latin treatise on alchemy ascribed to Frederick's astrologer, Michael Scot. Contacts of the Western world with Byzantium are illustrated in the fields of relic-hunting, doctrinal controversy, hagiology, and the occult. The rise of the new Latin rhetoric of the Middle Ages is briefly traced in Italy and beyond the Alps. Chapters X and XI are concerned with heresy and the Inquisition in Northern France. In the concluding chapter the progress of mediaeval studies in the United States is exemplified by brief memoirs of the two leading American mediaevalists of the past generation, Henry Charles Lea and Charles Gross.

Much of the material comes from manuscripts, much from printed texts of a sort which has received too little attention from historians, so that references to the great editions of the chroniclers are comparatively few (except in Chapter X), and those to the standard collections of theology and law are still fewer. Of course these great repositories of narrative, documentary, and theological texts are fundamental for our knowledge of the structure of mediaeval society and the content of the mediaeval mind, but, taken by themselves, they give too bald and conventional an impression of mediaeval life and thought; and they need to be supplemented not only by vernacular literature and art but also by the more informal and imaginative portions of the Latin literature of the age. Men joked and sang and told stories and made love in Latin, students wrote home for money in Latin, sports and games were described in Latin, astrologers and alchemists foretold the future and tried to make gold in Latin; and all of this is essential to a picture of the totality of mediaeval civilization. This volume seeks to emphasize the importance of these less used sources, as well as the necessity of combined effort on the part of historians, philologists, archaeologists, and other students of the art, philosophy, and literature of the Middle Ages.

Three of the studies have not before been printed, namely, those comprised in Chapters III, IX, and XI, while Chapter VIII is chiefly made up of fragments already published. The other chapters are republished, with detailed revision and sometimes with considerable amplification, from the *American Historical Review*, *Speculum*, *Isis*, and the *Proceedings* of the Massachusetts Historical Society, publications to which the author's thanks are due.

Among the many libraries whose hospitality I have enjoyed in gathering the materials for this volume, my indebtedness is greatest to the authorities of the Bibliothèque Nationale, the Vatican, and the British Museum, not to mention many other collections, consulted by photographs or on the spot, which will be found enumerated in the Index of Manuscripts and Libraries. For personal suggestion and help, my obligations to MM. Charles-Victor Langlois and Henry Omont are deep and of long standing.

To Harvard University I am grateful for grants from the Milton Fund for Research, as well as for President Lowell's personal encouragement of research. To the scholarship and editorial competence of Mr. George W. Robinson and to his unfailing help at all times I owe more than I can hope to express.

The many courtesies of the Clarendon Press are deeply appreciated.

C. H. H.

CAMBRIDGE, MASSACHUSETTS,
    April 1929.

CONTENTS

LIST OF ABBREVIATIONS

A. H. R. . . . . . *American Historical Review.* New York, 1895- .

Archiv (Neues Archiv) *Archiv* (from 1876 *Neues Archiv) der Gesellschaft für ältere deutsche Geschichtskunde.* Frankfort, etc., 1820–24; Hanover, etc., 1838- .

B. E. C. . . . . . *Bibliothèque de l'École des Chartes.* Paris, 1839- .

B.M. . . . . . British Museum.

B.N. . . . . . Bibliothèque Nationale, Paris.

E. H. R. . . . . *English Historical Review.* London, 1886- .

Hauréau . . . . Barthélemy Hauréau, *Notices et extraits de quelques manuscrits latins de la Bibliothèque Nationale.* Paris, 1890–93. 6 vols.

H. F. . . . . . . *Recueil des historiens des Gaules et de la France.* Paris, 1738- .

MS. lat. . . . . Bibliothèque Nationale, MS. lat.

Mediaeval Science . C. H. Haskins, *Studies in the History of Mediaeval Science,* 2d ed. Cambridge, Mass., 1927.

Migne, *P. L.* . . . *Patrologiae cursus completus,* accurante J. P. Migne. Series prima, secunda. [*Patrologia Latina.*] Paris, 1844–64.

M. I. O. G. . . . *Mittheilungen des Instituts für Oesterreichische Geschichtsforschung.* Innsbruck, etc., 1880- .

Notices et extraits . . *Notices et extraits des manuscrits de la Bibliothèque Nationale et autres bibliothèques, publiés par l'Institut National de France.* Paris, 1787- .

Q. E. . . . . . *Quellen und Erörterungen zur bayerischen und deutschen Geschichte.* Munich, 1856- .

SS. . . . . . *Monumenta Germaniae Historica. Scriptores.* Hanover, 1826- .

S. B. . . . . . *Sitzungsberichte* of the Berlin, Heidelberg, Munich, and Vienna Academies. Unless otherwise stated the philosophisch-historische Klasse is understood.

CHAPTER I

THE LIFE OF MEDIAEVAL STUDENTS AS ILLUSTRATED BY THEIR LETTERS[1]

THE early history of universities is one of the most interesting and fruitful of the many questions of origins with which historical inquiry has in recent years been occupied. Through the efforts of Denifle, Rashdall, and others, the subject of mediaeval universities has been lifted out of the realm of myth and tradition and placed upon a solid basis of established fact, so that, while many perplexing problems still remain unsolved, we can now trace with measurable confidence the main outlines of their early development. As yet, investigation has centred chiefly about what may be called the anatomy of the mediaeval university and its external history—its privileges and organization, its relations to king and pope, and similar questions—while much less attention has been given to its inner life and history or to the daily life and occupations of its students, topics manifestly of the greatest importance if we are to form an accurate and comprehensive idea of what a university of the Middle Ages really was. The life of mediaeval students is, however, a large and complex subject, exhibiting wide differences at different times and in different places, and no treatment of it will be in any sense adequate which does not rest on the detailed study and comparison of the conditions at each centre of learning and the changes they underwent at different periods. Such an investigation demands the careful examination of a great variety of sources, literary, documentary, and narrative, which are at present in large measure unpublished and whose value and interest for this purpose are by no means generally understood.[2]

[1] Revised and expanded from *American Historical Review*, iii. 203–229 (1898).

[2] For a good example, see Guido Zaccagnini, *La vita dei maestri e degli scolari nello Studio di Bologna nei secoli XIII e XIV* (Geneva, 1926), who draws in part from unpublished material, and prints in an appendix various student letters from a collection of Pietro de' Boattieri. See below, p. 7, note.

On the proper methods to be followed in studying the history of mediaeval civilization, too often treated in a dilettante and uncritical fashion, see the excellent observations of Langlois in the *Revue historique*, lxiii. 246 ff. (1897).

The present chapter is designed to call attention to one class of these sources, student letters, and to point out how far they throw light on the academic conditions of their time.

The intellectual life of the Middle Ages was not characterized by spontaneous or widely diffused power of literary expression. Few were able to write, still fewer could compose a letter, and the professional scribes and notaries on whom devolved the greater part of the labour of mediaeval correspondence fastened upon the letter-writing of the period the stereotyped formalism of a conventional rhetoric. Regular instruction in the composition of letters and official acts was given in the schools and chanceries, and numerous professors, called *dictatores*, went about from place to place teaching this valuable art—"often and exceeding necessary for the clergy, for monks suitable, and for laymen honourable," as one rhetorician tells us.[1] Beginning with the latter part of the eleventh century we find brief manuals of epistolography in which definite rules of composition are laid down and the order and form of the various parts of a letter fixed.[2] According to the usual theory there should be five parts

[1] Albert of Samaria, in L. von Rockinger, *Q. E.*, ix. 84.

[2] On mediaeval treatises on rhetoric and collections of forms in general (*artes dictaminis, summae dictaminis*, etc.), see W. Wattenbach, "Ueber Briefsteller des Mittelalters," *Archiv für Kunde österreichischer Geschichtsquellen*, xiv. 29–94 (an appendix to his article "Iter Austriacum 1853"); Rockinger, *Ueber Formelbücher vom dreizehnten bis zum sechszehnten Jahrhundert als rechtsgeschichtliche Quellen* (Munich, 1855); id., *Ueber Briefsteller und Formelbücher in Deutschland während des Mittelalters* (Munich, 1861); id., *Ueber die* ars dictandi *und die* summae dictaminis *in Italien*, *S. B.* of the Munich Academy, 1861, i. 98 ff.; id., *Briefsteller und Formelbücher des eilften bis vierzehnten Jahrhunderts*, in *Q. E.*, ix (the fullest single collection); N. Valois, *De arte scribendi epistolas apud Gallicos Medii Aevi scriptores rhetoresve* (Paris thesis, 1880); A. Gaudenzi, "Sulla cronologia delle opere dei dettatori Bolognesi," in *Bullettino dell' Istituto Storico Italiano*, xiv. 85–174; C.-V. Langlois, "Formulaires de lettres du XIIᵉ, du XIIIᵉ, et du XIVᵉ siècle," in *Notices et extraits*, xxxiv, xxxv, 1890–96; A. Bütow, *Die Entwicklung der mittelalterlichen Briefsteller bis zur Mitte des 12. Jahrhunderts, mit besonderer Berücksichtigung der Theorieen der* Ars dictandi (Greifswald diss., 1908); G. Manacorda, *Storia della scuola in Italia*, i, 2 (1914), pp. 255–279; C. S. Baldwin, *Medieval Rhetoric and Poetic* (New York, 1928), ch. 8.

An excellent brief survey of the subject is given by H. Bresslau, *Handbuch der Urkundenlehre*, ii, 1 (1915), pp. 225–281, who brings the bibliography down to 1915. On subsequent German publications, see K. Burdach, *Schlesisch-Böhmische Briefmuster aus der Wende des Vierzehnten Jahrhunderts* (Berlin,

arranged in logical sequence. After the salutation—as to which the etiquette of the mediaeval scribe was very exacting, each class in society having its own terms of address and reply— came the exordium, consisting of some commonplace generality, a proverb, or a scriptural quotation, and designed to put the reader in the proper frame of mind for granting the request to follow. Then came the statement of the particular purpose of the letter (the narration), ending in a petition which commonly has the form of a deduction from the major and minor premises laid down in the exordium and narration, and finally the phrases of the conclusion.

The construction of a letter in accordance with this elaborate scheme was, however, possible only for those who had attained some proficiency in the epistolary art; for the ordinary man the writing of a letter meant, not the composition of an original epistle of his own, but the laborious copying of a letter of some one else, altered where necessary to suit the new conditions. It is in this way that the greater part of mediaeval correspondence has come down to us, preserved not as personal mementoes or sources of historical information, but as models for future letter-writers. Frequently these models would be copied and added to until they grew into considerable collections, which might find use as independent compilations of forms or be joined as illustrations to the various current treatises on the art of composition. It must not be supposed that all of the letters contained in these useful collections were actual pieces of correspondence. The authors of rhetorical manuals did not hesitate to compose models of their own or to incorporate exercises of their pupils, possible letters, but not actual ones, and they needed to make large use of such inventions when they proposed, as did many, to provide 'complete letter-writers' containing examples suited to every station and condition in life. Where real letters were used the names were often omitted or altered beyond recognition, while sometimes bits of pure fancy—letters to or

1926), p. 7; and in general, see the current notices in the *Neues Archiv*. For the early development of the art in Italy, see Chapter IX, below; and for the reign of Frederick II, Chapter VI.

from Venus, Lent, Rhetoric, the Devil, and similar personages [1]
—would find their way into these strange compilations.

It is evident that the collections of letters which have come
down to us from the Middle Ages differ widely in character and
contents and, consequently, in the nature of the information
they afford the historian. The correspondence of known indi-
viduals has obviously a very different value from a series of
anonymous or invented models, and the difficulty of distinguishing the real from the fictitious is one reason for the relatively
small use that has been made of these formularies. While,
however, the student of diplomatics in his search for authentic
and datable acts cannot exercise too great caution in utilizing
material of this sort,[2] the danger to the student of social conditions is much less. To him a possible letter may yield as valuable information as an actual letter, provided he can satisfy
himself as to the place and time of its composition and the good
faith of its author. He will not seek in these formulae trustworthy details of biography or of political history, but he may
well expect them to reflect faithfully, because unconsciously,
the conditions of the age in which they were composed, and thus
add to the stock of material, none too large at best, available
for the history of mediaeval civilization. The models were
written to be used; and the more closely they corresponded to
the needs of the user the greater the popularity of the *dictator*
and his manual. Most of all is this true in models relating to
student affairs, since the collections of forms and the treatises
on rhetoric were generally put together in the schools and for

[1] See the interesting paper of Wattenbach, "Ueber erfundene Briefe in
Handschriften des Mittelalters besonders Teufelsbriefe," in the *S. B.* of the
Berlin Academy, 1892, pp. 91–123. Exercises of this sort occur frequently;
several are mentioned by Valois, p. 43, from MS. lat. 1093 of the Bibliothèque
Nationale, and examples may be seen in Wattenbach, "Iter Austriacum,"
p. 92; *Fontes rerum Austriacarum*, second series, xxv. 466; *Rendiconti dei
Lincei* (1888), iv, 2, p. 404; *Oxford Collectanea*, i. 42–49; Chapter VI, below,
pp. 137–139.
[2] On this question, and particularly on the necessity of examining each collection as a whole before utilizing any of the documents it contains, see Wattenbach, "Iter Austriacum," and "Ueber erfundene Briefe"; Pflugk-Harttung,
in *Forschungen zur deutschen Geschichte*, xxiv. 198; Delisle, *Catalogue des Actes
de Philippe-Auguste*, p. xxx; Bresslau, ii, 1, pp. 225–226.

the use of scholars—some of the most famous are directly connected with Orleans and Bologna—so that even where they were the product of direct invention they would be likely to represent correctly the life of the academic environment in which they arose.

The number of extant letters and forms of letters which concern the life of the mediaeval student is very great. Of the hundreds of formularies and collections of letters preserved in the larger European libraries, probably the greater number contain some reference to student affairs, and several seem to have been composed with special regard to the needs of students and their parents. All kinds of schools and all parts of Europe are here represented: cathedral schools like Hildesheim [1] and Chartres,[2] lower schools like those of Arbois[3] and Saint-Denis,[4] and nearly all the important university centres—Bologna, Pavia, Padua, and Naples, [5] Vienna and Leipzig, Prague and Erfurt and Louvain, Oxford and Cambridge, Salamanca, Toulouse, Montpellier, Orleans, and Paris. An exhaustive critical study of this mass of student correspondence is not at present possible, as the greater part of it is still unpublished and many

[1] H. Sudendorf, *Registrum*, iii. 30–36. Cf. the exercises from Worms, likewise of the eleventh century, in Pflugk-Harttung, *Iter Italicum*, pp. 382–389. For later letters from Hildesheim, see B. Stehle, *Über ein Hildesheimer Formelbuch* (Sigmaringen, 1878), and Otto Heinemann, "Hildesheimer Briefformeln des zwölften Jahrhunderts," in *Zeitschrift des Historischen Vereins für Niedersachsen*, 1896, pp. 79–114.

[2] *B. E. C.*, 1855, pp. 454 ff.; Wattenbach, "Iter Austriacum," p. 44. The schools of Rheims are mentioned in a MS. of the Bodleian (Laud Misc. 569, f. 187) which contains a version of the treatise known as the *Aurea gemma*: 'Remensi studio legum—*vel* dialetice—alacriter et sane die noctuque adherere.' Rheims is here substituted for the Pavia of the original model of Henricus Francigena (cf. *Archiv*, ix. 632; *Zeitschrift der Savigny-Stiftung für Rechtsgeschichte*, vii, romanistische Abtheilung, 2, p. 66). Cf. Chapter IX, no. 4.

[3] MS. lat. 8653A; a student's notebook of the fourteenth century from Arbois in Franche-Comté, containing, besides a collection of proverbs and a vocabulary (published by U. Robert in the *B. E. C.*, xxxiv. 33–46), a number of forms of correspondence composed about the year 1316. Some relate to the schools of Arbois, others to scholars from Besançon studying at Orleans. Cf. *Histoire littéraire*, xxxii. 274–278.

[4] Letters in MS. lat. 15131, ff. 177–189. According to Hauréau, iv. 267 ff., they were composed by the schoolmaster of Saint-Denis; some of them refer to Orleans.

[5] *Infra*, Chapter VI, p. 135; *Mélanges Ferdinand Lot* (Paris, 1925), p. 246.

of the manuscripts have not been catalogued, while the sources
of the various letters and the relations of the collections to one
another have yet in most cases to be determined. The present
inquiry was originally restricted to printed works and to the
manuscripts of Paris, Munich,[1] London, and Oxford; it has been
extended to other collections, as opportunity has arisen, so that
the material examined has been sufficient to make the results
reasonably representative.[2]

[1] Student letters of the fifteenth century might form the basis of a special
investigation for some one who has easy access to German and Austrian
libraries.

[2] In order to present the results of the study in compact form, only the more
significant letters are printed, and many of these only in extract. In general
the quotations from manuscripts are published just as they stand in the
original; the occasional emendations necessary to render a passage intelligible
are noted wherever they have been made. If more than one MS. is mentioned,
the text is that of the first. The necessity for compression has prevented any
extended discussion of the nature of the different formularies utilized, but the
date and place have been noted in each instance. In the case of MSS. cited
but once or twice this information is given in connexion with the citation;
some collections, however, are referred to so frequently that they can be most
conveniently described once for all. They are:

Bernard de Meung, a *dictator* from the region of Orleans, author of an *Ars
dictaminis* of the close of the twelfth century which is found in a great number
of MSS., often with an appendix of models which vary in the different redactions, although the student letters are much the same throughout. See Langlois in *B. E. C.*, liv. 225 ff. (1893). Cf. particularly A. Cartellieri, *Ein Donaueschinger Briefsteller: Lateinische Stilübungen des XII. Jahrhunderts aus der
Orléans'schen Schule* (Innsbruck, 1898); Delisle, "Notice sur une 'summa dictaminis' jadis conservée à Beauvais," in *Notices et extraits*, xxxvi; Haskins, "An
Italian Master Bernard," in *Essays Presented to R. L. Poole*, pp. 211–226.

Rudolfus Turonensis, the supposed author of a *Summa dictaminis* preserved
in Munich, Cod. Lat. 6911, and printed in part by Rockinger, *Q. E.*, ix. 95–
114, who assigns it to the close of the twelfth century. The student letters
relate chiefly to Paris. The incomplete collection in MS. lat. 14069, ff. 181–
204 v, contains many of the same forms as the foregoing; the other models
concern chiefly the diocese of Mainz and are of the first half of the thirteenth
century. The date and authorship of the Munich MS. are discussed by H.
Simonsfeld in the Munich *S. B.*, 1898, i. 402–486.

Buoncompagno, professor at Bologna and author of numerous rhetorical
works of which the *Antiqua rhetorica*, composed in 1215, is the most important
for student affairs. A partial list of MSS. will be found in K. Sutter, *Aus Leben
und Schriften des Magisters Buoncompagno* (Freiburg i. B., 1894), p. 24; I have
used Munich, Cod. Lat. 23499; MSS. lat. 8654, 7732, and 7731; and B.M.,
Cotton MS. Vitellius C. viii. The table of contents of the *Antiqua rhetorica* is
published by Rockinger, *Q. E.*, ix. 133 ff.; cf. also *M. I. O. G.*, ii. 225–264.
The *Rhetorica novissima* has been edited by A. Gaudenzi in the *Bibliotheca*

By far the largest element in the correspondence of mediaeval students consists of requests for money—"a student's first song

iuridica medii aevi, ii. 249–297 (Bologna, 1892). On Buoncompagno's life and writings see the above mentioned monograph of Sutter, and particularly Gaudenzi in the *Bullettino dell'Istituto Storico Italiano*, xiv. 85 ff.

Guido Faba, a younger contemporary and rival of Buoncompagno. On the chronology of his life and writings see Gaudenzi in the monograph just cited. The forms of Faba were less bizarre than those of Buoncompagno and hence were more widely copied and imitated; the collections which contain material on student affairs have been published by Gaudenzi as follows: *Dictamina rhetorica* (1226–27), in *Il Propugnatore*, new series, v, 1, pp. 86–129; v, 2, pp. 58–109; *Epistole* (1239–41), *ibid.*, vi, 1, pp. 359–390; vi, 2, pp. 373–389; *Parlamenti ed epistole* (1242–43), in Gaudenzi, *I Suoni, le forme e le parole dell' odierno dialetto della Città di Bologna* (Turin, 1889), pp. 127–160. I have also examined the copy of the *Parlamenti* in B.M., Add. MS. 33221, which Gaudenzi does not appear to have seen. The models of Faba form the basis of a collection of the fifteenth century from Salamanca in MS. lat. 11386, ff. 55–60, and of a compilation from Orleans now at Avignon (MS. 831).

For the Bolognese *dictatores* of the succeeding period, see Zaccagnini, "Giovanni di Bonandrea dettatore e rimatore e altri grammatici e dottori in arti dello Studio Bolognese," in *Studi e memorie per la storia dell' Università di Bologna*, v. 145–204 (1920); "Le epistole in Latino e in volgare di Pietro de' Boattieri," *ibid.*, viii. 211–248 (1924); and "Grammatici e dettatori a Bologna," in *Il libro e la stampa*, n.s., vi. 113–132 (1912). Cf. G. Bertoni, *Il duecento* (Milan, 1911), pp. 145–150, 278 f., 295 f. Student letters from Bologna occur frequently in Italian manuscripts of the fourteenth century: e.g., Vatican, MS. Ott. lat. 1848 (Ugoninus Eugubinus); Florence, Biblioteca Riccardiana, MS. 669, ff. 288–307 (Iohannes Odonelli vocatus Batista de Sancto Iohanne Marianensi nativus sed studii Bononiensis alumpnus); University of Pavia, MS. 176, f. 22–22 v. See also J. Klapper, "Ein schlesisches Formelbuch des 14. Jahrhunderts," in *Zeitschrift des Vereins für Geschichte Schlesiens*, lx. 157–177 (1926).

Ponce de Provence, author of a well known *Summa de dictamine*, to which is joined a collection of letters dedicated to the students of Orleans. There are two redactions, dated 1249 and 1252. I have used the following MSS.: MSS. lat. 18595, 8653 (ff. 1–212), 11385; Bibliothèque de l'Arsenal at Paris, MSS. 3807, 1132; B.M., Arundel MS. 514, f. 54 (apparently the best text); Munich, Cod. Lat. 22293, f. 278 (redaction made in Germany in the fourteenth century); Troyes, MS. 1556. There are brief extracts in Munich, Cod. Lat. 16122, f. 11 v–16 v; other MSS. are in Arras (MS. 433), Vienna (MS. 2512), at the Laurentian in Florence (MS. Ashburnham 1545), and in the Archives of Aragon at Barcelona (MS. Ripoll 190). The beginning of a version composed for the students of Toulouse is in MS. lat. 11386, f. 13.

Laurentius of Aquileia (or rather from Cividale in the neighbourhood of Aquileia—cf. J. Loserth in *Neues Archiv*, xxii. 300) was one of the most prominent of the travelling rhetoricians of the type of Ponce de Provence. From his pompous addresses to students we learn that he visited Bologna, Naples, and Paris, while the models mention also Orleans and Toulouse. The student letters are rhetorical and commonplace and are generally adapted as well to

is a demand for money," says a weary father in an Italian
letter-writer, "and there will never be a letter which does not
ask for cash."[1] How to secure this fundamental necessity of
student life was doubtless one of the most important problems
that confronted the mediaeval scholar, and many were the
models which the *dictatores* placed before him in proof of the
practical advantages of their art.[2] The letters are generally

one university as to another. I have used MSS. lat. 11384 (ff. 1–78 v), 14174
(f. 16 v and foll.), 14766 (ff. 108–122), 16253 (ff. 5 v–26 v); B.M., Harleian
MS. 3593 (composed at Paris and dedicated to Philip the Fair). See *Speculum*, i. 102.

The Formulary of Tréguier, composed in the diocese of Tréguier in lower
Brittany about 1315 and now in the Bibliothèque Nationale (MS. lat. n.a. 426).
The letters relating to students at Orleans have been published by Delisle, *Le
formulaire de Tréguier et les écoliers Bretons à Orléans*, in volume xxiii of the
Mémoires de la Société Archéologique et Historique de l'Orléanais and separately ;
seven of them are reprinted by M. Fournier in the appendix to the third
volume of his *Statuts et privilèges des Universités Françaises*. See also the *Histoire littéraire*, xxxi. 25–35; and René Prigent, "Le formulaire de Tréguier," in
École des Chartes, *Positions des thèses*, 1921, pp. 95–97.

MS. lat. 8661, f. 95 and foll., succeeding a copy of Guido Faba and bearing
the heading, 'Quedam epistola de curtisia quesita a quodam canonico.' The
series of letters has to do chiefly with city affairs in the Romagna and the
Marches toward the middle of the thirteenth century. This seems to be the
collection alluded to by Gaudenzi, *Bullettino dell'Istituto*, xiv. 174, which he
dates *ca.* 1245.

Bibliothèque de l'Arsenal, MS. 854. M. Ch.-V. Langlois kindly called my
attention to a number of student letters contained in this MS., ff. 217–244,
dating from the early fourteenth century and relating to the University of
Toulouse. They are preceded, ff. 214–216, by a group of letters from Orleans
which belong to the close of the thirteenth century.

Munich, Cod. Lat. 2649, ff. 34–53. A treatise ('De arte dictandi breviter et
lucide . . .') with anonymous models belonging to the end of the thirteenth
century and dealing principally with Thuringian affairs.

Tarragona, MS. 6, ff. 17–96. Forms from France, England, and Italy of the
time of Gregory IX, with student letters from Orleans and Bologna. I hope
soon to publish a special study of this MS.

Archives of the Crown of Aragon, MS. Ripoll 190, ff. 73 v–84 (of 1326).
Student letters from Lérida and other places in this region.

Primum carmen scolarium est petitio expensarum, nec umquam erit epistola que non requirit argentum.' Buoncompagno, *Antiqua rhetorica*, in MS.
lat. 8654, f. 14 v; MS. lat. 7732, f. 9 v; Munich, Cod. Lat. 23499, f. 8 v.

[2] There is a decided sameness in the contents of letters of this kind, and
only the most interesting are given here. Examples of more commonplace
types may be found in Rockinger, *Q. E.*, ix. 71, 81, 372, 487; id., *Ueber Brief-steller*, p. 40; Guido Faba, *Dictamina rhetorica*, nos. 1, 22, 24, 63, *Epistole*, nos.
66 and 67, *Parlamenti ed epistole*, no. 83; Delisle, *Le Formulaire de Tréguier*,

addressed to parents, sometimes to brothers, uncles, or ecclesiastical patrons—a much copied exercise contained twenty-two different methods of approaching an archdeacon on this ever delicate subject.[1] Commonly the student announces that he is

nos. 1, 12, 16, 19; S. Günthner, *Geschichte der literarischen Anstalten in Baiern*, i. 217, 230; L. Biondi, *Le Dicerie di Ser Filippo Ceffi* (Turin, 1825), p. 65. Cf. also the authentic letters of Gui de Bazoches from Montpellier, *Neues Archiv*, xvi. 76, 77.

The manner of constructing one of these letters may be seen by the following extract from an anonymous treatise in the British Museum (Add. MS. 18382, f. 59): 'Assumatur ergo tale tema, quod quidam Parisius insistens studiis et nimis pauperrime vivens litteras dirigat matri sue ut in rebus neccessariis sibi provideat. Assumendum est *proverbium* in hunc modum: Mater moribus redolet novercam que filii non sublevat egestatem. *Nar*.: Diu est quod Parisius studiis inservivi et nummos meos in usus neccessarios iam expendi. *Petitio*: Mihi igitur necessaria propinetis et sic egestatem meam expensis minimis munere sublevetis. Ultimum *proverbium*: Domesticum est enim matri ut filio subveniat indigenti.' A similar example is found in Munich, Cod. Lat. 2649, f. 38 v, printed in a slightly different form by Rockinger, *Ueber Briefsteller*, p. 40. See also Langlois, *Formulaires de lettres*, iv. 14. The rhetorical elaboration of a simple letter of this sort is illustrated in Rockinger, *Q. E.*, ix. 487.

This commonplace of mediaeval student existence is also treated in verse. See *Carmina Burana*, p. 50; *Anzeiger für Kunde der deutschen Vorzeit* (1873), xx. 8; and particularly the poetical *dictamina* of Matthew of Vendôme, published by Wattenbach in the *S. B.* of the Munich Academy for 1872, pp. 561–631, which contain much interesting information on the student life of the twelfth century. Another begging letter of the same author is in M. Haupt's *Exempla poesis Latinae Medii Aevi* (Vienna, 1834), p. 31.

[1] Published by H. Bärwald in *Fontes rerum Austriacarum*, second series, xxv. 455–464, from a fourteenth-century MS. in Vienna. The earliest occurrence of this exercise that I have found is in a treatise in the Bibliothèque Nationale, MS. lat. 16252, ff. 39–41 v, composed, it would appear from the names on f. 34 v, between the years 1243 and 1249. Other copies are in MS. lat. 14357, f. 129 v (fourteenth century), and Munich, Cod. Lat. 5319, f. 182 v (fifteenth century).

Petitions to ecclesiastical dignitaries are usually either requests from students for benefices or petitions from beneficed priests for leave of absence for purposes of study, such leave to carry with it, of course, the enjoyment of the fruits of the living. Examples of such letters and the replies are common : e.g., Guido Faba, *Epistole*, nos. 25, 26; *Dict. rhet.*, nos. 88, 89; Historical MSS. Commission, *Fourth Report*, pp. 380, 394; *Codex diplomaticus Silesiae*, v. 161; Langlois, *Formulaires de lettres*, iv. 7; *Register of Archbishop Peckham* (Rolls Series), i. 3, 8; *Registrum Palatinum Dunelmense* (Rolls Series), iii. 307; Cartellieri, *Ein Donaueschinger Briefsteller*, nos. 257, 258. One poor scholar at Paris seeks to regain the favour of the prior of Canterbury by telling him about a highly useful book which he is so fortunate as to possess, "a summary of canon and civil law, called *tabula iuris*," and most jealously guarded by the Minorites. Historical MSS. Commission, *Various Collections*, i. 278 f. (1901).

at such and such a centre of learning, well and happy but in desperate need of money for books and other necessary expenses. Here is a specimen from Oxford, somewhat more individual than the average and written in uncommonly bad Latin:[1]

> B. to his venerable master A., greeting. This is to inform you that I am studying at Oxford with the greatest diligence, but the matter of money stands greatly in the way of my promotion, as it is now two months since I spent the last of what you sent me. The city is expensive and makes many demands; I have to rent lodgings, buy necessaries, and provide for many other things which I cannot now specify. Wherefore I respectfully beg your paternity that by the promptings of divine pity you may assist me, so that I may be able to complete what I have well begun. For you must know that without Ceres and Bacchus Apollo grows cold. . . .[2]

A more permanent provision is suggested by a Paris student, who wants to receive from Saint-Victor's ten loaves of bread a week, besides a mattress and sixpence.[3] Sometimes the supplies needed—books and parchment, clothing, linen, bedding, etc.—are sought directly from home.[4] In an interesting set of

[1] The text of the formularies of the Middle Ages is frequently quite corrupt; in many cases it is clear that the copyists did not understand the meaning of what they wrote. Langlois, *Formulaires de lettres*, v. 26, note.

[2] 'Venerabili domino suo A., B. salutem. Noverit universitas vestra quod ego Oxonie studeo cum summa diligencia, sed moneta promocionem meam multum impedit. Iam enim due mense transacte sunt ex quos mihi misisti expendidi [!]. Villa enim cara est et multa exigit; oportet hospicium conducere et utensilia emere et de multis aliis extra predicta que ad presens non possum nominare. Quare paternitati vestre pie suplico quatinus divine pietatis intuitu mihi succuratis, ut possim includere quod bene incoavi. Sciatis quod sine Cerere et Bacone frigescit Apollo (cf. Terence, *Eunuchus*, iv, 5, 6). Quare tum facite ut vobis mediantibus incoatum bene possim terminare. Vale.' B.M., Add. MS. 8167, f. 104 (collection dating from 1220 or soon after). Cf. H. Kalbfuss, "Eine Bologneser Ars Dictandi des XII. Jahrhunderts," in *Quellen und Forschungen*, xvi, 2, p. 33, nos. xlvi, xlix (Bologna).

[3] Angers, MS. 312, f. 18 v.

[4] 'Linea mea vestimenta simul lectisternia, pro studii oportunitate a vobis mihi longe procurata, iam a vetustate temporis corosa tendunt annichilari,' says a student at Vienna, and he asks for others, in order that 'me honesto more cum ceteris bursalibus valeam conservare'; Munich, Cod. Lat. 11799, f. 121 (fifteenth century). 'Mutatoria ac pelles' is the demand in the formulary of Hugh of Bologna (*Neues Archiv*, xxii. 300), while in the poetical *dictamina* of Matthew of Vendôme (ed. Wattenbach, p. 624) the student begs:
>> Delegare mihi mantilia, lintea, bracas
>> Accelera, matrem talia dona decent.

The needs of a student at Paris are thus stated in a monastic letter-writer

letters written from Chartres at the beginning of the twelfth century and quite unspoiled by the phrases of the rhetoricians, we find two brothers asking their mother for thick lambskins for winter clothing, parchment for making a psalter, their father's great boots, and some chalk, good chalk, since theirs is worth nothing.[1] A canon of Rouen sends his nephews ten sous, ten ells of linen cloth, a split ham, and a measure of white peas.[2] A Vienna student who writes to his father N., citizen of Klosterneuburg, that he has spent his money for books and other things that pertain to learning, receives in reply "by this present messenger ten Rhenish gulden, seven ells of cloth for a cloak, and one pair of hose."[3]

If the father was close-fisted, there were special reasons to be urged: the town was dear—as university towns always are!—the price of living was exceptionally high owing to a hard winter,[4] a threatened siege,[5] a failure of crops,[6] or an unusual number of

of the fourteenth century at Troyes (MS. 1992, f. 67): 'Parisiensis equidem scolaris non ad victum solum denariis indiget, sed ad multa, sicut libros emendos, ad exemplaria conducenda, ad pergamenum ceteraque necessaria que conveniunt ad notandum.'

[1] *B. E. C.*, 1855, pp. 454–455. Cf. A. Clerval, *Les écoles de Chartres au Moyen Âge* (Chartres, 1895), pp. 194, 195, 216–218; and R. L. Poole, "The Masters of the Schools at Paris and Chartres in John of Salisbury's Time," in *E. H. R.*, xxxv. 321–342 (1920). The elder brother, Arnaud, was dean of the chapter, and the younger, Jacques, was studying in the cathedral school.

[2] A. Luchaire, *Études sur quelques manuscrits de Rome et de Paris* (Paris, 1899), p. 120, no. 71.

[3] 'Dem allerliebsten so ich in auf erden hab, dem N. purger zu Newburg. . . . Das gelt das ir mir geben habt, das hab ich nun vertzert und hab mir auch davon pücher gekaufft und auch ander ding das zu der lernung gehört. . . .'

'Meinem hertzen lieben Sun N., studenten zu Wien. . . . Darumb, lieber Sun, sende ich dir pei disem gegenwartige poten x gulden reinisch und vii ellen tuch zu einem mantl und j parhosen.' Munich, Cod. Lat. 11799, ff. 4–5 (a brief collection of German *dictamina, ca.* 1447).

[4] 'Pro yemali frigore magis expendidi.' B.M., Harl. MS. 4993, f. 19 (a brief treatise, with examples, by an Oxford scholar, Thomas Sampson, dating in its present form from 1420 or thereabouts).

[5] 'Cum propter imperatoris adventum, quem Bononienses trepidanter exspectant, Bononia facta sit cara in victualibus ultra modum.' Guido Faba, *Epist.*, no. 6. Cf. Thymo of Erfurt in B.M., Arundel MS. 240, f. 123. So a foreign student in France asks for money at once because none can reach him after Easter, when war with England is to begin. Munich, Cod. Lat. 96, f. 38 v.

[6] 'Per grandinem et per alias tempestates importunas annone per totam

scholars; [1] the last messenger had been robbed [2] or had ab-
sconded with the money; [3] the son could borrow no more of his
fellows or of the Jews; he has been ill with the cold, and
tempted to run away; [4] the cold is so great that he cannot
study at night; [5] and so on. The student's woes are depicted

Thuringiam (MS. Thuringia) perierunt, ex quo caristia invaluit satis magna.'
Munich, Cod. Lat. 14660, f. 71 v: letter from Erfurt in a Silesian formulary of
the fourteenth century. Cf. M. Unterlauff in *Zeitschrift für Geschichte und
Alterthum Schlesiens*, xxvii. 310 ff. (1893). 'Propter ingruentem caristiam
temporis que in partibus supra modum invaluit gallicanis, non solum omnem
pecuniam quam mihi misistis utiliter iam expendi, sed etiam libros meos coactus sum pingnori obligare nomine usurarum.' Vienna, MS. 637, f. 74 (Orleans,
saec. xiii).

[1] So at Laon early in the twelfth century, according to the letter of an
Italian student, 'multis clericis Laudunum adventantibus, vix inveniri valde
cara poterunt.' *B. E. C.*, 1855, p. 466. A similar statement regarding Paris
toward the close of the twelfth century is in B. Pez, *Thesaurus anecdotorum*,
vi, 1, col. 427. In the *Dictamina rhetorica* of Guido Faba, no. 38, the citizens
of Bologna are accused of concealing the abundance which God has given
them and thus creating an artificial scarcity.

Uncommon dearness is a frequent excuse and comes from every quarter.
Thus, besides the passages just cited, we find for Bologna Guido Faba, *Dict.
rhet.*, no. 1; for Paris, Laurentius of Aquileia in MS. lat. 16523, f. 16, and
Rockinger, *Q. E.*, ix. 961; for Toulouse, Laurentius in MS. lat. 11384, f. 44, and
MS. lat. 14174, f. 26 v; for Vienna, Munich, Cod. Lat. 5667, f. 188 (MS. of the
year 1404); for Faenza, an extract in *Bullettino dell'Istituto Storico Italiano*,
xiv. 173; for Arbois in Franche-Comté, MS. lat. 8653A, f. 1 v; for Oxford,
B.M., Harleian MS. 670, f. 26 (fifteenth century); for Lérida, Archives of the
Crown of Aragon, MS. Ripoll 190, f. 74; etc. In how many cases a real
scarcity existed it would be impossible to say; Gaudenzi, *Bullettino dell' Istituto
Storico Italiano*, xiv. 131, thinks the model of Guido Faba (*Dict. rhet.*, no. 1)
refers to the severe famine of 1226–27.

[2] Munich, Cod. Lat. 22373, f. 207 (collection of the fifteenth century relating
to Prague).

[3] 'Reverendo patri suo ac per omnia merito diligendo A. suus filius studens
Parisius, filialis dilectionis constanciam et utriusque vite salutem. Paternitati
vestre reverende notum esse cupio quod cum nuncios Parisius mihi destina-
veritis cum equis et aliquanta pecunia [MS. aliquantam pecuniam], ex inoptato
eventu rerum se subtraxit unus nunciorum cum .x. maricis et cum equo qui
fuit ad valorem estimatus .c. maricarum, qui, ut dicitur, postmodum inter-
fectus fuit. Unde sicut multis positus anxietatibus, cum non possim habere
Parisius credenciam aliquam, supplico benignitati vestre quatinus alium equum
et pecuniam mihi sine obstaculo dilacionis aliquam mihi transmittatis, ne
tanquam feminam oporteat effugere et tanquam scirram vagari me contingat
aliqua dierum ad confusionem meam et vestrum opprobrium in vestra facie
comparere.' MS. lat. 14069, f. 194 v.

[4] Luchaire, *Études*, p. 135, no. 142.

[5] 'Tantum frigus nunc Cremone intenditur quod sine lessione pestifera noc-

in moving language, with many appeals to paternal vanity and affection. At Bologna we hear of the terrible mud through which the youth must beg his way from door to door, crying, "O good masters," and receiving nothing save a few scraps of refuse from the townsfolk and a "God go with you!" from his fellow students.[1] Another student blows on his frosty fingers while he remarks that it is two years since he has tasted wine, washed his face, or trimmed his beard.[2] In an Austrian formulary a scholar writes from the lowest depths of prison, where the bread is hard and mouldy, the drinking-water mixed with tears, the darkness so dense that it can actually be felt.[3] Another lies on straw with no covering, goes without shoes or shirt, and eats he will not say what—a tale designed to be addressed to a sister and to bring in response a hundred sous *tournois*, two pairs of sheets, and ten ells of fine cloth, all sent without her husband's

turno tempore non surgo in libris vigillare nimia paucitate pannorum.' *Floralius* from Modena, 1284, in the Vatican, MS. Vat. Lat. 6297, f. 43 v.

[1] 'Cogit me anxietas eximie paupertatis et abhominabilis inopia me compellit exordium promere lacrimosum et narrationum seriem pudorosam. Nam cum deberem lectioni vacare et studiosius insistere scholasticis disciplinis, per hostia scolarium clamito mendicando. Insisto quippe reiterans aliquando vigesies, O boni domini, vel huiusmodi, et non reporto nisi Vade cum Deo. Festino postmodum ad hostia laicorum, a quibus frequentius repellor cum clamoribus et garitu, et si quando dicitur, Expecta, exhibetur mihi panis de triplici mixtura quem canes comedere perorrescunt propter aristas spelte ibidem insertas. Olera quidem repudiata, cuticule, nervi qui commasticari non possunt, mucilagines carnium, abiectilia intestina, mice spinose, rapa, legumina contemptibilia, cibaria et vina dampnata sepius mendicantibus exibentur. Discurro de nocte per civitatem, in manu dextra baculum et in sinistra parasidem [other MSS.: piscidem, pixidem], peram iuxta cingulum et cucurbitam ad modum scarsellule deferendo, bacculo canibus resistendo, sed piscis oleribus, pera panibus, et cucurbita potibus deputatur. Cado frequenter in lutum Bononiense, cuius fetor est odori sepulcrorum similis, et ita fedatus ad hospitium revertor satisfaciens latranti stomacho de perceptis. . . .' Buoncompagno, *Antiqua rhetorica*, in Munich, Cod. Lat. 23499, f. 9 v. Also in MS. lat. 8654, f. 16; MS. lat. 7732, f. 10 v; B.M., Cotton MS. Vitellius C. viii, f. 96 v. Letters on the same folios of these MSS. describe the misfortunes of another begging student and of one who is lying in the hospital. The example cited is a good specimen of Buoncompagno's style; manifestly his descriptions are not to be taken as entirely typical. Cf. Zaccagnini, *Studio di Bologna*, p. 53. The mud of Bologna is also referred to by Matthew of Vendôme, ed. Wattenbach, p. 627.   [2] Buoncompagno, as in the preceding note.

[3] *Summa* of Petrus de Hallis, *ca.* 1337, in *Fontes rerum Austriacarum*, second series, vi. 117.

knowledge.[1] In another form of appeal to the sister's mercy the student asks for the loan of twenty sous from her, since he has been so short a time at school that he dare not make the demand of his parents, "lest perchance the amount of his expenses displease them." [2]

To such requests the proper answer was, of course, an affectionate letter, commending the young man's industry and studious habits and remitting the desired amount.[3] Sometimes the student is cautioned to moderate his expenses—he might have got on longer with what he had,[4] his uncle had less than an obol a day, and is still alive,[5] he should remember the needs of his sisters,[6] he ought to be supporting his parents instead of trying to extort money from them,[7] etc. One father at Besançon

---

[1] 'Soror discrepta [i.e., discreta] et callida suum debet maritum et parentes etiam ad amorem sui fratris indigentis et subsidium inflammare. Soror dulcis, tua noscat dilectio quod ego sum in tali studio sanus et lectus [i.e., laetus] per Dei gratiam et bene addisco et facio factum meum. Multas enim paupertates substineo: iaceo quidem in paleis sine linteaminibus et incedo discalciatus et male vestitus sine camisia, et solum de pane non loquor, de quo edigeo non possum reficere ventrem meum [the Arsenal MS. has: de quo non audeo ventrem meum satiare]. Precor igitur, soror dulcissima, ut diligenter et subtiliter tuum ducas maritum in quantum poteris ut iuvamen aliquod mihi mittat.' The sister cannot express her distress over his poverty; she has done what she could and got together '.c. solidos Turonensium et duo paria linteaminum et .x. ulnas de subtili tela, que omnia tibi dirigo per talem hominem presencium portatorem. Cave tamen cum summa diligentia ne hoc possit ad mei mariti noticiam pervenire, nam si hoc sciret mortua essem penitus et destructa. Ipse enim, prout credo firmissime, ad instanciam mei tuam in brevi tibi peccuniam destinabit.' Ponce de Provence in B.M., Arundel MS. 514, f. 76 v. Also in MS. lat. 18595, f. 22 v; MS. lat. 8653, f. 13; MS. lat. 11385, f. 73 v; Bibliothèque de l'Arsenal, MS. 3807, f. 61 v; Troyes, MS. 1556, f. 20.

[2] 'Ne mearum expensarum quantitas eos forte tedio afficiat.' Munich, Cod. Lat. 6911, f. 54 v.

[3] Examples in Rockinger, *Ueber Briefsteller*, p. 41; Guido Faba, *Dict. rhet.*, no. 2; Delisle, *Formulaire de Tréguier*, nos. 2, 5, 14, 17.

[4] 'Debuisses quidem per biennium primo fecisse moram in scholis antequam tam importune subsidia postulares.' To which the student replies: 'Qui remorantur domi iudicant de absentibus prout volunt, et dum sedent super ollas carnium in saturitate panem edentes illorum nullatenus recordantur qui fame, siti, frigore, ac nuditate opprimuntur in scholasticis disciplinis.' Buoncompagno in MS. lat. 8654, f. 14 v; MS. lat. 7732, f. 9 v; Munich, Cod. Lat. 23499, f. 8 v.

[5] Luchaire, *Études*, p. 108, cf. 117.

[6] Matthew of Vendôme, ed. Wattenbach, p. 622.

[7] 'Verecundari debet adultus et discretus filius cum a patre suo pauperrimo

—who quotes Horace!—excuses himself because of the failure of his vineyards, another, because of the drop in prices due to overproduction.[1] It often happened, too, that, the father or uncle has heard bad reports of the student, who must then be prepared to deny indignantly all such aspersions as the unfounded fabrications of his lying enemies.[2] If his parents could only see his tattered clothing and torn shirt, they would know that he did not spend his substance on royal raiment and costly furs in the pursuit of ladies' love.[3] Here is an example of paternal reproof taken from an interesting collection relating to Franche-Comté:

To his son G. residing at Orleans P. of Besançon sends greeting with paternal zeal. It is written, 'He also that is slothful in his work is brother to him that is a great waster.' I have recently discovered that you live dissolutely and slothfully, preferring license to restraint and play to work and strumming a guitar while the others are at their studies, whence it happens that you have read but one volume of law

credit et nititur pecuniam extorquere, cui deberet potius in necessariis provi-dere.' Munich, Cod. Lat. 22293, f. 280 v. Cf. also f. 281; and MS. 2775 of the Bibliothèque Sainte-Geneviève, f. 270 v.

[1] 'P. civis Bisuntinus suo precordiali filio G. in Montepessulano studenti, salutem et cure paternalis affectum.
      Insani sapiens nomen fert, equus iniqui,
      Ultraquam satis virtutem si petat ipsam,
sicut Horatius asseverat [*Epistles*, i. 6, 15]. Ut attumavi satis esse tibi sumptus hucusque suspedicavi pectore letabundo, sed hoc anno ymbres et uredo primi-tus, demum importune ulucres [i.e., volucres] vignearum fructus partibus istis adeo deterserunt quod in tribus vigneis sportas duntaxat dovam in quali-bet sigillatim collegi. Meos autem convicaneos par sterilitas reddidit conster-natos. Hac ratione non est michi suppetens qua te valeam relevare, nisi ultra quam satis immergar usurarum voragine, quo facto videar insanire. Igitur faciens de necessitate virtutem sustineas quousque nobis pinguiorem Omnipo-tens largiatur fortunam.' MS. lat. 8653A, f. 9 v. In a formulary from Toulouse, on the other hand, the parents cannot send money because of the low prices of produce: 'Cum de blado et vino nostro propter multitudinem que nunc est nullam poterimus pecuniam extorquere.' Arsenal, MS. 854, f. 232.

[2] 'Mentiti sunt per medios dentes qui de me talia predicaverunt,' says a student in the formulary of Ponce de Provence. B.M., Arundel MS. 514, f. 75; Munich, Cod. Lat. 22293, f. 282 v; MS. lat. 18595, f. 21. Specimens of the conventional reproof and denial may be seen in Guido Faba, *Dict. rhet.*, nos. 3, 4; *Epist.*, nos. 8, 9. In *Epist.* 8, the father calls down on the son's head "the maledictions of the Old and New Testaments." Cf. *Mélanges Ferdinand Lot*, p. 246; *Mélanges Pirenne*, p. 206, no. 15; Zaccagnini, pp. 210, 216.

[3] *Quellen und Forschungen*, xvi, 2, p. 33 (1914).

while your more industrious companions have read several. Wherefore I have decided to exhort you herewith to repent utterly of your dissolute and careless ways, that you may no longer be called a waster and that your shame may be turned to good repute.[1]

In the models of Ponce de Provence we find a teacher writing to a student's father that while the young man is doing well in his studies, he is just a trifle wild and would. be helped by judicious admonition. Naturally the master does not wish it known that the information came through him, so the father writes his son:

I have learned—not from your master, although he ought not to hide such things from me, but from a certain trustworthy source—that you do not study in your room or act in the schools as a good student should, but play and wander about, disobedient to your master and indulging in sport and in certain other dishonourable practices which I do not now care to explain by letter.[2]

The arrival of students at school is frequently the occasion of letters to parents describing their new surroundings, as in the following illustration, which comes from Moravia:

After my departure from your gracious presence the circumstances of my journey continued to improve until by divine assistance I arrived safely in the city of Brünn, where I have had the good fortune to obtain lodgings with a certain citizen who has two boys in school and provides me with food and clothing in sufficient amount. I have also found here an upright and worthy master, of distinguished reputation and varied

---

[1] 'P. Bisuntinus G. filio suo Areliensis—*vel* Aurelianis—residenti, salutem cum zelo paternali. Scriptum est, Qui mollis est et dissolutus in opere suo frater est sua opera dissipantis [Proverbs, xviii. 9]. Te nuper intellexi ⟨te⟩ molliter et dissolute adeo vivere ut petulanciam plus celibatu diligas et ludicra seriis anteponas, nec non cum ceteri lucubrationi vacant in cithara diceris concrepare; unde contingit unum volumen legeris, quamquam tui choetanei plura condecentius legerint commentaria [MS. comitaria]. Igitur te duxi presentibus exortandum quod [MS. qq] a tuis dissolutionibus insolenciis totaliter resipiscas, quod non dicaris bonorum dissipator sed in bonum nomen tua possit ignominia commutari.' MS. lat. 8653A, f. 9; a similar letter is on f. 13 v.

[2] 'Non per tuum magistrum, qui tamen non deberet mihi talia celare, sed per certam relacionem quorundam, didici quod tu non studes in camera tua nec in scolis sis ut bonus scolaris solet facere, sed extra vagabundus efficiaris atque lusor et tuo magistro non obediens et rebellis, indulgens ludis et quibusdam aliis inhonestis que ad presens nolo per litteras explicare.' Munich, Cod. Lat. 22293, f. 278 v; Cod. Lat. 16122, f. 11 v; MS. lat. 18595, f. 16 v. Cf. Buoncompagno, Munich, Cod. Lat. 23499, f. 4 v.

attainments, who imparts instruction faithfully; all my fellow pupils, too, are modest, courteous, and of good character, cherishing no hatred but giving mutual assistance in the acquirement of knowledge and in honour preferring one another.[1]

So a student from Paris writes his fair cousin at Ghent that he is well and happy, living with studious companions, and working industriously under a master of good life and suitable attainments.[2] The following, from Orleans, is more fresh and original:

To their very dear and respected parents M. Martre, knight, and M. his wife, M. and S. their sons send greetings and filial obedience. This is to inform you that, by divine mercy, we are living in good health in the city of Orleans and are devoting ourselves wholly to study, mindful of the words of Cato, "To know anything is praiseworthy," etc. We occupy a good and comely dwelling, next door but one to the schools and market-place, so that we can go to school every day without wetting our feet. We have also good companions in the house with us, well advanced in their studies and of excellent habits—an advantage which we well appreciate, for as the Psalmist says, "With an upright man thou wilt show thyself upright," etc. (Psalms, xviii. 25). Wherefore lest production cease from lack of material, we beg your paternity to send us by the bearer, B., money for buying parchment, ink, a desk, and the other things which we need, in sufficient amount that we may suffer no

---

[1] 'Postquam discessi a vestra facie graciosa, divino favente (MS. vavente) auxilio, meum iter ⟨convertitur⟩ de bono in melius se disposuit donec Brunnensis civitas incolomem me recepit. Ibidem apud quendam civem qui duos habet pueros scolas frequentantes sospes et cum gaudio sum locatus, qui sufficienter vestes et victualia aministrat; ibidem etiam inveni magistrum probum et honestum, suos subditos fideliter informantem, honestatis titulo ac diversis facultatibus presignitum. Preterea socii qui se in suis scolis recipiunt omnes sunt curiales, humiles, et honesti, inter quos nullum latet odium sed mutuo scientiis proficiunt et honoribus se exaltant.' Munich, Cod. Lat. 2649, f. 49; on f. 44 a student gives a similar account of his surroundings at Erfurt. The following, of much the same character, is from Buoncompagno: 'A vobis licentia impetrata et recepto benedictionis vestre munere, cepi ad studium properare sicque cum successive fortune incremento intravi Bononiam, ubi a sociis et amicis fui cum ingenti alacritate receptus et ab eis multipliciter honoratus. Postmodum vero conducxi hospitium, preelegi mihi magistrum et socios competentes, cum quibus lego et proficio iugiter in moribus et doctrina.' Munich, Cod. Lat. 23499, f. 5; MS. lat. 8654, f. 8. See also Guido Faba, *Epist.*, no. 54; and Ponce de Provence in Munich, Cod. Lat. 22293, f. 279, and MS. 3807 of the Arsenal, f. 57 v.

[2] N. de Pauw, "La vie intime en Flandre au moyen âge d'après des documents inédits," no. 11, in *Bulletin de la Commission Royale d'Histoire*, lxxxii. 34 (Brussels, 1913).

want on your account (God forbid!) but finish our studies and return home with honour. The bearer will also take charge of the shoes and stockings which you have to send us, and any news as well.[1]

The student's journey and arrival were not always so prosperous, and the famous Bolognese *dictator* Buoncompagno devotes a chapter of his collection to the accidents that may befall one on the way to the university.[2] Attacks from robbers seem to have been the chief danger: the scholar was hastening to Bologna, for the love of letters, but in crossing the Alps he was attacked by highwaymen, who took away his books, horses, clothing, and money, so that he has been obliged to remain in a neighbouring monastery till help can reach him.[3] So a Northern student on his way to Paris is stripped and left bound by four youths in clerical habit with whom he had fallen in upon the road.[4] In other instances the robbery, of fifteen marks of silver and grey furs, takes place in the forest of Bologna,[5] or in the

---

[1] MS. lat. 1093, f. 82 v, published by Delisle in the *Annuaire-Bulletin de la Société de l'Histoire de France*, vii. 149–150, 141 (1869). There is a reprint in the *Archivio della Società Romana di Storia Patria*, xi. 396 (1888).

With these may be compared such descriptions of Paris as are given by a German student at the beginning of the twelfth century (Jaffé, *Bibliotheca rerum Germanicarum*, v. 285); by Gui de Bazoches about fifty years later (*Bulletin de la Société de l'Histoire de Paris et de l'Île-de-France*, iv. 38; cf. *Neues Archiv*, xvi. 72); and by John, later archbishop of Prague, in 1375 or 1376 (*Archiv für österreichische Geschichte*, lv. 385).

[2] See the table of contents in Rockinger, *Q. E.*, ix. 134.

[3] 'Eram in procinctu itineris et Bononiam properabam ob amorem studii litteralis, unde si essent in homine vie illius meum ducxissem propositum ad effectum; sed comparuit evidens impedimentum quo cogor a proposito resilire. Sane cum essem in transitu Alpium occurerunt quidam ratopres [*sic*: MS. lat. latrones] qui peccuniam, libros, vestes, et equos mihi penitus abstulerunt, me nudum, verberatum, et vulneratum, lugubrem et abiectum in solitudinem dimittentes. Postmodum autem diverti ad quoddam monasterium, in quo tandiu proposui commorari donec quid mihi sit agendum vestris litteris intimetis.' Buoncompagno in Munich, Cod. Lat. 23499, f. 5; MS. lat. 8654, f. 8; B.M., Cotton MS. Vitellius C. viii, f. 93 v. In Matthew of Vendôme (ed. Wattenbach, p. 587) the same fate befalls a student of medicine on his way to Salerno.

[4] B.M., MS. Royal 8 A. vi, f. 25 (a brief collection of student letters from Paris in a hand of the late thirteenth century).

[5] 'Mirifice divinitatis nutu Vercellensis ecclesie religioso antistiti B. humillimus clericus . . . Cum enim nuper preter parentum velle philosofice discende liberalitatis gratia versus Bononiam iter incepissem et procuratorem habens itineris Bononiensium silvam ingressus essem, supervenientes quidam milites

highway near Aosta.[1] Sometimes advantage was taken of the greater security of forwarding by Italian merchants visiting the fairs of Champagne,[2] or Italian pilgrims to Santiago de Compostela.[3] Even a journey home from Bologna to Florence was not without its dangers, unless undertaken with a considerable armed company.[4]

Once safely arrived at a centre of learning, mediaeval students were slow to quit academic life.[5] Again and again they ask permission to have their term of study extended; war might break out,[6] parents or brothers die, an inheritance have to be divided,[7] but the student pleads always for delay. He desires to "serve longer in the camp of Pallas";[8] in any event he

de contiguis castrorum finibus ad depredandum, sicut re vero venerant habiles, me cum prefato itineris tutore ceperunt et cuncta seriatim investigantes cetera violenter abstulerunt .xv. argenti marcas, pelles grisias et xx nummorum sodilos [sic], exceptis subpellectilibus plurimis et diversis que scolares in terra extranea victuros portare cognoscitis.' *Precepta prosaici dictaminis secundum Tullium*, of the twelfth century, from Northern Italy, in B.M., Add. MS. 21173, f. 71 v; see below, Chapter IX, no. 14.

[1] 'Consultatione vestra Bononiam [MS. Bonaniam] proficiscebar iuris scientiam adepturus, verum in strata publica [MS. plubica] vispiliones me spoliaverunt, libros et pecuniam cum vestibus absportantes, unde pauperculus regressus sum ad Augustam ubi cum robore miserabili mendicitate sustentor.' MS. lat. 8653A, f. 3 v.

[2] 'Carissimo patri suo Nicholao de tali loco Martinus filius eius Bolonie moram faciens veram in Christo salutem. . . . Poscens humiliter quatinus per Gracianum mercatorem Bolonie satis expertum fidelitate qui nuper ad nundinas Latiniaci viam arripuit denarios ad sufficientiam, si placeat, transmittatis, mihi clauzis scribentes litteris quanta summa pecunie dicto commissa fuerit mercatori.' Tarragona, MS. 6, f. 34.

[3] Chapter IX, no. 7.   [4] Zaccagnini, *Studio*, pp. 207–208.

[5] Buoncompagno even tells of one who had spent twenty-eight years in study: 'Ecce iam xxviii. annorum spacium est elapsum quod te dedicasti scholasticis disciplinis.' Munich, Cod. Lat. 23499, f. 13; MS. lat. 8654, f. 21 v; MS. lat. 7732, f. 14 v.

[6] Guido Faba, *Dict. rhet.*, no. 53, *Epist.*, no. 84. Cf. Petrus de Hallis in *Fontes rerum Austriacarum*, second series, vi. 116; and *Bullettino dell'Istituto Storico Italiano*, xiv. 169.

[7] Munich, Cod. Lat. 2649, f. 50; Cod. Lat. 96, f. 38; Cod. Lat. 14708, f. 58, 58 v; *Zeitschrift für die Geschichte des Oberrheins*, n.s., xi. 34; Guido Faba, *Dict. rhet.*, nos. 15, 16.

[8] 'In castris Paladis disposui longiori spatio militare.' MS. lat. 8661, f. 98 v. So the nephews of Wolfgang of Altaich ask for more time (Berlin, MS. Lat. oct. 136, f. 112 v), and a beneficed student promises to return to his parish in the spring (Guido Faba, *Dict. rhet.*, nos. 84, 85).

cannot leave before Easter, as his masters have just begun important courses of lectures.[1] A scholar is called home from Siena to marry a lady of many attractions; he answers that he deems it foolish to desert the cause of learning for the sake of a woman, "for one may always get a wife, but science once lost can never be recovered."[2] In a similar case another student holds out against the charms of a proposed wife, who, "though she is dark, is clever and of placid demeanour and distinguished bearing, wise and noble, and moreover has a considerable dower and belongs to an influential family."[3] A married student is reminded that he has remained in the schools longer than the stipulated two years; his wife is sure he has been studying in some other *Code*, and proposes to read a little in the *Digest* on her own account![4] Sometimes, however, the student is taken ill and writes for money and an easy-going horse to take him home,[5] while occasionally he discovers his inability to learn and

[1] 'Ad presens te non possum presencionaliter consolari nec ante futurum Pascha tuam presenciam visitare, quia magistri quorum lectionibus me subiunxi quosdam libros mihi utiles legere inceperunt, quorum neglectio meo studio generaret irrecuperabile detrimentum.' Munich, Cod. Lat. 2649, f. 50 v; cf. Cartellieri, no. 246.   [2] Guido Faba, *Parlamenti ed epistole*, nos. 16–19.

[3] 'G., filiam Bernardi de Gualdo . . . que, quamquam bruna sit, abilis est et placida in conspectu, morum elegantia decoratur, nitet sapientia, magnaque nobilitate clarescit. Preterea nominata dotem exhibet grandi censu, caros habebit amicos plurimos et affines.' MS. lat. 8661, f. 98; on f. 96 v, on the other hand, a student writes that his approaching marriage will prevent his return to school.

[4] *Ibid.*, f. 99 v, from Buoncompagno; also published from an anonymous fragment at Rheims (MS. 1275, f. 40 v) by Wattenbach in the *S. B.* of the Berlin Academy for 1892, p. 93; it will be found, followed by another of similar character, in the copies of the *Antiqua rhetorica* in MS. lat. 8654, f. 22, and MS. lat. 7732, f. 14. Cf. Guido Faba, *Epist.*, no. 9, where a son assures his father that he has been studying in the Code of Justinian and no other.

[5] E.g., the letter of a French student at Bologna in the Formulary of Tréguier (MS. lat. n.a. 426, f. 17), cited by Delisle in the *Histoire littéraire*, xxxi. 30. The following letter from Angers in the same collection (f. 3) is not mentioned by Delisle: 'Reverendo pre omnibus suo patri reverencia filiali tali patrifamilias titulis domini talis opidi decorato, talis suus filius Andegavis in studio moram trahens [MS. traans] salutem corporis et anime, licet ipsa salute corporis iam privetur. Reverende pater, vobis tenore presencium innotescat me gravi valetudine corporis iam detentum taliter quod exercere studium nequeo, sed in lecto iacens egritudinis me rectis pedibus non valeo sustentare. Quare paternitati vestre carisime suplico, care- pater, visis presentibus unum de vestris clientibus cum equo suaviter ambulante et sufficienti pecunia ad

asks to enter the army or some other more congenial occupation.[1] One father promises the delights of manual labour to a son who complains that the Scriptures are too haṛd for him to understand and desires to do "some more useful work which leads to temporal gain."[2]

For the student who has finished his university studies there are naturally forms for soliciting cathedral prebends, benefices, or appointments as schoolmaster.[3]

As is indicated by letters already cited, one of the first cares of a student was to provide himself with a suitable room. Various models show that it was usual to secure accommodations in advance through acquaintances, a necessary precaution when the number of new students was uncommonly great.[4] The scholar is going to Paris at the feast of St. Rémy,[5] or he is

expensas pro me mittere non tardetis, quo ducente vestram gratuitam presenciam ante quam moriar valeam visitare. Spero etenim firmiter quod mea infirmitas mutacione locorum valeat immutari, alias timeo et oresco ne ossa mea terra contegat aliena.' In MS. lat. 15131, f. 177 v, a student at Orleans writes to the same effect. So in the B.M., Cotton MS. Vitellius C. viii, f. 141, where the writer wishes 'vehiculum et expensam.' Cf. Cartellieri, no. 128.

[1] 'Patri karissimo, etc. In labore scholastico sedi diucius ut mihi thesaurum scientie comparem, verum sed irritum laboravi et video quantum magis studeo tanto minus proficio nec ad memoriam possum reducere peraudita. Ad hoc ergo discretum habeat consilium vestra veneranda paternitas me ab officio clericali removendo et ad decus milicie, ad quod meus valde suspirat animus, transferendo; aliquin regnum Francorum gressibus visitabo regi donec me faciat militem cum diligencia serviturus.' The father tries to dissuade him, but adds that if in his simplicity he still insists on becoming a knight, he would better serve under his natural lord. Munich, Cod. Lat. 22293, f. 281. In other MSS. of Ponce de Provence (MS. lat. 18595, f. 19 v; MS. lat. 8653, f. 11 v; Arsenal MS. 3807, f. 59; B.M., Arundel MS. 514, f. 73 v) the request is more general—'filius patri quod non potest addiscere, et removeat eum ab officio clericali ad aliud aptum officium transferendo,' and in the reply the student, if he returns, is to go into business like his brothers—'negociando lucraberis, sicut faciunt fratres tui.'

[2] In the *dictamina* of Nicholas of Breslau (*Codex diplomaticus Silesiae*, v. 318).

[3] See *ante*, p. 9, n. 1, and, for an application for a schoolmaster's position, the letter from Orleans in MS. lat. 8350, f. 108 v.

[4] See the letter from Laon, written not long before 1117, in the *B. E. C.* 1855, p. 466.

[5] 'Ad festum beati Remigii est mihi propositum ire Parisius et vobiscum in eodem hospicio commorari. Unde vestram benivolentiam commoneo ut tam mihi quam vobis de bono hospicio curetis providere, quod in illud nostri socii utrumque confiteant ad honorem.' MS. lat. 8653, f. 32 v.

a monk whose prior has just granted him a year's leave of absence,[1] and he would like to live "away from the rush and noise of men,"[2] in the same room with his friend, if possible, or at least in the same hospice.[3] Frequently the student's father places him under the care of a relative or friend,[4] or he may ask the master to take special charge of the young man and his spending-money,[5] or to buy him a *Code*, if necessary, and to keep him off the streets on holidays lest he follow his brother

[1] 'De priore meo et meis confratribus pro anno sequenti scolatizandi licenciam optinens.' *Salutaciones secundum usum Oxonie*, in the Bodleian, Auct. F. 3. 9, f. 423 (fifteenth century). For the correspondence of monastic students, cf. V. Schmidt, "Ein Lilienfelder Formelbuch," in *Studien und Mitteilungen aus dem Benediktiner- und dem Cistercienser-Orden*, xxviii. 392–402, 577–595 (1907).

[2] 'Ab incursu hominum et strepitu separata.' Delisle, *Formulaire de Tréguier*, no. 15. 'Longe a tumultu hominum sequestratus,' says another model in the same formulary (MS. lat. n.a. 426, f. 13).

[3] 'Vobiscum in eodem hospicio et etiam in camera et propono et desidero, si vobis placuerit, commorari.' Ponce de Provence, in B.M., Arundel MS. 514, f. 77 v; MS. lat. 18595, f. 23 v; MS. lat. 8653, f. 13; Arsenal, MS. 3807, f. 62 v; Munich, Cod. Lat. 22293, f. 283.

[4] 'Mittitur filius ad amicum ut eum in pedagogio ponat.' *Epistolares quedam formule . . . extracte ex maiorum litterarum collectorio scolaribus Lovanii in pedagogio Lilii lectarum*, of the end of the fifteenth century, in Munich, Cod. Lat. 7082, f. 20 v (there is another copy in the Library of the University of Cambridge, Gg. v. 37). Cf. Munich, Cod. Lat. 96, f. 39 v; Cod. Lat. 14708, f. 59 v; Cod. Lat. 22294, f. 42 v. In a formulary from Orleans composed about the year 1230 (see Langlois, *Formulaires de lettres*, iii. 14), and preserved at Rouen, MS. 1468, f. 363 v, we find: 'Exoramus quatinus expensis tali filio nostro apud vos ad studium misso vobis placeat [MS. placat] providere et omnia bene computetis; nam parati sumus ad mandatum vestrum persolvere quicquid iustum fuerit cum actione multimoda gratiarum.' A Silesian student at Paris, near the middle of the fourteenth century, receives money weekly from the *hospes* with whom it is deposited (T. Jacobi, *Codex epistolaris Johannis Regis Bohemiae*, Berlin, 1841, p. 58). See further Guido Faba, *Dict. rhet.*, nos. 13, 14; *Zeitschrift des Vereins für Geschichte und Alterthum Schlesiens*, xxvii. 354; Wattenbach, "Iter Austriacum," p. 52 (formulary from Naples, *ca.* 1230); and Chapter VI, below.

[5] 'Et pourceo que jeo pensa qil demoura illeosques entre cy et Pasche sanz venir al hostel, si ay envoie oue lui vint soldes queux devers voillez prendre de luy et les gardre devers vous tanque soient ouelement despenduz, qar si la summe demouroit en son burse desmeme y les degastreit maintenant en chose qeu amonterent rienz.' B.M., Harleian MS. 4971, f. 20 v: a rhetorical treatise in French, with models, belonging to the reign of Edward III. Cf. Ellis, *Original Letters*, third series, i, p. x, note; and W. Uerkvitz, *Tractate zur Unterweisung in der anglo-normannischen Briefschreibekunst* (Greifswald diss., 1898). John, archbishop of Prague, who studied at Prague, Padua, Bologna,

into the Dominican order.[1] That indefatigable *rhetor*, Ponce de Provence, has left us models of all necessary correspondence between father and teacher—how the son is sent and received, the reports of his conduct and the appropriate parental admonition, statements of his progress and of the completion of his studies, and finally the letter sending the master his pay with the father's thanks.[2] In an example written at Cambridge a master is asked to permit a student to visit his parents,[3] while in another letter of the same collection a young man announces that he will bring his master home with him for two or three days at Christmas.[4]

The letters of students make frequent mention of their books and studies, but do not add much to our information on these subjects. Books were, of course, in steady demand, for purchase as well as for rent, and furnished a convenient occasion for appeals to the parental purse,[5] although it might also happen that they would be left in a chest at home until sent for.[6] Often

Montpellier, and Paris, in the latter part of the fourteenth century, says that in his student days the masters had charge of the scholars' money, so that they rarely had anything to spend and could never buy sweetmeats (*Archiv für österreichische Geschichte*, lv. 327). Note the regular payments to poor scholars in the "Livre de dépenses d'un dignitaire de l'église de Paris en 1248," published by Borrelli de Serres in *Mémoires de la Société de l'Histoire de Paris et de l'Île-de-France*, xxxi. 93–118 (1904). [1] Rheims, MS. 1275, f. 40–40 v.

[2] B.M., Arundel MS. 514, f. 70; MS. lat. 18595, f. 16 v; MS. lat. 8653, f. 9; Arsenal, MS. 3807, f. 56 v; Munich, Cod. Lat. 22293, f. 278. Letters of fathers sending their sons to school may also be found in Gaudenzi, *I Suoni*, p. 170; and in Hauréau, iv. 271. In Munich, Cod. Lat. 7082, f. 18, a master at Louvain returns a scholar 'in artibus graduatus,' but hopes he will continue his studies at Louvain or some other university.

[3] 'Et, tres gentil sire, vous plaise entendre que nous en avons tres grant voulantee et regret pour parler avec notre chier filz, sil vous plaist. Car vrayement ja grant temps a que nous ne lui vismes mais. Si vous prions chierement, tres doulz et tres gentil sire, que vous lui vueillez donner licence pour venir a lostel de parler avec nous au plus tost que faire se pourra bonnement.' B.M., Harleian MS. 3988, f. 49 v (forms of letters in French relating chiefly to affairs in the eastern counties in the reign of Richard II; cf. Ellis, *l.c.*).

[4] 'Mon tres doulz pere, sauve votre grace il nest pas vray ce que vous mavez certifiee par votre lettre, comme mon tres honeuree maistre vous dira plus plainement á Noel, quar il venra avecque moy pour sojourner et prendre desduit avec vous par deux jours ou trois, sil vous plaist.' Ibid., f. 45 v.

[5] Compare the warning to certain students in Pez, *Thesaurus anecdotorum*, vi, 2, p. 186.

[6] 'Dilectioni tue notum esse desidero quod, cum me Parisius transtulerim

the particular work needed is ordered through some friend. Thus if the writer is studying grammar, he wants a *Grecismus* and a *Doctrinale* with the glosses copied in a large and accurate hand,[1] or more rarely a Priscian and *Argentea lingua*.[2] When well advanced in grammar, he may aspire to study law,[3] and thus become a "tower of refuge to his friends and a source of terror and confusion to his enemies."[4] Then, if a civilian, he will need "ten livres *tournois* for a certain book called *Digestum Novum*,"[5] or forty livres *parisis* for the *Code, Digest,* and *Institutes*,[6]

ad hoc ut studiis vacem omni qua possum diligentia, libros quos in archa tua habes repositos habeo necessarios ad propositum studiorum,' writes a student to his mother: Munich, Cod. Lat. 6911, f. 53; MS. lat. 14069, f. 201. Cf. the request for 'anomynale and a bok of sofystre of my brother Emundes' in the *Paston Letters* (ed. Gairdner), i. 82.

¹ Thus a student at Orleans sends to his friend 'P. de tali loco,' 'Doctrinale cum magnis glosulis de litera veraci et legibili tam in nota quam in textu.' Arsenal, MS. 854, f. 214 v. In the *Formulaire de Tréguier*, no. 10, a *Doctrinale* of this sort is sought by the schoolmaster of Prat. So in the same MS. of the Arsenal, f. 215, the student wants 'Doctrinale . . . et Grecismum et ceteros libros gramatice oportunos'; and in Ponce de Provence the *Grecismus* and *Doctrinale* are desired: B.M., Arundel MS. 514, f. 72; MS. lat. 18595, f. 18; MS. lat. 8653, f. 11; Arsenal, MS. 3807, f. 58. Cf. also *Zeitschrift für die Geschichte des Oberrheins*, new series, xi. 34.

On the *Doctrinale* of Alexandre de Villedieu and the *Grecismus* of Évrard de Béthune, the popular grammatical text-books of the thirteenth and fourteenth centuries, see D. Reichling, *Das Doctrinale des Alexander de Villa Dei* (Berlin, 1893), and J. Wrobel, *Eberhardi Bethuniensis Graecismus* (Breslau, 1887); and cf. Thurot in the *Notices et extraits*, xxii, 2, especially pp. 98–102, and the excellent studies of L. J. Paetow. A facsimile of a portion of a MS. of the *Grecismus*, showing the glosses, is given by Prou in his *Manuel de Paléographie*, fourth edition, plate xiii.

² Hugh of Bologna, in *Neues Archiv*, xxii. 300; cf. Chapter IX, no. 5, *infra*.

³ Guido Faba, *Dict. rhet.*, no.´61. Ponce de Provence, in B.M., Arundel MS. 514, f. 72 v; Munich, Cod. Lat. 22293, f. 280; Troyes, MS. 1556, f. 16.

⁴ 'Tuorum turris et refugium amicorum et inimicorum confusio atque terror.' Ponce de Provence, *l.c.* Cf. *Codex diplomaticus Silesiae*, v. 318, and the letter from Orleans cited below.

⁵ 'Quatinus michi in .x. libris Turonensium pro quodam libro emendo qui Digestum Novum dicitur dignemini subvenire.' Laurentius of Aquileia, in MS. lat. 11384, f. 36 v; also in MS. lat. 16253, f. 12, except that here the text reads 'libris Parisiensibus' (*sic*).

⁶ 'Patri ac domino metuendo B. civi Parisiensi, C. humilis eius natus scolaris [MS. scolari] Ariliensis salutem cum reverencia filiali. Cum scientia sit nobilis possessio, illa est maxime appetenda que nobilissima reputatur. Hinc est quod in legum honorabili facultate propono ulterius desudare, quia sui possessores multum honoris consequuntur. Quare dominationi vestre suplicat devotio

while if he forsakes these "clamorous subterfuges"[1] for the canon law, he must have the *Decretals* at least[2] and perhaps the *Summa* of Gaufridus.[3] From Orleans a student writes that he has become famous in dialectic, and desires to study theology if only his father will send him enough money to buy a Bible.[4] The father praises his ambition but cannot afford the great expense of a theological course—let the son turn to some of the 'lucrative' professions.[5] There are, of course, numerous letters in praise of the *ars dictaminis* and its study,[6] and the "frivolous and empty quarrels" of the logicians are not forgotten.[7] The preoccupations of the twelfth century are reflected in the "little glosses" with which one master has filled thirty-two volumes.[8]

Usually the writers of these letters study their law at Bologna

filialis quod [MS. qq] causa emendi Codicem et Digestum cum Institutionibus quadraginta libras Parisiensium michi mitere procuretis, scientes pro certo quod iste labor vobis et amicis nostris honorem et gloriam reportabit.' Arsenal, MS. 854, f. 214.

[1] 'Clamosis tergiversationibus legistarum.' Laurentius of Aquileia, MS. lat. 11384, f. 59 v.

[2] 'Decretales in textu et glosa sufficienter correctas ad usum meum pro competenti precio emere procuretis.' Id., MS. lat. 14174, f. 126; MS. lat. 11384, f. 55; MS. lat. 16253, f. 23.

[3] A. Starzer and O. Redlich, *Eine Wiener Briefsammlung* (Vienna, 1894), pp. 245 f.

[4] 'Demonstratione presentis cedule noscat vestra paterna bonitas, pater karissime, quod ego sum Aurelianis sanitate corporea per Dei gratiam predictatus et in dyalectica taliter fundatus quod omnes scolares et etiam magistri dicunt me fore disputatorem optimum et sophistam, et multum desidero in sancta theologia de cetero prostudere. Michi mittat igitur, precor et moveo, paterna pietas unde possim Bibliam comparare et expensas habere, quamvis non plenarie, quoquo modo.' Ponce de Provence, B.M., Arundel MS. 514, f. 73; MS. lat. 18595, f. 19 v; MS. lat. 8653, f. 11 v; Arsenal, MS. 3807, f. 59; Troyes, MS. 1556, f. 17. In Pez, *Thesaurus anecdotorum*, vi, 2, p. 185, a student who has secured a benefice is required to learn the Psalter by heart.

[5] 'Hoc requirit, sicut mihi dicitur, magnos sumptus. Audias ergo artes, fili karissime, vel actores vel phisicam vel aliquam scientiam lucrativam, quia non possem tibi magnam pecuniam ministrare.' Ponce de Provence, Arundel MS. 514, f. 73 v, and other MSS. as above. Cf. also K. Burdach, *Schlesisch-Böhmische Briefmuster*, pp. 89–90, no. 57.

[6] For examples see Valois, *De arte scribendi epistolas*, pp. 25–27; *Archiv*, x. 559; Cartellieri, nos. 287–289. Cf. also a letter in the Arsenal (MS. 854, f. 233), where 'scolaris studens Parisius significat socio studenti Tholose quod dictator optimus venit Parisius, et ibi ad studendum venire non postponat.'

[7] Petrus de Hallis, in *Fontes rerum Austriacarum*, second series, vi. 117.

[8] Cartellieri, nos. 274, 275, 279.

or Orleans, their medicine at Montpellier, and so on, but sometimes their statements add to our knowledge of the mediaeval
curriculum and the branches that flourished at different institutions. Thus Thurot concludes from the models of Ponce de
Provence that logic was not necessary for the study of law, but
was demanded of students of medicine and was indispensable
for theology,[1] and it is on such forms that Fitting bases his argument for the early pre-eminence of Pavia over Bologna as a
centre of legal instruction.[2] The arrival of the new French theology at Bologna can be traced in the same way.[3] Similar evidence has enabled Delisle to establish the existence of a flourishing school of rhetoric and literature at Orleans in the twelfth
century,[4] while the later decline of the *trivium* there is seen in
a letter of the early fourteenth century.[5] A careful study of the
formularies would also show something as to the regions upon
which the various universities drew most largely for students,[6]

[1] *Notices et extraits*, xxii, 2, p. 93, note. For the studies preliminary to
'physical science' at Naples, see the letter printed below, Chapter VI, p. 136.

[2] *Die Anfänge der Rechtsschule zu Bologna* (Leipzig, 1888), pp. 80, 105.

[3] Chapter IX, no. 3, 3, *infra*.

[4] 'Les Écoles d'Orléans au XIIe et au XIIIe siècle,' in *Annuaire-Bulletin de
la Société d'Histoire de France*, vii. 139–154 (1869). Cf. the letter of certain
Flemish scholars expressing their dissatisfaction with the instruction they
found at Orleans. Valenciennes, MS. 483, f. 96 v; printed below, Chapter
IX, p. 186.

[5] A certain P. of Salins (Jura) desires to give instruction in rhetoric and
logic at Orleans, 'ubi plures dicuntur trivialibus assidentes,' but in response to
his inquiries 'G. Arelianis studens' writes: 'Scicitatus sum quot et quanti
forent Arelianis in trivialibus auditores, tandem pro facto compertum est hos
scolares esse paucos et indigos nec non superficia rudimenta sectantes, quod
eorum doctores intuiti ad reliquas convolant disciplinas. Igitur quamquam
meus animus vestram gliscat presenciam, nullominus vobis instinctu consulo
caritatis quod [MS. qq] Arelianis non curetis pro trivialibus edocendis venire,
ubi non sunt plures qui subtiliter audirent sermonis vestri dogmata ⟨venienda⟩
veneranda.' MS. lat. 8653A, f. 16.

[6] Thus Delisle has pointed out on the basis of the Formulary of Tréguier
that the youth from that part of Brittany frequented Orleans rather than
Paris. The collection from Arbois (MS. lat. 8653A), to which reference has
frequently been made, indicates that Orleans was also the favourite resort of
scholars from Franche-Comté, although Paris, Montpellier, and Bologna are
also mentioned in the letters. We find Paris occupying a prominent place in
forms from the upper Rhine (*Zeitschrift für die Geschichte des Oberrheins*, new
series, xi. 34; *Archiv*, xi. 503), and from more remote parts of the Empire
(Pez, *Thesaurus anecdotorum*, vi, 1, col. 427; vi, 2, pp. 14, 185; Jacobi, *Codex*

and might throw some light upon the matter of inter-university migration. Thus in 1291 an English student who hopes to lecture on canon law at Oxford has, by the advice of a member of the papal curia, begun his legal studies at Bologna—where a thieving servant made away with his *Decretals*, and almost led him into the irregularity of cutting off the thief's head.[1]

Letters from all parts of Europe testify to the expense attendant upon securing a degree. Thus a student at Paris asks a friend to explain to his father, "since the simplicity of the lay mind does not understand such things," how at length after much study nothing but lack of money for the inception banquet stands in the way of his graduation.[2] From Orleans D. Boterel writes to his dear relatives at Tours that he is labouring over his last volume of law and on its completion will be able to pass to his licentiate provided they send him a hundred livres for the necessary expenses.[3] A student of medicine at Montpellier asks for "more than the usual amount of money" in view of his promotion.[4] A

---

epistolaris Johannis Regis Bohemiae, p. 58; etc.), while German students are often represented as attending Bologna (*Das Baumgärtenberger Formelbuch*, Vienna, 1866, p. 317; *Codex diplomaticus Silesiae*, v. 318; B.M., Arundel MS. 240, ff. 122–123). In general, evidence of this sort must be used with caution, as names of universities might be retained from older models, or well known *studia* like Paris or Bologna might be inserted without their having any close connexion with the region where the formulary took its present shape.

[1] Historical Manuscripts Commission, *Various Collections*, i. 260.

[2] Rockinger, *Q. E.*, ix. 487. Cf. *Romanische Forschungen*, xiii. 914 f. (1902). On inception feasts at Oxford compare the *Literae Cantuarienses*, i. 416; and the *Paston Letters*, iii. 248.

[3] 'Viris providis et discretis consanguineis peramatis A. et B. et C. cognomine Roterellis, civibus Turonis, D. Boterel Aurelianis in ultimo legum volumine lectionibus elaborans, cum salute vite cursum prosperum et longevum. . . . Vestra noverit dilectio mihi cara quod infra mensem, favente Deo, finiem librum meum, quo finito licentiam in legibus adipisci potero, qua obtempta conscribi desidero venerabili collegio professorum. Sane cum tunc oporteat me facere sumptus graves, vobis supplico quod [MS. qq] in .c. libris Parisiensium vos habeam provisores, taliter quod, meo principio subventione vestra laudabiliter celebrato, vestre dilectionis affectum recoligens per effectum vobis impensius magis tenear obligatus.' Arsenal, MS. 854, f. 215. Cf. the Italian models published by Gaudenzi, *I Suoni*, p. 168.

[4] 'Venerabili patri in Christo suo P., civi Bisuntino, G. studens in Montepessulano . . . Porro nostis quod dudum theoricis et practicis laborans [MS. laborant] ad elicona medicine provear, cuius messis est copiosa. Propinquat nunc tempus quo predicatus honore magistrali repatriare decrevi. Placeat

successful inception at Bologna is thus described by Buoncompagno:

Sing unto the Lord a new song, praise him with stringed instruments
and organs, rejoice upon the high-sounding cymbals, for your son has
held a glorious disputation, which was attended by a great number of
teachers and scholars. He answered all questions without a mistake,
and no one could get the better of him or prevail against his arguments.
Moreover he celebrated a famous banquet, at which both rich and poor
were honoured as never before, and he has duly begun to give lectures
which are already so popular that others' classrooms are deserted and
his own are filled.[1]

Buoncompagno also tells of an unsuccessful candidate who
could do nothing in the disputation but sat in the chair like a
goat while the spectators in derision called him rabbi; his guests
had such eating that they had no will to drink, and he must
needs hire students to attend his classes.[2]

If we were to judge them by their own accounts, mediaeval
students were models of industry and diligence, hearing in some
instances at least three lectures a day and expecting soon to
excel their professors as well as their fellows.[3] The *dictatores*,

igitur paternitati vestre mihi plus solito pecunia subvenire.' MS. lat. 8653A,
f. 9 v.

    [1] 'Cantate Domino canticum novum, psallite in cordis et organo, cum cim-
balis benesonantibus iubilate [Psalms, cl. 4, 5], quia filius vester venerabilis-
simum celebravit conventum, in quo fuit innumerosa magrorum et scolarium multitudo. Ipse vero querentibus et questionibus absque defectu aliquo
satisfecit, nullus ei concludere potuit obiciendo, sed ille universis obiciendo
conclusit et nemo fuit qui suis potuerit argumentis instare. Preterea famosum
convivium celebravit, in quo tam pauperes quam divites melius quam unquam
auditum fuerit honorati fuerunt. Item cum sollempnitate scolas regere
celebres incepit, vacuavit scolas multorum, et habet plurimos auditores.'
Munich, Cod. Lat. 23499, f. 6 v; MS. lat. 8654, f. 11; B.M., Cotton MS. Vitellius
C. viii, f. 94 v.

    [2] 'Celebravit conventiculum, non conventum, in quo sedit tanquam hircus
in cathedra et rabbi [MS. arabbi] fuit derisorie appellatus, quia non erat puer
qui sibi de quolibet sophismate non concluderet manifeste et ipse in obiciendo
procedere non sciebat. Invitati autem ad convivium taliter comederunt quod
non habuerunt voluntatem bibendi. Item incepit regere cum quibusdam con-
ductitiis et novitiis, quia nullum valet habere profectum nisi velit illum pretio
numerario comparare.' *Ibid.* (Cf. the *Novissima rhetorica* in Gaudenzi, *Bibliotheca iuridica Medii Aevi*, ii. 273, 282.) This is followed by an account of a
candidate who answered satisfactorily the question set him, but, to the
amusement of the audience, proved unable to explain a proposition which he
himself had propounded to others.

    [3] 'Scolas commaneo frequenter, omni die ad minus tres lectiones mihi utiles

however, were well acquainted with other types of academic youth, who needed to be reminded that reward came, not from having been at Paris, but from profitable study there,[1] and many are the forms of warning or reproof that they have left us. Buoncompagno indeed has a rebuke for him who studies too much—who rises before the morning bell, is first to enter and last to leave the schools, spends the day in his room reading, ponders his lectures at meal-time, and even reviews and argues in his sleep—but he significantly adds that the same letter may be addressed in irony to one who studies too little.[2]

Letters to fellow-students occupy a considerable place in these collections, but they are confined for the most part to messages of condolence, introductions, requests for news, protestations of friendship, and similar commonplaces.[3] We also find students urging friends to join them at Paris, "that flourishing centre of the arts, with all their turns and twists, theology, and canon law," where corn and wine and masters abound,[4] arranging to

a magistro et sociis audiendo, et spero dum ad partes natales rediero quod tantum profecerim quod non solum meos coetaneos sed eciam quosdam meos magistros in facultate scholastica valeam superare.' Munich, Cod. Lat. 2649, f. 50.

[1] Philippe de Harvengt, in *Chartularium Universitatis Parisiensis*, i. 53; Konrad von Mure, in Rockinger, *Q. E.*, ix. 440; Wolfgang of Altaich, in Pez, *Thesaurus anecdotorum*, vi, 2, p. 185, and Berlin, MS. Lat. oct. 136, f. 112.

[2] 'Littere quibus notantur gravamina que possunt de nimietate studii provenire. . . . Dicitur autem quod ante pulsationem initialis tintinabuli surgis preter consuetudinem ad legendum, in ingressu scolarum es primus et ultimus in regressu; postquam autem reverteris ad hospitium diem totum continuas in lectionibus quas audisti; immo, quod plus est, variis cogitationibus dum comedis anxiaris, et etiam in sompno, in quo animalium virtutum quies esse deberet, sub quadam imaginatione disputas et lectiones repetis dormiendo.' Then, after describing the student's neglect of his personal appearance, he adds: 'Nota quod premissa narratio destinari potest etiam illi qui huc et illuc vagatur et studere contempnit, et dicitur hoc species ironie in qua delinquens efficitur maiori pudore.' Munich, Cod. Lat. 23499, f. 4; B.M., Cotton MS. Vitellius C. viii, f. 93.

[3] These are particularly common in the various redactions of Bernard de Meung. Thus: 'Socius socio consolans eum de morte socii sui' (MS. lat. 1093, f. 62); 'Scolaris sociis suis ut latores presentium secum in hospicium habeant' (B.M., Add. MS. 8167, f. 179 v); 'Scolaris amico suo' for news (Munich, Cod. Lat. 96, f. 38). Cf. Cartellieri, nos. 78, 79, 287–304; P. Wolff, *Der Briefsteller des Thymo von Erfurt und seine Ableitungen* (Bonn diss., 1911), pp. 17–21; and Burdach, *Briefmuster*, pp. 85 ff., nos. 54 ff.

[4] Ponce de Provence in MS. lat. 18595, f. 24 v. Bernard de Meung in MS

make the journey together to Bologna in the autumn,[1] or inquiring concerning the advantages of other places of study.[2] Reference has been made above to the practice of securing rooms through friends already at school; in case of the death or sudden departure of a student his effects were sent home by one of his fellows.[3] At Bologna, at least, it was customary for the companions of a departing student to accompany him on horseback some miles on the way, and we even find outlines [4] of a

lat. 1093, f. 61 v (also B.M., Add. MS. 18382, f. 94 v; Cotton MS. Vitellius C. viii, f. 140): 'Tuam ergo commoneo caritatem ut, relicta soli natalis dulcedine, mature te conferas ad urbem Parisius, ubi florent ambages artium et profunda scientia divine pagine cum decretis.' An exhortation to come to Paris is also noted in *Zeitschrift für die Geschichte des Oberrheins*, new series, xi. 34; and in MS. lat. 14069, f. 185, we read: 'Cum igitur circumstancias ville Parisiensis scire meoque rescripto super hiis certificari desideres, innotescat tue dilectioni quod status terre bonus est, vinum et annona pro modico precio sui plenam exibent ubertatem, magistrorum etiam copia tanta super quod scolarium indigentia supprimatur, et—quid plura referam?—omnia se prospera sociis studere volentibus offerunt et iocunda.' So from Leipzig in the fifteenth century 'quidam scribit quodam socio hortando eum ut ocius beanorum spretis inepciis ad universitatem quampiam sese recipere festinet' (Munich, Cod. Lat. 14529, f. 357). See also the *Rethorica Poncii* (no place, 1486; Hain, no. 13255), ff. 18, 20, where a friend is exhorted to come to Basel.

[1] See for example the correspondence of two German students planning to study canon law at Bologna, in B.M., Arundel MS. 240, f. 122. One writes: 'Patefecit mihi quorundam relatio quod tue voluntatis in hoc stabiliatur propositum ut ad Bononiense proficiscatis studium postquam estivi fervoris virtus per successionem auctumpni fertilis fuerit mitigata.' The other will be glad to have his company; 'in crastino beati Michaelis proximo tuum adventum desiderabiliter prestolabor.'

[2] See the MS. just cited, f. 123, and particularly Guido Faba, *Dict. rhet.*, nos. 38, 39, where a student at Bologna is compelled to leave because of the dearness of living and writes for information concerning conditions at Naples. Laurentius of Aquileia (MS. lat. 14766, f. 119) represents a student at Naples making similar inquiries with respect to Bologna, while a Spanish redaction of Guido Faba (MS. lat. 11386, f. 56) substitutes Salamanca for Bologna and Paris for Naples in the example cited from the *Dict. rhet.* Cf. the letters in Burdach, *Briefmuster*, nos. 70–76, exchanged among students of Paris, Prague, Vienna, and Cracow, *ca.* 1404.

[3] Delisle, *Le Formulaire de Tréguier*, no. 18; cf. also no. 11 and an unpublished letter in the MS. (MS. lat. n.a. 426, f. 9). An analogous letter to a student at Oxford, *ca.* 1331, is printed in the *Literae Cantuarienses*, i. 417, and in the same collection (iii. 334) is a long and interesting letter of the reign of Henry VII, written in English and describing the property to be packed and the commissions to be performed for a former student. See also the *Rethorica Poncii* (1486), f. 20 v.

[4] 'Arenga qua utitur de studio litterali revertens inter illos qui eum causa

proper speech of thanks to be made to these *transcursibiles amici* [1] when they turned back.

In the Orleanese collections the group of letters between fellow-students is often followed by a group of correspondence between lovers—*amicus amice, amasius amasie*, etc.[2] The lady is warned to beware of the boys (*ne credat iuvenibus*); under the name of Thisbe, she is exhorted to elude her guards by night; she is reproached for having parted with the girdle which the writer had given her; the examples of Helen and Leda should incite her to tenderness,[3] etc. A fervid group of such letters is found in an early Italian collection, full of tender reproaches and passionate farewells, and closing with a missive to 'my only rose' in a curious kind of loose rhyme.[4]

Like his modern successor, the mediaeval student seems to have been an inveterate borrower. Sometimes it is a book for which he asks, such as the glosses on Virgil and Lucan, more commonly a loan of money until a messenger arrives from home, and models are not lacking for demanding back the money or the book.[5] We hear of a certain faithless Peter who borrowed ten livres *tournois*

honoris per aliquot miliaria vel leucas associant in regressu.' *Arenge composite a magistro Petro de Loro*, in the *Liber epistolaris* of Richard of Bury, p. 25 of the copy in the Bibliothèque Nationale (MS. lat. n.a. 1266). Similarly the *Arenge* of Guido Faba, MS. lat. 8652A, f. 30.

[1] The phrase is Buoncompagno's. Sutter, *Aus Leben und Schriften des Magisters Buoncompagno* (Freiburg i. B., 1894), p. 75.

[2] E.g., MS. lat. 1093, ff. 67 v, 68; Agen, MS. 4, f. 190; Valois, *De arte scribendi epistolas*, pp. 41 f.; Cartellieri, nos. 63, 64, 124, 125, 216–225; Delisle, in *Notices et extraits*, xxxvi. 200; Helen Waddell, *The Wandering Scholars* (Boston and New York, 1927), p. x.

[3] 'Dolor Paridis inflexit Helenam et Ledam Iupiter et matrem Herculis et plures alias quas modo taceo.' MS. lat. 1093, f. 67 v.

[4] 'G. unicę suę rosę A. vinculum dilectionis preciosę. Quę est fortitudo mea ut sustineam ut in tuo discessu pacientiam habeam? Numquid fortitudo mea fortitudo est lapidum ut tuum exspectem redditum que nocte et die non cesso dolere velut qui caret manu et pede? Omne quod iocundum est et delectabile absque te habetur ut lutum pedum calcabile. Pro gaudere duco fletus, nunquam animus meus apparet lętus. Dum recordor quę dedisti oscula et quam iocundis verbis refrigerasti pectuscula mori libet quod te videre non licet. Quid faciam miserrima, quo me vertam pauperrima? O si corpus meum terrę fuisset creditum usque ad optatum tuum redditum, aut si translatio mihi concederetur Abacuc ut semel venissem illuc . . .' Munich, Cod. Lat. 19411, f. 70.

[5] Bernard de Meung, in MS. lat. 8653, f. 32 v; MS. lat. 1093, ff. 61 v, 62; MS. lat. 14193, f. 27; Munich, Cod. Lat. 96, f. 37. Ponce de Provence, in B.M.,

one first of January and soon afterward quitted Paris for Orleans, where the lender's friends are requested to hunt him out.[1] The regular means of collecting such a debt seems to have been through the bishop of the debtor's diocese;[2] at Bologna, however, the matter was taken in hand by the municipal authorities, who threatened, unless the debt were promptly paid, to make it good from the property of such of the debtor's fellow-townsmen as came within reach.[3]

For obvious reasons, the letters of mediaeval students do not have much to say of what Rashdall calls "the wilder side of university life." We find a Paris scholar complaining of the disorders of the schools and expressing fear of personal violence,[4] and a student at Toulouse writes that a certain P., against

Arundel MS. 514, f. 78; MS. lat. 18595, f. 24; MS. lat. 8653, f. 13 v; Arsenal, MS. 3807, f. 63; Munich, Cod. Lat. 22293, f. 283 v. *Dictamen* from Louvain in Munich, Cod. Lat. 7082, f. 11 v. *Dictamen* 'magistri Johannis' in MS. lat. 16617, f. 224. Formulary from Toulouse, Arsenal, MS. 854, f. 223 v. Stehle, *Ueber ein Hildesheimer Formelbuch*, p. 9. Munich, Cod. Lat. 6911, f. 53; MS. lat. 14069, f. 201. Cartellieri, no. 283.

[1] 'Petrus, meus socius infidelis, cui decem libras Turonensium liberaliter mutuavi prima die ianuarii nunc instantis, furtive dimisso studio Parisiensi Aurelianum se transtulit ad studendum. Quamobrem sapientiam vestram, que, etc. [understand supplico], quatinus de predicto scolari cautius inquirentes, si eum poteritis invenire michi sine mora vestris litteris declaretis. Nam Parisius proficiscar vel certum nuntium destinabo recuperaturus pecuniam prelibatam vestro auxilio mediante.' Laurentius of Aquileia, in MS. lat. 11384; also with Toulouse in place of Paris and Paris in place of Orleans in MS. lat. 14174, f. 26, and MS. lat. 16253, f. 14 v. In MS. lat. 14766, f. 118 v, and in the B.M., Harleian MS. 3593, f. 49, the student has left Paris for Bologna. See also *Bullettino dell' Istituto Storico Italiano*, xiv. 167.

[2] 'Clericus episcopo ut cogat clericum reddere sibi pecuniam quam ei concessit.' Bernard de Meung, MS. lat. 1093, f. 57 v; MS. lat. 8653, f. 31; Munich, Cod. Lat. 96, f. 33 v. Similarly Ponce de Provence, in B.M., Arundel MS. 514, f. 83, and Add. MS. 8167, f. 172 v; MS. lat. 8653, f. 15 v; MS. lat. 18595, f. 2 8 v. Tarragona, MS. 6, f. 39 v: 'authors' pledged before starting against the Albigenses.

[3] Guido Faba, *Dict. rhet.*, nos. 97, 98; *Epistole*, no. 33. This is confirmed by the *Statuta Populi Bononiae*, ed. Frati, ii. 24, 29–32. On the collection of the debts of Bolognese students see also Giraldus Cambrensis, iii. 289; H. C. Lea, *A Formulary of the Papal Penitentiary in the Thirteenth Century* (Philadelphia, 1892), p. 124; Zaccagnini, *Studio di Bologna*, p. 67.

[4] 'Cum ad presens intentus esse deberem studiis, urgencia me protrahunt negotia bellorum quorundam, scilicet scolarium nephanda atque maligna perversitas qui studia dissipant, et timor cottidianus ingenium meum distrahit, quem habere me cogit anxietas de insultacionibus malignorum.' Munich, Cod. Lat. 6911, f. 54.

whom he had been warned before leaving his home in Narbonne, had taken forcible possession of his room and so disturbed him in his work that he would like permission to go home at Easter.[1] At Orleans a young man pleads for help from his father because, having quarrelled with a certain youth, as the devil would have it, he struck him on the head with a stick, so that he is now in prison and must pay fifty livres for his release, while his enemy is healed of his wounds and goes free.[2] That the pranks of students were not always severely judged we may perhaps infer from the letter of a professor of law at Orleans to a father at Besançon in which it is said that while no doubt the man's son G. was one of a crowd that had sung a ribald song on an organ, the matter was of no importance, as the young man's general record was good and he was making excellent progress in law.[3]

[1] 'Venerabili et discreto viro domino P., nobili burgensi Narbone, anchore spei sue, B. eius clericus, suus in omnibus. . . . Quando a vestra dominatione recessi, mihi districius precepistis ut P. societatem spernerem quantum possem; sed tanquam indiscretus vestrum salubre consilium non perfeci. Iustum est ut de hoc sentiam aliquod contra velle: ipse namque P. tam inique facere non expavit quod propriam cameram dimittere sum cohactus, et quosdam socios meos oportuit facere illud idem, ita quod nunc cum filio domini et cum quibusdam mercatoribus de comedere in eo est [?]. Unde cum occasione societatis predicti P. aliquantulum sum turbatus et quasi a studio deviatus, dominationi vestre supplico precibus subiectivis quatinus mihi dignetis declarare, si vobis placet, quod ad vos venire debeam in proximo festo Pasche.' Formulary from Toulouse, Arsenal, MS. 854, f. 232. A student makes a similar complaint of having been driven from his room at Paris: Munich, Cod. Lat. 6911, f. 55; MS. lat. 14069, f. 181.

[2] 'Cum essem nuper Aurelianis, pater karissime, rixatus fui cum quodam iuvene, sicut diabolus ministravit, et ipsum demum percussi cum baculo super caput, et propter vulnus sibi factum fui in Aureliani curia carceratus. Liberatus est quidem iuvenis et sanatus, et a me petunt pro expensis illius in banno curie libras Turonensium quinquaginta, nec antequam solute fuerint possum evadere carcerem supradictum.' Ponce de Provence, in B.M., Arundel MS. 514, f. 74; MS. lat. 18195, f. 20 v; MS. lat. 11385, f. 70 v; MS. lat. 8653, f. 12; Arsenal, MS. 3807, f. 59 v; Troyes, MS. 1556, f. 17 v. Similarly Laurentius of Aquileia, MS. lat. 16253, f. 13.

[3] 'Talis professor legum actu legens Aurelianis, laudabili viro P. civi Bisuntino salutem cum dilectionis amplexu. Lingua tertia multos perdidit, ut scriptura perhibet sacrosancta [Ecclesiasticus, xxviii. 16]. Proinde non debetis aurem inclinare credulam linguis obloquencium qui fame filii vestri G. mendoso [MS. mendenso] satagunt derogare susurro. Constat enim non fuisse diem profestum sed aprime festivum quo idem G. nec non plurimi scolares ⟨et⟩ organis armonicis decantarunt de scorto. Prorsus nihil est, cum ipse commendatur super mentis et corporis celibatu. Non igitur a prefato manum vestram

Naturally, too, the examples of parental reproof have something to say of the evils of the time, particularly gambling and
riotous living.[1] More rarely do we find mention of the more
innocent amusements of students, such as the loan of a horse
to ride on St. Nicholas' day at Oxford.[2] One scholar is told
that he gives too much time to chess;[3] and another's request
for a dog is refused, lest it furnish him occasion for waste of
time.[4] In general the formularies reflect the more virtuous side
of student life, and for a more adequate portrayal of its vice and
violence we must turn to the records of courts, the Goliardic
literature, and the vigorous denunciations of contemporary
preachers.

It is evident from this brief examination of the letters of
mediaeval students that their correspondence has to do chiefly
with the commonplace and everyday aspects of life at the school
and university, and that in substance, though not in form, much
of it would be almost as representative of the Harvard or Yale
of to-day as of mediaeval Orleans or Bologna. Lambskin cloaks

pro linguis obtrectantium retrahatis, scientes quod in utroque iure proficit
eleganter.' MS. lat. 8653A, f. 10. What is meant by the contrast between
'diem profestum' and 'aprime festivum' is not entirely clear.

[1] E.g., 'Lupanar in scolis et ludum exerces alee, litteralis scientie profectum
abhominans': B.M., Cotton MS. Vitellius C. viii, f. 141. 'Nam omnino labore
scolastico postrigato tempus tuum et alia que habes consumis, ut dicitur, pilas,
Dianam, et meretricia frequentando': letter to student at Orleans, MS. lat.
15131, f. 180 v. Cf. also Guido Faba, Dict. rhet., no. 3, and the Bohemian collections of the fourteenth century analysed by Palacky in the Abhandlungen
der königlichen böhmischen Gesellschaft der Wissenschaften, fifth series, ii. 259,
and by Schlesinger in the Mittheilungen des Vereins für die Geschichte der
Deutschen in Böhmen, xxvii. 16. See also Matthew of Vendôme, ed. Wattenbach, pp. 620–621.

[2] 'Constanciam vestram quam diligo cordis et anime puritate deprecor incessanter quatinus equum vestrum in honore sancti Nicholay equitandum
dignetur vestra dilectio mihi accomodare, super quem honorifice valeam equitare.' Bodleian, Auct. F. 3. 9, f. 427 (fifteenth century). On the feast of St.
Nicholas—the patron saint of scholars—as celebrated in the schools of Saint-
Denis, see the form printed by Hauréau, iv. 276. A letter, entitled 'Scolaris
patri significans se eligendum episcopum puerorum' (Stehle, Über ein Hildesheimer Formelbuch, p. 9; Zeitschrift des Historischen Vereins für Niedersachsen,
1896, p. 108) seems to allude to the same occasion. Cf. infra, p. 69.

[3] Luchaire, Études, p. 103, no. 19.

[4] Liber epistolaris of Richard of Bury, MS. lat. n.a. 1266, p. 81; also in a
Cistercian formulary, MS. lat. 11384, f. 195.

and parchment, the glossed *Doctrinal* and the inception banquet, belong plainly in the Middle Ages and nowhere else, but
money and clothing, rooms, teachers, and books have been subjects of interest at all times and in all places. This characteristic of the letters is in some respects disappointing—we might
have known quite independently, it may be urged, that the
mediaeval student wanted money and tried to extort it from his
father, borrow it from his fellows, or beg it from others; we
might have known that he was robbed by highwaymen and
rebuked by his parents. What a pity that out of such a mass
of letters there are none that tell us in simple and unaffected
detail how a young man studied and how he spent his day! To
all this the answer is that under the conditions then prevailing
very few such letters could have been written, and, if written,
there was no reason why a matter of such individual and temporary interest should be preserved. It was precisely because·
they were trite and banal, because they voiced the needs of the
great student body everywhere and always, that these letters
and models were considered useful to others and hence were
copied and kept. It is certainly worth something to us to know
what were the commonplaces of existence in the schools of the
Middle Ages, and to realize more vividly those phases of student
life which we might otherwise lose from view. One may, of
course, easily be deceived by the modern atmosphere with which
such letters, read without reference to other sources of information, surround the mediaeval student, and yet from one point
of view their value lies just here. The contrasts between the·
Middle Ages and the twentieth century are broad and striking,
in universities as well as in the world at large, and we need to be
reminded again and again that the fundamental factors in man's
development remain much the same from age to age and must
so remain as long as human nature and physical environment
continue what they have been. A just historical view requires
accurate appreciation of both the constant and the varying
elements in the history of civilization; the present chapter may
perhaps serve to illustrate something of their relative importance
in the life of the mediaeval student.

CHAPTER II

THE UNIVERSITY OF PARIS IN THE SERMONS OF THE THIRTEENTH CENTURY [1]

In the intellectual life of the Middle Ages the University of Paris occupies a place of pre-eminent importance. "The Italians have the Papacy, the Germans have the Empire, and the French have Learning," ran the old saying; and the chosen abode of Learning was Paris. "Let us suppose," says a preacher by way of illustration, "that all the sky is parchment, all the sea is ink, and all the stars are Paris masters." [2] The University of Paris was generally recognized as the 'parent of the sciences' and the first school of the church, and its supremacy was manifest not only in its position as the centre of scholasticism and the bulwark of orthodoxy, but also in the large number and wide distribution of its students, in its influence upon the establishment and the constitutions of other universities, and in its large share in the political and ecclesiastical movements of the later Middle Ages.[3] So prominent were the constitutional and theological aspects of the university and so violent the controversies which raged about it, that, amid the confusion of chancellors and faculties and nations, and the conflicts over the new Aris-

---

[1] Revised and expanded from the *American Historical Review*, x. 1-27 (1904).

[2] J. Klapper, *Exempla aus Handschriften des Mittelalters* (Heidelberg, 1911), no. 87. Glorifications of Paris as the great centre of learning are common in mediaeval literature. See for examples the bull *Parens scientiarum* of Gregory IX (*Chartularium Universitatis Parisiensis*, i. 136) and the anonymous sermon printed by Hauréau (ii. 105), where Paris is called the mill where the world's corn is ground and the oven where its bread is baked.

[3] Cf. Rashdall, *The Universities of Europe in the Middle Ages*, i. 518 ff.; Valois, *La France et le Grand Schisme*; Gross, "The Political Influence of the University of Paris in the Middle Ages," in *A. H. R.*, vi. 440-445; Jean Bonnerot, "L'ancienne Université de Paris, centre international d'études," in the *Bulletin* of the International Committee of Historical Sciences, i. 659-681 (1928). The interesting subject of foreign students at Paris is treated by A. Budinsky, *Die Universität Paris und die Fremden an derselben im Mittelalter* (Berlin, 1876), but there is room for a more thorough study on the basis of the materials since published in the *Chartularium*. The proportion of foreigners among the distinguished doctors of the university was remarkably high. Cf. Hauréau, iv. 47-48.

totle and the 'Eternal Gospel,' there is some danger of losing sight of the more human element and forgetting that an adequate idea of a university can be got only when its teaching and organization are seen against the background of the daily life of its student body. Unfortunately, the sources of information concerning the student life of mediaeval Paris are by no means abundant. There is of course much to be gleaned from the great *Chartularium Universitatis Parisiensis*, so admirably edited by Denifle and Chatelain, and from the proctor's book of the English nation printed as an appendix to it—our knowledge of the various taverns of mediaeval Paris, for example, being largely derived from this nation's minutes of the drinking up of its surplus revenue [1]—; but most of the documents in this invaluable repository relate to the organization and external history of the university rather than to its inner life. The records of the courts of law, so rich a mine of information for student manners at other universities, fail us entirely at Paris,[2] and the collections of student letters, which reflect the decent commonplaces of existence among mediaeval scholars, are of little specific help here.[3] For the early years of the university the Goliardic poetry and other products of the renaissance of the twelfth century are, it is true, of considerable value, but this movement was soon crushed by the triumph of scholasticism, and in the thirteenth century, when Paris was the undisputed

[1] Sixty such resorts of this nation, which comprised the students from Northern and Eastern Europe, are mentioned in its records. See E. Chatelain, "Notes sur quelques tavernes fréquentées par l'Université de Paris aux XIVe et XVe siècles," in *Bulletin de la Société de l'Histoire de Paris et de l'Île-de-France*, xxv. 87–109 (1898); cf. P. Champion, "Liste de tavernes de Paris d'après des documents du XVe siècle," *ibid.*, xxxix. 259–267 (1912); and G. C. Boyce, *The English-German Nation in the University of Paris during the Middle Ages* (Bruges, 1927). For other records of the nations, see H. Omont, "Le 'livre' ou 'cartulaire' de la nation de France de l'Université de Paris," in *Mémoires de la Société de l'Histoire de Paris et de l'Île-de-France*, xli. 1–130 (1914).

[2] For illustrations from Bologna see the documents published in the appendix to F. Cavazza, *Le scuole dell'antico studio bolognese* (Milan, 1896), and for Oxford the coroners' inquests published by J. E. Thorold Rogers, *Oxford City Documents*, pp. 145 ff.; C. Gross, *Coroners' Rolls*, pp. 87–91; J. F. Willard, *The Royal Authority and the Early English Universities* (Philadelphia, 1902), pp. 82–85. [3] See Chapter I, above.

intellectual centre of Christendom, very little Latin poetry of any sort was produced.[1] But while not an age of poetry, the thirteenth century was an age of preaching, and in the scarcity of other sources the enormous mass of sermons which has come down to us from that period is well worthy of examination for the light it throws upon the University of Paris and its life.

The material is at first sight not promising. By their very nature sermons are not historical but hortatory; their purpose is to edify, not to record; and the preaching of the thirteenth century, with its elaborate subdivisions, its piling of text upon text, its senses literal and allegorical, tropological and anagogical, would seem peculiarly barren of information upon the life of its age.[2] In the midst, however, of the scholastic sermonizing of this period, and soon reacting upon it, there came a genuine revival of popular preaching, due largely to the influence of the Mendicant Orders. In order to hold the attention of the people the preachers found it necessary to be entertaining, as well as simple and direct, and to make abundant use of marvels, anecdotes, and pointed illustrations from everyday life. If his audience showed signs of nodding, the speaker would begin, "There was once a king named Arthur," or shout suddenly, "That fellow who is asleep will not give away my secrets,"[3] or "For

[1] The poems of most interest in relation to the University of Paris in the thirteenth century are those of Rutebeuf (ed. Kressner, Wolfenbüttel, 1885). John of Garland can hardly be called a poet, but the large amount of prose and verse which he turned out contains not a little of interest to the student of university conditions. His *Morale scholarium*, however, which promises something of the interest of the German student-manuals of the fifteenth century, proves on examination distinctly disappointing; cf. Chapter III, below. It has now been edited, with great patience and learning, by L. J. Paetow, "Morale Scolarium of John of Garland," in his *Two Medieval Satires on the University of Paris* (Berkeley, 1927). Cf. in the same volume his edition of *La bataille des VII ars* of Henri d'Andeli.

[2] See the general works of L. Bourgain, *La chaire française au XIIᵉ siècle* (Paris, 1879), and A. Lecoy de la Marche, *La chaire française au Moyen Âge, spécialement au XIIIᵉ siècle* (2d ed., Paris, 1886). There is an excellent résumé of the subject by Langlois, "L'Éloquence Sacrée au Moyen Âge," in the *Revue des deux mondes*, January 1, 1893, pp. 170–201. See now also the interesting volume of G. R. Owst, *Preaching in Medieval England* (Cambridge, 1926).

[3] Caesar of Heisterbach, ed. Strange, i. 205; T. F. Crane, *The Exempla of Jacques de Vitry* (London, 1890), p. xlii, note.

God's sake, if any one has a pin let him wake up that old dame!"[1] Such sallies might easily pass the bounds of reverence and even of decency,[2] and Dante had good ground for complaining of those "who go forth with jests and buffooneries to preach" and swell with pride if they can but raise a laugh.[3]

Questions of propriety apart, however, it is this very freedom and unconventionality on the part of many of the preachers which gives them their historical interest. The stories, or *exempla*, with which the sermons are embellished come from all kinds of sources—fables and folk-lore, bestiaries, lives of saints, historical manuals, and personal experiences—and comprise the greatest variety of legends and miracles and contemporary anecdotes, so that they afford a most valuable insight into the popular religion and superstitions of their day, besides preserving a considerable amount of curious information concerning the manners and customs of all classes of society.[4] Still, the great body of mediaeval sermons is not interesting reading, especially in the condensed and desiccated form in which most of them have come down to us. The *exempla* and the allusions to contemporary life constitute but a small portion of the whole, and it is a long and arduous task to separate these from the mass of scholastic theology and pulpit commonplaces in which they lie embedded. In the case of the *exempla* much of this labour of sifting was performed by the mediaeval purveyors of sermon-helps, who not only provided the lazy or ignorant preacher with complete series of sermons for the ecclesiastical year under such suggestive titles as *Sermones parati* or *Dormi secure*, but also furnished material for enlivening these dry outlines in the form of collections of *exempla* conveniently arranged by subjects— manuals of clerical wit and anecdote which enjoyed great popularity in the later Middle Ages and have survived in numerous

[1] Owst, *op. cit.*, p. 186.

[2] For illustrations see the extracts printed by Hauréau, iv. 17 ff.; and the citations in the *Histoire littéraire de la France*, xxvi. 417 ff.

[3] *Paradiso*, xxix. 115-117. Gautier de Château-Thierry says of the sending of the disciples by John the Baptist to Christ, 'Audiebat verba oris eius, non opera regum vel renardi vel fabulas.' MS. lat. 15959, f. 59, col. 4.

[4] See the sketches in Bourgain and Lecoy de la Marche entitled "La société d'après les sermons."

manuscripts and early imprints. The importance of these compilations for the history of mediaeval culture is now recognized,[1] and a good deal of the more scattered material has been

[1] Upon *exempla* and their use see T. F. Crane, "Mediaeval Sermon-Books and Stories," in the *Proceedings* of the American Philosophical Society, xxi. 49–78 (1883); his "Mediaeval Sermon-Books and Stories and their Study since 1883," *ibid.*, lvi. 369–402 (1917); the introduction and notes to his edition of the *Exempla* of Jacques de Vitry; and Frenken's edition (see below); C. G. N. de Vooys, *Middelnederlandsche Legenden en Exempelen* (The Hague, 1900); J. A. Mosher, *The Exemplum in the Early Religious and Didactic Literature of England* (New York, 1911); the *Catalogue of Romances in the Department of Manuscripts in the British Museum*, vol. iii, ed. by J. A. Herbert (London, 1910); and now especially J. T. Welter, *L'Exemplum dans la littérature religieuse et didactique du Moyen Âge* (Paris, 1927), who discusses the whole subject on the basis of wide knowledge of the printed and manuscript material. Translations of typical stories of this sort have been made into English by Munro, *Monastic Tales of the XIII. Century*, in the *Translations and Reprints* published by the University of Pennsylvania, ii, no. 4; and into French by Lecoy de la Marche, *L'Esprit de nos aieux* (Paris, 1888). The most important collections from Northern France and neighbouring lands in the thirteenth century are as follows, Jacques de Vitry and Étienne de Bourbon being, as former students at Paris, the most valuable for university life (on all these see now Welter, *L'Exemplum*):

Jacques de Vitry, *Exempla or Illustrative Stories from the Sermones Vulgares*, edited by Crane for the Folk-Lore Society (1890); also in J. B. Pitra, *Analecta novissima spicilegii Solesmensis* (Rome, 1885–88), ii. 443–461. Extracts from his *Sermones vulgares* are also published by Pitra, ii. 344–442; the library of Harvard University possesses a manuscript of these sermons which was once the property of the monastery of S. Jacques at Liége (MS. Riant 35). *Die Exempla aus den Sermones feriales et communes des Jakob von Vitry* have now been edited by J. Greven (Heidelberg, 1914) in the *Sammlung mittellateinischer Texte*, no. 9, and, with a fuller commentary, by G. Frenken, *Die Exempla des Jacob von Vitry* (Munich, 1914) in *Quellen und Untersuchungen zur lateinischen Philologie des Mittelalters*, no. v, 1.

Caesar of Heisterbach, *Dialogus miraculorum*, ed. Strange, Cologne, 1851; fragments of the *Libri VIII miraculorum*, ed. Meister, Rome, 1901; stories from the *Homeliae*, ed. A. E. Schönbach, Vienna *S. B.*, cxliv, no. 9 (cf. also his review of Meister, *M. I. O. G.*, xxiii. 660 ff.). On the life and writings of Caesar, see also Schönbach, "Studien zur Erzählungsliteratur des Mittelalters: Ueber Caesarius von Heisterbach," in Vienna *S. B.*, cxliv (1901), no. 9; clix (1908), no. 4; clxiii (1909), no. 1; and J. Greven, "Kleinere Studien zu Cäsarius von Heisterbach," in *Annalen des historischen Vereins für den Niederrhein*, xcix. 1–35 (1916).

Thomas de Cantimpré, *Bonum universale de apibus*. Various editions; see W. A. van der Vet, *Het Biënboec van Thomas van Cantimpré en zijn Exempelen* (The Hague, 1902).

Étienne de Bourbon, *Anecdotes historiques*, ed. Lecoy de la Marche (Paris, 1877).

Anonymous *Compilatio singularis Exemplorum*, MS. 468 of the Bibliothèque

rendered available by the patient scholarship of the late Bar-thélemy Hauréau, whose studies must form the starting-point of any other investigations in this field.[1]

In endeavouring to bring together such information as the sermons contain upon the life of the University of Paris in the thirteenth century we must give up from the first any idea of an exhaustive investigation. Of all countries France was the most productive in sermons, and probably most of the dis-tinguished French preachers of this period were at some time in their careers connected with the University of Paris; and while few of their sermons have been, or ever will be, published, the number preserved in manuscript reaches far into the thou-sands. Some practical limit must evidently be set by confining the study to the printed texts and to such portions of the manu-script sources as seem likely to yield fruitful results. Accord-ingly, besides the collections of *exempla* and the extensive materials published or indicated by Hauréau,[2] attention has

de Tours. Welter, *L'Exemplum*, pp. 236–244, has also found MSS. at Berne and Upsala.

Anonymous *Tabula Exemplorum secundum ordinem Alphabeti*, edited by J. T. Welter (Paris, 1926). Cf. the related collection at Auxerre (MS. 35).

A Franciscan collection, in part from Paris. L. Oliger, "Liber exemplorum Fratrum Minorum Saeculi XIII," in *Antonianum*, ii. 203–276 (1927).

A collection compiled by an anonymous Dominican at or near Cambridge, preserved in the British Museum, Royal MS. 7 D. i, and analysed by Herbert, pp. 477–503.

Reference should also be made to the *Latin Stories* edited by Wright for the Percy Society (1842), and to the fables of Odo of Cheriton in the edition of Hervieux, *Fabulistes latins*, iv (1896).

[1] See particularly his *Notices et extraits de quelques manuscrits latins de la Bibliothèque Nationale*; and numerous articles in the *Histoire littéraire* and the *Journal des savants*. The catalogue of *Incipits* of sermons and other Latin works of the Middle Ages upon which Hauréau based many of his conclusions as to authorship can now be consulted at the Bibliothèque Nationale.

[2] Hauréau's studies were chiefly confined to manuscripts in Paris. Besides the various manuscripts in other libraries noted below under individual preachers, I have found of special interest the following miscellaneous collec-tions of Paris sermons: Bodleian, Ashmolean MS. 757; Merton College, MS. 237; Munich, Cod. Lat. 23372; Library of St. Mark's at Venice, Fondo Antico, MS. 92. See also the analysis by Langlois of MS. 691 at Arras, containing Paris sermons of the first half of the thirteenth century: *Journal des savants*, 1916, pp. 488–494, 548–559; and the extracts from Graz MSS. of Jacques de Lau-sanne printed by A. E. Schönbach, "Miscellen aus Grazer Handschriften. 6. Jakob von Lausanne," in *Mittheilungen des historischen Vereines für Steier-*

been directed especially to those preachers who had personal knowledge of academic conditions at Paris and were in the habit of alluding to them in their sermons, particularly to that altogether delightful cleric, Robert de Sorbon,[1] the companion of St. Louis and founder of the Sorbonne, and to the chancellors of the university. Originally simply the official of the church of Notre-Dame who was charged with keeping the chapter's seal and drawing up its documents,[2] the chancellor was early given

mark, xlviii. 120–192 (1900). Cf. the general remarks on university education by Humbert de Romans, general of the Dominican order from 1254 to 1263, in his *Expositio Regulae S. Augustini, Maxima bibliotheca patrum*, xxv. 632–634. I have not seen the *Sermones Parisienses* at Erlangen, MSS. 320, 321, 322. Cf. Hans Fischer, *Die lateinischen Pergamenthandschriften der Universitäts-bibliothek Erlangen* (Erlangen, 1928), pp. 377–380.

[1] See Hauréau, "Les Propos de Maître Robert de Sorbon," in the *Mémoires de l'Académie des Inscriptions*, xxxi, 2, pp. 133–149; and the bibliography and list of Robert's works in the introduction to F. Chambon's edition of the *De conscientia* (Paris, 1903). The library of the Sorbonne formerly possessed 'Sermones magistri Roberti de Sorbona de tempore, de festis, et ad status' (Delisle, *Cabinet des manuscrits*, iii. 113), but the manuscript seems to have disappeared. The most considerable collection of his sermons which survives is found in the Bibliothèque Nationale, MS. lat. 15971, ff. 68–198, a collection for Sundays and holy days throughout the year, delivered, as appears from the concordance of the fixed and movable feasts, in 1260 and 1261. A large number of these sermons are in his name and many of the others are in his style. Scattered sermons are in MSS. lat. 14952, f. 53 (printed by Hauréau, iv. 69); 15951, f. 374; 15952, ff. 14, 119, 119 v; 15954, ff. 172, 272; 15955, f. 179; 16482, ff. 309–312, 318; 16488, ff. 437 v, 457 v; 16499, f. 272; 16505, ff. 155 v, 157, 217, 220 v; 16507, ff. 30, 267, 268, 421; and in Munich, Cod. Lat. 23372, p. 124.

[2] On the early functions of the chancellor, see Guérard, *Cartulaire de Notre-Dame de Paris*, i, pp. civ–cv; Mortet, "Maurice de Sully," in the *Mémoires de la Société de l'Histoire de Paris*, xvi. 150 ff. On the later development of the office, see the *Chartularium*, i, pp. xi–xix; Rashdall, *Universities*, i. 305–313, 333–334, 339–342, 393–396, 448–452, 456–458, 472–474.

The chancellors of the thirteenth century are enumerated, with their approximate dates, in the *Chartularium*, i, p. xix, note; ii, p. xv. The following list of their sermons includes all that I have been able to find after a somewhat protracted search. Unless otherwise indicated, the manuscripts are those of the Bibliothèque Nationale:

Pierre de Poitiers, chancellor as early as 1193 and as late as 1204 or 1205. See Bourgain, *Chaire française*, p. 54; Hauréau, ii. 240; iii. 67 ff.; and Lacombe, as cited below, pp. 36, 120–130. The only important collection of his sermons to which attention has been called is in MS. lat. 14593, where several numbers of the series are repeated. Some of these are also in MSS. lat. 3563, f. 114; 3705, f. 129; 12293, ff. 99–107; 13586, p. 330; Bibliothèque Mazarine, MS. 1005.

Prévostin (Prepositinus), a Lombard, chancellor from 1206 to 1209 or there-

supervision over the schools which sprang up about the cathedral, and as these grew in numbers and importance and de-

abouts. On his life and works see Hauréau in the *Mélanges Julien Havet*, pp. 297–303; and now G. Lacombe, *La vie et les oeuvres de Prévostin* (Kain, 1927: *Bibliothèque Thomiste*, xi), the first volume of a projected complete edition of Prévostin's works. His sermons contain exceedingly little on the life of the time.

Étienne de Reims, chancellor from 1214 or 1215 to 1218. Only one of his sermons is known, MS. lat. 16505, f. 190.

Philip de Grève (?), 1218–36, the most distinguished chancellor of this period, often called simply 'The Chancellor.' His poems and theological writings do not concern us here; on the man and his sermons see Oudin, *Commentarius de scriptoribus ecclesiae*, iii. 121; Peiper, in the *Archiv für Litteraturgeschichte*, vii. 409 ff.; the index to the first volume of the *Chartularium*; and Hauréau in the *Journal des savants*, July, 1894. H. Meylan, in the *Positions des thèses* of the École des Chartes, 1927, makes two persons of Philip de Grève and Philip the Chancellor, ascribing to the latter all the sermons and other writings; judgement must be suspended until his evidence is made available. The sermons fall into four groups:

1. *Sermones festivales*, for Sundays and holy days throughout the year. MSS. lat. 2516A, 3280, 3543, 3544, 3545, 12416, 15933, 16469 (last portion of series only); Bibliothèque Mazarine, MS. 1009; MSS. Troyes, 1417; Rouen, 615; Alençon, 153, 154; Bourges, 117; B.M., Royal MS. 8. F. 13; Siena, MS. F. x. 5. According to Omont (*Cabinet historique*, 1882, p. 568), this series was also found in the seminary library at Autun, MS. 139B. Scattered sermons of this series are in MSS. lat. 15951, 15954, 15955, 15959, 16466, 16471, 16488, 16505, 16507; MSS. Amiens, 284; Bourges, 115, ff. 74–84; Arras, 329, f. 54.

2. *Expositiones Evangeliorum Dominicorum*, also called simply *Omelie*, really a theological commentary on the Gospels throughout the year (cf. Hauréau, vi. 56). MSS. lat. 3281, 18175; Vatican, Fondo Vaticano, MSS. 1246, 1247; Lincoln Cathedral, MS. A. 2. 5; Cambridge, Peterhouse, MS. I. 3. 9; Munich, Cod. Lat. 3740; Erfurt, MS. Q. 97; Troyes, MS. 1100, ff. 206–227 v.

3. *In Psalterium Davidicum CCCXXX sermones*. Numerous manuscripts (see Lacombe, p. 156); published at Paris in 1522 and at Brescia in 1600.

4. A number of occasional sermons delivered at Paris and various places in Northern France and possessing considerable historical interest. Two are in MS. lat. n.a. 338 (ff. 152, 236), where they were seen and their importance noted by Hauréau (vi. 239; *Journal des savants*, August, 1889). The others, unknown to Hauréau, are found in MSS. Avranches, 132; Troyes, 1099; and Vitry-le-François, 69. The Avranches manuscript is the most complete collection of Philip's sermons, containing also the first and second series. See Chapter XI for a fuller discussion.

There is no apparent reason for attributing to Philip the *Sermones cancellarii Parisiensis* of MS. 403 of the State Library at Berlin (cf. Rose, *Verzeichniss*, ii. 237) or the *Sermones cancellarii Parisiensis* at Erfurt (MS. F. 103). For a French sermon on the Virgin composed in part by him see Valois, *Guillaume d'Auvergne*, pp. 220 ff.

Guiard de Laon, chancellor from 1237 to 1238, when he became bishop of Cambrai. On his writings see the *Histoire littéraire*, xviii. 354–356; and Hau-

veloped into a university he still asserted his right to license masters and his jurisdiction over scholars. Stubborn conflicts

réau, in the *Journal des savants*, June, 1893. His numerous sermons, many of which are shown by the manuscripts to have been preached at Paris, have not come down to us in any single collection (the *Summula sermonum* seen by Oudin at Dijon seems to have been lost), but are found in several manuscripts, scattered among those of Eudes de Châteauroux, Guillaume d'Auvergne, and others of his contemporaries. Taken together, MSS. lat. 15959, 15955, and 15964 offer a fairly complete series for Sundays and festivals throughout the year, often with several for the same day. MSS. lat. 15951 and 16741 and Arras, MS. 329, contain a large number of sermons *de sanctis*. Various sermons are in MSS. lat. 12418 (five, not three, as Hauréau states), 15952, 15953, 15954, 16488, 16502, 16505, 16507, n.a. 338, and in Amiens, MS. 284 (which contains some in addition to those enumerated in Coyecque's catalogue). A French sermon of Guiard is printed in the *Revue des sciences ecclésiastiques*, iv. 124 (1861). Some of his sermons in MS. lat. 16471 were ascribed by Hauréau to Gautier de Château-Thierry because of the opinion, which he was finally compelled to abandon, that Guiard was never chancellor.

Eudes de Châteauroux, chancellor 1238–44 and afterward cardinal bishop of Tusculum. The time at my disposal has not permitted an investigation of the very numerous manuscripts of Eudes, apparently the most prolific sermonizer of all the chancellors of his century. Cardinal Pitra (*Analecta novissima spicilegii Solesmensis*, ii. 188–343) has published extracts from a collection of 765 of his sermons in the possession of the Dominicans at Rome and has enumerated a large number of other manuscripts; many of the Paris manuscripts have been noted by Hauréau. See also Delisle in *B. E. C.*, xlix. 268–272. The printed sermons and such others as I have read bear out Hauréau's statement that they contain few allusions to the customs or events of the time. On Eudes see Pitra, ii, pp. xxiii–xxxv; Hauréau, in the *Journal des savants*, August, 1888, and in the *Notices et extraits*, xxiv, 2, pp. 204 ff.

Gautier de Château-Thierry, chancellor from 1246 to 1249, when he became bishop of Paris. Scattered sermons by him are found in MSS. lat. 15951, 15953, 15955, 15959, 16471, 16488, 16507; Arras, MS. 329, ff. 1, 53 v, 72, 152; and MS. 691, f. 139 v. In a volume of *Quaestiones theologicae* in the Biblioteca Antoniana at Padua (MS. 152) his name appears on ff. 150 v and 153; on f. 152 v, apropos of the question whether a master reading at Paris can preach without the bishop's license, he has something to say of the chancellor's office. Some account of Gautier and his writings will be found in *Gallia Christiana*, vii. 100; *Histoire littéraire*, xxvi. 390–395; Lecoy de la Marche, *Chaire française*, p. 95.

Etienne Tempier, also known as Étienne d'Orléans, chancellor from 1262 or 1263 to 1268, when he became bishop of Paris. See *Gallia Christiana*, vii.108–115; Hauréau, in *Journal des savants*, 1890, p. 255. Three sermons by him are in MS. lat. 16481, ff. 77 v, 136 v, 214 (cf. Quétif and Échard, *Scriptores Ordinis Praedicatorum*, i. 269).

Jean d'Orléans, also known as Jean des Alleux, chancellor from 1271 to 1280, when he became a Dominican. See *Chartularium*, i. 494; Quétif and Échard, i. 499; *Histoire littéraire*, xxv. 270–280. His sermons are scattered through MSS. lat. 14899, ff. 46, 83, 86, 132; 14947 (see Quétif and Échard, i.

arose over these claims in the earlier years of the thirteenth century, and various papal bulls placed important restrictions upon the chancellor's powers, but he continued to style himself the head of the university and to direct the examinations leading to the master's degree. As the chancellors were themselves masters and generally distinguished preachers as well, it is evident that their sermons, though they are naturally of the learned and dignified type and need to be used with due allowance for the official and often unfriendly attitude of the authors, represent close acquaintance with university affairs and possess special importance for our purpose.

With regard to the studies pursued at Paris we must not expect to find much information in the sermons. Various chancellors do indeed draw out elaborate comparisons between the seven liberal arts and the seven gifts of the spirit,[1] between the

385); 14952, f. 188 v; 15005 (contained also in MS. lat. 14947); 15956, ff. 279 v, 301 v, 313 v; 16481 (see Quétif and Échard, i. 268); 16482, ff. 178 v, 204, 275 v (ascribed to him by Quétif and Échard and the *Histoire littéraire*); Soissons, MS. 125, f. 60 (Molinier's catalogue is wrong in attributing to him the four that follow, of which two are anonymous and two in the name 'fratris Petri de Remerico Monte'); Troyes, MS. 1788, f. 82 v; Munich, Cod. Lat. 23372, pp. 8, 15, 19, 29, 39, 47, 53, 88, 129, 130; Bodleian, Ashmolean MS. 757, ff. 81, 349, 359; Merton College, MS. 237, ff. 32 v, 94 v, 110; Venice, Library of St. Mark's, Fondo Antico, MS. 92, ff. 228 ff. (six sermons); University of Erlangen, MS. 326, no. 33; MS. 327, f. 3 v.

Nicolas de Nonancourt, 1284–88. Sermons in MSS. lat. 15952, ff. 277 v (also in 14961, f. 135), 279; 16252, f. 279. A 'sermo cancellarii' in MS. lat. 15952, f. 113 (and anonymously in MS. lat. 14899, f. 109), is attributed to him by Hauréau.

Bertaud de St. Denis, 1288–95. But one of his sermons is known: MS. lat. 14947, f. 210 (also in MSS. lat. 15005, f. 113, and 15129, f. 191). Cf. *Histoire littéraire*, xxv. 317–320; xxvi. 439; *Journal des savants*, 1889, p. 303; 1891, p. 302.

Sermons of anonymous chancellors who have not been identified are in MSS. lat. 568, f. 190; 10968, f. 104; 12418, ff. 109, 110; 15527, f. 1; 15952, ff. 107–108; 16502, ff. 26, 84 v, 124. The editors of the *Chartularium* declare that various sermons of Aimery de Veire, chancellor from 1249 to *circa* 1263, are extant, but none were known to Hauréau nor have I been able to discover any. The sermons in MS. lat. 2516A, of which Lecoy de la Marche conjectures Aimery to have been the author, are the work of Philip the Chancellor (*Journal des savants*, 1890, p. 249).

[1] Prévostin, B.M., Add. MS. 18335, f. 14; Gautier de Château-Thierry, MS. lat. 15955, f. 429; and Arras, MS. 329, f. 3 v; Eudes de Châteauroux, MS. lat.

lessons of the Lord's school and those of the Devil's,[1] but in
such cases the audience is assumed to be sufficiently familiar
with the studies mentioned, and the weight of exposition is put
upon the corresponding virtue or vice; and even where the account is more specific, it offers interest as an expression of the
preacher's attitude toward learning rather than as a description
of particular subjects. The all-important study, according to
the preachers, is of course theology, 'Madame la Haute Science'
of the thirteenth century,[2] supreme above all other studies,
which may be valuable as disciplines but do not deserve to be
studied for their own sakes.[3] The arts are merely preparatory
to theology; [4] indeed the *trivium* affords a sufficient preparation,
since "the branches of the *quadrivium*, though containing truth,
do not lead to piety." [5] "The sword of God's word is forged by
grammar, sharpened by logic, and burnished by rhetoric, but
only theology can use it." Some students, however, use up the
blade in putting on the edge; [6] others give the best years of
their life to fine speaking [7] or to the study of the stars,[8] coming

15959, f. 240 v; Barthélemy de Tours, Hauréau, iv. 35. Cf. Philip 'de Grève,'
In Psalterium, i, f. 311 (Paris, 1522); Jacques de Vitry, in Pitra, ii. 365.

[1] Jean d'Orléans, Munich, Cod. Lat. 23372, p. 39; anonymous Dominican,
Journal des savants, 1916, p. 553.

[2] Henri d'Andeli, *La bataille des Sept Arts*, line 79 (ed. Paetow, p. 43).

[3] 'Exercitandus et exercendus est animus in aliis scienciis, et in logicis et
in naturalibus et in moralibus, secundum uniuscuiusque possibilitatem. Ipsa
etiam scientia iuris, maxime iuris canonici, non parum neccessaria sacre scripture doctoribus. Licet autem predicta discantur ante ipsam, finaliter tamen
addiscenda sunt propter ipsam.' Philip the Chancellor (?), 'ad scolares,' Troyes,
MS. 1099, f. 38.

[4] See the passages from sermons cited by Denifle, *Universitäten*, i. 100.

[5] Jacques de Vitry, in Pitra, *Analecta novissima*, ii. 368, and Lecoy de la
Marche, *Chaire française*, p. 458, note.

[6] 'Gramatica fabricat gladium verbi Dei, logica ipsum acuit, rethorica ipsum
polit, et theologia ipso utitur et ipso percutit; sed quidam scolares superinten-
dunt fabricationi, id est gramatice, alii acutioni in tantum ipsum acuendo quod
totam aciem aufferunt ei.' Robert de Sorbon (?), MS. lat. 15971, f. 198.

[7] Gautier de Château-Thierry, MS. lat. 15959, f. 437, col. 1.

[8] 'Est alia quorundam sapientia qui scire complexiones argumentationum,
deceptiones sophismatum, secreta celi rimantur, motus astrorum, cursus
planetarum. In his tamen non adeo reprehensibiles invenio sacerdotes sed
quosdam qui etatem suam in his consumunt, quorum ingenium in talibus
desudant; semper discunt et nunquam ad scientiam veritatis proveniunt.'
Pierre de Poitiers, MSS. lat. 12293, f. 101 v; 14593, f. 146 v, 320 v.

in their old age with hard hearts to theology, which should be the wife of their youth.[1] Some neglect theology for geometry[2] or for the works of the philosophers,[3] so that even when they reach theology, they cannot be separated from their Aristotle,[4] but read his forbidden books in secret[5] and corrupt their faith.[6] The chief menace, however, to the pre-eminence of theology seems to have been the study of the canon law, after 1219 the only branch of jurisprudence regularly represented at Paris. The rapid development of the judicial and administrative side of the ecclesiastical system in this period created a considerable demand for men trained in law, and many are the denunciations uttered by the theologians against those who forsake the waters of sacred scripture for the Abana and Pharpar of the decretists[7] and are advanced to the best places in the church through the seductions of their Devil's rhetoric.[8]

[1] Philip 'de Grève' in *Journal des savants*, 1894, p. 430; anonymous Dominican, *ibid.*, 1916, p. 555.

[2] 'Multi proponunt librum geometrie libro theologie.' Guiard de Laon, MS. lat. 16471, f. 221.

[3] 'Tercia sollicitudo mala est nimie curiositatis studendo in libris philosophorum et pretermittendo theologiam.' Jean d'Orléans, MS. lat. 14889, f. 84 v; also anonymous Dominican, *Journal des savants*, 1916, p. 555. For the different view of an eminent philosopher, Jean de La Rochelle, see Hauréau, *Histoire de la philosophie scolastique*, part 2, i. 194. An amusing instance of the rivalry of Nominalists and Realists is given by Greven, *Jakob von Vitry*, no. 105, and by Frenken, no. 102.   [4] Jean de St. Gilles, in Hauréau, vi. 234.

[5] Guiard de Laon, in *Journal des savants*, 1893, p. 370.

[6] Jacques de Vitry, in Hauréau, *Philosophie scolastique*, part 2, i. 108, note. On the standard authorities in the various subjects at Paris cf. the following passage from a sermon of Friar Bartholomew of Bologna: 'Aristotili creditur in logica, Galieno in medicina, et Tullio in rethorica, et similiter de aliis; et esset opprobrium alicui quod in grammatica aliquid diceret contra precepta Prisciani et in logica contra precepta Aristotilis et sic de aliis scientiis.' Bodleian, Ashmolean MS. 757, ff. 367, 403 v.

[7] Philip the Chancellor (?), Troyes, MS. 1099, f. 37.

[8] 'Leges . . . multi audiunt ut volare possint ad dignitates.' Jean de Blois, MS. lat. n.a. 338, f. 110 v. Hauréau, vi. 226, 228; *Histoire littéraire*, xxvi. 394; *Journal des savants*, 1893, p. 368. Cf. Dante, *Paradiso*, ix. 133 ff., xii. 82–83; Caesar of Heisterbach, in Vienna *S. B.*, cxliv, no. 9, p. 79. Robert de Sorbon tells the story of a woman who supposed that her son was studying theology at Paris when he was really studying canon law, and who burst into tears on his return, saying, 'Credebam quod filius meus deberet esse in servicio Dei et deberet ire ad scientiam Dei et quod esse deberet unus magnus predicator, *e el vay a crotalas* (volebat dicere ad decretales).' MS. lat. 15971, f. 167.

On the general feeling toward lawyers in this period cf. Étienne de Bourbon,

The utilitarian motive appears not only in such obviously 'lucrative' studies as law and medicine,[1] but likewise in theology and arts, the study of which was the natural road to ecclesiastical preferment. The chief hope of many students lay in securing a good benefice or prebend,[2] to which end they would toil early and late, since a prebend of a hundred livres might depend upon remembering a single word at the examination.[3] Favouritism also played its part in the distribution of patronage, and great was the popularity of those masters who had the ear of bishops or could exert other influence on behalf of their scholars,[4] for one who had reached the episcopal dignity might easily forget his former room-mate at Paris.[5] Many who had the good fortune to get benefices remained at Paris to enjoy them,[6] a form of non-residence which seems to have become a serious abuse by the thirteenth century, so that some students even held more than one benefice at the same time.[7] Indeed a parish or cathedral appointment might come at the beginning as well as at the

nos. 438 ff.; the poem of Philip 'de Grève,' De advocatis, published in the Archives des missions, second series, iii. 288 (1866); anonymous Dominican, Journal des savants, 1916, p. 556; and the following passage from a collection of Paris sermons in the Library of St. Mark's (Fondo Antico, MS. 92, f. 193): 'Quondam ecclesia consuevit regi in pace per canones, modo regitur per advocatos, per quos fiunt plura mala quam per hereticos; et student in legibus dicentes quod canones non possunt sciri sine legibus.' Cf. Welter, Tabula exemplorum, p. 88.

[1] 'Omnes avaricie student, quia intermediis scienciis intendunt que sunt lucrative, scilicet medici, legiste, decretiste.' Robert de Sorbon (?), MS. lat. 15971, f. 198. On 'lucrative sciences,' cf. the bull Super speculam of Honorius III, Chartularium, i, no. 32.

[2] See the debate between the poor and the rich student published by Hauréau, vi. 306. Cf. also the forms of solicitation for benefices preserved in the student letter-writers: supra, p. 9, note 1.

[3] Robert de Sorbon, in Hauréau, iv. 70. Cf. iv. 38; Histoire littéraire, xxvi. 436. So Albert de Reims: 'Sic laborat aliquis .xx. annis in studio, et quis est finis eius? Certe ut capiat muscam, id est prebendam.' St. Mark's, Fondo Antico, MS. 92, f. 261 v.

[4] 'Scolares [curiositatem habent] de magistris qui habent favorem prelatorum.' Guiard de Laon, Amiens, MS. 284, f. 5 v. So Robert de Sorbon, De conscientia, p. 26; anon. in MS. lat. 16471, f. 118; Arras, MS. 329, f. 86.

[5] Welter, Tabula exemplorum, p. 131.

[6] Hauréau, vi. 209, 210, 213, 214, 230, 233, 237; Guiard de Laon, MS. lat. 15959, f. 14; Jean de Blois, MS. lat. n.a. 338, f. 111.

[7] Journal des savants, 1893, p. 368; 1894, p. 436; cf. Welter, Tabula exemplorum, p. 134.

end of one's university career, being sometimes conferred upon ignorant youths, who at once hastened to Paris to secure some sort of an education—"like a physician who should take his pay, leave his patient, and come to the university to learn his medicine," says one preacher.[1]

Too eager pursuit of learning for its own sake was in quite as much disfavour with the preachers as were ambition and non-residence. Scholars are constantly warned against the vanity of much study and against the sins of pride or false doctrine which may arise from wandering beyond the limits of modest attainment.[2] "Clerks busy themselves with eclipses of the sun, but fail to observe the darkening of their own hearts by sin." [3] Far better is it that they should seek to know themselves than to search out the nature of animals, the virtue of herbs, or the courses of the stars.[4] The doves know well the golden rule, yet they have never been at Paris or heard lectures on the *Topica*.[5] This doctrine is enforced by stories of masters struck dumb to punish their conceit [6] and of ambitious scholars dead before

[1] 'Contra illos qui tunc primo incipiunt studere et addiscere [MS. addicere] cum habent curam animarum, similes medico qui recepto salario dimisso infirmo vadit ad studium addiscere medicinam.' MS. lat. 15971, f. 198. Cf. Hauréau, iii. 243; vi. 58. An example of this practice from the early part of the twelfth century is that of Otto of Freising: SS., ix. 610. In 1254 two canons of Mainz, who were banished from Germany for stealing, were permitted to receive revenue from their prebends if they would study at Paris. Böhmer-Will, *Regesta archiepiscoporum Moguntiensium*, ii. 322, no. 78. Cf. the form of petition to the Pope for two benefices with permission to study at Paris or elsewhere in a brief formulary of the *officialité* of Rouen, MS. lat. 18224, f. 283 (on the MS. see my paper in the *Mélanges Paul Fournier*, Paris, 1929); and the papal registers, *passim*.

[2] Jacques de Vitry, in Pitra, *Analecta novissima*, i. 362; Guiard de Laon, MS. lat. 16488, f. 377 v; Prévostin, in *Mélanges Julien Havet*, p. 302; and Lacombe, p. 40.

[3] 'Querunt clerici de eclipsi solis sed de eclipsi solis spiritualis que contingit in cordibus eorum per peccatum non querunt.' Robert de Sorbon, MS. lat. 15971, f. 167. He alludes to the study of the stars and the movements of the heavens in the same MS., ff. 171 v, 195. So Gautier de Château-Thierry, MS. lat. 15955, f. 429; MS. lat. 16488, f. 410.

[4] Idem, MS. lat. 15951, f. 185; MS. lat. 16488, f. 399.

[5] 'Hanc regulam bene sciunt columbe que nunquam studuerunt Parisius nec audiverunt Thopica.' Idem, MS. lat. 16471, f. 79; MS. lat. 16507, f. 39.

[6] Robert de Sorbon, MS. lat. 15971, f. 198, translated in Lecoy de la Marche, *L'Esprit de nos aieux*, p. 279. Robert tells as the counterpart of this story the

their time, after they had studied so hard in the hope of becoming bishop that they would never go out into the fields with their companions,[1] or had put off entering monastic life till they should have completed their full course at Paris, the course in medicine at Montpellier, and seven years of law at Bologna.[2] The most popular story of this sort was that of a Paris student who appeared after death to his master, clad in a cope of parchment covered with fine writing. In reply to the master's question he said that the writing consisted of the sophisms and vain inquiries upon which he had spent his time, and that the cope was a heavier load to carry than the tower of Saint-Germain-des-Prés, near which he and the master stood. As proof of the inward fire which tormented him he let fall a drop of perspiration which pierced the master's hand like an arrow and left a permanent opening in it; whereupon the master abandoned the vain croakings and cawings of the schools and joined the Cistercians.[3] So a certain archdeacon who came to Paris to study theology, overcome by the number of books and the length of the course of study, declared that he could more easily become a good man than a good clerk, and forthwith took the vows of

instance of a successful master whose only preparation for lectures consisted in going to mass every morning.

[1] Hauréau, iv. 37.

[2] 'Clericus quidam Parisius scolaris cum quodam socio suo in una domo et camera manens inspiratus a Deo deliberavit intrare religionem et socium suum ad hoc inducere. Quod renuens socius ait se velle adhuc esse Parisius per triennium et fieri magister, iterum morari apud Montem Pessulanum et fieri magister in medicina, iterum morari Bononie per septennium et fieri dominus legum. Summo mane surgens alius et veniens ad lectum ut acciperet licenciam ab eo invenit eum morte subitanea percussum qui disposuerat vivere tantum.' Tours, MS. 468, f. 78; B.N., MS. Baluze 77, f. 175.

[3] Jacques de Vitry, ed. Crane, p. 12. On the widespread popularity of this *exemplum* see Crane's note (p. 146); Herbert, p. 30; and Hauréau, "Les Récits d'Apparitions dans les Sermons du Moyen-Âge," in *Mémoires de l'Académie des Inscriptions*, xxviii, 2, pp. 239 ff. It has been shown that the original of this story was a master at Oxford, Serlon of Wilton, and that the vision antedates 1154. See Schwob in *Comptes-rendus de l'Académie des Inscriptions*, 1898, p. 508.

There is also a curious story of a stupid student who is made miraculously clever by Satan. After his early death devils take his soul to a deep valley and torment it by playing ball with it, but he returns to life and becomes a holy abbot. Caesar of Heisterbach, ed. Strange, i. 36.

religion.[1] A current type of the conceited doctor was he who announced that early the next morning he would 'determine' a question of theology as subtly as Christ himself, but when the hour came had forgotten even the alphabet.[2] Another master, who declared that he understood the Pauline Epistles better than St. Paul himself, lost all his learning forthwith, until a girl was appointed as his tutor who with difficulty succeeded in teaching him the seven penitential psalms.[3]

Nothing in these Paris sermons is more interesting than the insight they afford into a phase of the university's life concerning which we have otherwise but little information, namely the nature of the examinations and the preparation for them. On this point evidence is found mainly in the sermons of Robert de Sorbon, and particularly in his treatise *On Conscience*,[4] which is really an expanded sermon based upon an elaborate and suggestive parallel between the examination for the master's degree and the last judgement. Taking as his text Job's desire that his "adversary had written a book,"[5] and outlining his headings in the approved fashion of his time, Robert begins with the statement that if any one decides to seek the *licentia legendi* at Paris and cannot be excused from examination—as many of the great, by special favour, are—he would much like to be told by the chancellor, or by some one in his confidence, on what book he would be examined. Just as he would be a crazy student indeed, who, having found out which book this was, should neglect it and spend his time on others, even so is he mad who fails to study the book of his own conscience, in which we shall

---

[1] Welter, *Tabula exemplorum*, p. 74, no. 278. Cf. Humbert de Romans, in *Maxima bibliotheca patrum*, xxv. 633.

[2] *Miscellanea Ehrle*, i. 181. Cf. *Antonianum*, ii. 213, no. 2.

[3] *Histoire littéraire*, xxxi. 54; *Études Franciscaines*, xxx. 662 (1913). See Herbert, p. 660; J. Klapper, *Erzählungen des Mittelalters* (Breslau, 1914), pp. 349–350.

[4] Robert de Sorbon, *De conscientia et de tribus dietis*, ed. Chambon (Paris, 1903). The old editions of Marguerin de la Bigne (*Maxima bibliotheca patrum*, xxv. 346–352) and Du Boulay (*Historia Universitatis Parisiensis*, iii. 225–235) are very faulty. Miss Dorothy L. Mackay has now written on "Le système d'examen du XIIIᵉ siècle d'après le *De conscientia* de Robert de Sorbon," in *Mélanges Ferdinand Lot* (Paris, 1925), pp. 491–500.

[5] Job, xxxi. 35, where the rendering of the Vulgate naturally suggests Robert's treatment: 'Librum scribat mihi ipse qui iudicat.'

all, without exception, be examined at the great day. Moreover, if any one is rejected by the chancellor, he may be re-examined after a year, or it may be that, through the intercession of friends or by suitable gifts or services to the chancellor's relatives or other examiners, the chancellor can be induced to change his decision; whereas at the last judgement the sentence will be final and there will be no help from wealth or influence or stout assertion of ability as canonist or civilian or of familiarity with all arguments and all fallacies. Then, if one fails before the chancellor of Paris, the fact is known to but five or six and the mortification passes away in time, while the Great Chancellor, God, will refute the sinner "in full university" before the whole world. The chancellor, too, does not flog the candidate, but in the last judgement the guilty will be beaten with a rod of iron from the valley of Jehoshaphat through the length of hell, nor can we reckon, like idle boys in the grammar schools, on escaping Saturday's punishment by feigning illness, playing truant, or being stronger than the master, or like them solace ourselves with the thought that after all our fun is well worth a whipping. The chancellor's examination, too, is voluntary; he does not force any one to seek the degree, but waits as long as the scholars wish, and is even burdened with their insistent demands for examinations. In studying the book of our conscience we should imitate the candidates for the license, who eat and drink sparingly, conning steadily the one book they are preparing, searching out all the authorities that pertain to this, and hearing only the professors that lecture on this subject, so that they have difficulty in concealing from their fellows the fact that they are preparing for examination. Such preparation is not the work of five or ten days—though there are many who will not meditate a day or an hour on their sins—but of many years.[1] At the examination the chancellor asks, "Brother, what

---

[1] 'Putatis vos quod si unus homo fuerit per .x. vel per .v. dies ad unam scientiam, quod cancellarius tam cito det licentiam? Certe non, immo oportet quod clerici multis diebus et noctibus et multis annis studeant. Sed multi sunt qui vix volunt una die vel una hora de suis peccatis cogitare.' MS. lat. 16481, f. 154; sermon of Amand de Saint-Quentin preached at the Madeleine on the fourth Sunday in Lent, 1273. Cf. *Histoire littéraire*, xxvi. 455.

do you say to this question, what do you say to this one and this one ? " [1] The chancellor is not satisfied with a verbal knowledge of books without an understanding of their sense,[2] but unlike the Great Judge, who will hear the book of our conscience from beginning to end and suffer no mistakes, he requires only seven or eight passages in a book and passes the candidate if he answers three questions out of four. Still another difference lies in the fact that the chancellor does not always conduct the examination in person, so that the student who would be terrified in the presence of so much learning often answers well before the masters who act in his place.[3]

If those who have studied their consciences thoroughly will have such difficulty in the great examination, how much worse will it be for those who have not studied at all ? The moralist is thus led to consider where the book of conscience may be read, namely in confession, and to compare the necessity of frequent confession with the student's need of regular attendance upon his master's lectures. At Paris only he who goes to the schools at least twice a week and hears 'ordinary' lectures is considered a student, and only such can expect a master to demand their release if captured by the *prévôt* and imprisoned in the Châtelet ;[4] yet many there are who confess but once a year or at best make only a hurried confession (*cursorie*) ; these are not God's scholars and for them there will be no release from the *prévôt* of hell. As at Paris the best clerk is he who by diligent attendance upon lectures becomes able to answer questions which silence the

---

[1] 'Scitis qualiter probantur clerici Parisius ? Queritur ab eo, Frater, qualiter diceretis ad istam questionem, et qualiter diceres tu ad hoc et ad hoc; et secundum hoc quod respondet licenciatur vel refutatur.' Amand de S.-Quentin, *loc. cit.*

[2] 'Item si quis sciret literam librorum corditenus et nesciret sensum, non transiret examinationem cancellarii.' Robert de Sorbon, MS. lat. 16482, f. 309 v. Another allusion of Robert to the chancellor's examination is printed in Lecoy de la Marche, *La chaire française*, p. 457, note.

[3] Robert here cites the instance of an abbot-elect examined before Guiard de Laon, bishop of Cambrai, who was so overcome that he could not even read his missal or say his *Pater noster*.

[4] On the distinction between 'ordinary' and 'cursory' lectures at Paris see Rashdall, i. 426 ff.; and on the method of securing release from the Châtelet, the *Chartularium*, i, no. 197.

great teachers, so on the day of judgement some simple monk or *béguine* who has well pondered the book of conscience and frequently confessed will put to shame and derision great masters of arts or law or medicine or theology who have neglected these duties. What will it profit a man then to possess the learning of Aristotle and Priscian, of Justinian and Gratian, of Galen and Hippocrates and the rest, preserved on the skins of sheep or goats? If a master were to give his scholars new robes or assure them good prebends in a cathedral, he would have such a throng of scholars that no room could hold them, and other masters, however excellent, would be obliged to shut up shop—"put their fiddles under the bench"—for lack of hearers. Yet God gives to all his followers the garment of the new man and the prebend of his grace the day they enter his school, and, unlike certain proud masters who will lecture only to a large audience, he is willing to read to a single scholar. Many choose as confessors those who have been guilty of the same sin, yet only a fool would study his book with the poorest teacher of Paris, it being one of the glories of a student at his inception that he has studied under the best masters in the city. None but unworthy masters would imitate the jealousy of certain confessors who are unwilling to have their parishioners confess to others; indeed a good master will advise his pupils to attend the lectures of others, for it is scarcely possible to become a good clerk unless one has listened to several masters. Yet men should not avoid their own confessors and seek out strangers, but should follow the example of good students at Paris, who choose by preference masters who are compatriots and well known to them. In the day of judgement priests, as well as people, will be held responsible for the proper study of the book of conscience, just as the chancellor, when he hears on Saturday the lessons of the boys in the grammar schools, flogs the masters as well as the pupils if he thinks them to blame for the pupils' ignorance.

For the faults of the masters the preachers show little indulgence. Many begin to teach before they have studied long enough in the schools, an abuse which prevailsin all faculties but particularly in that of arts.[1] Such masters, says Jacques de Vitry, draw their lectures from books and closets, not from well stored minds, but they succeed in securing students none the less, by personal solicitation and friendship and even by hiring them to come.[2] The number of their scholars is the masters' pride,[3] wherefore their class-rooms should be large and easily accessible;[4] to crowd their class-rooms they preach new and strange doctrines,[5] and for money they will lecture even on Sundays and holy days.[6] Masters there are, too, who make life easy for the scholars who live with them, letting them sleep late in the morning and roam about and amuse themselves freely,[7] and even conniving at their vices.[8] The great aim of the master is not to instruct his pupils but to appear learned and be called rabbi;[9] many speak obscurely in order to appear more profound,[10] and even pay the beadles to magnify them and cover

[1] 'Quidam scolares ante tempus ablactari volunt et fiunt magistri, et hoc in quaque facultate.' Philip the Chancellor, sermon of 21 August, 1226, Avranches, MS. 132, f. 243 v. 'Multi qui adhuc deberent discere presumunt docere, quod vicium maxime in artibus inolevit.' The same, B.M., MS. Royal 8. F.13, f. 130 v. Cf. his Psalter, edition of 1522, f. 8 v; Nicolas de Nonancourt, MS. lat. 16252, f. 279 v.

[2] Pitra, *Analecta novissima*, ii. 359; Lecoy de la Marche, *Chaire française*, p. 452. The hiring of scholars is also found at Bologna; see Chapter I, *ante*, p. 28.

[3] Guiard de Laon, Amiens, MS. 284, f. 5 v. Cf. Robert de Sorbon, MS. lat. 15971, f. 176 v: 'Vidi Parisius multos magistros qui dimittebant legere quia non habebant multos auditores.'

[4] 'Scola est exposita cuilibet transeunti ut sciatur. . . . Item est fenestrata. . . . Item debet esse lata ut multos capiat.' Guiard de Laon, MSS. lat. 16471, f. 10; 16507, f. 8 v. Cf. Buoncompagno's description of an ideal Bolognese lecture-hall: Gaudenzi, *Bibliotheca iuridica medii aevi*, ii. 279.

[5] 'In discipulis coluntur magistri qui inaudita dicunt.' Guiard de Laon, MS. lat. 15959, f. 296 v. Crane, *Jacques de Vitry*, pp. 10, 11.

[6] 'Illi qui pro argento diebus dominicis et festivis legunt debent saluti anime sue intendere ut laicis bonum exemplum ostenderent.' Gautier de Château-Thierry, MS. lat. 15959, f. 437, col. 2.

[7] 'Magistri illi qui blandiuntur clericis suis et adulantur et dant eis licenciam spaciandi et ludendi et voluntatem faciendi habent plures scolares; sed illi qui artant suos timentur et paucos habent.' Philip the Chancellor, Bibliothèque Mazarine, MS. 1009, f. 123 v; B.M., MS. Royal 8.F.13, f. 271 v.

[8] Haureau, vi. 246. Cf. Jean de Montlhéry, Merton College, MS. 237, f. 227 v: 'Innocens iuvenis mittitur quandoque Parysius et exemplo mali socii vel forte magistri sui ita corumpitur et inficitur quod omnibus diebus vite sue non carebit illo vicio.'

[9] 'Nec magistri ad utilitatem audiunt, legunt, nec disputant, sed ut vocentur Rabbi.' MS. lat. n.a. 338, f. 197.   [10] MS. lat. 16507, f. 48 v.

up their ignorance.[1] Their quarrels are like cock-fights [2] and they are so jealous that they seek to draw away one another's scholars [3] and, even when detained by illness, will not suffer their pupils to hear lectures from another.[4] A more human figure is the master who stammered and could not pronounce the letter *r*.[5] Abaelard is still a vivid tradition in the *exempla*.[6]

When we turn from studies and teachers to the students themselves, we find the material contained in the sermons fuller and more satisfactory. The ideal scholar of the pulpits was a rather colourless personage, obedient, respectful, eager to learn, and keeping very much to himself.[7] In order to win the favour of the master and his personal instruction,[8] one should be assiduous at lectures, quick at learning, and bold in debate, and should also attract other pupils to the master.[9] When, in the Lenten season, a master in theology takes the chair and proposes a question, to which one of the bystanders replies, it is a mark of deference and honour to the respondent if the master determines the question in accordance with his reply.[10] Robert de Sorbon lays down six rules for successful study: a fixed time for each subject, concentrated attention, memorizing specific things, note-taking, conference with others, and finally prayer, "which availeth much for learning." [11] The good student should

---

[1] Hauréau, vi. 124.

[2] Philip 'de Grève,' *Notices et extraits*, xxi, 2, p. 193; *Journal des savants*, 1894, p. 431; Lecoy de la Marche, *Chaire française*, p. 452; Valois, *Guillaume d'Auvergne*, p. 52.

[3] Pitra, *Analecta novissima*, ii. 362.

[4] 'Contra magistros qui cum aliquando sint in vinculis infirmitatis vel alicuius occupationis non possunt sustinere quod discipuli sui alium audiant licet meliorem.' Guiard de Laon, MS. lat. 15951, f. 14.

[5] Greven, no. 88; Frenken, no. 85.   [6] Greven, no. 53; Frenken, no. 51.

[7] 'Magistri propter quatuor diligunt discipulos: . . . primo quia obedientes; . . . secundo quia timorosi; . . . tercio quia solitarii, non in strepitu et confabulacione cum aliis; . . . quarto quia de addiscendo solliciti.' Guiard de Laon, MS. lat. 16471, f. 112 v.

[8] 'Mos est apud scolares quod discipuli cariores ab ipsis magistris edocentur.' Guiard de Laon, MS. lat. 16471, f. 253.

[9] Anonymous, MS. lat. 16471, f. 118 v.

[10] Anonymous sermon cited by A. De Poorter, "Catalogue des manuscrits de prédication médiévale de la Bibliothèque de Bruges," in *Revue d'histoire ecclésiastique*, xxiv. 74 (1928). Cf. p. 114, *ibid*.

[11] Lecoy de la Marche, *Chaire française*, p. 453.

imitate Christ among the doctors, hearing many masters, always seeking good teachers without regard to their fame or place of birth, and listening as well as asking questions—unlike those who will not wait for the end of a question but cry out, "I know what you mean."[1] Even when he goes to walk by the Seine in the evening, the good student ought to ponder or repeat his lesson.[2]

It need scarcely be said that the students of mediaeval Paris did not as a rule spend their time in such studious promenades; indeed if further evidence were needed to dispel the illusion that a mediaeval university was an institution devoted to biblical study and religious nurture, the preachers of the period would offer sufficient proof. We have already seen how the theological faculty, the only one dealing directly with religious subject-matter, was suffering from the competition of the canon law and other 'lucrative' subjects, and it is on every hand apparent that the morals of at least a considerable portion of the student body were as profane as their studies.[3] Students, we are told, care nothing for sermons, and for most of them holy days are only an occasion for idleness;[4] they remain outside during mass, and like their masses short and their lectures and disputations long.[5] If their voice is in the choir, their mind is without, in the street, in bed, or at the table—as the rhyme ran,[6]

> Vox in choro, mens in foro
> Vel in mensa vel in thoro.

Confession they likewise neglect; instead of seeking to have his soul cleansed by confession on his arrival at Paris, the student hastens to the laundress.[7] Dominicans like Étienne de Bourbon

---

[1] 'Contra illos qui nolunt audire antequam respondeant sed clamant dicentes, Bene scio quid vultis dicere.' Robert de Sorbon, MS. lat. 15971, f. 146 v. Cf. Humbert de Romans, *Maxima bibliotheca patrum*, xxv. 632.

[2] 'Sic bonus scolaris sero debet ire spaciatum ad ripam Secane, non ut ibi ludatur sed leccionem repetat vel meditetur.' MS. lat. 15971, f. 198.

[3] Cf. Langlois, *Questions d'histoire et d'enseignement*, p. 5; Rashdall, ii. 700–702.

[4] Bourgain, *Chaire française*, p. 287; *Journal des savants*, 1893, p. 372.

[5] 'Contra illos qui gaudent de brevitate missarum et longitudine lectionum et disputationum et foris sunt dum cantatur missa.' Gautier de ChâteauThierry, MS. lat. 15955, f. 228, col. 4.   [6] MS. lat. 15971, f. 185.

[7] 'Scolaris quando venit Parysius statim currit ad lotricem ut lavetur, non vadit ad confessionem ut mundetur eius cor.' Jean de Montlhéry, Merton

attend vespers, at Notre-Dame or elsewhere,[1] but a miracle or special providence is often needed in order to bring students or masters into this order,[2] and one subprior complains that parents are more anxious to keep their sons away from the friars than from the brothel or the tavern.[3] "The student's heart is in the mire," says another Dominican, "fixed on prebends and things temporal and how to satisfy his desires."[4] "He is ashamed to sin against the rules of Donatus, but not to violate the law of Christ."[5] He is much more familiar, says Robert de Sorbon, with the text of the dice, which he recognizes at once, no matter how rapidly they are thrown, than with the text of the Old Logic—yet the gloss of the dice he forgets, which is, Swear, steal, and be hanged. "This very week within two leagues of Paris a priest hanged himself after gambling away ten livres and his horse. Such is the fate of gamesters."[6] Many students come to Paris like the prodigal to a far country, and indulge in practices they would not even think of at home, wasting in riotous living not only their own portion but the substance of their churches.[7]

College, MS. 237, f. 228. For other relations between students and *lotrices*, cf. the following, from the sermon of an anonymous chancellor: 'Sic hodie faciunt lotrices Parisius. Bene sciunt totundere fatuos clericos. Illos ergo qui in luxuria vivunt Dallida expoliat et isti tonduntur.' MS. lat. 16502, f. 86 v.

[1] Ed. Lecoy de la Marche, pp. 317, 363.

[2] *Ibid.*, pp. 44, 86, 222, 345.   [3] Hauréau, iii. 287.

[4] 'Scolaris habet cor ad lutum, ad temporalia, ad prebendas et huiusmodi, et quomodo possit suam explere libidinem [MS. libinem].' Jean de Montlhéry, Bodleian, Ashmolean MS. 757, f. 160 v.

[5] Quoted from St. Augustine in MS. lat. 15959, f. 437, col. 1; MS. lat. 15955, f. 430. Cf. Robert de Sorbon in Hauréau, v. 57.

[6] 'Hoc faciunt aleatores et ludentes cum taxillis hodie, namque multi sciunt melius textum taxillorum, id est numerum pungctorum. Quamcunque cito proiciantur statim vident asardum, et huiusmodi; unde melius sciunt textum taxillorum quam textum logice veteris. Tamen glosam nesciunt. Glosa taxillorum est hec: Iurabo, furabor, suspendar. Sic accidit ista septimana prope Parisius ad duas leucas de quodam sacerdote qui forte luserat in iuventute et modo non erat oblitus... Lusit .x. libras et equum suum, post suspendit se. Hic est finis taxillorum.' MS. lat. 15971, f. 68. So in the same MS., f. 117 v, he says: 'Ludis ad talos, ribaldus eris. Probatio: Qui studet in libris gramaticalibus gramaticus vult esse; ergo qui studet in libris ribaldorum, scilicet ludendo cum deciis, ribaldus vult esse.' Cf. Hauréau, "Les Propos de Maître Robert," p. 141.

[7] 'Sic scolares abeunt in regionem longinquam cum veniunt Parisius et expendunt aliquando non solum portionem propriam sed paternam et maternam

What the forms of riotous living were which prevailed among students the preachers do not hesitate to specify, sometimes with more particularity than modern taste permits. Gambling is mentioned,[1] even on the altars of churches,[2] and feasting and free indulgence in the wine-cup,[3] as well as wild carouses in the streets and the visiting of disreputable resorts,[4] which were often found in close proximity to the class-rooms.[5] Many of the students led a life that was by no means celibate,[6] and there are allusions to the darkest of monastic vices.[7]

et fraternam necnon bona ecclesie.' Guiard de Laon, Arras, MS. 329, f. 59 v; MS. lat. 16471, f. 39. Pierre de Poitiers, in Bourgain, *Chaire française*, p. 27, note, and p. 293 (where *inde* should be read in place of the *mihi* from which Bourgain infers the chancellor's feeling of responsibility for the scholars' morals); Hauréau, vi. 256; Gautier de Château-Thierry, MS. lat. 15959, f. 434 v.

[1] Besides the passages from Robert de Sorbon just quoted, see Crane, *Jacques de Vitry*, p. 8; and Tours, MS. 468, f. 80, printed below, p. 68, note 1. The more common offences committed by students against ecclesiastical discipline are illustrated by a comprehensive form of the papal penitentiary, or letter of 'Licet non credas,' covering acts which may have been committed by a clerk when a student and have afterward been forgotten: 'Quod olim in diversis terris, locis et studiis generalibus vel aliis fuisti, in clericos seculares, presbyteros vel alias religiosas et ecclesiasticas personas, interdum causa ludi, correctionis vel alia, irato animo manus temere violentas usque et citra sanguinis effusionem iniciendo absque alio excessu difficili vel enormi, arma portando, ad taxillos et alios illicitos ludos ludendo, tabernas, ortos, vineas, prata et alia loca vetita et inhonesta intrando . . . nec non doctoribus, magistris, bedellis et bacallariis salaria statutis terminis non solvendo.' Formulary of Benedict XII, in the Vatican library, MS. Ottoboni 333, f. 72 v. A somewhat different text is published from Tours, MS. 594, by Denifle in the *Archiv für Litteratur- und Kirchengeschichte des Mittelalters*, iv. 207. On these formularies see my article, "The Sources for the History of the Papal Penitentiary," in *American Journal of Theology*, ix. 421–450 (1905).

[2] *Chartularium*, i, no. 470.

[3] See, for example, Pierre le Mangeur in Bourgain, *Chaire française*, p. 292. The best evidence on this point is of course to be found in the drinking-songs and in the records of the nations.

[4] Prévostin, in Hauréau, iii. 166; *Mélanges Julien Havet*, p. 303; Lacombe, p. 40; Lecoy de la Marche, *Chaire française*, p. 460. See also the passages cited below in regard to the carrying of arms.

[5] See on this point the well known passage of Jacques de Vitry, *Historia occidentalis* (ed. Douai, 1597), p. 278; reproduced in Rashdall, ii. 690; and on its interpretation, Denifle, *Universitäten*, i. 672.

[6] Jacques de Vitry, *loc. cit.*; Pitra, *Analecta novissima*, ii. 434; Hauréau, iii. 319; Étienne de Bourbon, pp. 50, 402, 406; *Histoire littéraire*, xxvi. 458; and the characteristic story told in Auxerre, MS. 35, f. 127 v.

[7] Jacques de Vitry, *loc. cit.*; Gautier de Château-Thierry, in Hauréau, vi. 210, and *Histoire littéraire*, xxvi. 393; anonymous Minorite, Hauréau, vi. 257.

Whatever their other virtues, the students of mediaeval Paris were not distinguished for their love of peace and quiet. Theirs was a rough and violent age, and what with the *prévôt's* men and the townsmen, the monks of St. Germain and the friars, there was no lack of opportunity for a brawl, in which the students were only too likely to be the aggressors. "They are so litigious and quarrelsome that there is no peace with them; wherever they go, be it Paris or Orleans, they disturb the country, their associates, even the whole university." [1] Many of them go about the streets armed, attacking the citizens, breaking into houses, and abusing women.[2] They quarrel among themselves over dogs,[3] women, or what-not, slashing off one another's fingers with their swords,[4] or, with only knives in their hands and nothing to protect their tonsured pates, rush into conflicts from which armed knights would hold back.[5] Their compatriots come to their aid, and soon whole nations of students may be involved in the fray.[6] Some of these attacks

[1] 'Videbitis etiam aliquos sic rixosos, discolos, et litigiosos quod nullo modo potest cum eis haberi pax. Ubicunque sunt, Parisius vel Aurelianis, perturbant totam terram et totam societatem cum qua sunt, immo totam universitatem.' Jean de Montlhéry, MS. lat. 14955, f. 140 v; translated in *Histoire littéraire*, xxvi. 437. On the litigiousness of the time cf. Philip the Chancellor (Avranches, MS. 132, f. 242; Troyes, MS. 1099, f. 138); 'Tanta increvit malicia ut laicus laicum, clericus clericum, etc., scolaris scolarem ad remotos iudices trahat, non ut consequatur iusticiam sed ut adversarius redimat vexationem.'

[2] 'Qui portant arma . . . qui frangunt hospiçia, mulieres rapiunt, inter se aliquando se occidunt, hii sunt carnifices diaboli, non clerici.' Gautier de Château-Thierry, MS. lat. 15959, f. 436, col. 4. 'Hoc est contra petulantiam quorumdam vitulorum, id est scolarium, non Dei sed diaboli, qui quasi vituli prosiliunt de nocte discurrentes.' Guiard de Laon, MS. lat. 15959, f. 13 v. Philip ' de Grève,' *Journal des savants*, 1894, p. 430. Prévostin, in Hauréau, iii. 166; Lacombe, p. 40. On students who carry arms cf. the *Chartularium*, i, nos. 213, 426, 470; and on quarrels with tradesmen, John of Garland, *Dictionarius*, ed. Scheler, c. 35.   [3] Hauréau, vi. 250.

[4] 'Heu hodie non precinguntur scolares hoc lintheo sed potius gladio belli. . . . Nostri clerici sero cum gladiis invicem pugnarunt et quidam ex illis digitos alterius amputant.' Philip the Chancellor, MS. lat. n.a. 338, f. 155.

[5] Remark attributed to Philip Augustus. Hauréau, vi. 250.

[6] Anonymous Dominican, *ibid.*, and *Journal des savants*, 1916, pp. 554 f.; Nicolas de Nonancourt, Hauréau, iv. 157 (where, as in MS. lat. 16252, f. 279, the last sentence should begin, 'Ex certa malicia movent'). Hauréau strangely misunderstands the last passage as referring to the nations of Europe instead of to the nations of the university. Cf. also Rutebeuf, "Li Diz de l'Université de Paris," vv. 37–39 (ed. Kressner, p. 51).

are planned in advance at organized meetings of students,[1] which, according to Chancellor Philip, no impartial witness it is true, are largely given over to such matters. "In the old days," he says, "when each master taught for himself and the name of university was unknown, lectures and disputations were more frequent and there was more zeal for study. But now that you are united into a university, lectures and disputations are rare, things are hurried, and little is learned, the time taken from lectures being spent in meetings and discussions. In these assemblies, while the older heads are deliberating and legislating, the younger spend their time hatching the most abominable schemes and planning their nocturnal raids."[2] Outsiders might also indulge in these student escapades, donning the scholar's garb in order to escape arrest by the civil authorities.[3] A town and gown riot might even lead to a cessation of all lectures, as in the great dispersion of 1229, when many left Paris for Orleans and Angers.[4]

[1] Eudes de Châteauroux, *Journal des savants*, 1890, p. 305. Cf., for the fourteenth century, *Chartularium*, ii, no. 1072.

[2] Translated by Hauréau in *Journal des savants*, 1894, p. 430. Philip expresses his opinion of the university organization in another sermon: 'Circumiit scolas et invenit monstruositatem. Monstrum in uno corpore diversarum coniunctio naturarum. Quid est ergo ex diversis nationibus universitatem facere nisi monstrum creare? . . . Quattuor capita huius monstri sunt quattuor facultates, logice, phisice, canonici et divini iuris.' Mazarine, MS. 1009, f. 159 v; MS. lat. 15955, ff. 126 v–127.

[3] 'Falsorum scolarium qui sub nomine scolarium et habitu flagitia perpetrant licentius quam scolares, quia prepositi non audent manus immittere.' Philip the Chancellor, Mazarine, MS. 1009, f. 57 v; MS. lat. 15955, f. 96 v; Rouen, MS. 615, f. 53 v.

[4] The allusions of the preachers to the disturbances at Paris are seldom very specific (cf. Eudes de Châteauroux in Pitra, *Analecta novissima*, ii. 230, and Hauréau, ii. 119; Philip the Chancellor in Avranches, MS. 132, ff. 24, 263 v). There are, however, various references to the disorders of 1273 (Lecoy de la Marche, *Chaire française*, pp. 85, 451; Quétif and Échard, *Scriptores Ordinis Praedicatorum*, i. 269); and some points of interest in regard to the dispersion of 1229 are indicated in a contemporary sermon of Chancellor Philip: 'Habebant scolares tamquam apes domos exagonas Parisius, id est studio competentes, edificabant favos quibus demulcebant affectum et illuminabant intellectum . . . Sed aspersum est origanum super loca ipsorum, . . . fugerunt et florigeras regiones lustraverunt ut quietem invenirent, suspirantes nihilominus ad loca dimissa, quia spes est quod bonus et prudens paterfamilias, scilicet summus pontifex, purget amaritudinem origanni ut ad loca propria revertantur. Felix locus et felix civitas que filios dispersos pie collegit, pie dico scilicet ut eos

More interesting than these general characterizations in which the sermons abound are the incidental allusions to the ordinary life of the thirteenth-century student. The preachers take us into the very atmosphere of the Latin quarter and show us much of its varied activity. We hear the cries [1] and songs of the streets—[2]

> Li tens s'en veit,
> Et je n'ei riens fait;
> Li tens revient,
> Et je ne fais riens—,.

the students' tambourines and guitars,[3] their "light and scurri-.ous words," [4] their hisses [5] and handclappings and loud shouts of applause at sermons and disputations.[6] We watch them as they mock a neighbour for her false hair [7] or stick out their

nutriret et postmodum matri restitueret, quia signum est quod talis nutrix non diligit dispersionem. Non sic autem illa que quos nutriret sibi retinere intenderet, ut Andegavis, de qua impletur illud Ieremiae [xvii. 11], Perdix fovit que non peperit. . . . Videtur inter alias Aurelianis sic quos recepit habuisse, non tamquam emula sed tamquam nutrix et gerilla, et recte quia inter alias Parisiensis civitas soror est. . . . Ruben, filius visionis, scolares, . . . terra Moabitidis civitas Andegavis. . . . Bonus paterfamilias . . . scripsit regi ut scolaribus iusticie plenitudinem exhiberet et eos in Betleem, id est domum panis que est Parisius, revocaret ac libertates eisdem a felicis memorie rege Philippo pie indultas liberaliter et inviolabiliter conservaret.' 'Sermo cancellarii Parisiensis quem fecit Aurelianis ad scolares de recessu scolarium a Parisius, quem fecit in vigilia Pasche.' Avranches, MS. 132, f. 340 v; Troyes, MS. 1099, f. 160 v. On the little known history of Angers in this period, cf. J. C. Russell, "An Ephemeral University at Angers (1229–34)," in *Colorado College Publication*, December, 1927, pp. 47–49.

[1] See the story in Étienne de Bourbon, p. 185, of the poor scholar who substituted the cries of dealers in old clothes for the words of the church service; and cf. the poem of Guillaume de la Villeneuve, "Les crieries de Paris," in Franklin, *Les cris de Paris* (Paris, 1887), p. 133.

[2] Hauréau, iii. 341; Étienne de Bourbon, p. 346.

[3] *Histoire littéraire*, xxvi. 458.

[4] 'Verba levia et scurrilia. Talia sunt verba multorum scolarium.' Richard, Minorite, in MS. lat. n.a. 338, f. 54. Cf. the story of the student who blasphemed against Abraham, Caesar of Heisterbach, ed. Strange, i. 192.

[5] 'Dico de scolaribus, quia multi peccant lingua aliter quam loquendo, sicut illi clerici qui sibilant.' Philip the Chancellor, Alençon, MS. 153, f. 58. Cf. Du Cange, under *sibillacio*.

[6] Anonymous sermons in Hauréau, ii. 108; vi. 257.

[7] 'Isabel, ceste queue n'est pas de ce veel.' *Ibid.*, iv. 177; Étienne de Bourbon, p. 239. Cf. *Miscellanea Ehrle*, i. 181.

tongues and make faces at the passers-by.[1] We see the student studying by his window,[2] talking over his future with his roommate,[3] receiving visits from his parents,[4] nursed by friends when he is ill,[5] singing psalms at a student's funeral,[6] or visiting a fellow-student and asking him to visit him—"I have been to see you, now come to my hospice." [7]

All types are represented. Of three Flemish students who discuss their future, one plans to become a master at Paris, one a Cistercian monk, and the third a jongleur.[8] There is the poor student, with no friend but St. Nicholas,[9] seeking such charity as he can find [10] or earning a pittance by carrying holy water [11] or copying for others, in a fair but none too accurate hand,[12]—as thin as if he had just come from hell, or poor enough to sell his soul to the Devil,[13]—sometimes too poor to buy books or afford the expense of a course in theology,[14] yet usually surpassing his more prosperous fellows, who, with every opportunity, have an abundance of books at which they never look.[15]

[1] 'Idem potest dici de scolaribus qui linguam protrahunt et naso subsannant et supercilium supprimunt digitum extendentes in derisione coram se transeuntium.' Guiard de Laon, MS. lat. 15959, f. 135.

[2] Hauréau, iii. 341; Étienne de Bourbon, p. 346.

[3] Tours, MS. 468, f. 78, printed above, p. 50, note 2.

[4] See the story of the student who was ashamed to receive a visit from his father and made him eat with the servants. Munich, Cod. Lat. 23420, f. 170; Herbert, p. 649.

[5] Odo of Cheriton, in Hervieux, *Fabulistes latins*, iv. 295.

[6] Caesar of Heisterbach, ed. Strange, i. 37.

[7] 'Nota quod socius quando socium visitavit, Veni ad vos, modo venite ad nostrum hospicium.' Anonymous, MS. lat. 16505, f. 203 v.

[8] Greven, no. 84; Frenken, no. 80.

[9] 'Hinc est quod pauperes clerici qui non habent qui figant illos in ecclesia Dei, beatum Nicholaum invocent.' Eudes de Châteauroux, MS. lat. 16471, f. 48.

[10] *Journal des savants*, 1887, p. 122; Lecoy de la Marche, *Chaire française*, p. 462.

[11] Jacques de Vitry, ed. Crane, p. 47, ed. Pitra, p. 451; Étienne de Bourbon, p. 446.

[12] 'Pauperes enim scolares manu sua propria sibi vel aliis scribunt, quod sibi fideliter, quod aliis pulcre et velociter.' Guiard de Laon, MS. lat. 15951, f. 372 v.

[13] Herbert, pp. 83, 545.

[14] Lecoy de la Marche, *loc. cit.* On the expense of a theological course cf. *supra*, p. 25.

[15] 'Sepe visum est Parisius quod clerici qui vivunt de beneficio istorum clericorum divitum multi plus proficiebant in scientia et vita quam ipsi divites

There is the well-to-do student, who besides his books and desk will be sure to have a candle in his room,[1] and a comfortable bed with a soft mattress and luxurious coverings,[2] and will be tempted to indulge the mediaeval fondness for fine raiment beyond the gown and hood and simple wardrobe prescribed by the statutes.[3] Then there are the idle and aimless, drifting about from master to master and from school to school and never hearing full courses or regular lectures, but spending their time looking out of the windows and watching the passers-by.[4] Even among the laborious copyists are those, some of them Irish (*et maxime Ybernici*), who will drink up in one day all they have earned by a week of labour.[5] Some, who care only

de quibus vivebant et a quibus victum recipiebant, et ita probi et magni clerici fiebant quod postea ipsi divites eis serviebant. . . . Non propter hoc dico quod vir religiosus non possit plus sibi proficere si sit sollicitus circa se quam secularis, sicut videmus de clerico divite. Non dico quin plus possit proficere in scientia et virtute si velit esse sollicitus de profectu suo quam pauper possit. Nec hoc est mirum, *car il a plus davantages* et melius habet victum suum et libros sibi neccessarios et magistros magis paratos circa se.' Robert de Sorbon, Munich, Cod. Lat. 23372, pp. 124–125. 'Quidam habent multos et pulcros libros et bene paratos et nunquam ibi respiciunt. . . . Debent libros suos qui in eis nichil faciunt tradere pauperibus scolaribus qui libenter addiscunt.' Idem, MS. lat. 15971, f. 198.

[1] 'Si quis daret alicui scolari Parisius lumen per annum, multum diligeret eum.' Lecoy de la Marche, *Chaire française*, p. 461, note.

[2] Étienne de Bourbon, p. 29. There is an *exemplum* of a Paris student who dies and leaves his mattress to his companion to be given to the poor for the repose of his soul. The companion keeps the mattress for himself,whereupon he has a vision of the former owner lying in torment upon the hard, rough cords of a wooden bed; after he gives the mattress to the poor, he sees his friend lying in comfort upon a mattress. Jacques de Vitry, ed. Crane, p. 53, ed. Pitra, p. 452. Auxerre, MS. 35, f. 80 v.
On the furniture found at Paris in this period, see John of Garland, *Dictionarius*, ed. Scheler, cc. 55, 56. It is not so clear as Rashdall (ii. 668) supposes that c. 55 refers to student hostels.

[3] *Chartularium*, i, nos. 20, 201, 202, 448, 501. See also the beginning of the poem 'De presbytero et logico,' in Hauréau, vi. 310; Wright, *Latin Poems attributed to Walter Mapes*, p. 251. There are allusions to the cope and hood in Hauréau, iv. 51; Étienne de Bourbon, p. 406; Jacques de Vitry, ed. Crane, p. 12. Jean de Montlhéry says: 'Scolaris bene custodit capam novam: pueri quandoque infigunt tibias suas in luto et dicunt se esse bene calciatos.' Merton College, MS. 237, f. 227 v. Cf. Humbert de Romans,*Maxima bibliotheca patrum*, xxv. 594.

[4] Schönbach, in *Mittheilungen des historischen Vereines für Steiermark*, xlviii. 151; Owst, p. 332. Cf. Humbert de Romans in *Maxima bibliotheca*, xxv. 632.

[5] 'Hoc maxime faciunt ebriosi quales sunt Parisius multi et maxime Ybernici,

for the name of scholar and the income which they receive while attending the university, go to class but once or twice a week, choosing by preference the lectures on canon law, which do not begin till nine in the morning [1] and thus leave them plenty of time for sleep.[2] Many eat cakes in the morning when they ought to be at study,[3] or go to sleep in the class-rooms, spending the rest of their time drinking in taverns or building castles in Spain (*castella in Hispania*); [4] and when it is time to leave Paris,[5] in order to make some show of learning such students get together huge volumes of calfskin, with wide margins and fine red bindings, and so with wise sack and empty mind they go back to their parents. "What knowledge is this," asks the preacher, "which thieves may steal, mice or moths eat up, fire or water destroy?"; and he cites an instance where the student's horse fell into a river, carrying all his books with him.[6] Some never go home, but continue to enjoy in idleness the fruits of their benefices.[7] Even in vacation time, when the rich ride off with

qui quicquid scribendo in septimana conquirunt, totum una die potando consumunt. Nec de hoc corrigi possunt.' Servasanto da Faenza, *Liber de virtutibus et vitiis*, dist. vii, c. 4, printed by L. Oliger in *Miscellanea Ehrle*, i. 180.

[1] Ordinarily the first lecture of the day seems to have come at six. Rashdall, ii. 652.

[2] Jacques de Vitry, ed. Pitra, p. 363.

[3] Hauréau, iv. 39, 248; Schönbach, *loc. cit.*, pp. 151 f. Hauréau (p. 39) quotes an adage from MS. lat. 16089:

Parisius locus egregius: mala gens, bona villa,
Nam duo pastilla pro nummo dantur in illa.

Cf. an anonymous Minorite, MS. lat. 15005, f. 160 v: 'Sunt enim solliciti in cibos delectabiles, unde libenter pastillant et huiusmodi.'

[4] Eudes de Châteauroux, in Lecoy de la Marche, *Chaire française*, p. 463. Cf. Humbert de Romans, *Maxima bibliotheca*, xxv. 633.

[5] Cf. Robert de Sorbon (MS. lat. 15971, f. 84): 'Quando clerici diu fuerunt Parisius et volunt recedere, ipsi corrigunt libros suos quia extra Parisius non invenirent exemplaria ad corrigendum.'

[6] 'Dixit quidam de quibusdam fatuis scolaribus sic: In nugis sunt subtiles, in neccessariis tardi et ebetes, et ne nichil fecisse videantur cum repatriaverint, de pellibus vitulinis cum latis spaciis magna componunt volumina eaque pellibus rubeis et pulcris vestiunt, et sic cum sapienti sacculo sed cum insipienti animo ad parentes redeunt. Que est ista scientia quam fur subripere, mus rodere, tinea demoliri, aqua delere, ignis comburere potest?' MS. lat. 15971, f. 198; translated in *Histoire littéraire*, xxvi. 465.

[7] Gautier de Château-Thierry, in Hauréau, vi. 210; translated in *Histoire littéraire*, xxvi. 392.

their servants [1] and the poor trudge home under the burning sun,[2] many idlers remain in Paris to their own and the city's harm.[3] Mediaeval Paris, we should remember, was not only the incomparable 'parent of the sciences,' but also a place of good cheer and good fellowship and varied delights,[4] a favourite resort not only of the studious but of country priests on a holiday; [5] and it would not be strange if sometimes scholars prolonged their stay unduly and lamented their departure in phrases which are something more than rhetorical commonplace.[6]

We get glimpses, too, of the troop of hangers-on who always thrive in a university town, bedels and servants and furnishers and other 'emptiers of purses'[7]—like the vendors of fancy wafers (nieules), who make a handsome profit by visiting the students at meal-times and spreading their tempting wares on the table.[8] The bedels are represented as imposing but ignorant persons, fond of good eating and drinking,[9] whose multifarious duties put them in a position of considerable influence and gave them many opportunities for acquiring money.[10] They levied

[1] 'Quidam scolaris nobilis et iuvenis multum Parisius morans tempore vacationis ivit in equis suis cum magistris et familia circumquaque Parisius spaciatum et declinans ad quandam abbaciam Cisterciensis ordinis.' Tours, MS. 468, f. 75.

[2] 'Quando ego veni semel de scolis in estate, pater meus vix cognovit me, ita fui denigratus in via propter solem.' Robert de Sorbon, MS. lat. 15971, f. 116.

[3] Jean de Montlhéry, Histoire littéraire, xxvi. 437.

[4] Cf. Hauréau, iv. 248; and the poem printed in Raynaud, Motets français, i. 277.

[5] See chapter 26 of the synodal statutes of Eudes de Sully, bishop of Paris, in Migne, P. L., ccxii. 66.

[6] See for example the lament of a Picard scholar published by Langlois, Revue internationale de l'enseignement, xxiii. 561 ff.

[7] John of Garland, Dictionarius, ed. Scheler, c. 69. Cc. 19, 30, 31, 34, and 35 mention various tradesmen who had frequent dealings with the Paris students. See also Chapter III, infra.

[8] 'Consuetudo est in aliquibus terris, ut Parisius, quod lo neuliers qui facit nebulas veniet ad domum clericorum vel aliorum, et si potest intrare in hora comestionis veniet et proiciet nebulas per mensam et tunc dicet quod nesciret modum et consuetudines. Dicitur de isto homine, Quam largus est! sed certe antequam recedat ipse pro illo debili encenio reportabit quod valebit in quadruplo.' MS. lat. 15971, f. 155 v. Cf. John of Garland, loc. cit., c. 30.

[9] 'Tales . . . similes sunt bedellis qui semper sunt in scolis sine libris et nihil addiscunt nisi curias querere et bene comedere et bene bibere.' Guiard de Laon, MS. lat. 16471, f. 248 v.

[10] On the duties of bedels see particularly the Chartularium, i, no. 369.

toll on the scholars for good seats in the lecture-halls,[1] exacted a goodly purse at inceptions,[2] and for a sufficient sum were ready to glorify ignorant masters.[3] The well-to-do student might have a servant of his own, to carry his books to class,[4] etc., but ordinarily one servant seems to have sufficed for a number of students of more modest needs.[5] By all accounts these servants were a thieving lot, and Jacques de Vitry has a good story to tell of their skill in defrauding their masters. The servants, it appears, had a sort of chief or captain, who one day brought them together and began to question them as to their professional attainments. One after the other explained how he could make one, two, even three farthings on the penny, until the cleverest of all declared that he could pocket a penny for each farthing. "I buy," he said, "mustard from the dealer who furnishes me the vegetables, candles, and so on for my masters, and every time I get mustard I divide a farthing's worth into four portions and set each down as a farthing. Then, as I am a regular customer, the dealer throws in a fifth portion, which I also reckon at a farthing, and so I gain four farthings for one." [6]

Other aspects of everyday life are illustrated in various stories of the students and their doings which the preachers have preserved. One clerk has a dog which he calls Rose and teaches to walk on its fore legs; another clerk steals it, names it Violet and teaches it to walk on its hind legs, so that it refuses to obey its former master when he claims it in the bishop's court.[7] Certain students amuse themselves over their dice by putting one of the dice in a cat's paws; if the cat wins, they give it something to eat, if not, they kill it and sell its skin.[8] In another *exemplum*

---

[1] Hauréau, vi. 125; Schönbach, *loc. cit.*, p. 152.

[2] *Chartularium, loc. cit.*   [3] Hauréau, vi. 124.

[4] *Ibid.*, p. 311; Pitra, *Analecta novissima*, ii. 363.

[5] 'Mulier est quasi serviens pluribus scolaribus qui vix potest satisfacere, sed virgo cogitat que Deo sunt.' Guiard de Laon, MS. lat. 15959, f. 455 v. Cf. E. Berger, *Registres d'Innocent IV*, no. 2525; and the next note.

[6] Jacques de Vitry, ed. Crane, p. 87, ed. Pitra, p. 456; Étienne de Bourbon, p. 372; Wright, *Latin Stories*, p. 113; translated in Lecoy de la Marche, *L'Esprit de nos aieux*, pp. 187 f.

[7] Auxerre, MS. 35, f. 96; printed by Delisle in *Histoire littéraire*, xxxi. 59, and by Welter in *Tabula exemplorum*, p. 14, no. 43.

[8] Crane, *Jacques de Vitry*, p. 8; Welter, *Tabula exemplorum*, p. 53, no. 194.

the students were playing for a dinner, when one of them seized
a neighbour's cat which frequented the house, and said: "He
eats here and never pays his reckoning. He shall play." So they
made the cat throw, and when he lost they tied to his neck a
bill for a quart of wine and sent him home, threatening to take
his skin if the owner did not pay. The owner sent back the cat
with the money, but begged them not to force him to play
again, as he could not count.[1] A student is drinking in his room
with some friends, when he sees a thief under the bed. He asks
them, "Did you give our brother there anything to drink?"
Then they beat the thief.[2] A companion of Étienne de Bourbon
is at vespers on Christmas eve, when a thief enters his room and
steals his law-books. When the student comes to use the books
after the holidays, he cannot find them and seeks help from a
necromancer, who accuses an innocent relative of the student.
Finally the real thief is forced to take sanctuary in a church
tower and confesses to the theft, giving the residence of the Jew
with whom he had pawned the books.[3]

One cannot read these tales without being reminded of that
precious rogue of the *fabliau* who drank and diced away his
clothing and his *clergie* throughout France: his A.B.C. and books
of devotion, his grammars and 'authors'—Ovid the great, Lucan, Juvenal, Statius "and Virgil lost at dice at Abbeville,"—
while Paris has his books of divinity, of arts, physic, and music:

> Li tremeriaus m'a abatu,
> Par ma folie ai tout perdu,

[1] 'Clerici quidam Parisius ludebant ad talos pro quadam cena, et quidam
amittens [MS. admittens] accepit catum cuiusdam vicini eorum stantem iuxta
eos qui frequentabat domum, et ait, Iste ludet vobiscum qui frequenter hic
comedit et nunquam solvit simbolum; et ponens taxillum [MS. taxillo] intra
iiiior pedes cati eum fecit proicere, et amisit. Et ponens cedulam ad collum eius
scripsit amisisse quartam vini, quam nisi sólveret pellem dimitteret, quod
videns dominus eius ligavit peccuniam in collo cati, rogans ne compellerent
eum ludere de cetero, *car il ne savoit compter sa chance.*' *Compilatio singularis
exemplorum*, Tours, MS. 468, f. 80.
[2] 'Clerici scolares Parisius bibebant in camera unius sociorum, et vidit unum
latronem asconditum sub lecto et ait, Dedistisne illi socio ad bibendum? quem
egregie correxerunt.' *Ibid.*, f. 79 v.
[3] Étienne de Bourbon, p. 317; translated in Lecoy de la Marche, *L'Esprit de
nos aieux*, p. 289.

Tout mon avoir et toz mes livres
Grant pieça que j'en sui delivres.
En duel ai torné mon revel,
Quar je cuit que il n'ait chastel
En France que je n'i alaisse,
Et de mes livres n'i lessaisse.

.   .   .   .   .

Mes livres de Divinité
Perdi à Paris la cité,
Et cels d'art et cels de fisique,
Et mes conduis et ma musique.[1]

The principal student festivals mentioned in the sermons are
Saint Nicholas's day, Christmas, and inceptions. The feast of
Saint Nicholas, the patron saint of scholars, was one of the great
days in the student calendar. There was a drama, in which
clerks or maidens impersonated the saint and his miracles,[2] and
then came feasting[3] and games and dancing and the rest.
"Some scholars swell the crowd of the Nicolaitanes [Rev., ii.
6], which men of authority always hate, and rise up at the
voice of the cock, but in them the daughters of music are
brought low."[4] Christmas eve was likewise made an occasion
for revelry, with dicing and drinking and wild Bacchic processions,[5] so that some "committed more sins at Christmas time
than during all the rest of the year."[6] The inception celebra-

[1] See the poem in full, "Le departement des livres," in D. M. Méon, *Nouveau
recueil de fabliaux et contes inédits* (Paris, 1823), i. 404–406; and the spirited
English version of Helen Waddell, *The Wandering Scholars*, pp. 242–243.

[2] Hauréau, iv. 76.

[3] See the story in Étienne de Bourbon, p. 51, of the barber who stole a pig
for the clerks whom he was to entertain on this day.

[4] 'Quidam enim scolares qui student vimencie ad turbam vadunt Nico-
laitarum, quam viri catholici semper oderunt, et surgunt ad vocem volucris
que gallus dicitur, sed obsurdescunt in eis filie carminis.' Prévostin, sermon
'in epiphania,' B.M., Add. MS. 18335, f. 13 v. See particularly Étienne de
Besancon, in Hauréau, iv. 208. On cock-fights among scholars, cf. Hauréau, iv.
274; Lecoy de la Marche, *Chaire française*, p. 452, note. Another game, probably
also among the students of the grammar schools, is alluded to in a Lenten sermon
of a chancellor (Nicolas de Nonancourt?), MS. lat. 15952, f. 113 v: 'Sicut in
ludo scolarium, gallice *avoir*, *dire*, *et amentir*.' Cf. also MS. lat. 15959, f. 191.

[5] 'Sed ve illis scolaribus qui vigilias bacancium et furiosorum cum tirsis et
facibus candelarum ei [Deo] exhibent bachalia festa celebrantes.' Guiard de
Laon, sermon 'in vigilia Nativitatis,' MS. lat. 15959, f. 132.

[6] Anonymous subprior, Hauréau, iii. 287–288. Cf. Eudes de Châteauroux,
ibid., vi. 209.

tions also fell under the displeasure of the moralists of the pulpit, for besides the inevitable banquet there were likely to be masquerades [1] and processions, with songs and garlands and tapers, and round dances (*choreae*) [2] in the streets and squares—the last-named form of amusement being in such disfavour with the church [3] and with the university authorities that candidates were obliged to swear that they would permit no *choreae* about their houses nor suffer anything improper at their inception. [4] Such infractions of strict discipline might even leave their echoes in the chroniclers, as when Guillaume le Breton tells us that the victory of Bouvines (1214) was celebrated by the scholars in dancing, singing, and feasting for eight days and as many nights. [5] So in 1233 the Pope finds it necessary to legislate against canons and clerks of Paris who dance and gesticulate at Easter time in the cloisters of Orleans cathedral. [6]

The account of Paris student life which has been thus put together from the sermons is not of course a rounded picture. There is much truth in Mark Pattison's aphorism that "history cannot be written from manuscripts," and in presenting the material contained in a single class of sources many aspects of university life must necessarily be neglected. To the preachers the university and its members are primarily a theme for moralizing, and they emphasize what best points their moral. [7] It is

[1] 'Sed heu ! modo non est disciplina Christi in clericis sed disciplina histrionum, quod patet in principiis magistrorum quando scolares diversificant se; portant enim in capite signum crucis sed in corpore portant dyabolum portando vestes histrionum.' John Peckham, Library of St. Mark's at Venice, Fondo Antico, MS. 92, f. 205.

[2] 'Sicut Deus habet suam processionem in qua portantur cerei flores et crux et vexilla, ita dyabolus suas habet processiones, scilicet choreas et circuitus per vicos etiam de nocte. Fiunt enim choree cum cantilenis et floribus rosarum et violarum in capellis capitis et in manibus. Item circuitus fiunt per vicos cum cereis maxime a scolaribus in principiis et a laicis in nuptiis.' Gautier de Château-Thierry, MS. lat. 15955, f. 98, col. 3. Pierre de Bar-sur-Aube, in Hauréau, vi. 243. Cf. Jacques de Vitry, in Étienne de Bourbon, ed. Lecoy de la Marche, p. 162, note.

[3] See the stories of demons afflicting the dancers, in Étienne de Bourbon, pp. 161, 226, 232, 397 ff.; and Hauréau, iv. 161. Cf. Welter, *Tabula exemplorum*, p. 96.   [4] *Chartularium*, i, nos. 202, 501.

[5] *Philippis*, xii. 265–279 (ed. Delaborde, p. 358).

[6] Auvray, *Registres de Grégoire IX* (Paris, 1896–), no. 1077.

[7] Cf. the observations of Langlois in Lavisse, *Histoire de France*, iii, 2, p. 354.

not their business to tell of the orderly working of university institutions, the eager enthusiasm for learning, the wholesome routine of academic life; they give only what suits their purpose, and we must be thankful for that. Furthermore, much of what the sermons contain on university matters is interesting as showing the state of mind of their authors rather than as yielding specific information, and allowance must of course be made for the official position of some of the preachers as well as for the pulpit equation in general. What the preachers set out to say is usually of less historical importance than what they tell us unintentionally and incidentally. Still, when all deductions have been made, there remains a substantial residuum of fact which adds materially to our knowledge of academic conditions in the thirteenth century and to our sympathetic understanding of the human background of a great mediaeval university.

CHAPTER III

MANUALS FOR STUDENTS

THE mediaeval student, we have found in the preceding chapters, is an elusive person. He is numerous, he is noisy, a standard subject for the commonplaces of the class-room and the pulpit, but he meets us almost entirely in the mass, generic and impersonal. The individual student remains silent and inexpressive. He left behind him no "Diary of a Freshman," no compositions on the theme, "Who I am and why I came to Paris." Even Chaucer's incomparable clerk of Oxenford some would make only a type, 'souning in moral vertu' like the preachers. Types certainly the clerks are to their fellows, the authors of the Goliardic rhymes and the *fabliaux*. The next world, too, will know them in the mass, if we are to believe *Aucassin et Nicolete*—

> Car en infer vont li bel clerc.

While the student literature of the Middle Ages is a literature of types, it is not on that account entirely barren for the historian of culture and social conditions, and one group of such sources of knowledge, the student manuals, may briefly claim our attention. Manuals of advice and information for students, it is true, may be found at all times, from the Graeco-Roman dialogues of the Pseudo-Dositheus to our current handbooks of deportment and of conversation in foreign tongues; nor should we forget that eighteenth-century Cambridge has left us Waterland's *Advice to a Young Student*,[1] containing edifying directions for a religious and sober life and days and nights of systematic study, or that nineteenth-century Oxford produced that amusing satire, *The Adventures of Mr. Verdant Green* as freshman and as undergraduate at 'Brazenface College.' The didacticism of such handbooks was, however, peculiarly welcome in the Middle Ages, when the schoolmaster ran at large through literature and even carved the seven liberal arts in stone. Mediaeval, too,

---

[1] C. Wordsworth, *Scholae Academicae* (Cambridge, 1877), pp. 330–337.

was the literary characterization of the several classes of society, with its mirrors of princes, of monks, and of fools. It is very possibly an accident that we have no adequate 'mirror of students' by that title—and, after all, the *Mirror of Fools* of Nigel Wireker is chiefly concerned with students at Salerno and Paris, its hero an ass whose bray resists all academic remedies. In any case there are various manuals which hold up the mirror to the mediaeval student and reflect one or another phase of his life, and, without attempting to exhaust this class of materials, we may illustrate it by characteristic examples.

The most popular of mediaeval manuals, the *De disciplina scholarium* of the Pseudo-Boethius, doubtless owes much of its popularity to the honoured name which it bore, for Boethius, last of the ancients and first of the schoolmen, carried great authority throughout the Middle Ages, when the fame of his text-books easily spread to anything else which was ascribed to him. The extraordinary diffusion of this work in the later Middle Ages is attested by at least eighty-two manuscript copies and numerous early imprints. Nevertheless, no modern critic is misled by the author's attempt to dress the work up in a Boethian garb by means of allusions to "the inhuman king of the Goths" and the mythical student days of Boethius at Athens, or by the numerous examples of such imaginary ancients as Ganymede, son of the dictator Pyrrhus. Both internal and external evidence clearly place the treatise at Paris in the first half of the thirteenth century, though its author is unknown.[1]

According to the author's advice, grammatical studies, which are begun at the age of seven, are to be followed by the Roman poets, and when the rudiments of such a training have been duly completed, the youth proceeds to climb, by careful attention to logical terminology and method, and a liberal use of the

[1] The text will be found most conveniently in Migne, *P. L.*, lxiv. 1223–38. The treatise is discussed by Jean Porcher in the *Positions des thèses de l'École des Chartes* for 1921, preliminary to a critical edition. He sets the date at 1230–40. Cf. J. T. Welter, *L'Exemplum* (Paris, 1927), pp. 188–189. Paul Lehmann, *Pseudo-antike Literatur des Mittelalters* (Berlin, 1927), pp. 27–28, 101, argues that the author's name was Conrad, as shown by the acrostic at the end of the treatise. Manacorda, who still accepts the Boethian authorship, cites a copy as early as 1247 (*Storia della scuola in Italia*, i, 2 (1914), p. 88).

text-books of Boethius, to "the knowledge of the five universals, which is the mistress of the sciences of the *trivium*, the power of the *quadrivium*, and the plenitude of the collateral sciences." If he would attain this end, the scholar should not be restless (*dyscolus*), as are many "in the city of Julius Caesar which was called Paris," wandering through the streets and squares with roving eye and unbridled tongue, visiting taverns and low resorts, and frequenting dances, public spectacles, and banquets. He should avoid luxury in all its forms and should limit himself to that moderate use of wine which gives keenness to the intellect. The wise scholar will choose a good chum and be on his guard against the wiles of scouts and laundresses. Before making final arrangements with a master, it is well to visit his lectures for three days. Once selected, the master should be treated with all respect, acts of violence, in particular, being avoided, to which the choleric temper is always prone, since "he who rises up against the imparter of knowledge is not worthy of knowledge." The poverty of masters and scholars comes in for discussion, in the course of which some general precepts are given for overcoming "the detestable close-fistedness of parents." The student who looks forward to becoming a master should begin to accumulate books of his own and not rely slavishly upon lectures. Oral expression and actual teaching should be practised and a wide acquaintance be cultivated, so that when the day of inception comes there may be a goodly concourse at the festivities and the lectures which follow. It is also well so to demean one's self as to secure the goodwill of those "by whose favour one is to be crowned." Before his promotion a new master ought also to be sure that he has sufficient means to support himself throughout the first year, for some have had to beg and others have found it necessary to hire students in order to have well filled class-rooms. The closing chapter is thus brought to consider "the venerable majesty of masters" and the principles which should govern their conduct, especially in the early years of their career when the judicious teacher must walk softly and tolerate the interruptions of those who come late to his lectures.

Much briefer, and quite without pretence to antiquity, is the manual *De regimine et modo studendi quem debent habere scolares* of Martino da Fano, a pupil of Azo at Bologna, and professor of law at Arezzo and Modena in 1255.[1] If, he begins, you are seeking how to study, a purpose for which I am glad to give you credit, you must first find the right sort of master, one who teaches the necessary things and answers questions readily and satisfactorily, suffering contradiction willingly and giving for his assertions sound reasons based on holy writ. Try to harmonize case and text, and to understand the text as fully as possible. Search out the reasons for the case, answering objections and seeking parallels. Commit carefully to memory in each instance one or two laws which seem most appropriate. Do not waste your time in saying these over by rote, but seek the meaning of the laws and be sure to go over them in your mind as you walk the streets or lie awake, saying, "To-day I have had so many laws, beginning so and so."

My children, favour equity and love justice; see the Code *De pactis*, law *Hac lege*.[2] Avoid vice, lest you appear unworthy in the eyes of other authors of the laws; see the Authentica *De triente et semisse*: *Sin autem*.[3] Reverence chastity, for the emperor has decreed that it is ever to be reverenced; see the Authentica *Si qua mulier*, in the *Consultum Orfitianum*.[4] For chastity alone is able to bring the souls of men into the presence of God; see the Authentica *De lenonibus*: *Sancimus*;[5] and we

[1] See the text in L. Frati, "L'epistola *De regimine et modo studendi* di Martino da Fano," in *Studi e memorie per la storia dell' Università di Bologna*, vi. 19–29 (1921). That Martino taught also at Naples and Milan has been brought out by E. M. Meyers, *Iuris interpretes saec. XIII* (Naples, 1924), pp. xxvi ff.

[2] *Code*, bk. v, tit. xiv, *De pactis conventis*, law 8 : 'Hac lege decernimus . . . quoniam conditores legum aequitatis convenit esse fautores,' etc.

[3] *Novels*, collatio iii, tit. v, novel 18, *De triente et semisse*, c. 5 : 'Si autem confusa concupiscentia ita fiat, et alias superinducat priori concubinas . . . odibilis quidem nobis iste qui talis est, procul autem omnibus modis ab hac lege expellatur.'

[4] *Code*, bk. vi, tit. lvii, *Ad senatus consultum Orfitianum*, law 5 : 'Si qua illustris mulier . . . hanc legem ipsi pudicitiae, quam semper colendam censemus, merito dedicamus.'

[5] *Novels*, coll. iii, tit. i, novel 14, *De lenonibus*, c. 1 : 'Sancimus igitur omnes quidem secundum quod possint castitatem agere, quae etiam sola Deo cum fiducia possibilis est hominum animas praesentare.' Cf. Psalms, xxiv. 3, 4; Matthew, v. 8.

do not love our soul unless we live chastely; see the Authentica *Quomodo oportet episcopos*: *Haec de Deo*.[1] Practise clemency, for by it alone is won the likeness of God; see the Code *De nuptiis*, law *Imperialis*.[2] Avoid pride, for God resisteth the proud, and giveth his grace to the humble.[3] Do not practise avarice, which is the root of all evil[4] and is therefore to be smitten by the penalties of the law; see the Authentica *Ut iudices sine quoquo suffragio*, in collatio ii.[5] If you do all these things, the light of learning will shine within you, for, as Solomon says, "into a malicious soul wisdom shall not enter, nor dwell in the body that is subject unto sin."[6]

A precise legal authority cited for every precept of ordinary morality, what could be more lawyer-like? We are very near that University of Bologna where an assault with a cutlass in the class-room was charged as a loss of time and money to the assembled scholars,[7] and where the examples in the law lectures of Odofredus[8] afford the best picture of the life of students in their idle hours, even to their giving false names to the police, the *Code* to the contrary notwithstanding.[9]

The *Morale scolarium* of John of Garland takes us back to the University of Paris and the thirteenth century; indeed, it has been definitely placed in the year 1241. Its author was a pedantic professor of grammar who imagined himself a poet and turned out verse on every subject from etymologies and supines to the miracles of the Virgin and the mysteries of the faith.[10] Stilted

---

[1] *Novels*, coll. i, tit. vi, novel 6, *Quomodo oporteat episcopos*, secunda pars, *Haec de Deo*: '. . . ipsam castitatem eligentem, primum principium et fundamentum manifestum secundum divinas regulas et residuae virtutis constitutam.'

[2] *Code*, bk. v, tit. iv, *De nuptiis*, law 23, *Imperialis benevolentiae*: 'Nam ita credimus Dei benevolentiam et circa genus humanum nimiam clementiam quantum nostrae naturae possibile est imitari.'

[3] 1 Peter, v. 5.   [4] 1 Timothy, vi. 10.

[5] *Novels*, coll. ii, tit. 2–3, novel 8, *Ut iudices sine quoquo suffragio fiant*.

[6] Wisdom of Solomon, i. 4.

[7] F. Cavazza, *Le scuole dell' antico studio bolognese* (Milan, 1896), no. 29.

[8] On Odofredus see the memoir of G. Tamassia, in *Atti e memorie della R. deputazione di storia patria per le provincie di Romagna*, 3d series, xi. 183–225: xii. 1–83, 330–390, especially 71–83; cf. Zaccagnini, *Studio di Bologna*, pp. 78 f.

[9] *Code*, bk. ix, tit. xxv, *De mutatione nominis*.

[10] Hauréau, *Notice sur les oeuvres authentiques ou supposées de Jean de Garlande*, in *Notices et extraits des manuscrits*, xxvii, 2 (1879), pp. 1–86, has now been superseded by the elaborate introduction of L. J. Paetow to his edition of the *Morale Scolarium*, published in *Two Medieval Satires on the*

in their diction and generally obscure in style, the numerous works of John of Garland sometimes contain material of interest for the university life of his day, like the lines addressed by a Parisian student to the warden of the bishop's prison,[1] or the remarkable circular which sets forth the manifold advantages of the newly founded University of Toulouse,[2] in a way that would do credit to any modern educational promoter. John of Garland had some knowledge of student life at Paris, and we have a right to expect something from a treatise of six hundred and sixty-two lines which bears the title *Morale scolarium* and, along with the "insertion of the mystery of theology and the explanation of the cause of certain natural phenomena," promises to "eliminate the original rudeness of scholastic life by setting virtue over against vice and courtesy against boorishness in satirical reprehension." Nevertheless the poem is distinctly disappointing. Not only does this "new satire" deal wholly in generalities, "lest it may arouse wrath," but it is soon plain that the term satire is in fact used in the sense of a collection of miscellaneous poems. Instead of "a manual of *savoir-vivre* for the use of the ill bred and turbulent youth of the schools of Paris"[3] we have a disconnected lot of Garland's occasional verse. The decline of the liberal arts and theology before the more popular lucrative sciences, the defects of the newer text-books in grammar, the patience of the Mendicant Orders and the crown which awaits them, the vices and virtues of prelates, the generosity of parents and noble givers, the niggardliness of the rich in time of famine, the medicinal qualities of herbs, the praise of Rome, as well as the personal merits of St. Louis, the

---

University of Paris (Berkeley, 1927) and also separately. My own acquaintance with the *Morale scolarium* is based upon an examination of the Bruges, Cambridge, and Oxford manuscripts, but I have profited largely by the results of Paetow's researches.

[1] Printed in part by L. Rockinger in *Q. E.*, ix. 488.

[2] Johannes de Garlandia, *De triumphis ecclesiae libri octo*, ed. T. Wright (Roxburghe Club, 1856), pp. 96–98; Académie de Toulouse, *Mémoires*, 5th series, i. 209–211 (1857), accompanied by a French translation; *Chartularium Universitatis Parisiensis*, i, no. 72, pp. 129–131; M. Fournier, *Les statuts et privilèges des universités françaises*, i (1890), no. 504, pp. 439–440.

[3] Hauréau, *loc. cit.*, p. 15.

bishop and the chancellor of Paris, and that example for honest
imitation, John le Blund, "once the flower of Paris and now
the flower of York"—when all these have been celebrated there
is small room for counsel to students and still less for explaining
the early and tantalizing allusions to the rectorship, determina-
tions, and the 'hazing' of freshmen. The student should learn
while he is at Paris, lest he be found wanting when he goes
to Rome:

Parisius discas ne Rome forte deiscas.

"He should not be a fornicator, a robber, a murderer, a deceitful
merchant, a champion at dice." The best models of deportment
are the graven images of the churches. The lot of the poor
scholar is not so hard: the life is honourable, and beets, beans,
and peas, perhaps a quart of wine, make a good dinner for a
tableful of scholars. If you give a feast, receive your guests with
a glad countenance and in an honourable manner; give them
clean seats and a fresh tablecloth. Carve the meat skilfully,
and have a clean knife before you begin to hunt for the tender
morsels. Don't drink when your mouth is full. After dinner
wash your hands and refill the glasses, but first say grace. Learn
to keep your mouth shut, and do not scratch yourself.

The two chapters of the *Morale scholarium* which deal with
behaviour at table have given John of Garland, and his students, a place in the long list of mediaeval books on deportment.[1] Occupying a position somewhere between the moral
Distichs of the Pseudo-Cato on the one hand and the "Perfect
Butler" and the cookery books on the other, these manuals of
manners are particularly concerned with table manners, and if
their utility is not limited to clerks, their substance is already
suggested in the clerkly handbooks of the earlier twelfth century, the *De institutione novitiorum* of Hugh of St. Victor and
the *Disciplina clericalis* of Petrus Alphonsi. Well before John
of Garland's time, this teaching was crystallized in a short poem

---

[1] The most considerable collection of such handbooks is that edited by
F. J. Furnivall for the Early English Text Society under the title *Manners and
Meals in Olden Time* (London, 1868); the best critical study is the article of
S. Glixelli, "Les *Contenances de Table*," in *Romania*, xlvii. 1–40 (1921).

of twenty-three lines which serves as the starting-point of a long
series of such treatises:[1]

Quisquis es in mensa,	primo de paupere pensa:
Nam cum pascis eum,	pascis, amice, Deum.
Nescit homo plenus,	quam vitam ducat egenus.
Nemo cibum capiat,	donec benedictio fiat,
Nec capiat sedem,	nisi quam vult qui regit edem.
Donec sint posita	tibi fercula mandere vita,
Et mundi digiti	tibi sint unguesque politi.
In disco tacta	non sit bucella redacta.
Non tangas aures	nudis digitis neque nares.
Non mundes dentes	ferro acuto ad comedentes.
Sal non tangatur	esca quo vase locatur.
Si potes hec repeto	in mensa ructare caveto.
Esse scias vetitum	in mensa ponere cubitum.
Lege mandatur	ne parapsis ad osque ponatur.
Qui vult potare	debet prius os vacuare
Et sint illius	labia tersa prius;
Nec tacere possum,	ne dentibus laceret ossum.
Non dicas verbum	cuiquam quod ei sit acerbum,
Ne possit quis irasci	vel discordia nasci.
Vultu sis hilaris,	nullum tamen irridearis.
Si pauce loqueris,	gratior sodalibus eris.
Mensa submota,	manus ablue, postea pota.
Privetur mensa,	qui spreverit hec documenta.

Such concise counsel lends itself easily to expansion and adaptation both in Latin and the vernacular: by the beginning of
the fourteenth century the Lombard Bonvesin da Riva has
written a poem of two hundred and four lines, four for each of
his "Fifty Rules of Courtesy of the Table," *De quinquaginta
curialitatibus ad mensam*,[2] and by the sixteenth century the
length of such poems runs into thousands of lines. They are
found in practically all of the European vernaculars, in French,
Provençal, and Italian, in German, Swedish, and Polish, as well
as in English under such self-explanatory titles as "The Babees
Book," "Lerne or be Lewde," "The A B C of Aristotle," "The
Book of Curtisie," etc. All have a certain sameness, not to say

[1] F. Novati, *Carmina Medii Aevi* (Florence, 1883), pp. 47–50; Glixelli,
loc. cit., pp. 28–29.

[2] Best edited by A. I. Bekker, *Monatsberichte* of the Berlin Academy, 1851,
pp. 85–90; Italian and English versions, Early English Text Society, 1868.

obviousness. "Wash your hands in the morning and, if there is time, your face; [1] use your napkin and handkerchief; eat with three fingers only, and don't gorge; don't be boisterous or quarrelsome at table; don't stare at your neighbour or his plate; don't criticize the food; don't pick your teeth with your knife or wipe them on the cloth; don't butter your bread with your finger; don't whisper or go to sleep; don't spit on or over the table!" Here and there we find a further touch of the age: "Scrape bones with your knife but don't gnaw them; when you have done with them, put them in the bowl or on the floor!"

Behaviour at table covers but a small part of the territory occupied by the works of advice and counsel addressed to the mediaeval student, but it is often the most specific and informing part, for much of what was written on the whole duty of students is quite general and commonplace. Thus Bonvesin da Riva, who is often interesting in his fifty rules of courtesy for the table, wrote a banal *Vita scholastica* [2] "in which are contained the five keys of wisdom, namely, the fear of the Lord, respect for the master, assiduous reading, frequent questioning, and discipline of the memory." A better reflection of the age meets us at the end of the fifteenth century in the various *Statuta vel Praecepta scolarium* written in the form of couplets to be impressed on the memory of German youth. [3] The beginning of wisdom was to remember God and obey the master, but the student had also to watch his behaviour in church and

---

[1] 'Ablue mane manus, faciem si tempus habebis.' Vatican, MS. Ottoboni lat. 3325, f. 16.

[2] Extracts printed by Bekker, Berlin Academy, *Monatsberichte*, 1851, pp. 450–456. Closely similar is a 'Liber scolastice discipline editus a magistro utili Parisiensi,' in the Vatican, MS. Ottoboni lat. 3325 (saec. xv), ff. 27–37, beginning
Utilis est rudibus presentis cura libelli.
In the manuscript this is preceded, ff. 1–24, by another 'Liber discipline scholastice,' also in verse, beginning
Hic rudium primo vivendi forma docetur.
The Wolfenbüttel catalogue lists under MS. 2444, f. 66 v, an 'Admonitio scolarium' and a 'De moribus beanorum atque studentium carmen.'

[3] See the editions of Maurus Weingart, printed as a *Beilage zum Jahresberichte des humanistischen Gymnasiums Metten*, 1893–94, and of P. Bahlmann, "Schüler-Regeln aus dem Ende des 15. Jahrhunderts," in *Mitteilungen der Gesellschaft für deutsche Erziehungs- und Schulgeschichte*, iii. 129–145 (1893).

lift up his voice in the choir—compulsory attendance at church and singing in the choir being a regular feature of these schools —keep his books clean, and pay his school bills promptly. Face and hands should be washed in the morning, but the baths should not be visited without permission, nor should boys run on the ice or throw snowballs. Sunday was the day for play, but this could be only in the churchyard, where boys must be careful not to play with dice or break stones from the wall or throw anything over the church. And whether at play or at home, Latin should always be spoken.

> Ne graventur nimium per studium scolares,
> Ipsi solent ludere dies per solares.
>
> Ludus his permittitur causa recreandi,
> Et idioma sedulo latinum usitandi.
>
> In nullo loco tu debes ludum exercere,
> Quam in cimiterio, hic debes manere.
>
> In hoc ludas, ut decet, omni abs clamore,
> Nullum malum a tuo audiatur ore.
>
> Non ludas pro re aliqua talos neque tractes,
> Non rumpe muri lapides nec supra templum iactes.[1]

John of Garland was the author of another work which helps us to understand the mediaeval student, namely, his *Dictionarius*,[2] in which, it is said, our modern word 'dictionary' first makes its appearance. This is a descriptive vocabulary, topically arranged and devoting a large amount of space to the

---

[1] Couplets 55–59.

[2] The *Dictionarius* has been edited four times. (1) Hercule Géraud, "Dictionnaire de Jean de Garlande," in his *Paris sous Philippe-le-Bel* (Paris, 1837), pp. 580–612: in the *Documents inédits sur l'histoire de France*. (2) Baron Kervyn de Lettenhove, in Société d'Émulation pour l'Étude de l'Histoire et des Antiquités de la Flandre, 2d series, viii. 160–176, 219–220 (1850). Incomplete. (3) Thomas Wright, "Dictionarius of John Garland," in *A Volume of Vocabularies* (London, 1857), pp. 120–138. (4) Auguste Scheler, in his essay "Trois traités de lexicographie latine du XIIe et du XIIIe siècle," *Jahrbuch für romanische und englische Literatur*, vi. 142–162, 287–321, 370–379 (1865). The best of these editions is that of Scheler, but there is much need of a critical edition which shall use all the manuscripts and glosses. For the manuscripts see Paetow's list, in his edition of the *Morale Scolarium* (Berkeley, 1927), pp. 128–129.

Much of the material which follows in the text has already been utilized in my *Rise of Universities* (New York, 1923), pp. 90–95, 97–102.

objects to be seen in the course of a walk through the streets of Paris. The reader is conducted from quarter to quarter and from trade to trade, from the bookstalls of the Parvis Notre-Dame and the fowl-market of the adjoining Rue Neuve to the money-changers' tables and goldsmiths' shops on the Grand-Pont and the bow-makers of the Porte Saint-Lazare, not omitting the classes of *ouvrières* whose acquaintance the student was most likely to make. Saddlers and glovers, clothiers and furriers, cordwainers, cobblers, and apothecaries, the clerk might have use for the wares of all of them, as well as the desk and candle and writing-materials which were the special tools of his calling; but his most frequent relations were with the purveyors of food and drink, whose agents plied their trade vigorously through the streets and lanes of the Latin quarter and worked off their poorer goods on scholars and their servants. There were the hawkers of wine, crying their samples of different qualities from the taverns, at four, six, eight, and twelve pence per measure; the fruit-sellers, deceiving clerks with lettuce and cress, cherries, pears, and green apples; and at night the vendors of light pastry, with their carefully covered baskets of wafers, waffles, and rissoles—a frequent stake at the games of dice among students, who had a custom of hanging from their windows the baskets gained by lucky throws of the six. The *pâtissiers* had also more substantial wares suited to the clerical taste, tarts stuffed with cheese and eggs (good and bad) and well peppered pies of pork, chicken, and eels. To the *rôtissiers* scholars' servants resorted, not only for the pigeons, geese, and other fowl roasted on their spits, but also for uncooked beef, pork, and mutton, seasoned with garlic and other strong sauces. Such fare, however, was not for the poorer students, whose slender purses limited them to tripe and various kinds of sausage, over which a quarrel might easily arise and "the butchers be themselves butchered by angry scholars."

From the student dictionary the way is short to the student dialogue, indeed both dialogue and descriptive vocabulary are closely associated in the Graeco-Roman tradition handed down to the Middle Ages. Thus grammar took on a catechetical form in the *Ars minor* of Donatus and in the brief grammatical introductions of the later Middle Ages like *Es tu scolaris*, as well as in Greek compends like the Greek grammar of Roger Bacon and the *Erotemata* of Chrysoloras. There were manuals of conversation for travellers, both commercial and uncommercial, whether German merchants in Italy, Western voyagers to Constantinople,[1] or the Englishmen of many sorts who had occasion to learn French, be it the French of Paris or of Stratford-atte-Bowe.[2] Then the earlier Middle Ages had their own Latin dialogues such as the *Debate between Pippin and Alcuin* [3] and the *Colloquium* of Aelfric.[4] Nothing was more natural than to develop the vocabulary of a grammatical lesson by references to daily life, and in a didactic age it was easy to add something on religion or something on daily duty. Thus the grammatical *Es tu scolaris* started with *sum*, that 'root of all verbs' whose three letters represent the Trinity, but soon found occasion to ask concerning the six *opera scolarium*, namely, to get up in the morning, dress, brush one's hair, wash one's hands, say one's prayers, and go willingly to school.[5] Such school dialogues are in no wise peculiar to the Middle Ages; they are a well known feature of the heritage of Graeco-Roman education [6] and they were popular with the humanists of the sixteenth century, one of whom, Francisco Cervantes Salazar, carried the Latin type

[1] *Cabinet historique*, xxiii, 1 (1877), pp. 11–15.

[2] See Kathleen Lambley, *The Teaching and Cultivation of the French Language in England during Tudor and Stuart Times* (Manchester, 1920), pp. 3–57, 403–404. Cf. F. Callaey, "La vie belge au temps jadis d'après les Manuels de conversation," in Institut Historique Belge de Rome, *Bulletin*, v. 119–136 (1925).

[3] In Migne, *P. L.*, ci. 975–980. For a still earlier example, see M. Förster, "Das älteste mittellateinische Gesprächbüchlein," in *Romanische Forschungen*, xxvii. 342–348 (1910).

[4] Printed in Benjamin Thorpe's *Analecta Anglo-Saxonica*, new ed. (London, 1868), pp. 18–36.

[5] J. J. Baebler, *Beiträge zu einer Geschichte der lateinischen Grammatik im Mittelalter* (Halle, 1885), pp. 189–195.

[6] See particularly the dialogues of the Pseudo-Dositheus in G. Goetz, *Corpus Glossariorum Latinorum*, iii. 635–659; cf. C. H. Moore, "Latin Exercises from a Greek Schoolroom," in *Classical Philology*, xix. 317–328 (1924), and, for parallels in other languages, W. Schubart, "Ein lateinisch-griechisch-koptisches Gesprächbuch," in *Klio*, xiii. 27–38 (1913), and H. F. J. Junker, "Ein mittelpersisches Schulgespräch," Heidelberg *S. B.*, 1912, no. 15.

across the seas to the earliest American university, founded in the city of Mexico in 1553.[1] Nor was there much in the dialogues which was characteristic of their time. If Salazar takes us on a promenade to Chapultepec, most of his predecessors keep well within the limits of the classroom, and the classroom is much the same in all ages. The greater part of the Graeco-Roman school dialogues might have been written yesterday, or even this morning, and so might a little manual composed in 1467 for the instruction of the future Emperor, Maximilian I, with its "Good morning, master, how are you?" and its hair-pulling and fisticuffs interspersed with biblical quotations.[2] Very modern, too, is much of the *Paedologia* of Peter Mosellanus, written by a professor of Greek at Leipzig in 1518 and now turned into colloquial English by Professor Seybolt.[3] Still the colloquies of the humanists contain information which serves as a basis for reconstructing the academic conditions of the sixteenth century,[4] and we may expect something from such materials respecting the preceding age.[5] Let us take two examples, both from Germany in the fifteenth century, one describing university conditions, the other coming from a lower school.

The most interesting of such handbooks, the *Manuale Scholarium*, is entitled a "Manual of Scholars who propose to attend universities of students and to profit therein,"[6] and while in

---

[1] L. Massebieau, *Les colloques scolaires du seizième siècle* (Paris, 1878), pp. 178–203.

[2] G. Zappert, "Über ein für den Jugendunterricht Kaiser Maximilian's I. abgefasstes lateinisches Gesprächbüchlein," in Vienna *S. B.*, xxviii. 193–280 (1858).   [3] Urbana, Illinois, 1927 : with a bibliography.

[4] See particularly A. Bömer, "Lernen und Leben auf den Humanistenschulen im Spiegel der lateinischen Schülerdialoge," in *Neue Jahrbücher für Pädagogik*, ii. 129–141, 204–220 (1899); "Ein unbekanntes Schülergesprächbuch Samuel Karochs von Lichtenberg," *ibid.*, iii. 465–476 (1900) ; and *Die lateinischen Schülergespräche der Humanisten* (Berlin, 1897–99, 2 parts) ; and compare the works of Massebieau and Seybolt cited above.

[5] No one has made a list of such material for the Middle Ages. Indeed the mediaeval history of the prose dialogue still awaits a study of the type of H. Walther's *Das Streitgedicht in der lateinischen Litteratur des Mittelalters* (Munich, 1920). R. Hirzel, *Der Dialog* (Leipzig, 1895, 2 vols.), is worthless for the Middle Ages, while G. Niemann's dissertation, *Die Dialogliteratur der Reformationszeit* (Leipzig, 1905), treats only of the period named in its title.

[6] Most conveniently accessible in Friedrich Zarncke, *Die deutschen Universi-*

its most common form it is designed for the students of Heidelberg about the year 1480, it could be adapted with slight changes
to any of the German universities. "Rollo at Heidelberg," we
might call it. Its eighteen chapters conduct the student from
his matriculation to his degree, and inform him by the way on
many subjects quite unnecessary for either. When the young
man arrives he registers from Ulm; his parents are in moderate
circumstances; he has come to study. He is then duly 'hazed'
after the German fashion, which treats the candidate (*beanus*)
as a foul beast with horns and tusks which must be removed
by officious fellow-students, who taunt him as 'mother's dar-
ling' and subject him to much rough language and violent horse-
play; they also hear his confession of sin and fix as the penance
a good dinner for the crowd, but at the end come up and wish
him good luck. He begins his studies by attending three lectures
a day on the works of Aristotle, and learns to champion nominalism against realism and the comedies of Terence against the
law, and to discuss the advantages of various universities and
the price of food and the quality of the beer in university
towns. Thus:

Camillus. Where do you come from?
Bartoldus. From Erfurt.
Cam. What news do you bring?
Bar. Nothing at all, absolutely nothing.
Cam. I supposed that Erfurt was the harbour of all news.
Bar. That fact has escaped me; in fact, I must admit that I don't
care to hear gossip.
Cam. Where are you going?
Bar. To Heidelberg.
Cam. What are you going to do there?
Bar. I've often been told that the instruction in the liberal arts is
very good there, so I wanted to try out the usage of the university. As
good luck would have it, I've met you. Tell me, what are the customs
of your school?
Cam. I'll tell you. But first answer my question.

täten im Mittelalter (Leipzig, 1857), pp. 1–48. See the translation into colloquial
English by R. F. Seybolt, *The Manuale Scholarium* (Cambridge, Mass., 1921);
and cf. W. Fabricius, "Die ältesten gedruckten Quellen zur Geschichte des
deutschen Studententums: I. Das sogenannte 'Manuale Scolarium,'" in
Zeitschrift für Bücherfreunde, i. 178–182 (1897).

Bar. What is that?

Cam. Tell me the manner of your university.

Bar. I'll do so gladly. First, they revere the method of the nominalists; if there are any realists, they're not admitted, and they're not permitted to lecture or to hold recitations.

Cam. Why?

Bar. On account of quarrels; for disputes are stirred up, from which enmity arises and hatred is born. But to avoid disputes of this sort they think best to have one method only.

Cam. That isn't the right way; for if there were more than one method, the students would become keener, and more versed, and more ready in argument.

Bar. That's very true.

Cam. But you asked me to explain the usage of our university to you. It's very different from yours, from what I hear. First, we don't shut out the nominalists; if we can get any good out of them, we're perfectly willing to do so. Second, masters of each method are admitted. Each is permitted to state what he may have in his demonstrations. Indeed, among us there are some who follow Albert, some who esteem Thomas, some who admire the most subtle John the Scot, and follow in his footsteps; and the teaching of all these doctors contributes to the exercise of the understanding.

Bar. To tell you the truth, you've now aroused in me a great desire for study. Nothing is sweeter to me, nothing more enjoyable, than to hear what most excellent men think. Worthy patron, be kind enough to direct me to a lodging house in which study is held in great respect.[1]

Then we find our student and his room-mate quarrelling over a mislaid book; rushing at the first sound of the bell to dinner, where they debate the relative merits of veal and beans; or walking in the fields beyond the Neckar, perhaps by the famous Philosophers' Road which has charmed so many generations of Heidelberg youth, and exchanging Latin remarks on the birds and fish as they go. Then there are shorter dialogues: the scholar is reported for breaking the statutes; he has bad news from home, and no remittance; he borrows money from his room-mate; he falls in love and recovers; he goes to hear a fat Italian friar preach or to see the jugglers and the jousting in the market-place; he knows the dog-days are coming—he can feel them in his head! Finally our student is told by his parents that it is high time for him to take his degree and come home. At this

[1] Chapter vii (Seybolt's translation).

he is much disturbed: he has gone to few lectures, and he will have to swear that he has attended regularly; he has not worked much and has incurred the enmity of many professors; his master discourages him from trying the examination; he fears the disgrace of failure. But his interlocutor reassures him by a pertinent quotation from Ovid and suggests that a judicious distribution of gifts may do much—a few florins will win him the favour of all. Let him write home for more money and give a great feast for his professors; if he treats them well, he need not fear the outcome. This advice throws a curious light upon the educational standards of the time; it appears to have been followed, for the manual closes with a set of forms inviting the masters to the banquet and the free bath by which it was preceded:[1]

Reverend master, may we ask Your Reverence not to refuse to accept the entertainment of Master N.'s collation, and that you be mindful of us in the disputation, and we shall always be most studious to please you.

Reverend master, does it please Your Grace to enter the bath? For I am going to pay the fee for you. I pray, moreover, that you accept it with good will. Indeed, if I could show you greater reverence or honour, I would do so most eagerly.

More systematic is a school manual of the fifteenth century from the neighbourhood of Saxony, preserved in a manuscript of the Bibliothèque Nationale at Paris.[2] "Since by reason of imbecility youths cannot advance to a knowledge of the Latin tongue by theory alone," the author has for their assistance prepared a set of forms which contain the expressions most frequently employed by clerks.[3] Beginning with the courtesies of school life (for obedience and due reverence for the master are the beginning of wisdom), the boy learns how to greet his master and to take leave, how to excuse himself for wrong-doing, how to invite the master to dine or sup with his parents

---

[1] Chapter xviii (Seybolt).   [2] MS. lat. n.a. 619, ff. 28–34 v.

[3] 'Latinum ydeoma duplici via potest cognosci scilicet arte et usu. Sed quia ratione imbecillitatis iuvenes per viam artis ad studium latini sermonis nequeant perficisci, ideo ad subveniendum eorum tenuitati dignum duxi [MS. tenacitati dignum dixi] tabulas conscribere in quibus per ordinem quidam ponuntur sermones qui a clericis sepius proferuntur' (f. 28).

—there are half a dozen forms for this! [1] He is also taught how
to give proper answers, both jocose and serious, to those who
seek to test his knowledge, "that he may not appear an idiot
in the sight of his parents." [2] "If the master asks, 'Where have
you been so long?'" he must be ready, not only to plead the
inevitable headache or failure to hear the bell, but also to express the causes of delay well known to any village boy. He
was busy at home; he was sent on an errand; he had to look
after the house or feed the cattle or water the horse; he took a
bath; he was detained by a wedding, by picking grapes, by
dyeing, or making out accounts, or—for these were German
boys—by helping with the brew, fetching beer, or serving drink
to guests. [3]

In school after the "spiritual refection" of the morning
singing-lesson [4] comes refection of the body, which is placed
after study hours because "the imaginative virtue is generally
impeded in those who are freshly sated." [5] In their talk at table
or on the playground "clerks are apt to fall from the Latin
idiom into the mother tongue," and for him who speaks German
rather than the language of a rational being the high discretion of the master has invented a dunce's symbol called

[1] 'Domine reverende, parentes mei diligenter petunt vos ut cras cum illis
prandium faciatis. . . . Pater commisit mihi vos rogare ut sitis hoc vespere
secum in collacione' (f. 28).   [2] F. 28 v.

[3] 'Fui in domo occupatus. Pater misit me monitum. Ego propinavi hospi-
tibus. Ego tuli cervisiam. Ego noviter commedi. Dolorem capitis passus eram.
Ex iussu patris mei adaquavi equum. Ego signavi debita. Balneatus eram.
Vel sic: Ego obaudivi pulsum. Ego putabam quod fuisset 5ª pro certe surrexi
hora 4ª. Ego dedi animalibus pascua. Ego fui in mercatorio. Ego custodivi in
domo. Ego eram cum parentibus ad nupcias. Ego portavi brasium. Ego iuvi
braxare. Ego uvas collegi. Ego laboravi in sandice' (f. 29).

[4] 'Magister reverende, est hodie cantandum vel legendum? Est ordo
versuum faciendus? Quot pueri sunt ad utrum [MS. vᵐ] versum ordinandi?
Sunt versiculi cum alleluia dicendi? Quis erit versiculus? Sub qua nota
Benedicamus cantabitur? . . .' (f. 29 v).

[5] 'Et quia secundum consuetudinem scolarium expedi⟨a⟩tis lectionibus
scolares solent prandere ut post spiritualem refectionem sequatur corporalis,
et rationale est quod prius student antequam commedent, quia virtus ymagi-
nativa plerumque impeditur in hominibus noviter saturatis, sic itaque dum
commedunt colloquuntur: Care socie, impertire mihi prandium, *vel* Da mihi
porcionem prandii. . . . Vis habere caseum? Non commedo illum; ceteris bene
vescor lacticiniis' (ff. 29 v, 30).

an ass, which the holder tries hard to pass on to another.
"Wer wel ein Griffel kouffe[n]?" "Ich wel ein Griffel kouffen."
"Tecum sit asinus." "Ach, quam falsus es tu!" Sometimes the
victim offers to meet his deceiver after vespers, with the usual
schoolboy brag on both sides until it is silenced by the arrival
of the master.[1] As it is forbidden to come to blows in school,
the boys are taught to work off their enmities and formulate
their complaints in Latin dialogue. "You were outside the
town after dark. You played with laymen Sunday. You went
swimming Monday. You ran about the market on Tuesday.
You stayed away from matins. You slept through mass. You
missed vespers. You beat some of the boys and stirred up
trouble. You lost my pen and carried off a book." "Reverend
master, he has soiled my book, he shouts after me wherever I
go, he calls me names, he dragged me by the legs, he never
leaves me in peace."[2]

Besides the formal disputations, the scholars discuss such
current events as a street fight, a cousin's wedding, the coming
war with the duke of Saxony, or the means of getting to Erfurt,
whither one of them is going, via Halle, when he is sixteen, to

[1] 'Frequenter in huiusmodi confabulacione et in ceteris clerici de latino
ydeomate incidunt in maternum ydeoma. Ideo discrecio magistralis conve-
nientem modum excogitat quod illi vendetur [sic] azinus qui velud azinus
teutonicum respondet nec velud homo rationalis fatur latinum. Vendens
igitur azinum sic loquens insidiatur: Wer wel ein griffel kouffe[n]? Ich wel
ein griffel kouffen. At ille, Habeas tibi azinum, vel Tecum sit azinus. Ach
quam falsus es tu! Quare non es circumspectus? Ego non adverto quia
dictis vesperis ego tecum disputabo. Quid ad me? estimas quod timeam te?
Tu magnus es artifex, neminem curas. Utique non timeo te. . . . Qui te timeat
fugiat. Ecce, quantum gloriatur iste dominus. . . . Sitis compositi, magister
venit' (ff. 30, 30 v, 31).
[2] 'Post diversa negocia pertracta accidit inter scolares discordia et dum unus
laudat aliquem tunc alter vituperat et dum inimicicias verberibus ostendere
non possunt tunc verbis odium ostendunt alter alteri dicens:
'Ego accusabo te quod visus es de sero foris civitatem. In die solis lusisti
cum laycis. In die lune in aquis balneatus es. In die martis discurrebas in
foro. Matutinis non interfuisti. Pueros verberasti. Contra statuta magistri
murmurasti. Ad discordiam plures concitasti. Opprobriosa verba contulisti.
Insanias exercuisti. Libros cantandi maculasti. Vesperas neglexisti. Missam
obdormivisti. Michi stilum perdidisti. Libro[rum] unum subtraxisti.
'Ex hiis et consimilibus verba accusacionis formare possunt dum ad
magistros in necessariis illatis currunt sic dicentes:
'Reverende magister, ille me semper vituperat. Me transeunte undique

study at the university.[1] The great ordeal of the day was the master's quiz on Latin grammar, when every one was questioned in turn (*auditio circuli*). The pupils rehearse their declensions and conjugations and the idle begin to tremble as the hour draws near. There is some hope that the master may not come. "He has guests." "But they will leave in time." "He may go to the baths." "But it is not yet a whole week since he was there last." "There he comes. Name the wolf, and he forthwith appears." Finally the shaky scholar falls back on his only hope, a place near one who promises to prompt him.[2]

"When the recitation is over and the lesson given out, rejoicing begins among the youth at the approach of the hour for going home," and they indulge in much idle talk "which is here omitted, lest it furnish the means of offending." Joy is, however, tempered by the contest which precedes dismissal, "a serious and furious disputation for the *palmiterium,*" until one secures the prize and another has the *asinus* to keep till next day.[3]

After school the boys go to play in the churchyard, the sports mentioned being hoops, marbles (apparently), ball (during

inclamat. Cognomina michi donat. Verbis opprobriavit me. Textum meum maculavit. Cruribus me traxavit. Nunquam in pace me permittit' (f. 32 v).

[1] 'Postquam ero sedecim annorum mittar ad studium. Ego peragam tecum. Unde [?] recipias expensas? Deus providebit. Quo ibimus primo? Ad Erfordiam. Si haberemus currum! In Hall[is] sufficiencia curruum reperitur. . . . ' (f. 32).

[2] 'Clerici insuper specialibus sermonibus sunt usi ante tempus audicionis circuli. Tunc enim incipiunt pavere et tedere discoli sed gaudent studiosi. Sic mutuo colloquuntur:

'Estne cito hora audiendi? Ymmo inmediate sed adhuc est modicum intervallum; estimo quod non audiemur. Utinam vellet Deus! Quare deberet obmitti? Magister est occupatus. Ut quomodo? Ipse hospites habet. Quid ergo? subito recedunt et possibile est quod tunc protinus audiet. Forte intrabit balneum. Nuperrime est balneatus. Quamdiu est hoc? Nondum plene ebdomada est transacta. . . . Nonne vides ipsum venientem? Dum lupus nominatur sine mora presentatur. Bene dic mihi ignota in circulo. Si possis circa me locum obtinere' (f. 33).

[3] 'Audicione facta leccioneque accepta leticia crescit in iuvenibus quia appropinquat hora ut vadant ad domum, illo quoque tempore multos truffaticos tractant sermones de quibus sileo ne detur eis peccandi occasio. Et quamvis ex spe dimissionis crescit leticia, tamen aliqualiter miscetur cum tristicia vel mesticia quia tunc pro palmiterio incipit certacio et seriosa et furiosa disputacio. Venit enim alter ad alterum: Disputa tu mecum. Libenter . . . ' (f. 33 v).

Lent), and a kind of counting game. The author distinguishes hoops for throwing and for rolling, spheres of wood and of stone, but the subject soon becomes too deep for his Latin, and in the midst of this topic our text comes to an abrupt conclusion.[1]

[1] 'Recreatur puerorum animus in cymiterio post dimissionem per ludos diversos. Idcirco in cymiterio exercitio ne [MS. non] careant, iuxta hunc casum sermones faciunt illo modo ut sic :

'Nemo de cymiterio currat. Nullus faciat. Iuvenes, quibus placet ludere ? Per quem modum ? Cum cottis. Solvam ? Accomodabitur. Ad libitum tuum. Quot optas ? Sto contentus. Capias solidum. Quot dabis pro nummo ? Quis cupit emere ? Adde duos. . . .' (f. 34).

'Preterea ludorum scolarium alii sunt trocorum alii globorum. Primum Cathonis concessit auctoritas cum dicit, Troco lude [*Distichs*, ed. W. J. Chase (Madison, 1922), p. 14]. Item docet temporis oportunitas, Trocorum ludus singula tempora occupat, pila vero quadragesimale, globorum autem ludus estivale, cui ludo annectitur ludus nucleorum. Trocorum ergo [alii] iaciles, alii vertiles. Sic fingere eis nomina necesse est quorum sic formandi sunt sermones. . . . Globorum alii lignei alii lapidei et cum utrisque ludunt scolares sic tempus deducentes. Circa ludum ligneorum speciales habent terminos teutonicales, velud sunt *velle reyne* etc. Hii non faciliter possunt exprimi sed circumlocutione proferuntur sub hac forma' (f. 34 v).

CHAPTER IV

THE SPREAD OF IDEAS IN THE MIDDLE AGES [1]

IN the general history of ideas an important chapter deals with the means by which ideas are carried from individual to individual and from group to group. The story is a long one, with the club and the sword and similar instruments of sweet reasonableness at one end, and the headline, the aeroplane, and the radio at the other, while slower and possibly more efficacious agencies lie between. The Middle Ages present a special phase of the subject, combining as they did static rural conditions and primitive modes of travel with a social structure which required a certain amount of communication between widely separated units of the same type, so that extreme localism in some respects coexisted with a common European civilization in others. Certain historians have accordingly stressed the regional, others the general, elements in mediaeval culture, with a tendency toward a vague and mystical *Volksgeist* on the one hand or an equally vague and mystical *Zeitgeist* on the other. A more realistic view of mediaeval society may be reached by considering briefly the more common ways by which ideas passed, and noting some matters toward which investigation may profitably be directed. This essay seeks to suggest and illustrate by examples to which any one can easily add, rather than to present the results of a specific piece of research.' The word 'idea' is used, for lack of a better, to include not only abstract conceptions but new information of every sort, new themes and modes in literature, and new types in art.

In the Roman empire the ease of intercourse and communication was proverbial. What with the system of roads and bridges, the constant passing of troops, officials, and messengers, the

[1] Reprinted from *Speculum*, i. 19–30 (1926), having been read before the American Academy of Arts and Sciences, 12 November 1924, and before the American Historical Association, 30 December 1924. Some aspects of the topic have been further developed in my *Renaissance of the Twelfth Century* (Cambridge, Mass., 1927), ch. 2.

free interchange of wares between distant provinces, and the habit of long journeys by sea and land, the amount of travel has been declared greater than was to be found again before the nineteenth century.[1] For specific illustrations it is enough to recall the voyages of Paul of Tarsus; the vogue of Antioch, Athens, and Alexandria for Western students; the Phrygian merchant who made seventy-two journeys to Rome; and the man of Cadiz who travelled all the way to Rome and back merely to set his eyes on the historian Livy. The result was a singularly uniform and cosmopolitan civilization throughout the Roman world, from which the local and provincial spirit was strikingly absent and through which ideas passed with singular ease and swiftness, as exemplified in the 'ubiquitous professor' and in the spread of Christianity and other forms of Oriental religion.

This unity of life and ideas came to an end in the West with the Germanic invasions, and in the region of the Mediterranean with the Saracen conquests.[2] Roads fell into disrepair, commerce dried up, education declined, and book-learning almost disappeared. ⟨ Localism was writ large across the Europe of the early Middle Ages, the localism at first of the tribe and the estate, later shaping itself into those feudal and manorial units upon which mediaeval society rested. Both politically and socially these units were very nearly independent, and the exchange of products and ideas was reduced to a minimum. Under these conditions culture became regional, at the widest, and we witness the slow formation of those provincialisms which still survive so tenaciously—types of cottage roofs and schools of ecclesiastical architecture, local products of the soil and local cuisines, local costume and local custom, local saints and local beliefs, local dialects and folk-lore and literary traditions—all

[1] L. Friedländer, *Roman Life and Manners under the Early Empire* (New York, 1908–13), i. 322. Cf. M. P. Charlesworth, *Trade Routes and Commerce of the Roman Empire* (Cambridge, 1924).

[2] On the relation of the Saracen conquests to commerce and communication, cf. the recent papers of H. Pirenne, "Mahomet et Charlemagne," in *Revue belge de philologie et d'histoire*, i. 77–86 (1922) ; "Un contraste économique: Mérovingiens et Carolingiens," *ibid.*, ii. 223–235 (1923); "Le commerce du papyrus dans la Gaule Mérovingienne," in Académie des Inscriptions et Belles-Lettres, *Comptes rendus*, 1928, pp. 178–191.

that mass of deep-rooted and full-bodied localisms which give to European life its variety and flavour and sense of age-long contact with the soil. Naturally ideas and information spread only slowly, and against great resistance, from one district to another; custom determined everything, and the type altered little from age to age. If this were all of mediaeval life, our theme were soon exhausted.

As a matter of fact, the spread of ideas in the Middle Ages is only in part a history of slow diffusion through the resisting medium of local habit and custom. It is mainly concerned with the relations of scattered centres of another sort, stations of high tension, if you like, communicating with other stations of the same type with comparatively little reference to distance or the nature of the intervening space. Such centres, representing different social strata, consisted chiefly of monasteries and cathedrals, courts, towns, and universities.

That the church was the chief source of unity for mediaeval society is a commonplace which is not open to dispute. When, however, we pass beyond the fundamentals of law and creed and ritual to the cultural side of the church's influence, we must make certain distinctions. The church drew men to Rome, but only in small numbers before the twelfth century, when the growth of the canon law and the centralization of the papal monarchy began to compel or at least encourage the presence of ever-increasing numbers of litigants and petitioners and other visitors *ad limina Sanctorum Apostolorum*. The church sent men on distant pilgrimages, but the pilgrims moved to specific places by definite routes whose significance we are only beginning to appreciate. The church fostered ecclesiastical architecture, but the types of building and decoration show a strange combination of regional influences and of imitation of far distant types through the intermediary of pilgrims and travelling prelates and architects, like that Villard de Honne-court whose surviving sketch-book shows him at Chartres and Lausanne and in Hungary as well as in his native Picardy. The history of ecclesiastical travel has much to teach us.

In the earlier Middle Ages the chief centres of intellectual life were the various monasteries, set like scattered islands of knowledge in a sea of ignorance and barbarism, and the spread of knowledge was chiefly from one such centre to another. Much of this intercourse was naturally local, but much of it also was at long distance, by routes which we do not yet fully understand. Thus the annals of a group of Anglo-Norman establishments were based on annals which came from the Rhine by way of Burgundy and went back ultimately to the Easter-tables of Bede. A detailed description of the opening of Charlemagne's tomb at Aachen by Otto III turns up unexpectedly at Novalese on the Mount Cenis pass.[1] A noteworthy report of King John's condemnation by the court of Philip Augustus appears in the annals of Margam, on the Welsh border.[2] Bury St. Edmunds in 1181–82 has a six-months' visit from the Norwegian archbishop Eystein.[3] Matthew Paris at St. Albans had detailed information respecting the Tartars.[4] The monks of Mont-Saint-Michel in Normandy were in close touch with those of Monte Santangelo on the east coast of Italy, where St. Michael was also the patron. Saint-Évroult in Normandy sent out daughter monasteries to Mileto, Venosa, and S. Eufemia in Italy, where its local ritual, the *cantus Uticensis*, was sung long afterward.[5] The miracles of St. Nicholas, so important in the history of the religious drama, passed from the East via St. Nicholas of Bari as far as Bec and Hildesheim, not only to churches dedicated to this patron saint but also to others along the road like S. Salvatore at Lucca,[6] as attested by its portal. The monastic *confraternitates* often joined widely separated communities, and the mortuary *rotuli* travelled long distances. One of the best illustrations of the fallacy of a merely regional view is Traube's study of the so-called 'national hands,' in which he demonstrated

---

[1] Th. Lindner, *Die Fabel von der Bestattung Karls des Grossen* (Aachen, 1893).

[2] F. M. Powicke, *The Loss of Normandy* (Manchester, 1913), pp. 463 ff.

[3] H. G. Leach, *Angevin Britain and Scandinavia* (Cambridge, Mass., 1921), pp. 89–95.   [4] *Chronica Maiora, passim.*

[5] Ordericus Vitalis (ed. A. Le Prévost, Paris, 1838–55), ii. 89–91.

[6] A. K. Porter, *Romanesque Sculpture* (Boston, 1923), nos. 224, 225; and, in general, G. R. Coffman, *A New Theory concerning the Origin of the Miracle Play* (Menasha, Wis., 1914), pp. 45–66; and in *Manly Anniversary Studies* (Chicago, 1923), pp. 269–275.

that there was no such thing as a Merovingian or a Lombard book-hand, but only the handwriting of the several monastic *scriptoria*, with occasional monks passing from one to another, so that the manuscripts of Corbie in Gaul show closer resemblances to manuscripts of Northern Italy than to those of Frankish neighbours.[1]

As time went on, the possibilities of monastic intercourse were enlarged and systematized by the formation of the great organizations of Cluni and Cîteaux with their chapters and visitations and systematic colonization; and the share of these orders in the spread of French culture to Germany and Spain has long been recognized by historians of art. In the Franciscan and Dominican orders the local element almost disappears in a European organization which emphasizes uniformity and migration. At the hands of the friars historiography becomes general rather than local, while works of theology and erudition, as well as collections of *exempla*, circulate freely among their new centres of study and teaching. Even the suppression of heresy by the Dominican Inquisition tends indirectly to favour the wide and rapid circulation of the standard manuals of doctrine and procedure.

The importance of the cathedral as an intellectual centre dates from the ninth century, when the maintenance of cathedral schools and the adoption of the common life of the canons were prescribed by the Carolingian legislation. In spite of their growing divergence of interests, bishop and chapter constituted for most purposes a single intellectual group, having affinities on the one hand with monastic communities and on the other with the feudal courts, while the ecclesiastical organization insured a certain amount of communication within each province. The intellectual influence of the cathedral centres reached its height in the revival of the twelfth century, as seen in the spread of translations from the Arabic under Archbishop Raymond of

---

[1] See particularly his "Perrona Scottorum," Munich *S. B.*, 1900, pp. 472–476: and in his *Vorlesungen und Abhandlungen* (Munich, 1909–20), iii. 97–99. See now Ph. Lauer, "Recherches sur l'écriture de Corbie dite lombardique," in *Bulletin philologique et historique* of the Comité des travaux historiques et scientifiques, année 1924 (Paris, 1926), pp. 59–68.

Toledo, in the continental relations of Canterbury under Archbishops Theobald and Thomas Becket, and in the resort from
all parts of Europe to the cathedral schools of Northern France.

The court, feudal, episcopal, or royal, is important primarily
for the circulation of the courtly type of literature, through the
intermediary of jongleurs, trouvères, and Goliardi, those 'jongleurs of the clerical world.' Such composers and colporteurs
required patrons, and only the richer courts could offer them
permanent support, so that they were perforce migratory, passing from court to court or moving about with a migratory
patron, like the 'Archpoet' with the archbishop of Cologne in
the wake of Frederick Barbarossa. In this way the subject-
matter of French poetry spread over Western Europe; original
French and Provençal lyrics acquired currency in Italy; and
French became the courtly language of a large part of Latin
Christendom. Even the larger courts shared their men of letters:
Peter of Blois was the 'intimate friend' of the rulers of England
and of Sicily;[1] the poet Henry of Avranches, who has a pension
and a livery of wine from Henry III of England, is also found
writing Latin verse for Frederick II.[2] And when whole courts
wandered, as on the Crusades or the *Römerzüge* of the German
emperors, the possibilities are obvious. Nor was the interchange
of courts limited to belles-lettres. Otto III receives his Byzantine ideas of government through his mother; Manuel Comnenus
sends Ptolemy's *Almagest* as a present to the king of Sicily;
while Frederick II is in scientific correspondence with various
Saracen sovereigns. King Roger draws to Palermo men of learning from every land, and one of his officials, Master Thomas
Brown, is afterward found sitting at the Exchequer of Henry II.[3]

[1] Stubbs, introduction to Roger of Hoveden, ii, p. xcii.
[2] *Forschungen zur deutschen Geschichte*, xviii. 482–492 (1878); *Monatschrift
für die Geschichte West-Deutschlands*, iv. 336–344 (1878); Josiah C. Russell,
"Master Henry of Avranches as an International Poet," in *Speculum*, iii.
34–63 (1928).
[3] See *Mediaeval Science*, chs. 9, 12; and, for Anglo-Sicilian relations, my
articles in *E. H. R.*, xxvi. 433–447, 641–665 (1911). On the foreign relations
of the court of Henry II, see Stubbs, *Seventeen Lectures on Mediaeval and Modern
History*, chs. 6 and 7; and my paper in the *Essays in Medieval History presented
to Thomas Frederick Tout* (Manchester, 1925), pp. 71–77.

Henry's Assize of Arms was, we are told, one of the administrative expedients imitated by Philip Augustus.[1] French royal institutions were used as models in creating the central government of the Burgundian state, while this in turn served as a type for the Hapsburgs when Maximilian brought skilled officials from the Netherlands to Vienna. In a still different field lies the well known fact of the spread of Wiclif's doctrines to Bohemia by the marriage of Richard II. Historians ought frequently to heed, not only Lavisse's reminder that kings, like other people, inherit from their mothers, but also the fact that kings and their courts are influenced by their wives and their wives' relatives and followers.

The towns of the Middle Ages were, like the monasteries, islands, islands, in this instance, of political and social freedom in a sea of rural bondage. While they grew in part by drawing to their free air serfs from the adjacent country, their relations were chiefly with other towns. Here again, as in the early spread of Christianity from city to city, geographical proximity was not the only occasion for contact. If the urban constitution of Soissons was imitated chiefly by its immediate neighbours and in Burgundy, the *Établissements* of Rouen spread through the Plantagenet dominions to the Spanish frontier, while the customs of the Norman *bourg* of Breteuil have been traced as far as the Welsh border and Ireland.[2] The intercourse of towns was primarily commercial, and it is not easy to discern the manifold connexions between the exchange of wares and the exchange of ideas.[3] Significant illustrations may be seen in the spread of Albigensian doctrines from Italy to France and the Low Countries through the industrial population—weaver (*textor*) and heretic were often synonymous in the North—and in the share of the Italian cities in the transmission of Byzantine learning to

---

[1] Haskins, *Norman Institutions* (Cambridge, Mass., 1918), p. 193.

[2] G. Bourgin, *La commune de Soissons* (Paris, 1908) ; A. Giry, *Les Établissements de Rouen* (Paris, 1883–85) ; Mary Bateson, "The Laws of Breteuil," *E. H. R.*, xv–xvi (1900–01).

[3] On the travel of merchants, see H. Pirenne, *Mediaeval Cities* (Princeton, 1925), and his references; and J. W. Thompson, *An Economic and Social History of the Middle Ages* (New York, 1928), ch. 23. On their education, Pirenne, in *Annales d'histoire économique et sociale*, i. 13–28 (1929).

the West through Italians resident at Constantinople (Burgundio
the Pisan, Moses of Bergamo, James of Venice, etc.). The intellectual role of the cities is, however, hard to follow in the case
of the Crusades, for alongside the general enlargement of experience and of the subject-matter of romance there is little to
set in the way of new scientific knowledge from the East. The
Crusaders were, in the nature of the case, not scholars or men
of ideas: the amount of translation from the Arabic in Palestine
and Syria is surprisingly small, and even the new geographical
learning filters very slowly indeed into the manuals of the thirteenth century.[1] Fairs are an especially important phase of
urban intercourse, while toward the close of the Middle Ages
the growth of capitals and metropolitan markets in the case of
London and Paris introduces a new relation whose intellectual
implications need further study.[2] By this time, too, there was
a bourgeois literature and art to communicate from town to
town.

The importance of the mediaeval universities in the spread
of knowledge may be taken for granted. By its very definition
a *studium generale* was open to scholars from every country,
and students and professors passed freely from one institution
to another, carrying with them books and lecture-notes and
whatever else their heads contained. These conditions secured
easy communication between distant seats of learning, while
they also favoured the quick diffusion of knowledge through the
educated class. Moreover, the universities were the earliest
centres of the book trade as we understand it, and the provisions for the multiplication, sale, and rent of standard works
helped these at least to travel by their own momentum. In
these respects the university life of the later Middle Ages reached
a comparatively close approximation to early modern conditions; the chief difference, to use Shaw's phrase, lay in the
iconography. From the thirteenth century onward we can

[1] *Mediaeval Science*, chs. 7, 10; J. K. Wright, *Geographical Lore of the Time
of the Crusades* (New York, 1925), pp. 77, 87, 292.
[2] T. F. Tout, *The Beginnings of a Modern Capital* (British Academy, 1923);
the volumes of Marcel Poëte on mediaeval Paris; and the studies of N. S. B.
Gras on the metropolitan market.

register with some definiteness the knowledge of the university world, and the principal scholastic writers have been the subject of minute investigation. The obscurer problems lie rather in the period immediately preceding—the sources and the course of the new Aristotle, the new medicine, and the new Euclid and Ptolemy; the origin and career of the Northern translators who appear unheralded in Spain and Sicily; the routes by which their work passed northward, and its reception in the monastic and cathedral schools of the twelfth century. Michael Scot suddenly makes his appearance at Toledo in 1217; what was his earlier career? Daniel of Morley toward 1200 returned to England from Spain with "a precious multitude of books"; what did they contain? Did the Fourth Crusade have any discoverable relation to the spread of Greek learning? [1] How much does Christian music owe to the Arabs?

The migration of books is always an important phase of the migration of ideas, and this was peculiarly true in the Middle Ages, when scholarship depended in so large a degree upon antecedent authority. The choice spirits of all ages have influenced one another with surprising disregard of time and space, the spirit leaping from one to another as it listeth through the medium of the written page; but in the Middle Ages everything turned on the transmission of the written page. "Plato," says Coulton,[2] "might have shaken hands with Anselm," but actually he could not, for Anselm had access to no work of Plato save a part of the *Timaeus*. For various reasons books had very little independent movement of their own. Being valued neither as furniture nor as fuel, they were closely connected with the centres of intellectual activity, and the migration of books is for the most part a phase of the intercourse between such centres.

I do not mean to claim exhaustiveness for the foregoing list of centres active in the spread of ideas and information, still less to imply that each worked at long range only and in entire

[1] We need more studies like that of Miss Dorothy Stimson, *The Gradual Acceptance of the Copernican Theory* (Columbia University thesis, 1917), or of J. W. Thompson on Arabic science in Lorraine, *Isis*, xii. 184-193 (1929).

[2] G. G. Coulton, *Five Centuries of Religion* (Cambridge, 1923-   ), i. 21.

isolation from the others. Recent studies show interrelations between the regular and the secular clergy in the same neighbourhood,[1] and interpenetration of the lay and ecclesiastical worlds in art and music and literature to an extent once deemed impossible. Nevertheless, the main problem lies in tracing the connexions within these respective sets of centres, the paths along which ideas moved from place to place. These obscurer topics require investigation at once more thorough and more comprehensive than heretofore. On the side of detailed research we need to know more of mediaeval roads viewed as lines of communication, and their relations to the centres of learning and literature. "In the beginning was the road," says Bédier.[2] The general course of the roads is known,[3] but the historical facts have not been sufficiently grouped about them and analysed, their 'wayfaring life' has not been sufficiently explored.[4] We also need to study more closely the 'wanderings and homes of manuscripts,' the catalogues of mediaeval libraries, the content of the European mind at definite intervals.

A realistic study of the spread of knowledge must also take account of the rapidity of movement, the rate as well as the route. The report of Frederick Barbarossa's death in Asia Minor required four months to reach Germany, while the news of Richard's captivity in Austria reached England in about as many weeks. At this period the normal time from Rome to Canterbury was seven weeks, but urgent news could make the journey in four.[5] Was the rapidity with which books crossed Europe really so remarkable as it seemed to Renan?[6] How

---

[1] E.g., G. R. Coffman, "A New Approach to Mediaeval Latin Drama," *Modern Philology*, xxii. 239–271 (1925).

[2] *Les légendes épiques* (2d ed., Paris, 1914–21), iii. 367.

[3] There is still room for local monographs of the type of E. Sthamer's "Die Hauptstrassen des Königreichs Sicilien im 13. Jahrhundert," in *Studi di storia napoletana in onore di Michelangelo Schipa* (Naples, 1926), pp. 97–112.

[4] The example set by the charming book of J. J. Jusserand, *English Wayfaring Life in the Middle Ages* (3d ed., London, 1925), has not been sufficiently followed.

[5] R. L. Poole, *The Early Correspondence of John of Salisbury* (British Academy, 1924), p. 6. F. Ludwig, *Untersuchungen über die Reise- und Marschgeschwindigkeit im XII. und XIII. Jahrhundert* (Berlin, 1897), is useful so far as it goes.   [6] E. Renan, *Averroès* (Paris, 1869), pp. 201 f.

fast did a book or a scholar actually travel? What do we know about the exchange of letters in the days before the post?

We also need to apply to the Latin literature of the period more of the searching investigation of origins and connexions which has been applied to the vernacular, and to consider more closely the mutual relations of Latin and vernacular. Above all, for many of these problems we need the combined effort of the historian, the geographer, the philosopher, the philologist, and the archaeologist, specialists who have too often, especially in the United States, worked in the isolation of separate compartments.

May I re-enforce this argument by citing two pieces of synthetic research performed by scholars outside the conventional field of history yet yielding results of wide significance to the historian? One is the work of Bédier on the mediaeval epic, the other the recent study of Romanesque sculpture by Arthur Kingsley Porter.[1] Bédier, by a brilliant combination of evidence drawn from literature, history, topography, and archaeology, places the French epics in an entirely new light, both as literary and as historical documents. Instead of resting upon songs and sagas of the earlier Middle Ages, these poems are shown to belong to the eleventh and twelfth centuries, whose point of view and conditions of life they reflect, and to represent specific sources of information, not the vague and elusive *tout le monde* of popular tradition. They were composed in large measure for the travelling public of pilgrims and frequenters of fairs, and to a considerable degree out of local materials furnished by those concerned with specific shrines and relics, especially shrines situated along the great routes of pilgrimage, Roman roads then marked by masses of Roman ruins in which many of the imaginary scenes are localized. Written by travellers and for travellers, they must be interpreted in relation to Rome and Com-

---

[1] Bédier, *Les légendes épiques, ed. cit.*; A. K. Porter, *Romanesque Sculpture on the Pilgrimage Roads* (10 vols., Boston, 1923). I do not mean to imply that all the conclusions of these scholars have won universal acceptance. For a good example of the application of Bédier's method to other mediaeval material, see Ezio Levi, "Troveri ed abbazie," in *Archivio storico italiano*, serie vii, iii. 45–81 (1925).

postela, while they show the closest co-operation of classes once deemed entirely distinct, the monks and the jongleurs, and a free interpenetration of vernacular and sacred literature. Even Charlemagne, grim conqueror of the Saxons and the Avars yet unknown to the Northern epic, is annexed by the pilgrim and the crusader and turned toward the South and the pilgrims' roads, defending Rome from Saracens who had never been there in his time, celebrated above all for the three journeys consuming fourteen years in Spain, which he visited but once, blazoned forth on the windows at Chartres for the journey to Constantinople and Jerusalem, which he never took at all. And Einhard's sentence on Roland, sometimes considered an interpolation, becomes the plausible origin of the *Chanson de Roland*, which celebrates specific shrines on the pilgrims' and crusaders' road to Spain—a combination of the knightly and the clerical, of the Latin and the vernacular which breaks down all the watertight compartments of convention.

To this demonstration of the inadequacy of merely regional and traditional explanations in the fluid material of literature Porter's study comes as a sort of corollary in the stiffer medium of stone. Here the theory of provincial schools of Romanesque architecture had already admitted Byzantine influences in Périgord and evident relationship between the sculpture of both sides of the Pyrenees. By close study of the monuments along the pilgrimage roads Porter shows the northward spread of Byzantine influences and the type of the Holy Sepulchre; but his fullest demonstration traces the diffusion of Cluniac art, first in Burgundy, then to England, Galicia, Germany, Apulia, and Palestine, but especially by the great road to the shrine of St. James at Compostela, along which "there was a distinct tendency for Cluniac priories, for relics, and for monumental sculpture to gather."

This particular mode of inquiry is not, of course, to be imitated everywhere. The science of the Arabs came from Toledo, not Compostela; the religious ideas of St. Francis did not spring from the French songs which he loved in his worldly youth; the sources of the *Canterbury Tales* cannot be traced at wayside

stations on the Old Kent Road! What is of general validity
for the spread of ideas is the emphasis upon habitual lines of
communication, the fresh scrutiny of all available material, the
realistic and many-sided approach, the combined attack at once
by land and sea and air!

Finally, it may perhaps be suggested that the older modes of
communicating ideas have not, even now, entirely disappeared,
but survive in ways which are often overlooked. If the newer
psychology detects mediaeval survivals in the contemporary
mind of the individual, attention may also be called to their
persistence in our social mind in the mechanism by which ideas
pass from group to group. We are too prone to forget the
prevalence of intellectual stratification and non-communicating
groups. Ideas still move in part according to social and intellectual units. Thus universities and academies are still to a
certain extent, though in a far less degree, islands in the midst
of ignorance; scientists communicate with scientists, and professors with professors, without regard to the intervening medium.
So Greenwich Village speaks to Greenwich Village, while the
Ku Klux Klan may flourish in the shadow of great universities.
Chesterton says somewhere that the Englishman who goes
abroad to see different peoples could find greater surprises in his
own kitchen. So-called high-brow movements in politics are too
apt to think only of other high-brows and forget the 'low-brow'
voters of whom majorities are made. Illustrations could be
multiplied indefinitely; I have meant merely to suggest that
certain contemporary conditions can be more easily understood
in the light of the intellectual history of earlier times.

CHAPTER V

THE LATIN LITERATURE OF SPORT [1]

THE Mediaeval Academy of America, by the terms of its organization, is interested in every phase of mediaeval civilization. Literature, language, art, archaeology, history, philosophy, science, religion, folk-lore, economic and social conditions and matters of daily life—nothing is foreign to us. The whole breadth of the Middle Ages is ours, the only limits are chronological. While, however, the Academy has thus staked out a large field for itself, it has no desire to dislodge or interfere with previous cultivators. Its purpose is rather to break new ground where possible, to supplement existing agencies, and to serve as a clearing-house and meeting-point for investigators. Especially does it seek to promote combined and co-ordinated effort in the study of those aspects of the Middle Ages which need the united forces of historians, philologists, archaeologists, students of art, literature, and philosophy. It welcomes new material, new attacks on old problems, new points of view, new syntheses.

Inevitably one of the major concerns of the Academy is Mediaeval Latin. Not only is the Academy itself the outgrowth of a Committee on Mediaeval Latin Studies, but nothing can better express and illustrate its interest in a many-sided approach to mediaeval culture. Without Latin no understanding of the Middle Ages is possible. The international language of the epoch, it was the speech of treaties and formal international intercourse, of the international church in all its relations, and of religious observance in the several countries of the Occident. Men prayed in Latin, sang in Latin, preached in Latin throughout Western Christendom. It was the language of education, as reflected in text-books and lectures, in student conversation, and in the intercourse of educated men. Learned early, it was in such constant use that there was little likelihood of its being

[1] Presidential address delivered at the annual meeting of the Mediaeval Academy of America, 30 April, 1927; printed in *Speculum*, ii. 235–252 (1927), and here revised.

forgotten. It was the language of philosophy and theology and serious literature in general. Down into the thirteenth century it was the almost exclusive language of history and also of law, both in the form of legislation and of current record, the language of administration in charter and writ and fiscal account, whether on the part of royal treasurers or of local bailiffs. If it was the language of science, it was also a language of *belles lettres*, of poetry and parody, of tales and stories, of drama and romance. Though it ultimately yielded these more popular themes to the vulgar tongues, Latin literature long ran parallel to the vernacular, which in many fields it had preceded. There is no aspect of mediaeval life which does not leave its traces in Latin.

Nevertheless, so enormous is the amount of serious literature in Latin, theological, philosophical, religious, legal, and didactic, that its mere bulk creates the danger of taking the period too soberly, if not too sadly, and of falling into that gloom from which our President sought to release us in his address of last year.[1] I cannot hope to vie with Professor Rand as a dispeller of gloom, but I may perhaps re-enforce his point by an example drawn from a different field, the literature of sport. We shall understand the Middle Ages better if from time to time we glance at their lighter side, and we shall likewise understand the significance of Latin better if we recall that even in their gayer moments men did not shake off their Roman inheritance. If they played in Latin as well as prayed in Latin, we ought to know it, prepared for the worst. And if my theme appear trivial to the sober-minded, I can further plead in extenuation that it is now April, Chaucer's April, and Saturday.

> Tempus instat floridum,
> Cantus crescit avium,

sang the Goliardi, likewise in Latin.

In the long perspective of the literature of sport, from the victors' odes and systematic treatises of the Greeks to the contemporary glorifications of big game and big games, a place

[1] E. K. Rand, "Mediaeval Gloom and Mediaeval Uniformity," *Speculum*, i. 253–268 (1926).

must be found for what was written in Latin, since no international language could remain untouched by so universal a
human interest. Curiously enough, this phase of Latin literature
is mediaeval, and not Roman. The Romans had spectacles
rather than sport; they took their exercise vicariously on the
side-lines, applauding the professional gladiators and charioteers
who existed for their amusement. Under such circumstances it
was natural that they should produce no Pindaric odes, none
of those works on hunting and fishing which the Greeks turned
out naturally, not even any important translations of these.
Hunting, a servile occupation according to Sallust—and a chilly
one according to Horace—but popular among the provincials
of the Empire, inspired nothing beyond the meagre verse of
obscure writers like Grattius and Nemesianus.[1] The 'mule
medicine' of the later Empire served agriculture, not sport, and
sport has no place in agricultural literature, whether in prose
or verse. Thus Varro's chapter on wild boars is occupied merely
with fattening them in captivity, and leads up to a chapter on
fattening snails, at best a slow sport! The Romans wrote no
books on racing; inveterate gamblers, they did not even write
on betting. The arm-chair sportsman who went beyond such
works as Pliny's *Natural History* was forced to read Greek.

Even the circuses and spectacles which were so important in
the life of mediaeval Constantinople disappeared from the West.
The Western Church set its face against them as works of the
Devil, and their literary memory was preserved chiefly in Isidore's *Etymologies* and the flaming denunciation of Tertullian
On Spectacles. The arenas became ruins or castles, and men
went to church. The sports of the Middle Ages spring up anew
out of combat, out of hunting and hawking, and out of various
minor forms of amusement, sports of the nobility rather than
of the populace and reflected for it in the new courtly literature
of the time. They leave little record from the earlier Middle
Ages,[2] but by the twelfth and thirteenth centuries they have

---

[1] Cf. the utilitarian attitude of the Arabs toward sport. Louis Mercier, *La
chasse et les sports chez les Arabes* (Paris, 1927), p. 244.

[2] See G. W. Pfändler, "Die Vergnügungen der Angelsachsen," in *Anglia*,

begun to create a literature of their own, and first of all in the
chief language of the period, Latin. In general these Latin
writings antedate the better-known vernacular works of the
fourteenth and fifteenth centuries, but there is much overlapping and translation back and forth between the several idioms.
Still, back of the English period and the French period in the
literature of sport lies a Latin period. We must not, however,
infer from this that Latin had a place in the actual language of
sport analogous to that held by English in recent times and,
somewhat earlier and to a more limited extent, by French.
Those who knew Latin best, the clergy, were debarred from
most forms of sport, and the knights who made up the sporting
class rarely knew Latin. If men wrote on sport in Latin, they
commonly hunted and fought in the vernacular. The Latin
treatise usually codified vernacular practice. And when one
who knows both Latin and sport comes along in the person of
the scholar-emperor Frederick II, he complains that he cannot
find suitable Latin equivalents for the technical terms of falconry. So the more classically minded, who derived tournaments (*Troiana agmina*) from Troy via the games described in
the *Aeneid*, would have found serious gaps in the Virgilian
vocabulary.

The major sport of the Middle Ages was war, with its adjuncts
the tournament, the joust, and the judicial duel. War had its
open and closed seasons dependent upon conditions of climate
and upon the great festivals of Christmas, Easter, and Ascension, even its attempts at quiet week-ends in the Truce of God,
and the right of private war was the most valued of the sporting
privileges of the mediaeval barons; but war was after all grim
business rather than sport, the vocation rather than the avoca-
tion of the military classes, dominating their life and giving
colour to their amusements. Business or sport, war produced
no original literature beyond that recording deeds of valour and
military prowess. Vegetius was copied, excerpted, and imitated

xxix. 417–524 (1906); and for Old French the monographs listed by Ch.-V.
Langlois, *La vie en France au moyen âge*, i, nouvelle éd. (Paris, 1926), appendice
bibliographique, nos. 18, 19, 103, 195, 201.

in the monasteries, but no new mediaeval works on military science arose in his place,[1] whether in Latin or in the Western vernaculars, to parallel the great Byzantine works on tactics. Just as description of feudalism began when feudalism was declining, so treatises on tournaments meet us only when the institution is about to disappear, the best example being the *Traité de la forme et devis d'un tournoi* of that patron of the Renaissance, good King René of Provence. Appropriately enough for what was peculiarly a French sport (*ludi gallici*), this was written in French.[2]

The judicial duel, on the other hand, that crowning illustration of the sporting theory of justice, did produce a Latin literature, for it early fell into the hands of the lawyers, who wrote in Latin. This ancient institution not only canalized into legal channels something of the fighting instincts of the epoch, but it gave wide scope to those technicians of sport who have been in all ages concerned with the qualifications, equipment, and handicaps of contestants, particularly after the introduction of hired champions raised complicated questions of eligibility and professionalism. So in that age of *summae*, the thirteenth century, the eminent civilian Roffredo of Benevento composed a *Summa de pugna*, where he discusses the cases to which the wager of battle is applicable and the cases in which champions are allowed to take the place of those handicapped by youth, old age, illness, sex, servile rank, or ecclesiastical disabilities. The defects of the duel as a form of sport appear in his uncertainty as to the proper procedure when one of the contestants loses his weapons (c. 9):

Some say that if the weapons are broken others should be given, since the battle must legally be fought with clubs, but that if the weapons fall to the ground others shall not be supplied, and he who has dropped his

[1] On the predominant influence of Vegetius upon the tactical works which appear in the later Middle Ages, see M. Jähns, *Geschichte der Kriegswissenschaften* (Munich and Leipzig, 1889–91), i. 125, 186 f.; H. Delbrück, *Geschichte der Kriegskunst*, iii, 2d ed. (Berlin, 1923), pp. 669–677; the edition of Aegidius Romanus in R. Schneider, *Die Artillerie des Mittelalters* (Berlin, 1910), pp. 105–182; and the *Pulcher tractatus de materia belli*, ed. A. Pichler (Graz, 1927).

[2] See J. J. Jusserand, *Les sports et jeux d'exercice dans l'ancienne France* (2d ed., Paris, 1901), pp. 73 ff.

arms must blame himself and his evil fortune. For if arms are given back
to a man when he is losing, this would really be lifting him up and
starting him a second time, which would be unjust. Others say that
arms are not to be given back whether they break or fall. In this matter
we declare that the custom of the place should be observed and if there
is no custom then what seems most just and equitable to the judge
shall prevail.[1]

Already the judicial duel has begun to decline; Roffredo's
contemporary and one-time master, the sporting emperor
Frederick II, found it to be only "a sort of divination, out of
harmony with natural reason, common law, and equity." [2]

Next to war came the chase, that sport of all times and
places, which was considered the special delight of kings and
princes. The vernacular literature of the chase is well known,
at least from the fourteenth century: the *Livre du Roi Modus
et de la Reine Ratio*; the *Ars de venerie* of William Twici, master
huntsman of Edward II; the *Roman des déduis* of Gace de la
Buigne; and the famous *Livre de chasse* of that mighty hunter
and master of six hundred well-loved dogs, Froissart's patron,
Gaston Phébus, count of Foix.[3] The Latin literature is earlier,
going back apparently to the eleventh century, and clearly
antedating the great cyclopaedias of the thirteenth century in
which it is cited. Severely practical throughout, it is concerned
in the first instance with the animals which aid in the chase,
horses, dogs, hawks, and falcons, and especially with the diseases
of these and their remedies. It would be rash to deny any connexion between this and the veterinary medicine of antiquity,
but for the most part it shows a humbler origin, its precepts
drawn rather from the popular cures and leechdoms of current
practice. All kinds of ailments are included, even parasites re-

[1] Edited by F. Patetta, *Le ordalie* (Turin, 1890), pp. 478–492; and in A.
Gaudenzi, *Bibliotheca iuridica medii aevi*, ii (Bologna, 1892), pp. 75–83. Cf.
the Scottish examples in G. Neilson, *Trial by Combat* (London, 1890), cc. 65,
66, 73, 74; and B. Prost, *Traités du duel judiciaire* (Paris, 1872).

[2] Constitutions of 1231, ii. 33, ed. J. L. A. Huillard-Bréholles, *Historia
diplomatica Friderici Secundi* (Paris, 1859 ff.), iv. 105.

[3] See H. Werth, "Altfranzösische Jagdlehrbücher," in *Zeitschrift für romanische Philologie*, xii (1888), especially pp. 383–415. D. H. Madden, *A Chapter
of Mediaeval History: The Fathers of the Literature of Field Sport and Horses*
(London, 1924), is a popular account, devoted almost entirely to vernacular
writers.

ceiving careful attention to a degree which reminds one of the
course on 'Domestic Entomology' announced by an American
agricultural college. Those who practise this art, says Adelard
of Bath,[1] not only must be sober, patient, and chaste, alert and
of sweet breath, but must avoid those from whom hawks might
become infested with vermin, for which special remedies are
prescribed. These treatises, chiefly relating to falcons, claim an
ancient origin under such titles as the letters "of Aquila and
Symmachus and Theodotion to King Ptolemy" and "of Giro-
sius the Spaniard to the Emperor Theodosius," and they have
parallels in Byzantine literature. Those who derive falconry
from the East would doubtless trace them all to the Orient, but
in these days of multiple hypotheses it is not necessary to assume a common origin for the Norway falcons supplied annually
to King Henry II of England [2] and the hawking which Marco
Polo describes at the court of the Great Khan. Certainly the
treatise which Adelard of Bath in the early twelfth century
compiled from 'King Harold's books' and his own experience
shows no indebtedness to the East,[3] and the same is apparently
true of the work of one Grimaldus, 'Count of the Sacred Palace,'
which meets us in an eleventh-century manuscript at Poitiers.[4]
By the thirteenth century we have translations from the Arabic,
notably the work of Moamin on the diseases of falcons and
hawks turned into Latin *ca.* 1240 by Theodore, court philosopher of Frederick II, and the similar work of a certain Yatrib.
Another popular Latin treatise goes under the name of an
imaginary King Dancus but cites the precepts of William,
falconer of King Roger of Sicily, one of the earliest authorities
on this art. In spite of its brief account of the different species
of hawks and falcons, this is still a work on diseases rather
than on sport proper, and the same can be said of the earliest
mediaeval book on horses, compiled in Latin by Giordano Ruffo

[1] *E. H. R.*, xxxvii. 399 (1922).

[2] See the passages from the Pipe Rolls collected by A. Bugge, *Diplomatarium Norvegicum*, xix, nos. 35 ff.

[3] See *Mediaeval Science*, ch. 17, and cf. L. Mercier, *La chasse et les sports chez les Arabes* (Paris, 1927).

[4] MS. 184, ff. 70–73: 'Incipit opusculum Grimaldus baiuli et comitis sacri palatii ad Karulum regem de dieta ciborum et nutritura ancipitrum.'

of Calabria for Frederick II and soon translated into Italian and other languages.[1] So their contemporary, Albertus Magnus, while devoting most space to horses and hawks in his great treatise *On Animals*, concerns himself only with their diseases.[2]

The sport of falconry first comes fully to its own in the *De arte venandi cum avibus* of the Emperor Frederick II. Of Frederick as a man of science I have written elsewhere [3]—his spirit of free inquiry, his keen interest in animals, his tireless observation and experiment on birds, his wide-ranging activity as a collector, his extraordinary menagerie of beasts from other climes. In another age he might have stalked big game in Africa or explored the fauna of the Upper Amazon with the energy of a Theodore Roosevelt, but without sharing the Rooseveltian certainties or zeal for the betterment of his fellow men. In any event he was one of the great sportsmen of the Middle Ages and indeed of any age, a tireless devotee of hunting who delighted in the wings of a bird as well as in the strength of a horse and the legs of a man. A man of the open air, his sporting life can be followed in fragments of his administrative correspondence, but best of all in his own treatise on falconry to which he devoted the leisure of thirty years. This art, he tells us, "we have always loved and practised," and his high standard of sport stands out in his description of the ideal falconer:

Whosoever desires to learn and practise the art of hunting with birds, so as to be competent in feeding, keeping, taming, carrying, and teaching them to hunt other birds, in hunting with them, and if necessary in curing their diseases, should have with him the science of this book, both what is now said and what follows, and when he has this in sufficient measure from one worthier he may receive the title and name of falconer. [Of medium stature and medium weight] he must not weary of the art or the necessary labour, but should love it and persevere in it so that even in old age he shall be no less devoted to it, all of which will come from the love which he has for the art. For since the art is long and many new things happen in its pursuit, one should never desist from its practice but keep it up throughout life in order to attain greater perfection therein. The falconer should have great natural intelligence, since,

---

[1] *Mediaeval Science*, p. 256.

[2] *De animalibus*, ed. H. Stadler (Münster, 1916–20), xxii, 2, 1, cc. 52–93, xxiii, 1, cc. 1–24, pp. 1377–1400, 1453–93.

[3] *Mediaeval Science*, chs. 12, 14. Cf. *infra*, Chapter VI.

although he will learn much concerning birds from the experts in this art, he will still need to discover and devise many things out of his own head as occasion arises. For it would be impossible and it would in any case be tiresome to write down everything and consider all possible eventualities, both good and bad, in dealing with individual birds of prey of different temperaments, so let each man supply what is needed from his own mind and from the art of this book. . . . Of those who follow this art there are some who practise it neither to satisfy appetite nor for the sake of gain nor even for the joy of the eye, but only for the sake of having the best birds of prey which shall bring them surpassing fame and honour, and who take their delight in this, that they have good birds.[1]

Frederick's *De arte* has not reached us in its original form, which included material on hawks and on diseases of falcons which is absent from the surviving manuscripts, perhaps also books on other forms of hunting which he promises "if life permit." A book of his on hawks and dogs was captured at the

[1] 'Quicunque itaque vult discere et exercere artem venationis cum avibus ad hoc quod possit esse sufficiens in nutriendo, etiam custodiendo mansuefaciendo portando docendo ipsas ut venentur alias aves, in utendo eis in venationibus et in curando eas si opus fuerit, oportet ut in se habeat ea que dicentur iam et postea scientiam huius libri, que omnia cum sufficienter habuerit a digniori nomen accipiens falconarius poterit merito nuncupari. Qui sit mediocris stature ne propter magnitudinem superfluam plus lassus et minus agilis habeatur neque propter parvitatem nimiam sit minus agilis tam equester quam pedester. Sit mediocris habitudinis ne propter extenuatam maciem deficiat sustinere laborem aut frigus neque propter corpulentiam et pinguedinem nimiam fastidiat laborem et calorem et pigrior et tardior habeatur quam convenit huic arti. Non fastidiat artem neque laborem sed diligat et perseveret in ipsa in tantum quod etiam quando devenerit ad senectutem non minus intendat arti, quod totum procedit ex amore quem habebit in arte. Cum enim ars longa sit et plura in usu secundum eam noviter incidant, nunquam debet homo desistere ab exercitio huius artis sed perseverare quamdiu vixerit ut ipsam artem perfectius consequatur. Debet esse perfecti ingenii, ut, quamvis didicerit plura et a doctis huius artis circa ea que sunt necessaria avibus, tamen ex suo naturali ingenio sciat invenire et excogitare que necessaria fuerint incidenter. Non enim esset possibile scribere singula et noviter emergentia in operationibus bonis et malis avium rapacium, nam cum diversorum sint morum longe durum esset scribere omnia, pro qua re singulis [singulus ?] ex suo ingenio et ex arte huius libri quicquid erit expediens ministrare tenetur . . . Alii intendunt in hoc neque causa gule neque causa lucri alterius neque etiam causa delectamenti visus sui, sed tantum ut habeant suas aves rapaces bonas et meliores quam ceteri ex quo adquirant sibi famam et honorem pre ceteris, et in hoc habent magnum delectamentum, scilicet quod habent bonas aves.' Vatican, MS. Pal. Lat. 1071, ff. 68 r–69 v; Bibliothèque Mazarine, MS. 3716, pp. 173–177: *Reliqua librorum Frederici II Imperatoris de arte venandi cum avibus*, ed. J. G. Schneider (Leipzig, 1788–89), i. 107–109.

great defeat before Parma in 1248, and was in the hands of a certain William Bottatus of Milan in 1264; this *de luxe* copy then disappears, and King Manfred had access only to an incomplete text and scattered notes of his father's which he used in his revision of the first two books. Manfred's revision is the basis of the printed editions, although they lack the beautiful illuminations with their extraordinarily faithful depiction of birds which have come down to us in the Vatican manuscript. Four other books as yet unpublished are preserved in a different family of manuscripts, but we must repeat that we have not the work as Frederick planned it, perhaps not as he executed it.[1]

The first complete treatise on the subject of falconry, as its author tells us, the *De arte* is a big book, five hundred and eighty-nine pages in the Mazarine manuscript, and a detailed book. It is a scientific book, approaching the subject from Aristotle but based closely on observation and experiment throughout. *Divisivus et inquisitivus*, in the words of the preface, it is at the same time a scholastic book, minute and almost mechanical in its divisions and subdivisions. It is also a rigidly practical, even a technical book, written by a falconer for falconers and condensing a long experience into systematic form for the use of others. To the great regret of the modern reader, it is not discursive or narrative, for there are few specific references to time or place and no hunting stories. Only between the lines can we see the emperor rising betimes for a morning's sport beside Apulian watercourses, writing respecting the homes and haunts of herons in Sicily, ranging the country about Gubbio under a winter sky for those fat cranes which he describes in a letter to one of his falconers in the South.[2] Everywhere it is the work of a sportsman.

After a preface exalting the art of falconry, the first book is devoted to zoology, and very good zoology it is, treating of the structure and habits of birds in general and then of birds of prey in particular. Book Two then takes up the rearing, feeding, and

[1] I have discussed the manuscripts and editions of the *De arte* in my *Mediaeval Science*, ch. 14. The preparation of a critical edition has at last been undertaken by Professor J. Strohl of Zurich.

[2] Huillard-Bréholles, *Historia diplomatica*, v. 510, 698.

seeling of falcons, and the implements of the art, including the hood which the emperor borrowed from the Arabs on his Crusade and improved for Western use. Book Three is concerned with various kinds of lures and their use, especially those made of cranes' wings for that noblest of birds the gerfalcon, and the special training of the swift-footed dogs necessary to aid the falcon against large birds. In Book Four we reach the climax, the pursuit of cranes with gerfalcons, for "cranes are the most famous of all birds which birds of prey are taught to hunt, and the gerfalcon is the noblest of birds of prey and the bird which captures cranes better than other falcons and best goes after them." [1]

When a falconer goes out to hunt cranes with the gerfalcon his garments should be short, for the sake of greater agility, and of a single colour, preferably grey or an earthen hue such as farmers wear, for such clothing best stands exposure to changes of place and weather. If he wears fine and many-coloured raiment with striking colours, his prey will more quickly fly away. He should have on his head a broad hat, so as to conceal his face from the cranes and frighten them as little as possible, and, if need be, to shelter the falcon from sun, wind, and rain. He will also need heavy leggings as a protection against water and brambles. His horse should be gentle and quiet, running only at the rider's will and not quickening his pace if the reins are thrown on his neck when that hand is busy with the falcon, obedient and swift-footed and quick to turn to right or left when there is need. He should not be frightened by sudden or strange sounds nor should he whinny easily, for this scares the birds. He must not be hard in the mouth or difficult to curb, lest he injure the falcon in hastening to its aid, and there should be no bells on bridle or breastpiece, which would also frighten the birds.[2]

---

[1] 'Sed quoniam grues sunt famosiores inter omnes aves non rapaces ad quas docentur capiendas aves rapaces et girofalcus nobilior est avibus rapacibus et est avis que melius capit grues quam alii falcones, et que melius volat ad ipsas.' Mazarine MS. 3716, p. 282.

[2] 'Falconarius quando exire debet foras ad exercendum venationem cum girofalcis ad grues habeat pannos vestimentorum suorum curtos, ut agil[i]or sit cum eis, et si[n]t unius coloris qui color sit bisus aut similis coloris terre quali panno utuntur coloni, tales enim panni exponuntur convenientius oportunitatibus temporum et locorum. Si vero vestes haberet splendidas et variorum colorum per quos colores panni essent melius discernibiles, quando indutus talibus pannis exiret foras ad venandum aves quas capere intendunt cum falconibus, minus expectarent et facile aufugerent. Habeat pileum amplum super caput, ut per ipsum minus appareat facies eius gruibus et per hoc minus pavescant, et sub ipso defendat falconem a pluvia vento et sole si necesse

The habits of cranes are taken up in detail, their feeding according to climate, season, and time of day, the advantages and disadvantages of the various sorts of ground, the means employed to separate one or two or three cranes from the flock, the various methods of attack, the six reasons why a gerfalcon may be driven back by a crane. There is a concluding comparison of the gerfalcon with other falcons. The treatment in the two remaining books is closely parallel, dealing with the hunting of herons with the sacred falcon and of river birds with the peregrine falcon. Thus it is said that against herons, which nest in cane-brakes and in trees near the water, the best time to train falcons is the nesting season, which is early; the best terrain for hunting them is low, open places and small, tortuous rivers. They feed especially on fish, lizards, and young frogs ("worms with a large head and a small tail which are said to become frogs when they grow up"),[1] and move southward as the water-courses freeze over toward winter, though a few remain in the North about warm springs. Their migrations are discussed according to the seasons, and it is noted that they are most abundant in Egypt. All this is preliminary to a detailed discussion of the actual pursuit of herons, which closes again with a comparison of the characteristics of the sacred falcon with other birds.

The thirteenth century, which saw the climax of the Latin literature of sport in the *De arte*, also saw its disappearance before the vernacular, unless we make a place for some Latin

---

fuerit. Habeat ocreas crossas in cruribus suis que sint tutamen tibiarum et pedum contra aquam cardos et spinas et cetera nocumenta. Equus vero quem equitare debebit sit mitis stans quiete qui non currat nisi ad voluntatem equitantis et, si dimittantur habene sibi super collum causa faciendi aliquid circa falconem cum alia manu, ipse equus non acceleret propter hoc passum suum sed sit obediens et agilis ad girandum se de[x]trorsum et sinistrorsum ubi necesse fuerit et velox ad currendum. Non sit ad improvisa aut insueta pavescens neque hyniat libenter, nam aves ad auditum hinitus aufugerent. Non sit effrenis neque dure boce, quoniam quando curreretur ad succurrendum falconi posset de facili pesundari falconem. Non habeat frenum aut pectorale cum nolis seu campanellis quarum sonitu possent deterr[er]i aves.' Bibliothèque Mazarine, MS. 3716, pp. 373 f.: Rennes, MS. 227, p. 248.

[1] 'Vermium crossi capitis et pectoris subtilis caude de quibus dicitur quod fiunt rane quando crescunt.' Bibliothèque Mazarine, MS. 3716, pp. 423 f.

verse of the Cinquecento.[1] The beginning of the century pro-
duced the Provençal *Romans dels auzels cassadors* of Daude de
Pradas, which probably had predecessors in the vernacular, and
Frederick II's son Enzio was the patron of the translator of
Moamin and Yatrib into French. Before the end of the century
Frederick's *De arte* has been turned into French, and brief works
in French and Italian prefigure the more ambitious treatises of
the fourteenth century.[2]

Likewise, it would seem, of the thirteenth century is a brief
unpublished treatise on hunting the stag, *De arte bersandi*, which
goes under the name of Guicennas,[3] "most excellent hunter by
the testimony of the princes of Germany and especially of the
hunters of Emperor Frederick." It begins: [4]

Si quis scire desiderat de arte bersandi, in hoc tractatu cognoscere
poterit magistratum. Huius autem artis liber vocatur Guicennas et
rationabiliter vocatur Guicennas nomine cuiusdam militis Theutonici
qui appellabatur Guicennas qui huius artis et libri materiam prebuit.
Iste vero dominus Guicennas Theutonicus fuit magister in omni venacione et insuper summus omnium venatorum et specialiter in arte bersandi, sicut testificabantur magni barones et principes Alamanie et
maxime venatorés excellentis viri domini Frederici Romanorum imperatoris. Dixitque ergo hic dominus Guicennas quod qui vult scire et
esse perfectus in arte ista primo debet apponere cor et etiam voluntatem,
et debet esse levis et non piger. Debet etenim cogitare ad occidendum
bestiam quam venatur.

Audiatis ergo de ista venacione que quasi domina omnium venacio-
num reputatur. Primum oportet quod bersator sciat bene trahere et
bene menare bestias, et cum istis continentur bene multe alie, ut videlicet
quod bersator debet scire aptare brachetum ad sanguinem, et sciat bene
stare ad arborem et habeat bonam memoriam rememorandi ubi posuit
archarios, et hec est res que magis convenit bersatori quam alii vena-
tori. . . .

After further description of the qualifications of the hunter
we are told that he should also know how to make an arrow and

---

[1] See J. E. Harting, *Bibliotheca Accipitraria* (London, 1891), pp. 163–167.

[2] *Mediaeval Science*, ch. 17. See now Gunnar Tilander, "Étude sur les
traductions en vieux français du traité de fauconnerie de l'Empereur Frédéric
II," in *Zeitschrift für romanische Philologie*, xlvi. 211–290 (1926).

[3] For the possible identification of Guicennas as Konrad von Lützelhard,
see *infra*, p. 131.

[4] Vatican, MS. Reg. Lat. 1227 (saec. xv), foll. 66 v–70 r; MS. Vat. Lat. 5366
(*ca.* 1300), foll. 75 v–78 v: 'Incipit liber Guicennatis de arte bersandi.'

a leash as well as how to sound his horn and dress a stag. His equipment should contain among other things cord and flint (*petra focalis*) and hammer and nails for shoeing his horse in case of necessity. After several chapters on the training of brachets to follow the deer, the author ends with this account of an actual pursuit, even to such details as the disposition of the archers and the patting of the dog's head:

Postquam vero bersatores viderint bestias, illi qui debent menare debent equitare quasi ante faciem bestiarum et debent facere similitudinem quasi non videant eas, et postea circum eas, si bestie expectant, pone archatorem quasi contra primam spalam bestiarum et alium archatorem quasi ad pectus et tercium archatorem quasi ad alteram spalam sive ad pulmonem, et taliter sint ordinati quod unus non possit ferire alterum cum archabunt ad bestias. Si vero unus archator esset qui libentius trahat aliis, pone illum retro pectus bestie. Si vero recedunt bestie et fugerent multum a longe et non videres illas et velles ire retro illas, tunc pone brachetum in terra et reinvenies eas cum bracheto, et quando videbis eas surgere brachetum attira retro te et frica caput leviter cum manu et monstra ei bonam voluntatem, et istud est quare brachetus multum se letificat. Postea equita circumgirando bestias sicut superius diximus archatoribus ordinatis, et si bestie sunt bone pone archatores deprope et fac trahere taliter ut bestie non videant eos, quia si bestie viderent eos ipse irent tam solitarie quod non posses taliter facere alia vice quod ipse bestie non viderent te. Item debes equitare cum bestiis quamdiu potes, quia quanto cum illis equitabis tanto meliores erunt et quando equitabis post bonas bestias. *Explicit liber Guicennatis de arte bersandi.*

Fishing, on the other hand, has left no similar literary remains from our period, for it was not a recognized sport of the upper classes. There was, of course, the example of St. Peter— did not the Popes seal their breves *sub annulo piscatoris*?—and fish were a necessity during Lent, but neither the castle and monastery fish ponds nor the great herring fleets of the North tempted a mediaeval Izaak Walton to discourse upon angling as a fine art. Nor did the Middle Ages take kindly to other forms of aqueous diversion. No one wrote on swimming, although the Latin chroniclers recount such exploits as the feats of Lady Petronilla in the fish pond at Guines [1] or of a diver known as Nicholas the Fish who explored the watery fastnesses

[1] Lambert of Ardres, ed. J. Heller, in *SS.*, xxiv. 629.

of Scylla and Charybdis at the behest of Frederick II.[1] There
is a literature on bathing, notably verse on the baths of Pozzuoli,[2] but this is medicine, not sport. A bath in the Middle Ages
was a serious affair!

Serious, too, is the treatment of hawking, hunting, and fishing in the manual of country life by Petrus de Crescentiis, whose
Ruralium commodorum libri XII was written *ca.* 1300 and went
through many printed editions both Latin and vernacular.[3]
Serious, but hardly sporting, for to him wild beasts are either
food, or nuisances to be exterminated after taking them as best
one can. What shall we say of a man who catches fish with
nets, with quicklime, and—horror of horrors!—with a baited
hook? Somehow we do not visualize this sober Bolognese agri-
culturist as taking a day off with the patient anglers by the
banks of Seine, nor yet as registering Viscount Grey's self-
denying vow not to fish the trout streams in imagination before
the first of January. Still, his book has a traditional place in
the lists of collectors' books on sport, and it is germane to our
present purpose in reminding us that the oldest mediaeval
treatises on agriculture are written in Latin, like their models
Varro and Palladius.

Like everything else in the Middle Ages, hunting might become a theme for sermonizing, as in a Latin homily preserved
at Graz. The text, "Naphtali is a hind let loose" (Genesis,
xlix. 21), is explained on patristic authority as typifying Christ,
hunted as a stag through many passages of simile and with
copious references to the general vocabulary of the chase. Here
again Latin crowds close on the vernacular.[4]

---

[1] Salimbene, ed. O. Holder-Egger, in *SS.*, xxxii. 250 f.

[2] See Ries, in *M. I. O. G.*, xxxii. 576 ff. (1911), and the literature there cited.

[3] The most recent discussions of Petrus are by G. Zaccagnini in *Il libro e la
stampa*, n.s., vi. 133–136 (1912) ; Lodovico Frati, "Pier de' Crescenzi e l'opera
sua," in *Atti e memorie della R. deputazione di storia patria per le provincie di
Romagna*, 4th series, ix. 146–164 (1919) ; Anna Röding, *Studier till Petrus de
Crescentiis och hans antika källor* (Göteborg, 1927). I have not seen Luigi
Savastano, "Contributo allo studio critico degli scrittori agrari italiani: Pietro
dei Crescenzi," in *Annali della R. Stazione Sperimentale di Agrumicoltura e
Frutticoltura*, v (1922).

[4] A. E. Schönbach, "Miscellen aus Grazer Handschriften. 7. Eine Jagd-

Of all indoor games, chess easily took the lead in the Middle Ages. Indeed, we are told that "especially from the thirteenth to the fifteenth century chess attained to a popularity in Western Europe which has never been excelled and probably never equalled at any later date." [1] As the favourite pastime of lords and ladies chess leaves its trail throughout the mediaeval chronicles and at greater length in the feudal romances, while it develops a considerable literature of its own, and this largely in Latin. As an excellent survey of these texts exists in Mr. H. J. R. Murray's *History of Chess*, we shall confine ourselves to brief extracts by way of illustration. There are three principal types of these treatises: "didactic works, generally in verse, which are intended to teach beginners the moves and the most elementary principles of play, or to give a rapid description of the game"; moralizing works; and collections of chess problems. [2] The first and third of these have a modern sound, although Alexander Neckam in a Latin chapter on the rules of chess, *ca.* 1200, finds it necessary to begin with the statement that the game was invented by Ulysses, and in closing to illustrate the passionate devotion of the players by reference to the romance of *Renaud de Montauban*: "How many thousands of souls were sent to hell in consequence of that game in which Reginald the son of Eymund, while playing with a noble knight in the palace of Charles the Great, slew his opponent with one of the chessmen." [3] Even so did Homer sing of the many valiant souls of heroes which Achilles had sent to Hades before their time.

The 'moralities' are more characteristically mediaeval. An age which allegorized everything from the Bible to the spots on dice was not likely to neglect the opportunity presented by a popular game which suggested on the very surface the course of battle, the classes of society, and the vanity of all things

predigt," in *Mittheilungen des historischen Vereines für Steiermark*, xlviii. 192–201 (1900).

[1] H. J. R. Murray, *A History of Chess* (Oxford, 1913), p. 428.

[2] *Ibid.*, p. 418.

[3] *Ibid.*, pp. 501, 512, 741. See Neckam, *De naturis rerum*, ed. T. Wright (Rolls Series), pp. 324–326.

earthly. Thus we read in the so-called *Innocent Morality*, which is obviously of English origin:

The world resembles a chessboard which is chequered white and black, the colours showing the two conditions of life and death, or praise and blame. The chessmen are men of this world who have a common birth, occupy different stations and hold different titles in this life, who contend together, and finally have a common fate which levels all ranks. The King often lies under the other pieces in the bag.

The King's move and powers of capture are in all directions, because the King's will is law.

The Queen's move is aslant only, because women are so greedy that they will take nothing except by rapine and injustice.

The Rook stands for the itinerant justices who travel over the whole realm, and their move is always straight, because the judge must deal justly. . . .

The Pawns are poor men. Their move is straight except when they take anything; so also the poor man does well so long as he keeps from ambition. . . .

In this game the Devil says 'Check!' when a man falls into sin; and unless he quickly cover the check by turning to repentance, the Devil says, 'Mate!' and carries him off to hell, whence is no escape. For the Devil has as many kinds of temptations to catch different types of man, as the hunter has dogs to catch different types of animals.[1]

Much more elaborate is the enormously popular work of the Lombard Dominican, Jacopo da Cessole, of which we have perhaps a hundred manuscripts in Latin, not to mention early editions and vernacular versions, including an English one by Caxton. When we learn that these twenty-four chapters are really an expanded sermon, we are prepared to find that its chess is secondary to its moral teaching and that it is better described by its sub-title *Liber de moribus hominum et officiis nobilium*. It begins and ends with Babylon, the large, square city of Jeremiah, for the betterment of whose king Evil-Merodach chess was originally devised, and its description of the various classes of society is full of second-hand illustrations, chiefly out of John of Salisbury and the Bible. Thus the knights serve as a text for the military and knightly virtues, with quotations from Paul the Deacon and many Gentile writers, and mention of Alexander, David, and Codrus, Sulla, Damon and

---

[1] Murray, p. 530.

Pythias, and the laws of Lycurgus. The knight's victorious progress across the board shows that he who humbleth himself shall be exalted.

Finally it must be remembered that the game of chess was supposed, in England at least, to have another application, namely, to the reckoning of the king's Exchequer, the name of the Arabic chessboard having reached the royal treasury long before the Arabic numerals. The Exchequer unquestionably drew its name from the checquered table or chessboard (*scaccarium*) about which the royal reckoning took place, and it was easy to find a parallel with this royal game in which the king was never mated. Thus the *Dialogue on the Exchequer* says:

> For just as, in a game of chess, there are certain grades of combatants and they proceed or stand still by certain laws or limitations, some presiding and others advancing: so, in this, some preside, some assist by reason of their office, and no one is free to exceed the fixed laws; as will be manifest from what is to follow. Moreover, as in chess the battle is fought between kings, so in this it is chiefly between two that the conflict takes place and the war is waged,—the treasurer, namely, and the sheriff who sits there to render account; the others sitting by as judges, to see and to judge.[1]

To quote the *Dialogue* [2] is to remind ourselves that the Exchequer also had a Latin literature of its own, the earliest detailed description of fiscal operations of any Western government of the Middle Ages, and a very remarkable description for the twelfth or any other century. Later the Exchequer even inspired poetry, of a very mediocre sort, in the lines which describe the functions and the corruption of its members, *ca.* 1400:

> O scacci camera, locus est mirabilis ille;
> Ut dicam vera, tortores sunt ibi mille.
>
> .   .   .   .
>
> Dici miranda scacci domus ergo valebit,
> In qua si danda desint *chekmat*que patebit.[3]

---

[1] i, 1, as translated in E. F. Henderson, *Select Historical Documents of the Middle Ages* (London, 1892), p. 24. On the chessboard of the Exchequer, cf. R. L. Poole, *The Exchequer in the Twelfth Century*, pp. 100–101.

[2] The date of composition is usually given as 1178–79, but cf. H. G. Richardson in *E. H. R.*, xliii. 161–171, 321–340 (1928).

[3] Printed in full by Mrs. M. D. George and C. H. Haskins in *E. H. R.*, xxxvi. 58–67 (1921).

When Latin verse reaches this point, it is time to stop, check-mated.

This essay makes no claim to have exhausted the Latin literature of sport, even in its systematic forms, while of course there is much to glean from scattered references in the Latin chronicles, stories, and poetry of the epoch. I trust, however, that enough has been said to establish my main contention that there is a considerable body of such material in Latin, and that account must always be taken of Latin sources for the lighter as well as for the more serious sides of mediaeval life. *Omnia tempus habent*, said a book much read in the Middle Ages, and a *tempus ridendi* and a *tempus saltandi* are included in the Preacher's ensuing enumeration. There was a time for play in Latin as well as in the vernacular, as the copyists remind us:

Explicit expliceat, ludere scriptor eat.

CHAPTER VI

LATIN LITERATURE UNDER FREDERICK II [1]

THE personality and influence of the Emperor Frederick II have long constituted a fascinating problem for the historian.[2] *Stupor mundi* to his contemporaries, to Nietzsche he is still a *Rätselmensch*, along with Alcibiades, Caesar, and Leonardo da Vinci, "the first of Europeans according to my taste"[3]—one of the interesting men who will be absent from the Christian Heaven.[4] Poet, philosopher, zoologist, observer, experimenter, sportsman, enlightened legislator yet persecutor of heretics, intimate friend of Jews and Mohammedans, master of many tongues and devotee of all sorts of learning, he seemed a universal genius, *universale in tutte le cose*. "Had he but loved God and his church and his own soul," says his contemporary Salimbene,[5] "he would have had few equals." Early, too, he became the theme of legend, identified with Antichrist by ecclesiastical writers, so that even Dante finds him burning in Hell with the Epicurean heretics, while in popular tradition he forms the nucleus of the German *Kaisersage*, as he sleeps in his enchanted cavern in the mountains awaiting the fateful day when he and his knights shall come down to restore the Empire and deliver the oppressed. This many-sided figure has been variously judged from the different points of view of Empire or Papacy, Germany or Italy, scepticism or belief, politics or culture. Scholars still discuss whether he belongs to the Middle Ages or the Renaissance, to the beginning or end of an epoch, to his own time or to all time, ageless and universal.

[1] Revised from *Speculum*, iii. 129–151 (1928).

[2] See the excellent sketch of Karl Hampe, *Kaiser Friedrich II. in der Auffassung der Nachwelt* (Stuttgart, 1925). There has since appeared the stout volume of E. Kantorowicz, *Kaiser Friedrich der Zweite* (Berlin, 1927), stimulating but highly systematic and as yet giving no evidence for its assertions. On Frederick in prophecy and legend, see also A. de Stefano, *Federico II e le correnti spirituali del suo tempo* (Rome, 1922).

[3] *Beyond Good and Evil*, tr. Helen Zimmern (New York, 1923), c. 200.

[4] *Werke* (Leipzig, 1885–1926), xvi. 291; cf. viii. 310; xiii. 327, 335, 337; xv. 22.   [5] Ed. O. Holder-Egger, in *SS.*, xxxii. 349.

On the whole, understanding of Frederick has grown with understanding of the Middle Ages, especially as we see him in the light of the Sicilian tradition of his grandfather, Roger II, in his relations with the Arabic culture of his own epoch, and against the background of thirteenth-century Italy.[1] In attempting to fill in something more of this Italian background, we must be careful not to regard the Emperor as a merely Italian phenomenon, even as others have misunderstood him by judging him only as a German ruler. By the very fact of his Sicilian inheritance Frederick was born into the centre of Mediterranean politics and civilization, while the imperial dignity and the German kingship gave him a European position beyond the Alps as well. So cosmopolitan a personage inevitably left his impress in many languages. Thus Frederick is a clear figure in the Arabic writers of his time, as well as in his own scientific and diplomatic correspondence with Mohammedan sovereigns. The Jewish translator, Jacob Anatoli, praises Frederick as a 'friend of wisdom and its votaries,' and hopes the Messiah may come in his reign.[2] A king whose laws had to be issued in a Greek version for the benefit of his Greek-speaking subjects might well expect to be eulogized by Greek poets of Southern Italy such as John of Otranto and George of Gallipoli,[3] while his passing is mourned for Eastern Greeks in a funeral oration by Theodore Lascaris.[4] In the Western vernaculars he is celebrated by Provençal troubadours and German minnesinger and reflected in the Sicilian verse of his own *Magna Curia*, some of which apparently bears his own name.[5] Nevertheless, in

---

[1] See, in general, H. Niese, "Zur Geschichte des geistigen Lebens am Hofe Kaiser Friedrichs II.," *Historische Zeitschrift*, cviii. 473–540 (1912); and for palace life, A. Haseloff, *Die Bauten der Hohenstaufen in Unteritalien* (Leipzig, 1920 ff.).   [2] See *Mediaeval Science*, pp. 251–253.

[3] K. Krumbacher, *Geschichte der byzantinischen Litteratur* (2d ed., Munich, 1897), p. 769; N. Festa, "Le lettere greche di Federigo II," in *Archivio storico italiano*, 5th series, xiii. 1–34 (1894).

[4] J. B. Pappadopoulos, *Théodore II Lascaris* (Paris, 1908), pp. 183–189; Βυζαντίς, ii. 404–413 (1912).

[5] References on the vernacular writers of Frederick's time are conveniently brought together by E. H. Wilkins, "The Origin of the Canzone," in *Modern Philology*, xii. 135–166 (1915); for Provençal relations, cf. G. Bertoni, *I trovatori d'Italia* (Modena, 1915), pp. 25–27; O. Schultz-Gora, *Ein Sirventes von Guilhem*

Frederick's time Latin was still predominantly the language of history and law, of education and learning, and even of much imaginative writing, and it is in the Latin literature of his age that we may expect to find the fullest reflection of this many-sided personality. Something of this was directly called forth or encouraged by Frederick himself, on the part of members of his court or others; something he occasioned indirectly as the object of attacks from his enemies; while still more treated him but incidentally as one of the prominent men of his generation.[1] We shall try to bring together some facts concerning the litera-ture to which he gave positive encouragement, particularly in his southern kingdom, with some reference to that which was produced by way of hostile reaction, in the hope of understand-ing somewhat better the condition of Latin literature in the Italy of the thirteenth century, in relation to the age which followed as well as to Frederick himself.

To speak of Frederick II as a patron of literature and learning may easily give rise to a false impression, as if he represented the common type of Maecenas which satisfies its intellectual interests vicariously, by hiring writers and scholars rather than by personal effort. Whatever Frederick did, he did with his might, and his own initiative and participation are as apparent in discussion and experiment [2] as they are in war and sport.

Figueira gegen Friedrich II. (Halle, 1902), pp. 33–38. The latest account of the Sicilian school is G. A. Cesareo, *Le origini della poesia lirica* (2d ed., Milan, 1924). See F. Torraca, *Studi su la lirica italiana del duecento* (Bologna, 1902). For a critical edition and discussion of the poems ascribed to Frederick himself, see H. H. Thornton, in *Speculum*, i. 87–100 (1926); ii. 463–469 (1927).

[1] It would be interesting to follow Frederick through the Latin collections of *exempla* of the thirteenth and fourteenth centuries. Thus he appears in the two Franciscan collections recently brought to light by L. Oliger: "Liber exemplorum Fratrum Minorum saeculi XIII," in *Antonianum*, ii. 203–276 (1927), nos. 129–131; and "Servasanto da Faenza O. F. M. e il suo 'Liber de virtutibus et vitiis,'" in *Miscellanea Ehrle*, i. 148–189 (1924), p. 185, note 1 (this story is also cited in *Mediaeval Science*, pp. xiv, 263). Cf. J. T. Welter, *Tabula exemplorum*, p. 106.

[2] For an illustration, see the questions addressed by the Emperor to Michael Scot, published and translated in *Mediaeval Science*, pp. 266–267, 292–294; reprinted and discussed, with a German version, by Hampe, in *Festgabe für W. Goetz* (Leipzig, 1927), pp. 53–66, who proposes to date them 1227. Cf. E. F. Jacob, in *History*, xi. 243 (1926); and Kantorowicz, *Kaiser Friedrich der Zweite*, pp. 323 ff.

His autocratic government and large revenues gave him resources for pursuing his inquiries, but they did not set him
apart from his helpers and associates. Everything points to
Frederick as the most active force of the court as well as its
superior intelligence.

Accordingly, we must remember at the outset that Frederick
was himself a Latin author, quite apart from whatever Latin
writings he may have directed or inspired. Latin style was
probably one of the subjects in which as a youth he received
instruction from Willelmus Francisius,[1] and we later hear of
Latin orations [2] as well as Latin writings from his pen. How far
he was himself affected by the baroque Latin of the South it is
impossible to say, for the pompous language of his legislation
doubtless owes less to the Emperor than to his jurists and secretaries, nor can we safely seek his personal touch in what the
Pope called the *dictatoris facunditas* [3] of the correspondence
which emanated from his chancery. In the one work which is
clearly Frederick's, the treatise on falconry (*De arte venandi
cum avibus*),[4] the treatment is matter-of-fact, the style simple
and unadorned, with some looseness and repetition and much
evident influence of the vernacular, for whose technical terms
he has difficulty in finding Latin equivalents. Such glimpses of
the real Frederick do not, however, suffice to prove that he
may not have indulged in fine writing on other occasions or
that he looked with disfavour upon the Latin which his legislation borrowed from the *Code* of Justinian. Indeed, an autocrat
who cut off the thumb of a notary for misspelling his name [5] is
not likely to have tolerated a style foreign to his taste. Save in
the *De arte*, we cannot distinguish the imperial Latin from that

[1] Hampe, in *M. I. O. G.*, xxii. 575–599 (1901); and in *Historische Zeitschrift*,
lxxxiii. 8–12 (1899).

[2] Niese, in *Historische Zeitschrift*, cviii. 532; Wolfram von den Steinen, *Das
Kaisertum Friedrichs des Zweiten nach den Anschauungen seiner Staatsbriefe*
(Berlin and Leipzig, 1922), p. 15.

[3] Bull of Gregory IX, 15 July, 1233. J. L. A. Huillard-Bréholles, *Historia
diplomatica Friderici secundi* (Paris, 1852–61), iv. 444.

[4] See *Mediaeval Science*, ch. 14; *supra*, Chapter V; and the forthcoming
edition of J. Strohl.

[5] Salimbene, p. 350.

of Piero della Vigna and the other jurists and notaries of the court.

Respecting Frederick's encouragement of learning, the chronicler who passes by the name of Nicholas of Iamsilla, and who was perhaps a notary of Manfred,[1] tells us that at Frederick's accession there were few or no scholars in the Sicilian kingdom, and that it was his task by liberal rewards to attract masters from various parts of the earth. Concerning literature the classical passage is one in Dante's *De vulgari eloquentia* [2] which celebrates Frederick and his son Manfred—in intellectual history the two reigns belong together—as the illustrious heroes who, while fortune permitted, disdained lower occupations and followed humane pursuits, 'wherefore those of noble heart and gracious endowment tried to follow their majesties, so that whatever in their time the excellent minds of the Latins strove to produce, first saw the light in the court of these rulers.' Dante, however, is speaking from the point of view of vernacular letters, and the glory of the *Magna Curia* as the cradle of Italian poetry is sufficiently attested by the long list of Sicilian poets who held office under Frederick, not to mention his specific aid to German and Provençal versifiers. On the Latin side Frederick's court is less well known, but it must form the starting-point of our inquiry. Let us begin with a rough list of the Latin works known to have been dedicated to the Emperor or written by members of his court: [3]

1. Michael Scot, court philosopher from *ca.* 1227 to his death shortly before 1236, dedicated to Frederick (*a*) *Abbreviatio Avicenne de animalibus*, before 1232; and, after 1228, his three treatises on astrology and related matters: (*b*) *Liber introductorius*; (*c*) *Liber particularis*; and (*d*) *Physionomia*. See my *Mediaeval Science*, ch. 13; "Michael Scot in Spain," in *Homenaje á Bonilla y San Martin*

---

[1] L. A. Muratori, *Rerum Italicarum scriptores* (Milan, 1723–38), viii. 495–496. Cf. A. Karst, in *Historisches Jahrbuch*, xix. 1–28 (1898).

[2] i, c. 12.

[3] Cf. the longer list which I have drawn up for Henry II of England: *Essays Presented to Thomas Frederick Tout* (Manchester, 1925), pp. 71–77, to which may be added the medical treatise of Daniel Churche: E. Faral in *Romania*, xlvi. 247–254 (1920).

(Madrid, 1927-29), ii; "The Alchemy Ascribed to Michael Scot," *infra*, Chapter VII.

2. Theodore of Antioch, court philosopher and Arabic secretary, probably succeeding Scot and mentioned from 1238 till his death in or just before 1250, prepared for the Emperor's benefit (*a*) a treatise on hygiene extracted from the *Secretum secretorum* of the Pseudo-Aristotle; and (*b*) a translation of Moamyn, *De scientia venandi per aves*, corrected by the Emperor in 1240-41. See *Mediaeval Science*, pp. 246-248, 318 f. Theodore of Antioch is to be distinguished from his younger contemporary, the Dominican friar Theodoric the Catalan, on whose medical writings see Louis Karl, "Recherches sur quelques ouvrages scientifiques du moyen âge," in *Revue des bibliothèques*, xxxviii. 49-62 (1928).

3. Piero della Vigna, judge of the *Magna Curia* (1225-47), logothete and protonotary (1247-49). More or less doubtful letters addressed to the Emperor, including a eulogy (*Epp.*, iii. 44). See Huillard-Bréholles, *Vie et correspondance de Pierre de la Vigne* (Paris, 1865); and the literature cited below.

4. Terrisio di Atina, professor of rhetoric at the University of Naples. Poem addressed to the Emperor requesting a reform of judicial abuses. Edited in part by E. Winkelmann, *De regni Siculi administratione* (Berlin, 1859), pp. 55-56; completely by G. Paolucci, "Documenti inediti sulle relazioni tra chiesa e stato nel tempo Svevo," pp. 21-23, in *Atti* of the Palermo Academy, 3d ser., v (1900), and by F. Torraca, "Maestro Terrisio di Atina," in *Archivio storico per le province napoletane*, xxxvi. 251-253 (1911).

5. Petrus de Ebulo, court poet of Henry VI, to whom he dedicated the *Liber ad honorem Augusti* (see E. Rota's edition in the new edition of Muratori's *Rerum Italicarum scriptores*, xxxi, and G. B. Siragusa's in *Fonti per la storia d'Italia*, xxxix), and probably the 'magister Petrus versificator' whom Frederick mentions as dead by 1220; addresses to Frederick, 'Sol mundi,' 1211-20, a poem on the baths of Pozzuoli. A lost history, *mira Federici gesta*, to which he refers, seems to have dealt with Frederick Barbarossa. See R. Ries, *M. I. O. G.*, xxxii. 576-593, 733 (1911), and the works there cited.

6. Adam, chanter of Cremona, *Tractatus de regimine iter agentium vel perigrinantium*. With preface dedicated to Frederick *ca.* 1227. Ed. Fritz Hönger, *Aerztliche Verhaltungsmassregeln auf dem Heerzug ins Heilige Land für Kaiser Friedrich II. geschrieben von Adam von Cremona* (Leipzig diss., 1913).

7. Leonard of Pisa, *Liber quadratorum*, dedicated to Frederick in 1225 (?), besides other mathematical works discussed with the Emperor and members of his court. See *Mediaeval Science*, p. 249.

8. Henry of Avranches, three fulsome eulogies, in hexameters, addressed to Frederick *ca.* 1235–36. Ed. E. Winkelmann, *Forschungen zur deutschen Geschichte*, xviii. 482–492 (1878). On Henry as an international poet, see the unpublished Harvard thesis of J. C. Russell and his summary in *Speculum*, iii. 34–63 (1928); and *infra*, p. 145.

9. Richard, judge of Venosa, *De Paulino et Polla*, comedy dedicated to Frederick in the governorship of Raynaldus, 1228–29:

> Hoc acceptet opus Fredericus Cesar, et illud
> Maiestate iuvet atque favore suo!
> Cuius ad intuitum Venusine gentis alumnus
> Iudex Ricardus tale peregit opus.

Edited by E. Du Méril, *Poésies inédites du moyen âge* (Paris, 1854), pp. 374–416. To the six MSS. there mentioned, two have been added by R. Peiper, *Archiv für Litteraturgeschichte*, v. 540 (1875); and there is another in the Vallicelliana at Rome, MS. C. 91, ff. 45–67 v. For the contents and date, see W. Cloetta, *Beiträge zur Litteraturgeschichte des Mittelalters und der Renaissance*, i (Halle, 1890), pp. 94–96, 157–159; W. Creizenach, *Geschichte des neueren Dramas* (2d ed., Halle, 1911–23), i. 35–37; and *infra*, p. 144.

10. Orfino of Lodi, judge, *De regimine et sapientia potestatis*, a poem of *ca.* 1600 lines on the podestà, written under the patronage of Frederick of Antioch after 1244, and beginning with a laudation of Frederick II and his court. Ed. A. Ceruti, in *Miscellanea di storia italiana*, vii. 27–94 (1869); cf. F. Hertter, *Die Podestàliteratur Italiens im 12. und 13. Jahrhundert* (Leipzig, 1910), pp. 75–79, and V. Franchini, *Saggio di ricerche su l'instituto del podestà nei comuni medievali* (Bologna, 1912), p. 255.

11. Giordano Ruffo of Calabria, a marshal of the Emperor, prepared under Frederick's direction and completed after his death a treatise on the diseases of horses; the first mediaeval work on its subject in Latin, this was widely copied, translated, and imitated. Edited by H. Molin (Padua, 1818); see *Mediaeval Science*, p. 256, and the works there cited.

12 (?). 'Guicennas' (?), a German knight, 'master of all kinds of hunting, especially by the testimony of Emperor Frederick's huntsmen,' *De arte bersandi*. Unpublished. See *Mediaeval Science*, p. 256; *supra*, Chapter V. Professor Hampe suggests to me that Guicennas

is possibly to be identified with Konrad von Lützelhard, who is called Guizenardus in a letter of 1230 printed in *Acta pacis ad S. Germanum initae* (*M. G. H.*, *Epistolae selectae*, iv, 1926), pp. 52–53.

13 (?). Petrus Hispanus (later Pope John XXI), if 'we accept the doubtful ascription in Harleian MS. 5218, f. 1: *Epistola magistri Petri Hyspani missa ad imperatorem Fridericum super regimen sanitatis*. See L. Thorndike, *History of Magic and Experimental Science* (New York, 1923), ii. 489, and particularly M. Grabmann, "Mittelalterliche lateinische Aristotelesübersetzungen und Aristoteleskommentare in Handschriften spanischer Bibliotheken," pp. 98–113, Munich *S. B.*, 1928, no. 5.

14 (?). Friar Elias of Cortona, who went over to the imperial party after his deposition from the generalship of the Franciscans in 1239; certain of the doubtful alchemical works ascribed to him purport to be dedicated to Frederick. See *Mediaeval Science*, p. 260; Thorndike, *op. cit.*, ii. 308, 335; G. Carbonelli, *Sulle fonti storiche della chimica e dell' alchimia in Italia* (Rome, 1925); and Chapter VII, below, p. 158, note 3.

15 (?). Vididenus (?), *Liber septem experimentorum ad imperatorem Fridericum*. See Thorndike, *op. cit.*, ii. 803.

16 (?). *Epistola domini Castri dicti Goet de accidentibus senectutis missa ad Fridericum imperatorem*. An unidentified treatise which is no. 49 in a list of manuscripts copied at the direction of Ivo I, abbot of Cluni (1256–75). L. Delisle, *Inventaire des manuscrits de la Bibliothèque Nationale: Fonds de Cluni* (Paris, 1884), p. 379.

Such a list must in the nature of the case be far from a complete enumeration of the writers who can claim Frederick as their patron, but it is none the less significant and, to a certain extent, typical, both for what it contains and for what it omits. That most of these works should treat of science, or what then passed for science, is of course consonant with all that we know of the Emperor's tastes and experimental habit of mind, as revealed more fully in his own treatise on falconry and his scientific correspondence and questionnaires. Similarly the books on

---

[1] Cf. the various works which purport to have been translated into French for Frederick: *Mediaeval Science*, p. 254; Ch.-V. Langlois, *La connaissance de la nature et du monde* (Paris, 1927), pp. 198–208. The Vittorio Emanuele Library at Rome has a MS., no. 380, f. 6, containing 'Receptario de Galieno translatato de latino in vulgare per lo excellente medico maistro Johanne Saraceno medico etc. et mandato a lo imperatore.'

falconry and hunting are indicative of his well known love of sport. Neither of these aspects of his intellectual interests need detain us here, for they have been already studied elsewhere.[1] So we are prepared to find translations of scientific and philosophical writings, indeed Frederick's reputation as a promoter of translation from the Arabic would lead us to expect more of such versions than can actually be traced to his influence, even if we add to the versions of Michael Scot and Jacob Anatoli the pseudo-Aristotelian and astrological writings turned into Latin in Sicily at the command of King Manfred. The importance of Frederick's court as a centre of translation has plainly been exaggerated.[2]

On the other hand, the absence of any books of history is surprising. Recent investigation will have it that an important Ghibelline source for this reign has been lost in the work of Bishop Mainardino da Imola, who stood in close relations to Frederick and his court, and there may be other such losses to mourn.[3] There is, however, no evidence that Frederick II encouraged an official historiography in any sense parallel to that which flourished under Frederick Barbarossa, and to the paucity of Ghibelline histories we owe not only the predominantly hostile tone of the sources toward Frederick but also the scantiness of the record for many important phases of his reign. Frederick not only had a 'poor press' among his contemporaries, there were times when he had no press at all. His light went out suddenly in the midst of his career, and, as we see from the unfinished state in which he left his own work on falconry, there was no period of peaceful repose at the end when an account of his reign might have been rounded out with the Emperor's

[1] *Mediaeval Science*, chs. 12–14; *supra*, Chapter V.

[2] *Mediaeval Science*, pp. xiv, 260–261, 269–270; see also Huillard-Bréholles, *Pierre de la Vigne*, pp. 282–283. Cf. M. Grabmann, *Forschungen über die lateinischen Aristotelesübersetzungen des XIII. Jahrhunderts* (Münster, 1916), and his forthcoming paper on translation at the court of Frederick II.

[3] P. Scheffer-Boichorst, *Zur Geschichte des XII. und XIII. Jahrhunderts* (Berlin, 1897), pp. 275–283; F. Güterbock, "Eine zeitgenössische Biographie Kaiser Friedrichs II.," in *Neues Archiv*, xxx. 35–83 (1905); Hampe, *Kaiser Friedrich II. in der Auffassung der Nachwelt*, pp. 7, 60. Cf. also B. Schmeidler, "Der sogenannte Cusentinus bei Tolomeus von Lucca," in *Neues Archiv*, xxxii. 252–261 (1906).

approval. Nor did the next generation labour to fill this gap, for Frederick's line came to a swift end with Manfred and Corradino, and their Angevin enemies and successors had no desire to brighten its posthumous renown. For all succeeding generations Frederick's reputation was to suffer from the lack of any official biography. Furthermore, as Hampe has pointed out,[1] the ecclesiastical opponents of Frederick remained in possession of the historical field, and shaped the record in the great Guelfic compilations of the Franciscans and Dominicans, in which the whole life of the Emperor gets its colour from the bitter controversies of his later years, when he took on the semblance of Lucifer and Antichrist. The influence of Frederick on the writing of history was mainly the stimulus of opposition, and the phrases of the historians go back to the fulminations of Gregory IX and Innocent IV and the pamphleteers of their time.[2]

The answer to these, so far as there was an answer, lies in Frederick's own state papers, as drafted in large measure by his judge and secretary, Piero della Vigna.[3] The well known characterization of Dante, who makes Piero hold the keys to Frederick's heart, locking and unlocking it at his pleasure,[4] is matched by an earlier Latin eulogy by Piero's friend Nicola della Rocca.[5] What Piero closes, he says, "none can open, and what he opens none can close." He is another Moses who brought back the law from the Mount, another Joseph to whom the Emperor commits the government of the round earth, another Peter, a rock of security who has not denied his Lord. The letters of

---

[1] Hampe, op. cit., pp. 9–13.

[2] Friedrich Graefe, Die Publizistik in der letzten Epoche Kaiser Friedrichs II. (Heidelberg, 1909); cf. O. Vehse, Die Amtliche Propaganda in der Staatskunst Kaiser Friedrichs II. (Munich, 1929).

[3] See, besides the old editions of S. Schard (Basel, 1566) and J. R. Iselius (Basel, 1740), Huillard-Bréholles, Vie et correspondance de Pierre de la Vigne (Paris, 1865), who describes 82 MSS.; and cf. G. Hanauer, in M. I. O. G., xxi. 527–536 (1900); H. Kantorowicz, ibid., xxx. 651–654 (1909); and C. A. Garufi, in Archivio storico siciliano, n.s., xxv. 181–183 (1900). On Piero's family, see the documents recently published by Mattei-Cerasoli, in Archivio storico per le province napoletane, xlix. 321–330 (1924). The latest discussion of the disputed question of Piero's part in the constitutions of 1231 is that of F. G. Savagnone, in Archivio storico siciliano, n.s., xlvi. 141–156 (1925).

[4] Inferno, xiii. 58 ff.   [5] In Huillard-Bréholles, op. cit., p. 290.

Piero are naturally a prime source for Frederick's reign on the intellectual no less than on the political side, indeed their preservation, as they were copied and recopied for two centuries as models of Latin style, is due mainly to literary reasons. These collections, of which perhaps one hundred and fifty manuscripts are known, still await a comprehensive and critical edition. They differ widely in content and arrangement, containing many personal letters and exercises of Piero as well as a mass of official correspondence in the Emperor's name, not to mention some letters of Piero's friends and some pieces which are obviously posterior to his death in 1249.

Whether literary or legal in content, these letters bear the impress of Piero's style, which also appears in the body of the Emperor's constitutions. "Piero," says Odofredus, "spoke obscurely and in the grand manner," [1] using as he did so the artificial and overladen rhetoric of the Capuan school. The importance of this Capuan group in furnishing secretaries and other officials for the Hohenstaufen court has been made clear by the researches of Hampe and others, but its literary history has still to be written. [2] When it is written, there can be little doubt that Piero will be the most important member, by reason of his individual position and his influence on his own and succeeding generations. Kantorowicz goes so far as to call him the greatest Latin stylist of the Middle Ages and the last creator in the Latin tongue; [3] at least his style was much admired by contemporaries and retained a hold upon letter-writing until it was driven out by the Ciceronians. In any case Piero is the central figure in the Latin literature of Frederick's reign, when "he made the chancery a school of formal style." [4]

Two of Piero's associates represent the same style and school. One of these, Nicola della Rocca, author of more than a score of letters in the collection, including the eulogy of Piero from which we have already quoted, is in relations with various high

---

[1] *M. I. O. G.*, xxx. 653, note 1.

[2] Cf. Hampe, *Beiträge zur Geschichte der letzten Staufer: Heinrich von Isernia* (Leipzig, 1910), p. 34.

[3] *Kaiser Friedrich der Zweite*, pp. 275, 276.

[4] Niese, in *Historische Zeitschrift*, cviii. 526.

officials, and himself solicits an appointment as notary at the *curia*.[1] He also requests permission to give a public course on the *ars dictaminis*, perhaps at Naples. The other, Master Terrisio of Atina, is connected not only with the Emperor but with Naples and its new university by various compositions which range from a eulogy of Master Arnold the Catalan, late professor of philosophy, to a letter suggesting that the students appease this 'terror' (Terrisius) of the schools by suitable presents in Lent:

> Est honestum et est bonum
> Ut magistro fiat donum
> In hoc carniprivio.[2]

Certain of these epistolary collections of the Capuan school fall too early [3] or too late [4] for our purpose, but others illustrate various aspects of Frederick's time.[5] If Cardinal Thomas of Capua (d. 1239) belongs rather to the papal than to the imperial party, his much copied letters are still of considerable importance for the age in general.[6] Much fresh material for Frederick's early years has been found by Hampe in a Capuan letter-writer preserved at Paris,[7] including a description of the young

---

[1] Huillard-Bréholles, *op. cit.*, nos. 73–97, pp. 368–394.

[2] Torraca, "Maestro Terrisio di Atina," *Archivio storico per le province napoletane*, xxxvi. 231–253 (1911).

[3] P. Kehr, "Das Briefbuch des Thomas von Gaeta," *Quellen und Forschungen aus italienischen Archiven*, viii. 1–76 (1905).

[4] Hampe, *Beiträge zur Geschichte der letzten Staufer: Heinrich von Isernia* (Leipzig, 1910); K. Rieder, "Das sizilianische Formel- und Aemterbuch des Bartholomäus von Capua," *Römische Quartalschrift*, xx, 2, pp. 3–26 (1906).

[5] Whether a rhetorician named John of Sicily belongs to Frederick's reign, I am unable to say for lack of characteristic indications in his treatise, which appears in two manuscripts of the Bibliothèque Nationale: MS. lat. 14174, ff. 3–15 v (late thirteenth century); MS. lat. 16617, ff. 206–220 v (early fourteenth century), with some letters following. The treatise begins: 'Incipit rethorica magistri Iohannis de Sicilia in arte dictandi. Cum circa dictamen prosaicum sint multa prosequi volentibus inquirenda . . .'

[6] The elaborate Heidelberg dissertation of Frau Emmy Heller (1927) remains unpublished. On Thomas as the probable author of the earliest formulary of the papal penitentiary (ed. H. C. Lea, Philadelphia, 1892), see my discussion in the *American Journal of Theology*, ix. 429–433 (1905); and in the *Miscellanea Francesco Ehrle* (Rome, 1924), iv. 275–296.

[7] Heidelberg *S. B.*, 1910, nos. 8, 13; 1911, no. 5; 1912, no. 14; 1924, no. 10; *Historische Vierteljahrschrift*, iv. 161–194 (1901); vii. 473–487 (1904); viii. 509–535 (1905); *Zeitschrift für die Geschichte des Oberrheins*, n.s., xx. 8–18 (1905).

king about the age of thirteen, "in appearance already a man
and in character a ruler." [1] There is another collection at
Rheims which has been studied by various scholars, [2] and still
another at Pommersfelden. [3]

A copy of the Pommersfelden collection, preserved in a manuscript of *ca.* 1400 at Lübeck, still awaits detailed study, although
it was described by Wattenbach in 1853. [4] The letters belong to
the time of Frederick II and Gregory IX and centre about
Naples, Ischia, and Gaeta, while the name of Iohannes de Argussa, *notarius et curialis* of Ischia, occurs with sufficient frequency to suggest that he had a hand in the making of the
collection. We also meet with a certain R., professor of grammar at Naples and teacher of *dictamen tam metricum quam
prosaicum*, [5] a training which Iohannes seeks for his sons as a
preliminary to the study of 'physical science' with his brother
R. Pictus: [6]

Meritissimo d[o]ctori carissimo fratri suo plurimumque ad omnia
diligendo R. Picto egregio magistro studii fisicalis magister Iohannes de
Argussa eius frater valde devotus salutem et videndi desiderium. Si per-
sonarum absencia et diversorum locorum distancia nos sequestrant,

[1] *M. I. O. G.*, xxii. 598 (1901).
[2] MS. 1275. See C. Rodenberg, in *Neues Archiv*, xviii. 179–205 (1893);
W. Wattenbach, *ibid.*, 493–526; Hampe, in Heidelberg *S. B.*, 1913, no. 1;
1917, no. 6; *Historische Vierteljahrschrift*, xxi. 76–79 (1924); and in *Festgabe
Friedrich von Bezold* (Bonn, 1921), pp. 142–149; and now the full analysis of
Hampe and Hennesthal in *Neues Archiv*, xlvii. 518–550 (1928), who ascribe the
collection to Master Symon, clerk of Thomas of Capua.
[3] Hampe, in Heidelberg *S. B.*, 1923, no. 8.
[4] "Iter Austriacum 1853," in *Archiv für Kunde österreichischer Geschichts-
Quellen*, xiv. 33, 52–55 (1855). Cf. now Hampe, in Heidelberg *S. B.*, 1917,
no. 6; 1923, no. 8; *M. I. O. G.*, xl. 191 (1925); and *Acta Pacis ad S. Germanum
initae* (1926), pp. xii–xiii, 100 ff. The MS., which is quite corrupt, is no. 152
at Lübeck, from which I have specimen photographs through the kindness of
the Director of the Stadtbibliothek. Since these pages first appeared, I have
learned from Professor Hampe (cf. *Acta Pacis*, p. xii; *Neues Archiv*, xlvii. 519)
that the Lübeck MS. is only a copy, but a very exact copy, of that of Pommersfelden, which must, of course, be utilized in any definitive edition of the pieces
printed in the text.
[5] Wattenbach, *loc. cit.*, p. 33.
[6] Lübeck, MS. 152, f. 165. On f. 166, the sons write home for money. Cf.
the letter of condolence on f. 163 beginning: 'Fratribus suis carissimis Ber. et
A. et ceteris consanguineis plurimum diligendis Iohannes de Ar. dictus magister
insula Icē magister et publicus notarius constitutus.'

mens eadem viget in nobis et dilectio permanet illibata. Licet enim pro variis et diversis negociis desiderabilem personam vestram videre non possim, in sompnis et vigiliis ymaginando vos video et intrinsecus affectibus intuemur. Unum tamen semper et incessanter expecto, de salute vestra et iocundis successibus rectati, ut autem mei status integritas vos letos efficiat et iocundos. Noveritis me divini muneris gratia, a quo bona cuncta procedunt, iocunda corporis alacritate potiri et optatis eventibus iocundari, quod de vobis semper prestolor et expecto. Verum quia R. et N. filii mei, quos litterali scientie proposui penitus exhibendos, sine vestro auxilio ad optatum nequeunt pervenire effectum, dilectionem vestram, de qua plenam gero fiduciam, attentius deprecor et exoro quatinus inveniatis eis, si placet, magistrum ydoneum qui eos promoveat in grammatica et rethorica, quibus sufficienter indictis ad fisicalem scientiam eos inducere valeatis.

The fictitious nature of much of this collection is enhanced by bits of pure fancy, on themes which often go back to the Orleanese *dictatores* of the twelfth century.[1] Thus we here find exchanges between Life and Death, Soul and Body, the Universe and the Creator,[2] while a more satiric turn appears in the salutation *fornicacioni vestre* in place of the regular *fraternitati vestre* in a letter of Gregory IX to his prelates.[3] One example will illustrate the literary style as well as the general manner of these epistles; the use of the *ubi sunt* motif may be noted:[4]

Corpus separatum scribit anime

Corpus miserum omni solacio destitutum anime olim sue consocie et sorori pro salute tristiciam et merorem. Pene terribiles et tormenta varia me cohercent, bonis omnibus exuor, et humo glaciali frigore contremisco dum me video nudum terre humatum quam dum modo floreneam (?) conculcavi. Heu me, ubi est gloria mea? Ubi est dies nativitatis mee valde iocunda? Ubi sunt dulcissima matris ubera que sugebam et basia patris mei in puericia dulciter explorata? Ubi sunt iocunda parentum gaudia in meis nupciis feliciter dedicata, in quibus diversi cantus exiterant et varia genera musicorum?. Ubi est uxor pulcherrima velud stella cum qua cottidie lecto florido amplexibus et basiis delectabar? Ubi sunt equi arma et indumenta serica deaurata quibus cum militibus decorus cottidie apparebam? Ubi sunt varia fercula et vina

---

[1] E.g., MS. lat. 1093, ff. 68–69; Haskins, *The Renaissance of the Twelfth Century* (Cambridge, 1927), pp. 142–145. Cf. Chapter I, *supra*, pp. 3–4.

[2] Lübeck, MS. 152, ff. 162 v–163; Wattenbach, "Iter," pp. 54–55; *Neues Archiv*, xlvii. 520 ff.

[3] Lübeck, MS. 152, f. 164; Wattenbach, p. 55, where the text should read: 'ut in Cena Domini nostro vos conspectui presentetis.'

[4] Lübeck, MS. 152, f. 163.

gratissima quibus cottidie dulciter epulabar? Nunc autem me video miserum putridum sub terra iacentem variis plenum vermibus et fetentem. Sufficit ergo mihi ingens tribulacio mea. Dimitte me, rogo, ut paululum requiescam, nam cum in die iudicii te suscepero pene mi sufficient et tormenta. Si quid enim malum me memini commisisse, te operante et te duce nequiter adimplevi.

Such products of the imagination also meet us among the letters ascribed to Piero della Vigna and Terrisio di Atina: the wild beasts of Apulia celebrate a closed season proclaimed by the Emperor;[1] the courtesans of Naples complain to the university professors of their neglect by the students;[2] Rome writes to her daughter, Florence;[3] the qualities of an ideal horse are described;[4] writers debate the relative merits of birth and character, the rose and the violet.[5] The following satire on the power of money takes the form of parody of an imperial letter:[6]

Epistola notabilis de pecunia

Pecunia Romanorum imperatrix et totius mundi semper augusta dilectis suis filiis et procuratoribus universis salutem et rore celi et terre pi[n]guedine[7] habundare. Ego in altissimis habito,[8] in plateis do vocem meam,[9] girum celi circuivi sola,[10] feci surdos audire et mutos loqui.[11] Amen dico vobis, antequam Abraham fieret ego sum[12] in vestitu deaurato circumdata varietatibus.[13] Ego, inquam, sum illa preeminens imperatrix per quam genus humanum respirat ad gloriam, per quam multiplicata bonorum fecunditas exhibetur. Esurientes implevi bonis,[14] suscitans a terra inopem et de stercore erigens pauperem.[15] O vos omnes qui transitis per viam, attendite et videte si est honor sicut honor meus;[16] michi enim supplicant omnes reges terre et omnes populi, michi Romana curia famulatur. Ibi est requies mea in seculum seculi, hic habitabo quoniam preelegi eam.[17] Que maior leticia michi posset accidere quam

---

[1] Edited by Wattenbach, "Über erfundene Briefe in Handschriften des Mittelalters," in the Berlin *S. B.*, 1892, pp. 91–123. Cf. *Neues Archiv*, xlvii. 524.

[2] Ed. G. Paolucci, pp. 46–47, in *Atti* of the Palermo Academy, 3d ser., iv (1897); and by Torraca in *Archivio storico per le province napoletane*, xxxvi. 248–250.

[3] MS. Vat. Lat. 4957, f. 96 v.   [4] *Ibid.*, f. 42.

[5] Huillard-Bréholles, *Pierre de la Vigne*, pp. 319, 336.

[6] MS. Vat. Lat. 4957, f. 43–43 v.   [7] Genesis, xxvii. 39.

[8] Ecclesiasticus, xxiv. 7.   [9] Proverbs, i. 20.

[10] Ecclesiasticus, xxiv. 8.   [11] Mark, vii. 37.

[12] John, viii. 58.   [13] Psalms, xliv. 10.

[14] Luke, i. 53.   [15] Psalms, cxii. 7.

[16] Lamentations, i. 12.   [17] Psalms, cxxxi. 14.

ut cardinales michi colla subiciant et currant in odorem unguentorum meorum? [1] Levate in circuitu oculos vestros et videte [2] quia sacrorum verba pontificum (f. 43 v) sedium suarum per me posuit asti,[3] per me tremit, per me vacillat, per me concutitur orbis terrarum et universi qui habitant in eo.[4] Et quis enarrabit potencias meas? [5] Michi gremium suum non claudit ecclesia, michi summus pontifex aperit sinus suos et quotiens ad eum accedere voluero totiens in sinu suo colliget [6] et dextera illius amplexabitur me.[7] Transite igitur ad me omnes qui diligitis nomen meum et beatitudinibus meis implemini. Transite igitur, dico, ne sitis obprobrium homini et abiectio plebis,[8] non sequentes eos qui Christi vestigia sunt secuti, argentum suum expendebant non in panibus, laborem suum non in saturitate.[9] Accedite,[10] filii mei, et illuminemini et facies vestre non confundentur. Ego enim sum lux illa que illuminat omnem hominem venientem in hunc mundum,[11] et vos quidem non estis hospites et advene sed estis cives sanctorum, vel nummorum, et domestici mei,[12] quos diu diligere didicistis. Iam non plura loquor vobis-cum,[13] sed tamen concludo dum explicit sermo meus quia sinam vos. Dabo vobis de rore celi et de pi[n]guedine terre habundanciam [14] quam vobis conservare dignetur nostra nutrix dulcissima, scilicet avaricia, rerum timidissima dispensatrix.

Heavy with scriptural quotation, this letter suggests that earlier masterpiece of anti-clerical satire, the *Gospel according to Marks of Silver*,[15] to which it is, however, much inferior. The following, on the other hand, is strongly anti-imperial:

Fr[idericus] XXXVIIII., divina ingratitudine Remalorum depilator et semper angustus, Ierusalem et Sicilie reus, universis fidelibus suis pre-sentes apices generaliter inspecturis illam quam lupus capre salutem. . . .[16]

The letters of Master Terrisio and John of Argussa remind us that the Southern rhetoricians were in relations with the University of Naples as well as with the *Magna Curia*, indeed it was part of the Emperor's purpose that his new university

[1] Canticles, iv. 10.
[2] Isaiah, lx. 4.
[3] Text corrupt.
[4] Psalms, xxiii. 1.
[5] Job, xxxviii. 37; Psalms, cv. 2.
[6] MS. *colligat*.
[7] Canticles, ii. 6; viii. 3.
[8] Psalms, xxi. 7.
[9] MS. *santitate*. Isaiah, lv. 2.
[10] MS. *attendite*. Psalms, xxxiii. 6.
[11] John, i. 9.
[12] Ephesians, ii. 19.
[13] John, xiv. 30.
[14] Genesis, xxvii. 39.
[15] Ed. P. Lehmann, *Parodistische Texte* (Munich, 1923), no. 1 a; for a translation, see Haskins, *The Renaissance of the Twelfth Century*, pp. 185–186.
[16] Printed in full by Hampe in *Neues Archiv*, xxii. 619–620 (1897), from Add. MS. 19906, f. 79 v, of the British Museum, where it is followed by developments of similar themes, in the course of which we find, 'non Fidericus sed fide rarus.'

should train men for an official career.[1] Established in 1224, and renewed in 1234 and 1239, the University of Naples was designed by Frederick to offer such facilities for study to his own subjects as would obviate the necessity of any resort to the Guelfic *studia* of the North, from which they were commanded to return.[2] While the new university theoretically comprised all the studies which were then current, its strength lay in law and rhetorical composition, the very subjects in which Bologna excelled. To this end the importation of Bolognese masters like the jurist Roffredo of Benevento was almost a necessity; Piero della Vigna is himself said to have studied at Bologna,[3] with whose masters he was in correspondence; and Terrisio writes a letter of condolence on the death of the Bolognese professor Bene, who may have been his own teacher.[4] As Niese has pointed out,[5] the Latin culture of Frederick's kingdom was in large measure dependent on Northern sources.

A clear example of the transplantation of learning from Bologna to Naples meets us in the field of grammar in the person of Master Walter of Ascoli, author of an etymological dictionary bearing the title *Dedignomium, Summa derivationum*, or *Speculum artis grammatice*.[6] One of the four surviving manu-

---

[1] Huillard-Bréholles, *Historia diplomatica*, ii. 450; iv. 497; v. 493–496; H. Denifle, *Die Universitäten des Mittelalters* (Berlin, 1885), i. 452–456; Hampe, "Zur Gründungsgeschichte der Universität Neapel," in Heidelberg *S. B.*, 1924, no. 10; F. Torraca *et al.*, *Storia della Università di Napoli* (Naples, 1924), ch. 1; E. Besta, "Il primo secolo della scuola giuridica napoletana," in *Nuovi studi medievali*, iii. 7–28; E. M. Meyers, *Iuris interpretes saec. XIII* (Naples, 1924). [2] Cf. p. 30, note 2, *supra*.

[3] See Guido Bonatti in Salimbene, ed. Holder-Egger, p. 200.

[4] Huillard-Bréholles, *Pierre de la Vigne*, pp. 300–302; *Archivio storico nap.*, xxxvi. 243–244. For Frederick's invitation of Bene to his court, see R. Davidsohn, *Geschichte von Florenz* (Berlin, 1896–), i. 813. That, as late as the beginning of the fourteenth century, Frederick kept a place in the Bolognese collections of letters, appears from the collection of Pietro de' Boattieri, extracts from which are printed by G. Zaccagnini, *Studio di Bologna*, pp. 169–221; cf. his article on Pietro's letters, in *Studi e memorie per la storia dell' Università di Bologna*, viii. 211–248 (1924).

[5] *Historische Zeitschrift*, cviii. 513 ff. Cf. E. Monaci, "Da Bologna a Palermo," in L. Morandi, *Antologia della nostra critica letteraria moderna* (8th ed., Città di Castello, 1893), pp. 227–244.

[6] See my paper on "Magister Gualterius Esculanus," in the *Mélanges Ferdinand Lot* (Paris, 1925), pp. 245–257.

scripts says that 'this work was begun at Bologna when the army of the Pope entered the Terra di Lavoro, when Frederick was Emperor and sojourned in Syria, and was afterward completed at Naples,' so that we clearly have the date 1229. Walter of Ascoli is probably to be identified with the Master G. (Guaterus in one manuscript), professor of grammar at Naples, whose death is commemorated in a highly eulogistic letter of Piero della Vigna to the master's late colleagues. The Laon manuscript of the *Derivations* (*ca.* 1300) also contains syntactical notes of another Southern grammarian, Master Agnellus de Gaeta, who apparently belongs to the same period.

The Latin poetry of the South in this reign is less abundant and less known than its prose, indeed the whole subject of Latin poetry in thirteenth-century Italy still awaits detailed investigation. If we miss the more ambitious treatises of the close of the preceding century like the *Pantheon* of Geoffrey of Viterbo, the *Liber ad honorem Augusti* of Peter of Eboli, and the *Elegies* of Henry of Settimello,[1] there is still much evidence of interest in Latin verse. Readers of Salimbene will recall his frequent poetical quotations, whether from the Goliardic rhymes of the Primate or from the more serious compositions of his own master Henry of Pisa and others.[2] The habit of poetical quotation is also found in writers of a more sober turn, such as the jurist Roffredo of Benevento[3] and the chronicler Richard of San Germano,[4] a serious-minded notary who even drops into verse of his own. So the Southern *dictatores* pass easily into poetical *dictamen*, as we see in various pieces interspersed among the letters of Piero della Vigna and Terrisio of Atina.[5] Piero also has

[1] Cf. the recent edition of A. Marigo (Padua, 1926).

[2] Salimbene, ed. Holder-Egger, pp. 32, 34, 35, 43, 51, 72, 77, 78, 84–87, 99, 132–133, 135, 137, 144, 157, 182–184, 202, 219, 221, 227, 233, 241, 247–249, 255, 271, 292, 331, 340, 353, 361–362, 418, 430–432, 435, 437, 442–444, 474, 492–494, 512, 514, 539–542, 567, 572–573, 578, 590, 600–603, 605, 628, 644, 647, 651.

[3] *Studi medievali*, iii. 237 (1909).

[4] Ed. A. Gaudenzi (Naples, 1888), pp. 64, 68, 95, 104–107, 135, 147, 148, 151; *SS.*, xix. 324, 329, 338, 341, 343, 357, 373, 374, 378, 385.

[5] Huillard-Bréholles, *Pierre de la Vigne*, pp. 302, 402–424; *Neues Archiv*, xvii. 507; *Archivio storico nap.*, xxxvi. 244, 250–253; "Documenti inediti del tempo Svevo," pp. 43, 46, in *Atti* of the Palermo Academy, 3d ser., iv.

his traditional place in the Sicilian school of vernacular poets, though, as Monaci has pointed out,[1] the parallelism of theme in Latin is rather to be sought in certain of the imaginative debates in prose to which we have alluded.[2] On the other hand, the moral maxims of another Southern poet, Schiavo di Bari, were turned into Latin by Jacopo da Benevento, as the contemporary moral treatises of Albertano of Brescia were soon turned into Tuscan.[3] In this fluid period both themes and forms pass readily back and forth between Latin and vernacular and from one vernacular to another.

Now that the didactic poems of Schiavo di Bari, printed in the fifteenth century,[4] have been definitely placed in Frederick's reign[5] (before 1235), we are probably justified in assigning to the same period their translator, Iacobus de Benevento. In any event, the existence of thirteenth-century copies of the Latin version, or rather adaptation, places Iacobus of Benevento before 1300, and thus distinguishes him from a Dominican friar of the same name who meets us *ca.* 1360.[6] His relation to Schiavo is made clear in the heading and colophon:

> Incipiunt Sclavi de Baro consona dicta
> A Beneventano Iacobo per carmina ficta.
>
> .   .   .   .
>
> Expliciunt Sclavi huius proverbia Bari
> Que Beneventanus composuit Iacobus.[7]

---

[1] *Rendiconti dei Lincei*, 5th ser., v. 45–51 (1896).   [2] *Supra*, p. 138.

[3] G. Bertoni, *Il Duecento* (Milan, [1911]), pp. 228, 290–291. On the Latin works of Albertano, see especially A. Checchini, in *Atti del R. Istituto Veneto*, lxxi. 1423–95 (1912).

[4] See the account of older editions in the Bologna edition of 1865 (G. Romagnoli, *Scelta di curiosità letterarie*, xi).

[5] By P. Rajna, in *Biblioteca delle scuole italiane*, 3d ser., anno x, no. 18 (1904). Cf. M. Pelaez, in K. Vollmöller's *Jahresbericht*, viii, 2, pp. 98 f. (1904); G. Bertoni, *Il Duecento*, pp. 185, 282.

[6] J. Quétif and J. Échard, *Scriptores Ordinis Praedicatorum* (Paris, 1719–21), i. 648. The earlier Iacobus is also cited with Richard of Venosa by Geremia di Montagnone *ca.* 1290–1300: J. Valentinelli, *Bibliotheca manuscripta ad S. Marci Venetiarum* (Venice, 1868–73), iv. 187; and for the date, Rajna in *Studi di filologia romanza*, v. 193–204 (1891).

[7] Vatican, MS. Vat. Lat. 2868, ff. 67, 77 v (*ca.* 1300). I have also used the Vatican MS. Reg. Lat. 1596, ff. 21–36 v (*ca.* 1300), and Add. MS. 10415, ff. 1–17, of the British Museum (dated 1399), both of which lack the heading and read *cuius* in the first line of the colophon.

The poems themselves, in the form of a dialogue between father and son, begin and end thus: [1]

> Surexisse patet viciorum viscera flammas
> Urentes hominum que male corda fovent.
> Errant in morum nonnulli cale salubri,
> Sectantes miseri perditionis iter.
>
> . . . .
>
> Tu solus rex es nutu qui cuncta gubernas,
> Cuncta creas verbo, gloria lausque Tibi,
> Ergo Tibi virtus regnum decus atque potestas
> Imperiumque salus gloria lausque Tibi.

Iacobus of Benevento is perhaps to be identified with the Iacobus who is the author of an unpublished elegiac comedy of 416 lines *De cerdone*, preserved in certain Italian manuscripts of which the oldest is of the thirteenth century.[2] Like most such compositions in the Middle Ages, this is in the tradition of Plautus, or rather of the later Pseudo-Plautus, but the setting is mediaeval, though not localized—the priest who seeks through a procuress the beautiful young wife of the workingman (*cerdo*) and outwits the greedy husband who had hoped to extort money by a surprise *flagrante delicto*. It is not clear that Iacobus does more than put a familiar theme into Latin verse—*istud opus metrice descripsit*. His poem is chiefly dialogue, after the opening description of the lady's charms:

> Uxor erat quedam cerdonis pauperis olim
> Pulchra nimis, nunquam pulchrior ulla fuit.
> Huius erat facies solis splendentis ad instar.
> Fulgebant oculi sidera clara velut.
>
> . . . .

---

[1] Text based upon MS. Reg. Lat. 1596, ff. 21, 36 v. Further extracts, from the defective MS. Gadd. LXXI. inf. 13, are given by A. M. Bandini, *Catalogus codicum Latinorum Bibliothecae Mediceae Laurentianae* (Florence, 1776), iii. 718.

[2] The oldest MS., not later than 1300, is MS. Aldini 42 of the University of Pavia, ff. 1–5 v, of which I have photographs through the kindness of the Director, Signore Pastorello; the faint and illegible portions of the manuscript have been filled in by a modern hand. I have also used MS. E. 43 sup., ff. 105–114, and MS. O. 63, ff. 194–202, of the Ambrosian (both saec. xv), apparently those cited by Muratori, *Antiquitates*, iii. 916 (1740). There is a copy of the fifteenth century at Munich, Cod. Lat. 443, ff. 152–159, made by Hartmann Schedel in Italy: W. Creizenach, *Geschichte des neueren Dramas* (2d ed., Halle, 1911–23), i. 37. The colophon reads:

> Iacobus istud opus metrice descripsit ut omnis
> Qui leget hic discat spernere vile lucrum.
> Deo gratias Amen.

Time and place are more certain in the case of the better known comedy *De Paulino et Polla* which Richard, judge of Venosa, dedicates to the Emperor *ca.* 1228–29.[1] This is a much longer piece of 1132 lines, and the principal theme, the marriage of the two aged Venosans, Paulinus and Polla, is interrupted by moral disquisitions, and by much amusing by-play in the adventures of the judge Fulco, who serves as intermediary in the marriage negotiations only to lose his dinner to a cat, to be set upon by dogs, and to be stoned in a ditch where he has fallen. Still, like all these elegiac pieces, this does not seem to have been designed to be acted, though its popularity is indicated by the survival of at least nine manuscripts.

Frederick also had his place in the large body of prophecy and vision which, in both prose and verse, circulated widely in the Italy of the thirteenth century, under the cover of such names as Merlin, the Sibyls, Abbot Joachim of Fiore, Master John of Toledo, and his own astrologer Michael Scot.[2] In some of these the Emperor is the great beast of the apocalyptic visions in which the Joachite friars foretold the beginning of the new dispensation of the Holy Spirit in 1260, predictions which claimed to have been dedicated to his father Henry VI [3] but whose failure in the case of Frederick was a disappointment and a disillusion to the good Salimbene. Others are of astrological origin, going back to the planetary conjunction of 1186 and reappearing for the year 1229.[4] Still others, wise after the event, predict specific occurrences of Frederick's reign, like the fate of the Lombard cities after 1236 and the capture of the cardinals in the great sea fight of 1241. So Pope and Emperor, soon after 1245, are represented as exchanging predictions such as the following: [5]

---

[1] See the list above, p. 130, no. 9.

[2] O. Holder-Egger, "Italienische Prophetieen des 13. Jahrhunderts," in *Neues Archiv*, xv. 141–178; xxx. 321–386, 714 f.; xxxiii. 95–187; H. Grauert, "Meister Johann von Toledo," in Munich *S. B.*, 1901, pp. 111–325; and Hampe, in Heidelberg *S. B.*, 1917, no. 6; 1923, no. 8.

[3] Salimbene, p. 360.   [4] Grauert, pp. 165 ff.

[5] For the many forms of these verses see *Neues Archiv*, xxx. 335–349, 364, 714; xxxiii. 106–107; Salimbene, p. 362; and for other verses on Innocent IV and Frederick II, *Neues Archiv*, xxxii. 559–604.

Imperator ad papam

Fata monent stelleque docent aviumque volatus:
Totius subito malleus orbis ero.
Roma diu titubans, variis erroribus acta,
Concidet et mundi desinet esse caput.

Papa ad imperatorem

Fama refert, scriptura docet, peccata loquuntur
Quod tibi vita brevis, pena perhennis erit.

Guelf and Ghibelline alike made use of these prophetic materials; under the name of Cardinal John of Toledo they appear in relation to Manfred in 1256,[1] nor do they cease with the Hohenstaufen line.

Finally—to end on a Ghibelline note—Frederick was for a time patron of the international court-poet Henry of Avranches. Eulogist of Pope and Emperor, of the kings of England and France, and of prelates and lay lords in many parts of Christendom, recipient of grants from the English Exchequer which suggest those of the later poets laureate, the career of Henry as a Latin poet is an interesting phase of the intellectual life of the thirteenth century.[2] In the three poems addressed to Frederick [3] he speaks as the supreme poet approaching the supreme king,[4]

Simque poesis ego supremus in orbe professor.

Nor does he hesitate [5] to liken Frederick, master of Sicily, Rome, Acre, and Aachen, to Guiscard, Caesar, David, and Charlemagne, as he urges the Emperor to codify the civil law as the canon law has just been codified by Gregory IX. Pre-eminent as a peaceful ruler (*Frithe-rich*), Frederick would spare no expense to have the greatest masters at his court, be it an Orpheus or a Plato, a Euclid or a Ptolemy.[6] The Emperor himself has no superior in any art, liberal or mechanical; not satisfied with the art of

---

[1] Grauert, pp. 144–146, 319–321.

[2] See the article of my pupil, J. C. Russell, "Master Henry of Avranches as an International Poet," in *Speculum*, iii. 34–63 (1928).

[3] Ed. E. Winkelmann, *Forschungen zur deutschen Geschichte*, xviii. 482–492 (1878).

[4] P. 490, line 103.   [5] P. 491, lines 50 ff.

[6] P. 488, lines 35 ff.

ruling, he seeks the secrets of knowledge, and that not orally but by reading books for himself: [1]

Ingenioque tuo non sufficit ars moderandi
Imperium: quin ipsa scias archana sophie,
Consultis oculo libris, non aure magistris.
Nullus in orbe fuit dominans et in arte magister:
In te percipitur instancia.

The purpose of this survey has been to suggest, not to exhaust, yet enough has been said to show a many-sided literary activity in Latin in the South during Frederick's reign. In all this, poetry has its place as well as prose, products of the imagination as well as the exact sciences, literature as well as law and administration, Latin as well as the vernacular. While local centres appear, especially at Naples, the most active seat of culture seems to have been the *Magna Curia*, where none seems to have been more active than the Emperor himself. Especially at the court must we beware of isolating one kind of writing from another as if we were dealing with a period of intellectual specialization into separate compartments. Many poets of the Sicilian school appear also as notaries, judges, or falconers; Theodore of Antioch cast horoscopes besides drafting Arabic letters; and Piero della Vigna had his part in law as well as in literature. The connexion was particularly close between law and letters, and any study of the Latinity of the period must give due attention to the legal sources. Not only was much of this Latin literature written by lawyers, but the style of Frederick's legislation and official correspondence was deliberately literary. Much of the phraseology was also deliberately Roman, as when the Constitutions of 1231 are issued in the name of *Imperator Fredericus II Romanorum Cesar semper augustus Italicus Siculus Hierosolymitanus Arelatensis felix victor ac triumphator*. How far such titles represented a real attempt on Frederick's part to revive the Roman tradition, it is impossible to say, at least until the matter has been more thoroughly investigated. It is always easy to argue from phraseology,[2] and always unsafe, most of all when we are dealing

[1] P. 485, lines 34–38.
[2] Kantorowicz seems to me to exaggerate the importance of such Roman

with so realistic a mind as Frederick's. One thing seems fairly clear, and that brings us back to our special theme, there was no concerted attempt to revive the Latin classics. Naturally the Latinists of the Emperor's court were not ignorant of their Roman predecessors, such as Ovid, but there was not yet the systematic cultivation and imitation of the ancients which we find in Petrarch and Salutati. Whatever one may think of his style, Piero della Vigna was no Ciceronian, nor would the Ciceronians have claimed him.

Nevertheless this Latin culture of the thirteenth century has its place as a connecting link between the renaissance of the twelfth century and the Italian Renaissance. If the continuity is most apparent in the transmission of science and philosophy from the Greek and Arabic, it is also true that the *ars dictaminis* and the fictitious letters, the Goliardic verse and, especially, the Goliardic themes in prose, the elegiac comedy and anti-clerical satire, continued the tradition of the preceding age after these had declined north of the Alps, while the preoccupation with rhetoric and grammar foreshadows the humanism of the fourteenth and fifteenth centuries. In any investigation of the antecedents of the Quattrocento, account must be taken of the continuity of Latin studies in the South.

Finally, it should be noted that, from whatever point of view the matter be approached, one of the marked features of this literature of Frederick's kingdom is its sharply secular character. It is concerned with the world that is, not with the world to come. The absence of works of edification or ecclesiastical history from our list is striking, even if we make full allowance for loss and omission; and the exception proves the rule when the court poet Henry of Avranches writes saints' lives, for he takes such wares to another market. The secularization of literature under Frederick runs parallel to his secularization of the state, and in this respect his court prefigures the intellectual temper as well as the statecraft of the Quattrocento.

phrases and concepts. See also the discussions of A. de Stefano, *L'idea imperiale di Federico II* (Florence, 1927), pp. 64 ff.; and S. Ricci, "Gli 'augustali' di Federico II," in *Studi medievali*, n.s., i. 59–73 (1928). Cf. Franz Kampers, "Die Fortuna Caesarea Kaiser Friedrichs II.," in *Historisches Jahrbuch*, xlviii. 208–229 (1928).

CHAPTER VII

THE *ALCHEMY* ASCRIBED TO MICHAEL SCOT [1]

No phase of mediaeval science is more famous than alchemy, and none is so little understood. Mediaeval Europe, it is true, inherited a rich alchemical tradition from the classical world, transmitted partly directly and partly through the intermediary of Arabic writers; but this was only the beginning of Western alchemy. How much of their own the Arabs added in this process of transmission, and how much was due to Latin experimenters of the later Middle Ages, are questions which cannot be answered in the present state of our knowledge. Investigation can only advance as the result of a systematic inventory of Greek treatises on alchemy, which the International Union of Academies has begun; [2] by monographic studies of individual Arabic authors; [3] and by a comprehensive survey of the Latin and vernacular treatises of the later Middle Ages. [4] Meanwhile any study of individual Latin alchemists must be quite provisional, except so far as it discloses unpublished texts or brings to light new channels of transmission and previously unknown relations between experimenters.

Michael Scot, astrologer of the Emperor Frederick II and translator of Aristotle, Averroës, and Avicenna, [5] appears in certain mediaeval manuscripts as the author of works on alchemy. In this there is no intrinsic improbability for a man of Scot's occupation and surroundings, and a brief summary of

[1] Except for the opening and concluding paragraphs, this chapter is reprinted substantially unchanged from *Isis*, x. 350–359 (1928).

[2] *Catalogue des manuscrits alchimiques grecs*, published under the direction of J. Bidez *et al.* (Brussels, 1924–).

[3] See, for example, the note and bibliography concerning Jabir, in George Sarton, *Introduction to the History of Science*, i (Baltimore, 1927), pp. 532–533.

[4] Cf., e. g., Mrs. Dorothea Singer, *Catalogue of Latin and Vernacular Alchemical Manuscripts in Great Britain and Ireland Dating from before the XVI Century*, i (Brussels, 1928), published by the International Union of Academies at the expense of the British Academy.

[5] Cf. J. Wood Brown, *An Enquiry into the Life and Legend of Michael Scot* (Edinburgh, 1897); *Mediaeval Science*, ch. 13.

alchemical doctrine actually occurs in a chapter of one of his authentic works on astrology, written between 1227 and 1235 and thus affording an early example of such material in Latin.[1] This chapter, which sets forth the sulphur-mercury theory of metals and suggests the so-called elixir of life, runs as follows:

Metallum est quedam essentia que dicitur secunde compositionis, cuius species sunt 7, scilicet ferrum, plumbum, stagnum, ramum, cuprum, argentum, et aurum, sciendo quod generantur compositione argenti vivi, sulphuris, et terre. Et secundum unitam materiam eorum quibus componuntur sunt ponderis et coloris. Aurum plus tenet sulphuris quam argenti vivi; argentum tenet plus argenti vivi quam terre et sulphuris; ferrum plus tenet terre quam argenti vivi, etc. Valet quodlibet ad multa ut in compositione sophystica et in aliis virtutibus. Verbi gratia: aurum macinatum valet senibus volentibus vivere sanius et iuniores esse sumptum in cibo, et per eum comparantur multi denarii argenti causa expendendi, fiunt multa monilia, decorantur vasa, et pro eo acquiruntur femine ac multe possessiones. Argentum emit aurum et ex eo multa acquiruntur ut ex auro et fiunt ut denarii, vasa, etc. Stagnum valet ad faciendum vasa et aptandum ferrum laboratum et ramum. Idem dicitur de plumbo ramo etc. Sophysticantur metalla doctrina artis alchimie cum quibusdam additamentis pulverum mediantibus spiritibus quorum species sunt 4, scilicet argentum vivum, sulphur, auripigmentum, et sal ammoniacum. Ex auro cum quibusdam aliis fit plus aurum in apparentia, ex argento et ramo dealbato cum medicina fit plus argentum in apparentia, etc. De argento leviter [fit] azurum. De plumbo leviter fit cerusa. De ramo leviter fit color viridis cum aceto forti et melle. De plumbo et ramo etc. fit aliud metallum. De stagno et ramo fit peltrum cum medicina. Argentum vivum destruit omne metallum ut patet in moneta quam tangit et stagno cuius virgam rumpit tangendo, etc. De plumbo fiunt manubria lime surde quo sonus mortificatur. Argentum vivum interficit edentem et tollit auditum si cadat in aures. Metallorum aqua, ut ferri arsenici vitrioli calcis et videramini, corodit et frangit calibem. Ex vilibus et muracido ferro fit ferrum andanicum, et ecce mirrabile magnum.[2]

With respect to the other alchemical treatises ascribed to Scot, caution is imposed upon us by the various false attributions which appear in Scot's name, as well as by the confusion and uncertainty which still reign respecting the Latin literature

[1] Hampe, in *Festgabe W. Goetz* (Leipzig, 1927), pp. 53–66, proposes the date 1227 for this portion of Scot's *Liber particularis*.

[2] Bodleian Library, MS. Canonici Misc. 555, f. 49 v; Milan, Biblioteca Ambrosiana, MS. L. 92 sup., f. 76 v; Vatican, MS. Rossi ix. 111, f. 41 v. Printed in *Isis*, iv. 271 (1922); *Mediaeval Science*, p. 295, cf. pp. 280, 281.

of alchemy in general. We are still far from having attained a
secure footing in this field. Meanwhile this paper proposes to
describe more adequately a treatise, or pair of treatises, attributed to Scot which are too long for publication here *in extenso*,[1]
and to call attention to the collaboration which they reveal between Italian alchemists and Jewish and Saracen experimenters.

The *Alchemy* ascribed to Michael Scot has reached us in two
manuscripts. One is the well known fourteenth-century collection of alchemical works described by Carini when it was in the
possession of the Speciale family [2] and now MS. 4 Qq. A. 10 of
the Biblioteca Comunale at Palermo. This rich corpus of Latin
alchemy, which also comprises [3] a catalogue of the alchemical
library of seventy-two treatises belonging to a monk of S. Pro-
culo at Bologna, is a mine of unexplored information; its small
format (133 × 94 mm.) indicates that it was meant as a pocket
vade mecum of the art. The other manuscript, of the early fifteenth century, is in MS. 125 of the library of Corpus Christi
College, Oxford.[4] Neither scribe appears to have understood
all that he copied, and the text is in some places hopeless. I
have based the following extracts primarily upon the Palermo
codex (P) as generally more correct, giving the variants of the
Oxford MS. (C) only where they help toward a better reading.
Nevertheless, though offering a poorer text, C appears to stand
in one respect nearer the original in that Michael Scot there
speaks in the first person, while in P he is cited in the third.
The text begins:

Incipit liber magistri Miccaellis Scotti in quo continetur magisterium.
Incipit liber magistri Miccaellis Scotti de arte alchimie secundum quem in
diversis provinciis cum phylosophis huius artis est operatus. Incipit liber
magistri Miccaellis Scotti.[5] (I) Dum animadverterem nobilem scientiam

---

[1] For the *Liber luminis luminum* which Scot is said to have translated, and
a *Questio curiosa* which is clearly not his, see Brown, *op. cit.*, ch. 4, and his
appendix iii.

[2] I. Carini, *Sulle scienze occulte nel medio evo* (Palermo, 1872); description
repeated in G. Di Marzo, *I MSS. della Biblioteca comunale di Palermo* (1878),
iii. 220–243. For many kind offices in securing photographs I am indebted to
my friend, Professor C. A. Garufi. The treatise begins on f. 357.

[3] F. 370 v.   [4] Ff. 97–100 v.

[5] Titles and chapter-headings only in P. The numbering of the chapters is
mine. For a third MS. at Caius College, see the note below, p. 159.

apud Latinos penitus denegatam, vidi neminem ad perfectionem posse pervenire propter nimiam confusionem que in libris philosophorum reperitur, extimavi secreta nature intelligentibus revelare incipiens a maiori magisterio [1] et minori que inveni de transformatione metallorum et de permutatione ipsorum qualiter substantia unius in alteram permutetur. Hoc enim nullis vel paucis erat cognitum. Reperitur autem in libris philosophorum de permutatione et transformatione metallorum, sed [2] in eorum philosophia tanta erat obscuritas et oculi hominum caligine obfuscati et corda eorum velamento ignorantie oppilata quod ars alkimie [3] nullis vel paucis posset [4] revelari. Multi erant operantes ignorantia et obmittebant in operibus eorum et tempus eorum preteribat in obmissione [5] operum. Non potest aliquis sine magistro esse peritus, maxime is qui ignorat illud quod facit, si non est expertus, obmittit in eo. Cum prius enim animadverterem et perquirerem in libris philosophorum ut predictum, volui ipsam obscuritatem meo animo declarare gradiens et perquirens undique et ultramarinis partibus cum viris philosophis et sapientibus latinis iberiis [6] harabicis saracenis armenicis theophilis grecis et undique partibus provinciis et linguis, hiis omnibus perquisitis eorum prophetiam [7] meo corde notavi.

(II) *Item prologus in quo demonstratur secretum philosophorum.* Creator omnium Deus, qui ex nichilo [8] nova condidit universa, ante [9] ipsarum generationem de rerum [10] statu iudicans hoc quidem de universitatis sue tesauro largiri [11] dignatur et singulis distribuit unde omnis creatura eidem exibet obedientiam, ymaginavit [12] priusquam fierent cunta habens eorum notitiam arcano cordis qui suum spiritum cum intellectione [13] infundit habite tandem creature. Hic motus existit ut summentes et venientes [14] scriptorum instructiones huius compositionis industriam quasi quadam compagine sociaret, ut ablata totius alterationis rixa rationale animal positivamque iusticiam [15] nexu equali adinvicem federaret, universos itaque stolidos tamquam sapientes ad probandos facere contigisset quod nos eruditorum prudentium secreta computanda alkimie artem rationandi secreta nature [16] mentis arcano revocans, loca fixa [17] directos gradus ortus occasus permutationes et etiam distillationes et que sunt in eis alterationes admiranda vestigia attendens alchimie statum minus prudentium [18] deprehendendi [19] errores. Hac igitur permutatione ratione cogente compendium hoc certissimum ex hiis omnibus prudens invenit antiquitas. Deinde aput omnes filosoficas permutationes ratum arbitror [20] quicquid in hac arte conditum

---

[1] P, *ministerio.*
[2] Om. P.
[3] *hominum . . . alkimie* om. P.
[4] P, *poterant.*
[5] P, *admissione,* C, *amissione.*
[6] P, *iberniis.* Om. C.
[7] C, *philosophiam.*
[8] P, *ex⁰.* C, *cunta ex nichilo.*
[9] P, *qñ.*
[10] P, *illarium.*
[11] P, *largitu.*
[12] P, *ymaginavi.*
[13] P, *quod qui suspectum eum cum intelliget terre.*
[14] ? C, *ut sumat in hac.*
[15] Om. P.
[16] P, *vere.* C, *natura.*
[17] PC, *fixus.*
[18] P, *prudentem.*
[19] P, *deprehenditur.*
[20] P, *inter arbitrorum.*

subsistendi vicem alkemiarum [1] vel alkemistarum. Est autem difficile exemplar [2] in libris antiquis philosophorum contineri [3] quia [4] artificium alkimie antiquius forte antiquitas refert. Ego vero [5] magister Miccael Scottus interpretationem aggredior et tibi magistro Teophilo gayto Saracenorum tecum Tunixe [6] huius munusculum apporto et secreta nature et verba philosofica que audivi tecum volo alchimiam translatare. Hec est solutio caliditatis et roritatis et balneum aquosum et locus roridus et humidus et vaporosus. Hic est puteus solutionis et fimi acervus, et hic est fons in quo latet anguis cuius venenum omnia corpora interficit, et hoc est secretum omnium secretorum huius scientie, et hec est res quam in libris suis semper occultaverunt phylosophi ne facile possit ab aliquo tantum secretum haberi. Hic enim est [7] tesaurus rei et in hac arte et in re est omne secretum, et hec est res que erigit de stercore pauperem [8] et ipsum regibus equiparat et hec est res per quam pater Tholomeus et Hermes dixerunt [9] se super omnes mundi circulos esse exaltatos.[10] Te ergo, quicumque es, ad quem tantum secretum nature [11] pervenerit, per fedus [12] Dei te rogo et coniuro ne ostendas hoc et si ostenderis non aperias cuiquam in aliquo vel nescio vel stulto aut avaro vel regi vel [13] potenti, ne socies tibi in hoc opere quempiam malum,[14] prius referens gratias [15] Deo qui hoc te habere concessit operare, tum [16] secretissime perveniens ad illud quod amas et desideras cum auxilio Dei et potentia domini nostri Ihesu Christi qui vivit et regnat per omnia secula seculorum.[17]

(III) *Quomodo metalla assimilantur planetis.* Septem sunt planete, scilicet [18] Saturnus Iupiter Mars Sol Venus Mercurius et Luna. Signa planetarum sunt duodecim, scilicet [18] Aries Taurus Gemini Cancer Leo Virgo Libra Scorpio Sagittarius Capricornus Aquarius Pisces.

(IV) *De naturis planetarum et metallorum.* A Sole incipiamus qui est nobilior et dignior omnium planetarum.[19] Sol est calidus et siccus in quarto gradu, id est aurum.[20] Luna est [21] frigida et humida in quarto gradu, id est argentum. Iupiter est [21] frigidus et humidus in tertio [22] gradu, id est stagnum. Venus est [21] frigida et humida in quarto gradu, id est es. Saturnus est [21] frigidus et siccus in quarto gradu.[23] Mars est calidus et siccus in quarto gradu, id est ferrum. Mercurius est calidus et humidus in quarto gradu, id est argentum vivum.[24] Omnia ista sunt

---

[1] Om. P. [2] P, *dissimile ex^{tis}.* [3] P, *continere.*
[4] P, *quia ergo.* C, *et quia,* [5] Om. P.
[6] C, *magno Theophilo regi Saracenorum de Tunucii.* [7] P, *Huius namque.*
[8] P, *paupertatem.* [9] P, *philosophorum Hermes dixit.* [10] P, *exaltatum.*
[11] P, *tanti secreti naturam.* C, *tanta secreta nature pervenerint.*
[12] C, *fidem.* [13] Om. P.
[14] C, *ne facias tibi in hoc opere copiam malorum.* [15] P, *gratiam in.*
[16] P, *cum eo.* [17] P om. *domini ... seculorum.* [18] P om.
[19] C om. *A ... planetarum.* [20] P om. *id est aurum,* and other such.
[21] P om. [22] C, *quarto.* [23] C om. *Saturnus ... gradu.*
[24] P om. *Mars ... vivum.*

firmata et alligata quatuor elementis et inde retinent suam naturam et proprietatem in calido et sicco in calido et humido in frigido et humido in frigido et sicco.[1]

(V) *De maiori magisterio qualiter venus mutatur in solem.* Diximus superius de planetis et signis eorum cuius naturam et proprietatem habent, et in alio libro a nobis translato dissimus de naturis salium quomodo et qualiter in arte alkimie operantur maiori magisterio.[2] Ad presens qualiter venus in solem mutatur et quomodo et qualiter fit artificialiter et que in hac arte sunt necessaria, tibi, Frater Helya, diligenter et subtiliter enarravi. Accipe sanguinem hominis ruffi et sanguinem bubonis ruffi comburentem croceum vitriolum romanum colofoniam calcum bene pistatum allumen naturale vel [3] allumen romanum idem [4] allumen zuccherinum allumen de Castiglio tartarum rubeum markasidam [5] auream allumen de Tunixe quod est rubeum et salsum. Omnia ista pista simul in mortario eneo et subtiliter cribra cum panno subtili vel cum straminea.[6] Postea accipe pulverem istum et inpasta cum urina taxi vel cum succo cucumeris agrestis,[7] et illa urina sit bene cocta cum sale et optime per filtrum distillata et sucus similiter sit distillatus et optime coctus, et cum pulvis inpastatus fuerit ad celestem ignem fac ipsum bene siccare vel ad vehentissimum calorem si non esset estas, et cum siccatus fuerit optime iterum tere ipsum et subtiliter cribra. Postea accipe de pulvere isto et mitte in crucibulo cum venere et statim suffla cum manticello per unam horam et cum liquefactum fuerit prohice superius de urina vel de suco cucumeris ut dictum [8] et iterum abde in fortem ignem per horam maximam prohiciendo in crucibulo de comburente satis [9] et de arsenico rubeo si haberes. Postea extrahe ipsum de crucibulo et si non erit bene coloratum funde iterum [10] cum tuchia et arsenico [11] rubeo et parum de predicto [12] pulvere et tribus salibus que operantur in sole donec erit bene coloratum, et iste sol postea poterit substinere omne iudicium. Si vis scire si est perfectus,[13] pondera ipsum postea [14] funde ipsum fortiter ter vel quater et si tantum erit quantum erat in principio bonus et perfectus erit.

(VI) *De salibus.* Isti sunt sales qui in sole operantur: sal acrum, sal picrum de Poncto,[15] sal nitrum foliatum, sal alkali, sal rubrum,[16] sal nacticum, sal alembrot vel de marrech.[17] Ponas loco unius istorum salium de alumine rubro vel romano.[17] Hoc est documentum magistri Miccaellis Scotti quod ipse super solem fecit et hoc documentum ipse

---

[1] C om. *Omnia . . . sicco.*

[2] C, *Dicto de planetis de maiori magisterio et figuris, habita et notitia de salibus vel salium prout in aliquo libro a me translato dixi quomodo de salibus oportet in arte alkemie operari.*

[3] C om. *colofoniam . . . vel.*	[4] *item?*	[5] P, *martham.*
[6] P, *staminia.*	[7] P, *agresti.*	[8] P om.
[9] C, *pulverizato.*	[10] P, *ipsum.*	[11] P, *arte.*
[12] P om.	[13] P, *erit perfectum.*	[14] P, *prius.*
[15] C, *medium de puncto.*	[16] P, *rubeo.*	[17] P om.

docuit Fratrem Heliam et ego vidi Fratri Helie multis vicibus operari et hoc est experimentum a me probatum; verax inveni.[1]

Then follows (c. VII) a closely similar *Minus magisterium* for turning mercury into silver, ending, in the Oxford manuscript, 'prout Michael predictus probavi et docui Frater Helya,' and in the Palermo text, 'hoc est documentum magistri Miccaelis Scotti in mercurio.' The next chapter (VIII), on transforming copper into silver, is also parallel but bears no indication of authorship. Then comes a *congelatio* which begins (c. IX), 'Hoc est documentum Baesis Saraceni de Maiorica.' Chapter X contains 'Dealbatio eris perfecta secundum Barbanum Saracenum de Alap qui valde fuit sapiens et peritus in hac arte,' a process for turning copper into silver which ends with this note:

Nota quod dealbatio ista est perfecta et ego paucos inveni qui scirent ipsam facere sed ego vidi ipsam facere Fratri Helie et ego multotiens sum expertus et ipsam omnibus modis veracem inveni.

Chapter XI on making silver out of tin begins and ends as follows:

Hoc est documentum Theodori Saraceni de Tunixe [2] qui valde sapiens et peritus fuit in hac arte, operatio stangni ad stridorem perfecte tollendum et ipsum perfecte dealbandum. Accipe sucum jusquiami sucum sorbarum sucum malorum granatorum . . .

Nota quod pulvis iste est tesaurus pretiosus in arte. Ipse laborat perfecte in sole et optime constringit mercurium et ultra modum dealbat erem et defendit ipsum a suis superfluitatibus. Apud Sarzanum vidi ipsum facere a quodam Iudeo qui vocabatur magister Iacobus,[3] et ipse me docuit, et ego multotiens sum expertus hoc experimentum et ipsum veracem inveni. (Injunction of secrecy.)

Chapter XII describes the making of gold out of lead *secundum Modifar*, or (C) *Medibabaz, Saracenum de Africa.*[4] Here the attestation in the Palermo codex is in the name of Master G., but the Corpus manuscript has: 'et ego Michael Scotus multotiens sum expertus et semper veracem inveni.'

---

[1] C, *Et ego magister Michael Scotus sic operatus sum solem et docui te, Frater Elia, operari et tu mihi sepius retulisti te instabiliter multis vicibus operasse.*

[2] C, *Theodosius Sarracenus de Cunusani.*

[3] C, *et ego vidi istam operationem fieri apud Cartanam a magistro Iacobo Iudeo.*

[4] Translated by Brown, p. 93.

Chapters XIII and XIV deal with gums and *tuchie* respectively. Chapter XV on salts runs as follows:

(XV) *De salibus ad hoc magisterium.* Hec est affinatio salium qui in arte alchimie operantur. Accipe alba rotunda et in vase mundo mitte ubi sit aqua et postea pone ad ignem et fac subtus ignem donec sint dure et postea ipsas extrahe et optime munda ipsas album per se et rubeum per se et mitte album in petia subtili vel straminea et super turbidum calorem mitte et fac ita quod turbidus non ascendat et fac subtus postea bonum ignem. Accipe urinam tassi iuvenis et plenam manum [1] salis communis prohice ibi intus et fac ipsum totum liquefieri. Cum liquefactum fuerit totum prohice super alba rotunda et illud quod cadet prohice post in ea.[2] Postea stringe petiam et fac aquam exire [3] de alba substantia et aquam illam serva et cum aqua ista facta poteris affinare sales tuos qui in luna operantur, et de rubea substantia idem facies et poteris cum ista alia aqua quam extracseris de rubea substantia affinare sales qui in sole operantur. *Explicit tractatus magistri Michaelis Scoti de alk.*[4]

Here the treatise ends in the Oxford manuscript, while the Palermo codex goes on in another hand with a similar treatise which it ascribes at the end to Michael Scot, who is also mentioned once in the course of the text.[5] The heading of the first chapter tempts us to identify this with *alio libro a nobis translato . . . de naturis salium* cited above (c. V), but there is relatively little on salts, and the reference is more probably to the *Liber luminis luminum.*[6] The second work, of approximately the same length as the first, begins as follows:

(I) *De salibus qui operantur ad solem.* Maxime in alkimia invenitur ad convertendum venerem in solem, mercurium in lunam,[7] martem in lunam.[7] In permutando ista tria non indiget sublimatione nisi (?) fictio operum. Multi autem solverunt et sublimaverunt et cum difficultate invenerunt, multi autem non solverunt et melius invenerunt. Potest autem quelibet substantia in alteram resolvi, in oleo, aqua, et sale, et per resolutiones. Sublimationes penitus non commendo sed commendo fictiones. Multa corpora vim amittunt [8] et suam naturam; probatum est; experto crede magistro. Possunt enim corpora resolvi in aqua et oleo. Omnes autem sublimationes expertus fui sed parum utilitatis

---

[1] P, *plena manu.*   [2] P om. *post in ea.*
[3] P, *ex ere.*   [4] *Explicit* only in C.
[5] Folios 360–363, where it ends: . . . 'simili vase et dimittatur per totam. *Explicit liber magistri Miccaellis Scotti.*'
[6] Printed in Scot's name in Brown, appendix iii.
[7] MS. *luna.*   [8] MS. *admittunt.*

inveni nisi in lapidibus faciendis et congelandis. Sublimationes que opportune sunt in arte tibi ad intelligentiam enarrabo.

(II) *Capitulum vitri*. Tere et ablue vitrum cum aceto sorbarum et mali granati et aceto rubeo octo vicibus et sicca ad solem. Per activitatem illorum acetorum subtiliantur et depurantur omnes superfluitates partium. Deinde funde in fortissimo crucibulo ferreo et extingue in aqua salis communis et m^a. et ar^a. vii vicibus. Iuro tibi quod in septem vicibus erit calcinatum in calce solis cui non est par per activitatem salium.

The titles of the succeeding chapters are:
(III) Capitulum vitri. (IV) Capitulum vitri quod operatur in solem. (V) Capitulum sublimationis mercurii. (VI) Capitulum sublimationis. (VII) Capitulum distillationis. (VIII) Preparatio vitrioli. (IX) Capitulum olei albi fixi philosofici. (X) De alembrottis. (XI) Capitulum de acetis. (XII) Capitulum lune. (XIII) Capitulum dulcificationis. (XIV) Modus purgandi mercurium. (XV) Capitulum sublimationis. (XVI) Capitulum lune tingende in aurum verum. (XVII) De modo pulverizandi aurum sive calcinandi. (XVIII) Capitulum grossi de croco ferri. (XIX) De modo margassite. (XX) Capitulum congelationis saturni. (XXI) Congelatio mercurii cum herbis.

Hermes is cited in chapters VIII and XII, 'Barrecta Saracenus de Africa' in chapter III. In chapter VI we read:

Ego Balac Saracenus de Regis Cibilia Gauco Pogis acc[epi?] coagulationem tibi Fratri Elie transmisi et ipsam multotiens expertus fui, veracem inveni.

Chapter XX directs:

Pone in fornacem quam habuimus a magistro Iohanne Alexandrino designatam (?) que habet duos muros, unum de intus et alium de foris, sicut ego designavi discipulis magistri Ratoaldi Mediolanensis.

In chapter IX occurs the only reference to Michael Scot:

Nota quod Barac Saracenus et magister Boala de Alap philosophi concordati sunt cum magistro Miccaele Scotto quod terra que invenitur in allumine rubeo valde est bona mutando plumbum in optimum solem et lunam, albedinem perfectam dat eri, et optime constringit mercurium.

Chapter XVIII contains what may be a reference to Scot's studies at Toledo:

Illud estanum postea vidi Tollecti et contulit ista micchi et eadem contulit cuidam consanguineo suo seni et ille senex cum eodem crocio operati sunt Tollecti[1] secundum modum predictum.

[1] MS. *Celletti*. No subject for *contulit* appears in what precedes.

What we have here is not a comprehensive or systematic treatise like those ascribed to 'Geber' [1] or the briefer one of Master Simon of Cologne,[2] nor yet an orderly description of salts and alums like the *Liber luminis luminum*,[3] but rather accounts of particular experiments and processes such as Berthelot has indicated under the name of various Italians of the thirteenth century.[4] Any special study of these processes must be left to those familiar with other contemporary treatises. In general, the materials and methods are reasonably clear. Besides the metals themselves, the authors use earths, alums, glass, fruit acids and vegetable juices, gums, and *tuchie*. They are acquainted with solution, fusion, filtration, sublimation, distillation with the alembic, and calcination. The first treatise makes no use of weights and measures, the second frequently mentions specific quantities, usually pounds.

Besides illustrating the processes of alchemy in the thirteenth century, these two treatises may throw some light on its sources. They give us neither the translation of formal Arabic works nor the independent experiments of Latins working by themselves in the West. On the contrary the Latins are apparently in close contact with Jewish and Saracen experimenters. They watch Master Jacob the Jew at Sarzana; they cite specific experiments, or *documenta*, of Saracens of Africa, Tunis, Majorca, and Aleppo; they note the agreement of Barac and Boala with Michael Scot. Scot has been at Toledo, and if we can trust the preface, he dedicates his *Alchemy* to a Saracen official of Tunis, and has been in contact with alchemists of other lands. All this points to an amount of co-operation and interchange which has not heretofore been noted in the field of alchemy but which can easily be paralleled in other sciences in the same period. One need only recall the Jewish and Mohammedan scholars at the

[1] E. Darmstädter, *Die Alchemie des Geber* (Berlin, 1922; cf. *Isis*, v. 451–455); id., 'Liber Misericordiae Geber,' in *Archiv zur Geschichte der Medizin*, xviii. 181–197 (1925). Cf. p. 148, note 3, *supra*.

[2] Ed. Sudhoff, in *Archiv für die Geschichte der Naturwissenschaften*, ix. 54–67 (1922).

[3] Brown, app. iii. See now the important *De aluminibus et salibus* of Rasis, of which the Latin text is edited by R. Steele in *Isis*, xii. 10–46 (1929).

[4] *La chimie au moyen âge*, i. 75–78.

court of Frederick II and that emperor's correspondence and questionnaires addressed to the courts of Mohammedan rulers, including Tunis.[1]

With this milieu and these connexions the attribution to Frederick's astrologer Michael Scot offers no inconsistency. Furthermore, we know that Scot was familiar with the principles and practices of alchemy; that he had an experimental habit of mind; and that the form "ego Michael Scottus" appears in his authentic writings.[2] Comparison with his other works is inconclusive, since the *Alchemy* is unsystematic in form and has in any case been reshaped by another hand. Moreover, many false ascriptions gathered about Scot's name and reputation as a wizard, and his contemporary Friar Elias of Cortona, who also appears in the experiments noted above, became the centre of a suspicious alchemical literature;[3] so that it may be well to suspend our judgement as to the author until the discovery of further evidence. More important than the matter of individual authorship are the indications of collaboration with Jewish and Saracen experimenters in the West.

It should be added that Scot's relations with learned Jews and Mohammedans were not confined to Italy or the court of Frederick II. His acquaintance with Hebrew and Arabic is attested by Pope Gregory IX,[4] as well as by his translations from the Arabic, so far as these were his own. The aid of a certain Abuteus the Levite at Toledo in 1217 is acknowledged in the colophon of Scot's version of al-Bitrogi *On the Sphere*,[5]

---

[1] *Mediaeval Science*, chs. 12, 14, especially pp. 252–254, 290.

[2] *Mediaeval Science*, p. 272.

[3] Lempp, *Frère Elie de Cortone* (Paris, 1901); Golubovich, *Biblioteca bio-bibliografica della Terra Santa* (Quaracchi, 1906), i. 116–117, 223–224; and for relations with Frederick II, A. Haseloff, *Die Bauten der Hohenstaufen in Unteritalien* (Leipzig, 1920), i. 34–37. Of the alchemical works ascribed to Friar Elias two are in MS. 104 of the University of Bologna: f. 138 v, 'Liber Fratris Helye de Asisio Ordinis P. Minorum de secretis nature incipit feliciter. Amicum induit qui iustis amicorum petitionibus condescendit . . .' (de lapide). F. 241 v, 'Incipit magisterium Fratris Helye Ordinis Minorum de elixiris ad album et rubeum. Cum de infrascriptis aquis, distillationibus, et dissolutionibus cum igne et sine igne . . .'

[4] Auvray, *Registres de Grégoire IX*, no. 61; cf. *Mediaeval Science*, ch. 13.

[5] *Mediaeval Science*, pp. 273–274.

while Roger Bacon asserts that a Jew named Andrew (possibly the same as Abuteus) performed the greater part of the labour of Scot's translations.[1] This Andrew may plausibly be identified with a Master Andrew, formerly a Jew and now canon of Palencia, whom Pope Honorius III praises for his eminent learning, not only in the seven liberal arts but also in the Hebrew, Chaldee, Arabic, and Latin tongues. The bull, which was granted 15 April, 1225, while Scot was presumably at Rome and in any case high in papal favour, runs as follows:

Magistro Andree canonico Palentino. Ad persone tue dilectionem inducimur et ad exhibendum tibi specialem favorem et gratiam inclinamur. Accepimus enim et venerabilis frater noster Palentinus episcopus exposuit coram nobis quod veterem hominem, cum Iudeus fueris, penitus exuisti et, novo perfectius per misericordiam Salvatoris indutus, dimisso iudaice cecitatis errore, conversus ad Ihesum Christum lumen verum sacri unda baptismatis es renatus. Eminenti etiam diceris preditus esse scientia et per hoc, cum in sortem Domini sis assumptus, accessisse ad decorem ecclesie, que consuevit litteratis clericis venustari; septem namque, ut intelliximus, es liberalibus artibus eruditis, plenam habens intelligentiam diversorum idiomatum, ebraici et chaldei, arabici et latini. Verum tumorem habes quendam in gutture cuius occasione, siquando ad locum vel beneficium vocaris alicuius ecclesie, quidam te repellere moliuntur. Cum autem bonum tibi perhibeatur testimonium de conversatione laudabili et honesta, nos eiusdem episcopi supplicationibus incli[nati], devotioni tue de speciali gratia indulgemus ut, occasione huiusmodi non obstante, ad beneficia et dignitates ecclesiasticas, preterquam ad episcopatum, libere valeas, si canonice tibi offerantur, assumi. Nulli ergo nostre conces[sionis] etc. Siquis etc. Datum Laterani xvii. kal. Maii anno nono.[2]

[1] *Compendium studii*, ed. Brewer, p. 472; cf. *Opus tertium*, ed. Brewer, p. 91.
[2] Vatican Archives, registers of Honorius III, an. 9, f. 48 v, ep. 267; analysed in Pressutti, *Regesta Honorii Papae III*, no. 5445, to which my attention was called by Dr. Josiah C. Russell. Cf. my paper on "Michael Scot in Spain," in *Homenaje á Bonilla y San Martín* (Madrid, 1927–29); and *Mediaeval Science*, p. xv.

NOTE.—After this chapter was in type, I learned, through the kindness of Mrs. Dorothea Waley Singer, of a third copy of Scot's *Alchemy* at Gonville and Caius College, Cambridge, MS. 181, pp. 19–32 (saec. xiii). The MS. is anonymous in Dr. James's *Catalogue*, but mentions Michael Scot in the body of the treatise, so that the ascription to him is now carried back to the thirteenth century. The text confirms, in general, the other two MSS., but contains additional material of interest. A description by Mrs. Singer may be expected in a forthcoming number of *Isis*.

CHAPTER VIII

CONTACTS WITH BYZANTIUM

To the historian of Western culture in the Middle Ages, the Greek East is a subject of ever increasing importance. Long considered an alien and effete civilization, Byzantium has now come to be regarded as a great reservoir of material from which the less civilized West continued to draw throughout the mediaeval period. The channels of communication between East and West, however, often ran beneath the surface, and many of the contacts were occasional or accidental, so that the process of transmission often eludes us. Again and again our only evidence is a fine piece of craftsmanship, an obviously Byzantine type in art, a sacred relic from Constantinople, or a Latin translation of Greek hagiography or science, with no indication of how these came westward. Under such conditions the story of Byzantine influence must be built up by the slow accumulation of individual detail. The texts which are printed below illustrate the process in three of its more significant aspects, namely the search for relics on the part of pilgrims, the theological disputes between the two churches, and the translation of Greek hagiology and pseudo-science.[1]

A Canterbury Monk at Constantinople, c. 1090 [2]

The following account of a visit to Jerusalem and Constantinople is found on the last folio of a Rochester lectionary now in the library of the Vatican,[3] where the text breaks off abruptly at the foot of the page. The mention of Lanfranc's death fixes the date not long after May 1089. The pilgrim Joseph who is the subject of the narrative seems to have been a person of some importance at Christ Church:[4] a monk of this name appears

---

[1] For further discussion of the translators from the Greek, see my *Mediaeval Science*, chs. 8–11.   [2] Reprinted from *E. H. R.*, xxv. 293–295 (1910).

[3] MS. Vat. Lat. 4951, f. 220 recto, the verso being blank. The MS. is of the twelfth century; see Ehrensberger, *Libri Liturgici Bibliothecae Apostolicae Vaticanae Manu Scripti* (Freiburg, 1897), p. 150.

[4] He is not mentioned in W. G. Searle's *Lists of the Deans, Priors, and Monks of Christ Church, Canterbury* (Cambridge Antiquarian Society, 1902).

next after the prior and before Eadmer in a charter of Anselm for Rochester cathedral, and next after the archdeacons and likewise before Eadmer in a charter of Archbishop Ralph for the same church,[1] so that he was alive as late as 1114. Probably he is the Joseph whose obit is entered under 27 March in the Christ Church necrologies.[2] The journey to Jerusalem was undertaken with a considerable company, and, if we may infer anything from the silence of the narrative, met with no special difficulties. The friends whom our monk found at Constantinople in the emperor's household were doubtless among those English Varangians who entered the imperial guard after the Norman Conquest and were placed by Alexius in charge of the palace and its treasury.[3] The relics of St. Andrew, brought from Achaia in the fourth century, are frequently mentioned in the descriptions of mediaeval Constantinople,[4] as well as in the notices of the transfer of portions of them to Rome under

---

[1] Hearne, *Textus Roffensis*, p. 154, no. 93, p. 155, no. 94; *Monasticon*, i. 168. In both cases the abbreviation which follows Eadmer's name in the MS. should doubtless be resolved 'monachis.'

[2] Cotton MS. Nero C. IX., f. 8 v, printed in Dart, *Cathedral Church of Canterbury*, app., p. xxxv; Lambeth Palace, MS. 20, f. 175 v. Joseph heads the list of monks whose anniversary falls on this day, whereas the other Josephs in the necrologies (Dart, p. xxxvii; Lambeth MS., ff. 195, 196 v, 217) come in each case well down the lists, and hence probably belong to a later age. It is perhaps worth noting that a copy of Isidore of Seville in the British Museum (Royal MS. 5. E. I) was marked by the Rochester librarian 'De claustro Roffensi per Ioseph monachum.'

[3] 'Anglos igitur qui perempto Heraldo rege cum proceribus regni Albionem reliquerant et a facie Willelmi regis per Pontum in Thraciam navigaverant, Alexius in amicitiam sibi ascivit eisque principale palatium regiosque thesauros palam commendavit, quin etiam eos capitis sui rerumque suarum custodes posuit:' Ordericus, iii. 169; cf. p. 490, and ii. 172. On the English Varangians see Freeman, *Norman Conquest*, iv. 628–632; and especially Vasilievsky, in the *Journal of the Russian Ministry of Public Instruction*, clxxviii. 133–152 (1875). A passage from Gocelin's *Miracula S. Augustini Cantuariensis* does not seem to have been noted in this connexion: 'Primo ex Normannis regnatore Anglie Willelmo Angliam captante, vir honorificus de curia et nutritura B. Augustini cum multis optimatibus patrie profugis Constantinopolim transmigravit, tantamque gratiam apud imperatorem et imperatricem ceterosque potentes obtinuit ut super sapientes milites multamque partem sociorum ducatum acciperet, nec quisquam advenarum ante plurimos annos tali honore profecerit,' *Acta Sanctorum*, May, vi. 410.

[4] Riant, *Exuviae sacrae Constantinopolitanae*, ii. 211 ff. Two of these accounts are from English sources.

Pelagius II, to Scotland in the eighth century, and to Amalfi after the Fourth Crusade.[1] The cathedral for which Joseph desired the relics was of course Rochester, where Benedictine monks had recently been introduced by Bishop Gundulf, and the presence of the account in a Rochester service-book would imply that he was successful; but while there is evidence of the existence of relics of St. Andrew at Canterbury,[2] I can find no trace of them in Rochester records.[3] Perhaps the conclusion of the text can be supplied from another manuscript.

[T]empore quo Rex Willelmus iunior genti Anglorum preerat et ecclesia Christi Cantuarie morte Lanfranci archiepiscopi desolata fuerat, monachus quidam nomine Ioseph ex eadem ecclesia fuit qui gratia orationum Ierosolimam adiit. Cumque suum ibi desiderium complesset rectoque itinere cum magna sociorum multitudine rediret, rectum iter sociosque deseruit et cum suis tantum quibusdam famulis Constantino-polim secessit. Audierat enim ibi esse thesaurum reliquiarum incom-parabilem quarum patrociniis cupiebat se commendare presentem. Cum ergo illuc Deo ducente advenisset et quo in loco thesaurus ille haberetur perquireret, quosdam ibi viros de patria sua suosque amicos repperit qui erant ex familia imperatoris. Hos itaque cum statim recognovisset gaudensque allocutus fuisset, didicit reliquias illas esse in imperatoris capella et quia difficile quisquam illuc ingredi poterat. Imperator enim studiose volens custodire margaritas illas incomparabiles plures illic deputaverat custodes unumque precipue qui ceteris in custodia preesset. At tamen quia predicti monachi amici noti erant ipsi custodi et amici, factum est ut eorum interventu idem custos monachum in capellam introduceret eique maximam reliquiarum partem demonstraret. Cum-que has atque illas sibi ostenderet reliquias illeque monachus suppliciter adoraret singulas, contigit ut inter alias ei ostenderet quedam beati Andree apostoli ossa. Cum autem has esse reliquias illius apostoli di-ceret dicendo affirmaret, monachus, quia semper apostolum dilexerat carius, eius reliquias multo adoravit devotius. Mox etenim ut eas aspe-xit, terre se devotissime prostravit et inter alia hoc quoque oravit: "Placuisset," inquit, "omnipotenti Deo ut has reliquias nunc tenerem quo in loco eas habere desidero." Quod cum custos ille audisset sed, quia Grecus erat, minime intellexisset, quesivit ab uno ex amicis monachi, qui eorum interpres erat, quid esset quod monachus ille dixerat. Inter-

[1] For references to these translations, see the Bollandist *Bibliographia hagiographica Latina*, i. 72 f.

[2] Legg and Hope, *Inventories of Christ Church* (1902), pp. 37, 74, 81, 93.

[3] We should expect to find them mentioned in the biography of Bishop Gundulf, who was in great demand on the occasion of translations (*Anglia sacra*, ii. 285).

pres vero, quia votum huiusmodi non audebat manifestare custodi, prius a monacho requisivit an vellet ut hoc indicaret illi, cumque ab eo licentiam accepisset dicendi, tum demum ipsi patefecit custodi quia sic et sic monachus ille optaverit. Ille vero hec audiens monacho per eundem interpretem respondit: "Quid," inquit, "mercedis illi reconpensare velles qui ex eo quod optasti desiderium tuum compleret?" Et ille: "Parum," ait, "pecunie mihi de via remansit multumque vie restat adhuc peragendum mihi. Siquis tamen ex eo quod opto meam compleret voluntatem, ex eadem pecunia tantum sibi darem quanto carere tolerabiliter possem. Ipsas vero reliquias illum deportarem in locum ubi eis celeberrimum persolveretur obsequium. Est enim in patria mea sedes quedam episcopalis in qua fundata est ecclesia quedam in honorem beati Andree apostoli ubi noviter adunata monachorum congregatio Deo devotissime deservit. Ad hanc ergo ecclesiam, si Deus meam dignaretur adimplere voluntatem, aliquas ex apostoli reliquiis deportare cuperem." Tum custos, "Vade," inquit, "et ad hospicium tuum revertere, huncque nostrum interpretem et amicum tuum mihi remitte et per eum tuam mihi voluntatem remandans innotesce. Non enim expedit nobis ut ipse huc revertaris, ne de huiuscemodi negotio ani[madvertat?]."

CHRYSOLANUS OF MILAN [1]

The theological disputations of the twelfth century are sometimes the occasion of our most definite records of Graeco-Latin relations, indeed the reports of such discussion are often our only evidence of the presence of Western scholars at Constantinople. Thus in 1112, apparently on his return from the Holy Land, we find the archbishop of Milan, Peter Chrysolanus, or Grossolanus, disputing concerning the procession of the Holy Spirit with Eustratius of Nicaea and others before the Emperor Alexius, as recorded in various Greek texts and in the Latin *libellus*.[2] The Greek text of the address to the emperor,

[1] See my *Mediaeval Science*, pp. xiii, 195–197; and *Byzantion*, ii. 234–236 (1926).

[2] For the speeches of Eustratius and John Phurnes, see A. K. Demetracopoulos, *Bibliotheca ecclesiastica* (Leipzig, 1866), i. 36 ff. (cf. J. Dräseke, in *Byzantinische Zeitschrift*, v. 328–331 (1896)). Cf. F. Chalandon, *Les Comnène*, i (Paris, 1900), p. 263, note; K. Krumbacher, *Geschichte der byzantinischen Litteratur*, 2d ed. (Munich, 1897), p. 85; G. Tiraboschi, *Storia della letteratura italiana* (1787), iii. 324–327; J. Hergenröther, *Photius* (Regensburg, 1867–69), iii. 799–803; H. Hurter, *Nomenclator theologiae catholicae*, ii (1906), cols. 12 f. Recent writers on Chrysolanus, or Grossolanus, have nothing new on this debate: F. Savio, *Gli antichi vescovi d'Italia*, i (Florence, 1913), pp. 461–472; O. Masnovo, in *Archivio storico lombardo*, xlix. 1–28 (1922).

A sermon of Chrysolanus is preserved in the Biblioteca Nazionale at Florence,

found by Baronius (*ad an.* 1116, no. 7, with Latin version) in the Vallicelliana, and published with the same modern Latin version by Allatius (*Graecia orthodoxa,* i. 379–389) and Migne (*Patrologia Graeca,* cxxvii. 911–920=*P. L.*, clxii. 1005–16), is only a fragment containing the early part of the *libellus.* For the latter and longer portion there is an incomplete mediaeval Latin version at Monte Cassino, MS. 220, f. 149, printed in *Bibliotheca Cassinensis,* iv, florilegium, pp. 351–358. These two passages, it appears, supplement each other, and between them furnish the full text, save for an intervening passage of nineteen lines, as we see from the complete Latin text which is preserved in a manuscript of *ca.*`1200 in the University and Public Library of Prague, MS. 233, ff. 50–53 v.[1] Here the version begins and ends:

> Munere collatum divino pontificatum
> In Mediolano constat quondam Glosulano.
> Hic fidei clarę cupiens Grecos revocare
> Ad rectam formam scriptisque piis dare normam
> Orthodoxorum directo calle virorum,
> Numine de Trino quę sint credenda vel Uno
> Hunc per sermonem monstravit eis rationem,
> Quam qui sectatur bene credulus esse probatur.

Audi et intellige que ego Deo inspirante loquor ad te, sapiens et patiens potens et humilis imperator Alexi . . . Vale, bone imperator. Sit tibi pax et prosperitas. Concedat Flamen Sanctum quod poscimus. Amen.

The translation, after the manner of the twelfth century, is so literal that the Greek text can easily be recovered. The portion of the text which has not yet been printed in one form or the other reads in the Prague MS.:

[nisi alia fortasse dicatur] (f. 50 v). Ego certe agentis nullam adhuc huic similem rationem audivi, quamvis improprie ratio dicatur per quam nihil esse rectum [2] monstratur. Verum tamen de eadem nuper causa

---

MS. Conv. soppr. C. I. 2672, ff. 79–80 (saec. xv): 'Sermo sapientissimi Grosolani Mediolanensis episcopi [*sic*] de capitulo monachorum. Locus iste in quo vos . . .'

[1] Also at Florence, Conventi soppressi, I. IV. 21 (San Marco), ff. 95 v–101 v, without verses and incomplete at the end, followed (f. 99 v) by the reply of a Greek. Argelati, *Bibliotheca scriptorum Mediolanensium* (1745), i, 2, p. 712, cites a MS. then at San Salvatore in Bologna.

[2] The Florence MS. here has *ratum esse.*

loquebar cum quodam sapiente Greco, et audivi aliud ab illo et ego [1] aliud respondi illi. Volo itaque hic ponere illius opinionem et meam respon- (f. 51) sionem, ut bonus imperator bene possit discernere et quid de supradictis debeat iudicare. Grecus dicit: Si Spiritus ita procedit a Filio sicut procedit a Patre, ergo duo sunt principia Pater et Filius, et si duo sunt principia incidimus in heresim illorum qui dicebant unum principium esse ęternalium et alterum principium esse temporalium. Ad hęc ego respondi: Sancta et catholica ęcclesia dicit Spiritum procedere a Filio sicut a Patre, et dicit Patrem esse principium et Filium esse principium et [2] Spiritum Sanctum esse principium, nec tamen dicit esse tria vel duo principia sed unum principium, sicut ipsa dicit Patrem Deum et Filium Deum et Spiritum Sanctum Deum nec tamen dicit tres Deos vel duos Deos sed unum Deum. Si autem vis dicere Patrem esse principium Filii et Spiritus Sancti, consentio quidem, verum tamen aliter non intelligo [ipsum esse principium Filii et Spiritus Sancti nisi quia ipse genuit Filium et ab ipso procedit Spiritus . . .].

PASCHAL THE ROMAN [3]

One of the most curious figures among the Italians at Constantinople in the twelfth century is a certain Paschal the Roman. Unmentioned, so far as I am aware, in the narrative and documentary sources of the period, he can be traced by his own prefaces at the Byzantine capital at various times between 1158 and 1169. These tell us nothing of the occasion which originally took him to Constantinople, nor do they reveal his Western antecedents and associates except for the mention of Henry Dandolo, patriarch of Grado *ca.* 1130–86, who is known to have been in the East and who held a friendly theological dispute with Theorianus.[4] To Dandolo Paschal dedicated in 1158, or possibly in 1163, his translation, which has reached us in at least twelve manuscripts,[5] of a dialogue between a Jew

---

[1] Om. Florence.   [2] Om. Florence *Filium . . . et.*

[3] Based upon *Mediaeval Science*, pp. xiii, xiv, 218–221; and *Byzantion*, ii. 231–234 (1926).

[4] F. Ughelli, *Italia sacra*, v. 1192–1206; P. F. Kehr, *Italia pontificia*, vii, 2 (1925), pp. 61–70, nos. 113–141; Migne, *Patrologia Graeca*, xciv. 404–409.

[5] Vatican, MS. Vat. lat. 4265, ff. 197–199 (end of the fourteenth century); MS. 4847, ff. 207–208 (saec. xv); MS. 10068, ff. 151–154 (*Codices*, descr. M. Vattasso and E. Carusi, iv. 453); Vienna, MS. 590, ff. 172 v–176 (saec. xiv); MS. 4406, ff. 233–235 v (saec. xv); Munich, Cod. Lat. 5896, ff. 146–148 v (saec. xiv); Cod. Lat. 7547, ff. 48–51 v (saec. xv); Cod. Lat. 8184, ff. 122–132 v (*ca.* 1400); Cod. Lat. 15133, f. 192 (extract); Cod. Lat. 15956, ff. 116 v–118 v (saec. xv); Erfurt, MS. Q. 124, ff. 135–138 v (saec. xiv; see W. Schum, *Ver-*

and a Christian ascribed to Anastasius of Sinai. The title reads
as follows in the Vienna MS. 590, where the date is 1158:

Pascalis de Roma hoc opusculum [1] disputacionis Iudeorum contra
Sanctum Anastasium abbatem ad honorem venerabilis patriarche Gra-
densis Hainrici Deadoli [2] fideliter ac devote transtulit. Anno Domini
M⁰. c⁰. lviii⁰.[3]

The text proper begins and ends as follows:

Interrogavit Iudeus: Cum Deus precepit ligna non esse adoranda,
quare vos Christiani ea colitis vel adoratis facientes ex illis cruces et
ymagines? Christianus dixit: Dic mihi et tu quare adoratis librum legis
cum de pellibus immundis paratus sit . . . Christum verum Deum et
hominem confitentes cui gloria et imperium simul est cum Patre et
Spiritu Sancto in secula seculorum. Amen.

The treatise consists of a set of extracts, in different order,
from the *Disputatio* published by Mai [4] and reprinted by Migne.[5]
Krumbacher [6] argues that the *Disputatio* cannot be the work of
Anastasius of Sinai, as it says that more than eight hundred
years have elapsed since the destruction of Jerusalem. On this
point we need further manuscript evidence, for the copyists of
the Latin translations seem to have sought to bring this statement down to date, and the Greek scribe may have made a
similar emendation. Thus in three of the Latin manuscripts
we have 1281 years,[7] in another 1283,[8] in three others "per
MCCC et ultra annos." [9]

zeichniss, p. 383); MS. Q. 151, ff. 238 v–244 v (Schum, p. 416). Formerly at the
Escorial (G. Antolín, *Catálogo*, v. 183), and at Basel (B. de Montfaucon,
Bibliotheca nova, col. 608 d), where the Librarian, Dr. G. Binz, informs me it
has disappeared from the MS. (B. III. 1).

[1] MS. *opus secundum*. The correct reading is in most of the other MSS.

[2] The patriarch's name occurs thus also in Munich, Cod. Lat. 5896, and
Vienna, MS. 4406, and in corrupt form in Erfurt, MS. Q. 151; the other MSS.
omit it.

[3] So also Munich, Codd. Lat. 7547, 8184. MSS. Vat. lat. 4265 and Erfurt Q.
124 have 'M⁰.c⁰.lxiii⁰.' MS. Vat. lat. 4847: 'm⁰.c⁰.xl⁰ iii⁰.' MSS. Vienna 4406,
Vat. lat. 10068, and Erfurt, Q. 151: 'm⁰ cc⁰ quinquagesimo octavo.' Munich,
Cod. Lat. 15956: 'm⁰.ccc. 28'; Cod. Lat. 5896: '1240ᵗᵒ.'

[4] *Scriptorum veterum collectio*, vii. 207.

[5] *Patrologia Graeca*, lxxxix. 1203–72.   [6] *Geschichte*, 2d ed., pp. 64 f.

[7] Vienna, MS. 590, f. 175; MS. 4406, f. 235 v; Munich, Cod. Lat. 15956,
f. 118.   [8] Munich, Cod. Lat. 5896, f. 148.

[9] Munich, Codd. Lat. 7547, f. 50 v; 8184, f. 129 v; MS. Vat. lat. 4265,
f. 198 v.

With this clue in our hands, we shall have no difficulty in recognizing a further bit of Paschal's work in MS. 227 of Balliol College, Oxford, where as P. de Roma he addresses to the same patriarch a version of the life of the Virgin by Epiphanius.[1] The preface reads:

Incipit prologus in ystoria Beate Virginis Marie. Domino H. Dei gratia Dandolo patriarche dignissimo de Grado P. de Roma. Ex diuturna conversatione, carissime pater et domine, in omnibus liberalibus artibus vos optime studuisse, maxime etiam circa divinam scripturam curam[2] habere percognovi. Nunc, etsi parum in greco studuerim, tamen, ne latentem vitam silentio subducam, honore sancte Dei Romane ecclesie et vestro Christi Genitricis vitam et educationem, sicut a Beato Epiphanio archiepiscopo Cypri descriptam inveni, vobis fideliter transtuli. Quod si in aliquo forte a quibusdam scriptoribus discordat, quoniam non omnia exemplaria in manus omnium incidunt, non est meum tanto viro commendare vel exprobrare sed vestro [et] sancte Romane ecclesie iuditio illam relinquo. Sufficiat itaque mihi in uno verbo dumtaxat vestre sapientie posse placere.

A third and more important translation, of which Paschal the Roman can almost certainly be identified as the author, is the Latin version, made in 1169, of the curious Greek book known as Kiranides.[3] This strange compend of ancient lore respecting the virtues of animals, stones, and plants is well known in the Greek, from which it has been edited and translated by Mély and Ruelle, but the Latin version has not been specially studied. At least six Latin manuscripts are known, all with the same preface, dated 1169, addressed by Pa. to a certain Master Ka. In one of the manuscripts, namely Palatine

---

[1] Ff. 146 v–151 v (saec. xiii): 'De domina nostra Dei genitrice semperque virgine Maria multifarii precesserunt olim doctores . . . cui est honor et gloria in secula seculorum amen. Explicit ystoria gloriose semper virginis Marie.' For the Greek text see Migne, *Patrologia Graeca*, cxx. 185–216; for the author, Dräseke, in *Byzantinische Zeitschrift*, iv. 346–362.

[2] MS. *concuram*.

[3] F. de Mély, *Les lapidaires de l'antiquité et du moyen âge*, ii, iii (Paris, 1898–1902). For discussions of these confused texts, see P. Tannery, in *Revue des études grecques*, xvii. 335–349; F. Cumont, in *Bulletin de la Société des Antiquaires de France*, 1919, pp. 175–181; R. Ganszyniec, in *Byzantinisch-Neugriechische Jahrbücher*, i. 353–367, ii. 56–65, 445–452 (1920–21); idem, "Kyraniden," in Pauly-Wissowa, *Real-Encyclopädie*, xxiii. 127–134 (1924); Thorndike, *History of Magic and Experimental Science*, ii, ch. 46; *Catalogue des manuscrits alchimiques grecs*, i. 135–225; iii. 23–26; v. 73–94.

MS. 1273 of the Vatican, the monogram PASGALIS stands at the head.[1]

The translator of Kiranides knows of other works in Greek on the magical virtues of herbs and planets, which he even places before Kiranides itself. Latin versions of these appear in several manuscripts,[2] sometimes along with Kiranides,[3] but with no indication of the translator, who was perhaps also Paschal the Roman.

Meanwhile, in 1165, Paschal the Roman took advantage of his sojourn amid the occult lore of Constantinople to compile a work of his own on dreams under the title *Liber thesauri occulti*. The preface, which vaunts the superiority of the science of dreams over astrology, begins and ends thus: [4]

> *Incipit liber thesauri occulti a Pascale Romano editus*
> *Constantinopolis anno mundi .vi.dc.lxxiiii. anno*
> *Christi .m. c. lxv.*

Tesaurus occultus requiescit in corde sapientis et ideo desiderabilis, set in thesauro occulto et in sapiencia abscondita nulla pene utilitas, ergo revelanda sunt abscondita et patefacienda que sunt occulta. Quare de plurimis ignotis et occultis unius tantummodo elegi tegumentum aptamque revelacionem describere, videlicet sompnii secundum genus et species eius quo res profunda et fere inscrutabilis ad summum patenti ordine distinguatur. Eius namque doctrina philosophis et doctis viris valde necessaria est, ne forte cum exquisiti fuerint muti vel fallaces inveniantur. Nam omnis homo, ut ait Aristoteles in libro De naturis animalium,[5] a quatuor annis et supra sompnium conspicit atque ad contemplacionem mentis excitatur, et in sompno quidem fit sompnium

---

[1] The preface in full is printed in my *Mediaeval Science*, pp. 219–220, with an enumeration of five of the manuscripts and a mention of a fragment at Wolfenbüttel. Since then I have discovered a sixth at Florence, in the Laurentian Library, MS. Ashburnham 1520 (1443), f. 1 (saec. xiv), with the date 1169.

[2] Thorndike, ii. 233 f., who does not mention the edition of the seven herbs in K. N. Sathas, *Documents inédits relatifs à l'histoire de la Grèce au moyen âge*, vii, pp. lxiii–lxvii (from St. Mark's, Cod. gr. iv. 57, suppl.). See H. Haupt, in *Philologus*, xlviii. 371–374; Cumont, in *Revue de philologie*, 1918, pp. 85–108.

[3] E. g., Montpellier, MS. 277.

[4] Bodleian Library, MS. Digby 103, ff. 41–58 v; B.M., Harleian MS. 4025, f. 1 (first book only); Vatican, MS. Vat. lat. 4436, f. 1 (undated); B.N., MS. lat. 16610, ff. 2–24, anonymous, whence the contents have been analysed by Thorndike, *History of Magic and Experimental Science*, ii. 297–300. Part of the preface will be found in my *Mediaeval Science*, p. 218.

[5] *De animalibus*, iv. 10 (537 b), if indeed this be a direct citation.

et sompnus nichil est aliud quam quies et hebetacio animalium virtutum cum intensione naturalium (f. 41) . . . (f. 43) Collectus autem est liber iste ex divina et humana scriptura tam ex usu experimenti quam ex ratione rei de Latinis et Grecis et Caldaicis et Persis et Pharaonis et Nabugodonosor annalibus in quibus multipharie sompnia eorum sunt exposita. Fuerunt enim Pharao et Nabugodonosor amatores futurorum et quia prophetas non habebant velud gentiles dedit eis Deus per tegumentum sompnii futura conspicere. Nam in sompniis vita et mors, paupertas et divicie, infirmitas et sanitas, tristicia et gaudium, fuga et victoria levius quam in astronomia cognoscuntur, quia perceptio astronomie multiplicior est ac difficilior. Preterea sompniorum usus et cognicio maxime oraculorum vehemens ac aperta demonstracio est, contra eos qui dubitant de angelis et de animabus sanctis utrum sint vel non. Si enim non essent, quomodo eorum oracula vera essent? Nam quecunque anima sancta vel angelus aliquid in sompnio dixerit, absque omni interpretacione et scrupulo ita fiet ut predixit angelus vel anima. Non itaque longitudo prohemii nos amplius protrahat nec responsio aliqua impediat, set omni cura seposita succincte ad thesaurum desiderabilem aperiendum properemus.

Sompnium itaque est figura quam ymaginatur dormiens . . .

The introduction and body of the treatise give a curious jumble of Western and Eastern sources: the dreams mentioned in the Bible, the *Somnium Scipionis* of Macrobius, 'Cato noster,' Aristotle *On Animals*, Hippocrates, the *Viaticum* and *Passionarius* (probably the works respectively of Constantine the African and Gariopontus), and less definite Oriental sources, including perhaps the *Dream-book* of Achmet,[1] of which Leo Tuscus made a Latin version in 1176. None of this appears to have required a knowledge of Arabic writers, but much of the Greek material, including Aristotle *On Animals*,[2] was not yet accessible in the West, and the whole subject of dreams was as yet more fully developed in the Orient.[3]

It is quite possible that our list of Paschal's literary undertakings is far from complete, and that other discoveries may be made as the result of further exploration of manuscripts.

---

[1] *Mediaeval Science*, pp. 216–218. The treatise has now been edited by F. X. Drexl (Leipzig, 1925); cf. *Byzantinische Zeitschrift*, xxvii. 113–116, 171 (1927).

[2] First translated by Michael Scot from the Arabic shortly before 1220. *Mediaeval Science*, pp. 277 ff. I know of no other Latin citation of the *De animalibus* of so early a date.

[3] Cf. Thorndike, ch. 50, and *Byzantinische Zeitschrift*, xxvii. 113 (1927).

CHAPTER IX

THE EARLY *ARTES DICTANDI* IN ITALY

In the twelfth and thirteenth centuries the art of writing letters occupied a large place in the intellectual life of Western Europe. Maintained in the earlier Middle Ages chiefly as an adjunct to the drafting of legal documents, the study of epistolary composition, *ars dictaminis*, received a fresh stimulus from the revival of literature and learning in the twelfth century, in relation both to the study of law and to the cultivation of Latin letters. In the period immediately preceding, indeed, law had been almost a branch of rhetoric, and the establishment of law as an independent subject of instruction could not wholly break its close connexion with the drafting of official acts; while the greater attention now paid to Latin style was reflected in the freer forms of epistolary composition. Letter-writing, both in the monastic and cathedral schools and in the earliest universities and the contemporary chanceries, deserves the attention of the historian, not only as a phase of the development of rhetorical and literary studies, but also for the light which the collections of letters throw upon the narrative history and especially on the social and intellectual conditions of the epoch.[1]

Of course the ancient rhetoricians were not at once abandoned by the teachers and writers of this period. Cicero and Quintilian were still copied and pondered by advanced students, but we shall find them dropping gradually into the background before the more immediately practical manuals of letter-writing. In the desire to be directly useful, these newer treatises concentrated their attention upon the letter and its several parts, and gave little space to general questions of rhetorical form and ornament. They were regularly accompanied by examples and often by elaborate collections of letters public and private, suited to the principal classes in society and the principal occasions of life.

---

[1] See, for illustration, the discussion of student letters in the first chapter of the present volume.

Sometimes these collections of model letters became detached from the theoretical treatises and circulated independently in the manuscripts. They frequently contained authentic historical documents, as well as letters composed for use or imitation in actual life, while the proper names or initials help us to fix their time and place with a precision which is important in their utilization as specific historical sources, as well as in tracing the development and spread of the *ars dictaminis* throughout this period. The localization of these manuals and collections also helps us to study the intellectual currents flowing back and forth between the several countries of Western Europe. The new rhetoric originates in Italy toward the end of the eleventh century, and in the course of the following century it crosses the Alps and establishes itself most firmly in the region of Orleans, whose *dictatores* come to rival their Bolognese contemporaries in the schools and chanceries of Italy and exercise considerable influence in Germany as well. A survey of the Italian treatises and collections to *ca.* 1160 will help us to understand the nature and course of this development.[1]

1. ALBERICUS OF MONTE CASSINO. So far as we know,[2] the first exponent of the new *ars dictaminis* was Albericus, a monk of Monte Cassino in the later eleventh century, and Roman cardinal until his

[1] For the literature of the *ars dictaminis*, see above, Chapter I, particularly p. 2, note 2; p. 6, note 2. Of this the works most important for Italy in the twelfth century are the texts published by Rockinger, the excellent summary of the subject in Bresslau, and the sketch in Manacorda. A. Bütow, *Die Entwicklung der mittelalterlichen Briefsteller bis zur Mitte des 12. Jahrhunderts, mit besonderer Berücksichtigung der Theorieen der* Ars dictandi (Greifswald diss., 1908), is useful for a portion of the subject; see below, nos. 1–5, 8. The present chapter describes in summary fashion materials which I have collected at various times and which others may wish to examine and compare more fully in relation to the history of mediaeval rhetoric.

[2] The question of Alberic's predecessors and contemporaries still requires investigation. For the earlier treatises of the grammarian Urso, see C. Morelli, "I trattati di grammatica e retorica del Cod. Casanatense 1086," in *Rendiconti dei Lincei*, 5th series, xix. 287–328 (1910).

One of my students, Mr. Henry M. Willard, calls my attention to a fragment of an early treatise on *dictamen* on a leaf, possibly as early as the eleventh century, of Cod. Lat. 23496 at Munich, f. 11 v, beginning: 'Primo omnium consideranda est materia ordinanda . . .' Mr. Willard is planning to study this fragment specially. This treatise divides the letter into *salutatio, proemium, narratio, probatio, conclusio*.

death after 1079.[1] Author of a *Breviarium de dictamine*, Alberic had also a respectable background of classical education, and represented the broader tradition of the older Roman rhetoric and grammar, so that he stands at the turning-point of mediaeval rhetoric. He wrote a work on rhetorical ornament entitled *Flores rhetorici* or *Radii dictaminum*, preserved in three manuscripts,[2] and a group of short treatises under the general title *De barbarismo et solecismo, tropo et schemate.*[3] Moreover rhetoric and grammar did not represent the whole of Alberic's literary activity, as he is credited with saints' lives, sacred verse, sermons, theological and controversial pamphlets, letters, and treatises on dialectic, music, and astronomy.[4] To him is also ascribed the revival of the Roman *cursus*, in the form which his pupil John of Gaeta, chancellor of the papal see and later (1118–19) Pope Gelasius II, seems to have introduced into the papal curia.[5]

In the field of *dictamen* proper, Alberic's teaching is known to us solely from his *Breviarium*, preserved in two manuscripts, from which it has been published in part;[6] the *Rationes dictandi* printed in his name has now been placed in the region of Bologna a half-century after his time.[7] The *Breviarium* contains more grammatical and stylistic matter than is usual in the later books on *dictamen*, so that

[1] Besides the works of Bresslau and Bütow cited above, see L. von Rockinger, "Briefsteller und Formelbücher des eilften bis vierzehnten Jahrhunderts," in *Q. E.*, ix (1863–64), pp. xxvi–xxvii, xxxii–xxxiii, 1–46, 54; and cf. my paper on "Albericus Casinensis" in the anniversary *Miscellanea* published at Monte Cassino in 1929, where some unpublished extracts are given from Alberic's rhetorical and grammatical works. As to the lack of evidence respecting the exact date of Alberic's death, see Bütow, pp. 16–17.

[2] Munich, Cod. Lat. 14784, ff. 44–59 (66 v), entitled *Rethorici flores*; University of Breslau, MS. oct. 11, called *Radii dictaminum*; Copenhagen, MS. Gl. kgl. S. 3545, ff. 1–11, called *Dictaminum radii*. The preface is printed by Rockinger, *Q. E.*, ix. 4–5.

[3] Heiligenkreuz, MS. 257, ff. 103–122; Lilienfeld, MS. 98, ff. 91 v–111; MS. formerly at Zwettl, now lost; see T. Gottlieb, *Mittelalterliche Bibliothekscataloge Österreichs*, i (Vienna, 1915), p. 516. See also the fragment at Wolfenbüttel, MS. 2942, f. 118, "De orthographia Alberici."

[4] Petrus Diaconus, *Chronica*, in *SS.*, vii. 728; in Migne, *P. L.*, clxxiii. 766; *Liber de viris illustribus Casinensis coenobii, ibid.*, col. 1033.

[5] Cf. R. L. Poole, *Lectures on the History of the Papal Chancery* (Cambridge, 1915), pp. 83–88; R. Krohn, *Der päpstliche Kanzler Johannes von Gaëta (Gelasius II.)* (Marburg diss., 1918).

[6] Munich, Cod. Lat. 14784, ff. 67–104; Cod. Lat. 19411, pp. 115–130; printed in part by Rockinger, *Q. E.*, ix. 29–46. There is also a fragment at Pistoia: Bresslau, p. 248.

[7] Bütow, p. 17; Bresslau, pp. 249, 251–252; and see below, no. 8.

it is clear that the new epistolography has not yet become sharply differentiated from grammar and the older rhetoric. Thus Alberic here condenses from another of his treatises a discussion of the *vitia orationis*, and includes a *consideratio rithmorum* which takes us far from letter-writing. The new tendency appears in the emphasis upon the forms of salutation and in the invented examples of formal documents, in which both Gregory VII and Henry IV are made to speak in Alberic's style, to the confusion of certain modern critics.[1] The *Breviarium* is obviously not a complete treatise of the art, but is designed to supplement Alberic's oral instruction, being dedicated to two of his pupils, Gundfrid and Guido. Its influence and its relation to subsequent developments are seen in the citations by the Bolognese *dictatores* of the next generation.[2] Hugh of Bologna declares that while Alberic did not compose specimens of each type of *dictamen*, yet he is rightly considered superior to the others in writing letters and drawing up privileges.[3]

2. AGINOLFUS. Mentioned by Hugh of Bologna[4] as a critic of Albericus who introduces rash novelties, no works of Aginolfus have been identified.[5]

3. ALBERT OF SAMARIA, *ca.* IIII–18. Named with Aginolfus as a critic of Alberic,[6] Albert is the first teacher of *dictamen* who can be connected with Bologna, where the new art was established by the early years of the twelfth century.[7] Albert is known to us from two, or rather three, manuscripts. One is a codex of Reinhardsbrunn, now in a private library at Pommersfelden, containing *Precepta*

---

[1] See Bresslau, p. 249.

[2] *Q. E.*, ix. 41, 54; cf. Albert of Samaria in *Neues Archiv*, xxxii. 71–81, 717–719. This is probably the *Liber dictaminum et salutationum* of Petrus Diaconus.

[3] *Q. E.*, ix. 54.   [4] *Q. E.*, ix. 53.

[5] Wattenbach, "Iter Austriacum," in *Archiv für Kunde österreichischer Geschichts-Quellen*, xiv. 36 (1855), conjectures him to be the author of a fragment at Munich, Cod. Lat. 19411. Cf. Bütow, pp. 21–23; *infra*, p. 180.

[6] Hugh of Bologna, in *Q. E.*, ix. 53.

[7] Besides Bütow, pp. 21–30, see my paper, here summarized, on "An Early Bolognese Formulary," in the *Mélanges H. Pirenne* (Brussels, 1926), pp. 201–210; and W. Holtzmann, "Eine oberitalienische Ars dictandi und die Briefsammlung des Priors Peter von St. Jean in Sens," *Neues Archiv*, xlvi. 34–52 (1925). Unfortunately I did not see Holtzmann's study until after my paper was in print, but there is very little overlapping, since Holtzmann is concerned chiefly with the French portion of the collection, whereas my interest was primarily in the Bolognese letters. In general, the two papers confirm each other.

dictaminis with a preface, "Adalbertus Samaritanus superno munere monachus Ti. suo discipulo amantissimo," and a set of salutations which are apparently part of the same treatise, whence they have been published with the *Precepta* by Krabbo.[1] Even with this addition the treatise seems incomplete,[2] for it is disconnected and lacks the introductory classification and the rhetorical discussions which are usual in such works. Its date, if we may judge from the forms of address, is *ca.* 1111–18, in the time of Paschal II, Henry V, and Alexius Comnenus; the proper names point to Northern Italy— Parma, Modena, Reggio, Fermo, Pisa, Lucca—but not specifically to Bologna. The abbot of Monte Cassino and 'Albericus frater'[3] seem to have been taken over from Alberic. There is no information respecting the author or his home beyond the Samaritanus or de Samaria which regularly appears. As there is no known place of this name in Italy or adjacent countries, we are probably to assume some reference to the Samaritans of the Bible, apparently in the sense of poor or unfortunate.[4]

The second manuscript[5] is a codex of the twelfth century in Berlin, Cod. Lat. 181 (Phillipps, 1732), ff. 56 v–73, containing a brief treatise and an appendix of forty-five letters. The treatise begins, without title or author, as follows:

De dictamine tractaturus primum eius diffinitionem ostendere decrevi, quatinus ea cognita convenientius tractare queam. Dictamen est animi conceptio et recta oratione aliquid componere. Dictaminum duo sunt genera principalia. Omne namque dictamen aut est prosaycum aut metri-

---

[1] MS. 2750; see Krabbo, in *Neues Archiv*, xxxii. 71–81, 717–719.

[2] Cf. Bütow, p. 30.   [3] Cf. Krabbo, p. 75.

[4] Cf. Tiraboschi, *Storia della letteratura italiana*, iv. 448 (1788), for a similar explanation of Samariensis as applied to Henry of Settimello.

[5] The third manuscript, which I discovered after printing the article in the *Mélanges Pirenne*, is in the Royal Library at Copenhagen, MS. Gl. kgl. S. 3543 (saec. xii), ff. 19 to 22 verso (cf. Ellen Jørgensen, *Catalogus codicum Latinorum Medii Aevi Bibliothecae Regiae Hafniensis*, p. 300). It corresponds in general to the theoretical part of the Berlin manuscript, of which it offers a rather better text, omitting the section which in the Berlin manuscript covers ff. 59 v to 60 v. There are none of the letters which form the principal interest of the Berlin manuscript; the only letter being an exhortation (1130–37 ?) by a Pope I. to an Emperor L. (f. 21 v). The name Samaritanus appears but once (f. 21 v), 'ut Samaritanus nobili genere natus,' which corresponds to the Berlin manuscript, f. 61. In place of the 'ut Radulfus docet' of the Berlin codex, f. 60 v, the Copenhagen text has 'ut Iohannes docet' (f. 21), confirming Holtzmann's denial of any connexion with Ralph of Laon (*Neues Archiv*, xlvi. 37). In this MS. the treatise is likewise anonymous.

cum . . . Sub qua divisione sunt multe alie species . . . quibus omnibus in eo opere quod de metrica arte facere intendimus Deo nobis vitam tribuente tractabimus. Nunc de epistolari prosayco videamus . . .

The treatment is different from the *Precepta*, as the two for the most part cover different ground; where they overlap, as in the etymology of *epistola* and *cola*, the agreement is close but not exact. So there are resemblances without exact duplication in the later Bolognese treatises of Hugh, Henricus Francigena, and Bernard. The author limits himself to the prose epistle, but promises another work, *de metrica arte*. Samaria is mentioned three times for purposes of illustration (ff. 60 v–61).

On f. 61 v begins the appendix of letters, of which the first six read as follows:

1. Alberto doctori eximio divina sapientia referto morum honestate perspicuo G. scolarium infimus discipularem subiectionem. Tue sapientie ac probitatis fama, renovande [1] doctor, longe lateque diffusa a multis veridicis mihi relata me vehementer monuit ac tibi scribere persuasit et de fonte tue doctrine mellifluos haustus petere. Te namque nobili prosapia ortum, sapientia illuminatum, bonis consuetudinibus adornatum ut audivi in re cognovi. Magistralem igitur benivolentiam ad nostram [2] accedere urbem humiliter deprecor ac proxima hyeme cum .l. scolaribus vel eo amplius docere, qui dato pignore reddent te [3] securum per annuale [4] spacium tecum permanere et tui laboris ac doctrine debita reddere.

2. Albertus superno munere siquid est G. Cremonensi scolastico carissimo socio et ceteris sociis semper meliora proficere.[5] Vestrę dilectionis litteras, carissimi socii, ovanter accepimus ac benigna mente perlegimus. Quarum peticionem cum magno desiderio adimpleremus si qua ratione convenienter possemus. Pignoribus namque acceptis ac fide data nos per annum Bononie morari ac studium indesinenter regere proposuimus. Eapropter quod postulatis ad nos venire, vobis si libuerit ut carissimos filios suscipiemus et ut dilectos filios docebimus.

3. Dilectissimo socio et precordiali amico L. indissolubile dilectionis vinculum. Amicitia inter nos a cunabulis fere inchoata una cum etate incrementata magnam mihi fiduciam prebet a te necessaria petere et te monet postulata concedere. Quicquid enim usque modo habuimus una communicavimus sed quod fuit dignum dono alter alteri non denegavit. Quamobrem nimium confisus te multimoda prece deposco ut divinarum sententiarum excerptum [6] quod nuper de Francia detulisti per harum latorem mihi mittere necesses. Vicissim vero meis utaris ut propriis.

4. Necessariorum precipuo O. individue dilectionis unionem. Tue

---

[1] Read *reverende?*	[2] MS. *vestram*.	[3] MS. *reddente*.
[4] MS. *amnale*.	[5] MS. *profitere*.	[6] MS. *exertum*.

littere per Stephanum mihi delate in exordio me vehementer letifica-
verunt et in extremo mestificaverunt. Per eas enim tui animi affec-
tionem circa me animadverti et per earum portitorem salutem cognovi;
hac de causa ultra quam dici possit letatus sum. Quod autem tue peticioni inpresentiarum satisfacere nequeo omnimodo doleo. Nam librum
quem a me petisti [1] iam transacto mense Land. nostro accomodavi
amico, sed tuo presente latore meum direxi ut sine dilatione mihi mittat.
Quem postquam habuero tibi absque ulla cunctacione mittere curabo.

5. U. Bondinensi archiepiscopo [2] dilectissimo consanguineo Ada[lber-
tus] [3] Samaritanus superno munere si quid est voluntatis identitatem.
Nulla mea precesserunt officia pro quibus tua debeam flagitare beneficia,
sed quia caritatis zelo te fervere cognovi qua non modo notis verum
etiam ignotis es [4] subvenire, confidenter tibi meum pando infortunium
et tuum deposco suffragium. Bononiam kalendis Augusti divino iudicio
igne crematam et in eius combustione meam supellectilem me amisisse
sciatis et vix inde nudus evasi. Itaque tue propinquitatis dilectionem
humiliter deprecor quatinus tua copia mea sublevetur inopia, vel aliter,
tua opulentia aliquantisper mea sustentetur indigentia.

6. A. Samaritano adprime liberalibus disciplinis erudito carnis pro-
pinquitate coniuncto U. divina favente clementia Bonidinensis ecclesie
archipresbiter licet indignus salutem et eternam in Domino consolationem. Inspectis et superspectis et perlectis tuis litteris ob nimiam
tristiciam a lacrimis abstinere nequivimus. Cum enim divina scriptura
precipiat etiam extraneis compati, multo magis condolere tibi debemus
qui consilium et subsidium in nostris negotiis semper dedisti. Quo circa
pro nostra facultate tibi subvenimus et per nostros legatos unum ful-
crum et pulvinar linteumque atque duo plaustra honerata unum vino
alterum frumento tibi mittere curamus. Quę munuscula humiliter tuam
deprecamur dilectionem benigne suscipere sicut de promtuario karitatis
tibi studuimus mittere.

These and similar forms from Italy, which I have printed in the
Mélanges Pirenne,[5] make up the first seventeen letters of the collection,
but those which follow, analysed and studied by Holtzmann, form
two groups relating to Northern France in the region of Orleans,
Rheims, and Sens, *ca.* 1130–50, at least one of the letters anterior
to 1135, the earliest example yet indicated of the transmission of a
Bolognese rhetorical collection to France. From the point of view

---

[1] MS. *petistis*.
[2] Read *archipresbitero* as in the next letter. Hugo, archpriest of Bondeno
(prov. Ferrara), meets us in a papal bull of 1139: Jaffe-Löwenfeld, no. 8049.
[3] MS. *Adā*.   [4] *notus es?*
[5] Likewise of the time of Pope Paschal II (1099–1118) is a fragment in the
B.M., Add. MS. 16896, ff. 103 v–104 (early twelfth century), containing forms
of salutation from Italy.

of the *ars dictaminis*, the first part of the collection is the most interesting, the letters of Albert himself, who is specifically mentioned and clearly localized in Bologna in nos. 1, 2, 5, and 6. His dependence upon his predecessors is indicated in nos. 11 and 12, two letters concerning Bonizo as bishop of Sutri (1076–82), evidently taken over from an older collection relating to Central Italy—very possibly from that of Bonizo's contemporary Alberic of Monte Cassino, from whom a salutation has been taken in the *Precepta dictaminis*.

Albert's letters are the earliest so far discovered from the schools of Bologna. Hitherto evidence upon the study of the arts at Bologna in this period has been found only in the *Rationes* of the Bolognese canon Hugh,[1] *ca.* 1119–24, whereas, if we follow the dates indicated by the *Precepta*, Albert belongs to 1111–18. Albert confirms Hugh in emphasis upon the *trivium* in general and upon *dictamen* in particular, and in the omission of all reference to the study of law. His letters of aid and reproof and requests for the loan of books and writing materials (nos. 4, 7, 8, 13–15) have their parallel in Hugh and in many subsequent collections.[2] There are also some new points. Nos. 1 and 2 show a negotiation between Bologna and Cremona respecting a teacher of *dictamen*; the schools seem to be free of any connexion with the cathedrals, and in both cases there is a regular annual contract with guarantees for payment on the part of the students.[3] More significant is the reference in no. 3 to the *divinarum sententiarum excerptum quod nuper de Francia detulisti*. Not only does this show early communication between Bologna and the schools of Northern France, but it offers evidence particularly of the early spread of the new sentence literature, first worked out by Anselm of Laon and his school and, in the form which it received at the hands of Abaelard, exerting a definite influence upon the method of Gratian and the Bolognese theologians.[4] Theology is thus seen passing from France to Italy even earlier than the movement of the *ars dictaminis* from Italy to France which is illustrated by the latter part of our collection.

---

[1] *Q. E.*, ix. 47–94. See H. Fitting, *Die Anfänge der Rechtsschule zu Bologna* (Leipzig, 1888), pp. 80, 105; Rashdall, *Universities of the Middle Ages*, i, p. 111; G. Manacorda, *Storia della scuola in Italia*, i, 1, pp. 202–204, 223; i, 2, pp. 84, 134, 259.   [2] See Chapter I, *supra*.

[3] On cathedral and free schools in mediaeval Italy, see Manacorda, *op. cit.*

[4] M. Grabmann, *Geschichte der scholastischen Methode* (Freiburg, 1909–11), ii, especially pp. 213–229; J. de Ghellinck, *Le mouvement théologique du XII*ᵉ *siècle* (Paris, 1914).

4. HENRICUS FRANCIGENA, *Aurea gemma, ca.* 1119–24, Pavia.
This work is preserved in the following manuscripts:

A. Wolfenbüttel, MS. 5620, ff. 66–80.
B. Leipzig, University Library, MS. 350, ff. 132–146.
C. B. N., MS. lat. n.a. 610, ff. 27–52 v (saec. xii, incomplete at end).
D. Bodleian, MS. Laud Misc. 569, ff. 178 v–190 v (early thirteenth century), anonymous and without preface.
E. University of Erlangen, MS. 396, ff. 47–54 v, with letters from the Rhine valley and especially Schönau in the thirteenth century. See Hans Fischer, *Die lateinischen Pergamenthandschriften der Universitätsbibliothek Erlangen* (Erlangen, 1928), pp. 472–473.

Extracts from A are printed by Rockinger, *Q. E.*, ix. 41–46, 68–71, 90–91, 93–94; cf. H. Fitting, "Ueber neue Beiträge zur Geschichte der Rechtswissenschaft im früheren Mittelalter," in *Zeitschrift der Savigny-Stiftung für Rechtsgeschichte*, vii, romanistische Abtheilung, 2, p. 66 (1886); the same, *Die Anfänge der Rechtsschule zu Bologna* (Leipzig, 1888), pp. 80, 105. See Bütow, pp. 30–43, who uses A and B only and analyses the whole treatise.

The treatise is dedicated to Peter of S. Severino and mentions the author's late master Anselm, a teacher of *dictamen* otherwise unknown. The theoretical part borrows freely from Alberic and Albert of Samaria. The examples centre about Pavia; one is published by Fitting,[1] who seeks to establish from it the importance of Pavia at this time as a centre of legal studies.

MS. C begins:

Petro divino munere Severiane domus .M. sacerdoti glorioso Henricus Francigena amicorum eius amicissimus salutem et peticionem cum humanitatis familiaritate. Crebris vestre dilectionis, dilectissime Petre, fatigatus precibus, honestissime vestre peticioni opere precium duxi nullatenus denegare, quod meam parvitatem dudum scilicet opuscula dictandi componere promisisse recolo. Scribam itaque non invitus cum rogatu vestro quem sinceritatis brachiis Deo teste et consciencia mea complector[2] et in communi utilitate dictancium raciones dictandi prosaice, non tamen ex armariolo nostri ingenii verum etiam diversorum sentencias in unum colligendo. . . . Quocienscunque aliquis prosaice sine vicio egregias componere litteras desiderat, opere precium est ut primum

---

[1] "Ueber neue Beiträge," pp. 66–67; from MS. A.   [2] MS. *complectri.*

dictandi originem deinde ordinem et materiarum distinctionem perfecte
noscat, ut recto tramite vel ordine incedere per altos dictaminis montes
leviter valeat. Legat igitur studiosus dictatur [*sic*] hunc libellum qui
Aurea gemma intitulatur quem Francigena Henricus ad utilitatem de-
siderancium dictare Papie conposuit. . . .

MS. D, to which I called attention in 1898,[1] begins without
dedication but with a preface which holds up for imitation Cicero
and the Latin Fathers: [2]

(F. 178 v) Incipit ecce liber qui dicitur Aurea gemma. Librorum sicut
Cantica canticorum per excellentiam liber iste dicitur eo quod maxima
utilitas et maior quam in ceteris contineatur in eo. Intendit enim dictandi doctrinam perficere et construere et quodlibet imperfectum formare, Tullium in rethorica arte imitando, Gregorii, Augustini, Ieronimi,
atque Ambrosii vestigia in dictaminis varietatibus sequendo: Tullium in
faceta locutione et verborum compositione, Gregorium in dulcedine et
suavitate, Augustinum in callida et subtilissima argumentatione, Iero-
nimum in sententiarum pondere, Ambrosium in theorica disputatione.
Quanto ergo aurum cunctis metallis preciosius et gemma naturalis ceteris
lapidibus clarior et splendidior, tanto liber iste omnium [3] auctorum
abreviatior libris invenitur. Aurum itaque et gemma potest dici, sed
aurum gemme adiungas et utramque coniunctione qui[d]dam dulcius et
pulchrius et decentius idem auream gemmam facias. Vocetur itaque
Aurea gemma eo quod ex fontibus doctorum quasi ex auro et gemma sit
compositus et informatus. Sociorum assidua pulsatione coactus naturalis
et rationis incitamento astrictus aggressus sum rem arduam sed professionis officio non invictam et prosaycas orationes fingere cupientibus
satis idoneam, opus difficile sed tamen pro utilitate.

Under *colores rethorici* (f. 183) the doctrine of a Master Peter is
exalted.[4] The salutations (*temp.* Calixtus II, 1119–24, and Henry V,
1106–25) correspond to those in the other manuscripts, but there are
signs of retouching in France: W., bishop of Paris (f. 185 v), 'Galliana
ecclesia' (f. 187 v), and a church which appears variously as Menensis,
Viensis, and Venensis (ff. 187 v, 189). So the student who in the
other versions writes from Pavia is here studying law or dialectic
at Rheims (f. 187): 'Remensi studio legum—vel dialetice—alacriter
et sane die noctuque adherere.'[5] The treatise breaks off with a letter

---

[1] *A. H. R.*, iii. 206, note 2.   [2] Cf. Bütow, p. 43.   [3] MS. *omni*.
[4] 'Magistri Petri doctrine adherere decrevi, cuius est preclara doctrina, cuius
perpulchra facundia, cuius tenax memoria, cuius Attica vernat eloquentia,
cui tonat Tulliana rethorica, cui canit Romana fistula.' This Peter can hardly
be the author of a *summa* at Graz described by Loserth, *Neues Archiv*, xxii. 303.
[5] See the letter as printed from A by Fitting, "Ueber neue Beiträge,"
pp. 66–67.

in the name of an Emperor H. to Pope Alexander explaining that
the world is composed of four elements and man of four humours.[1]

Henricus Francigena seems to be the source of a collection of
letters from Pavia in Munich, Cod. Lat. 19411, ff. 65–68 v, where the
passage attacking Alberic is verbally reproduced from Henricus:
Bütow, p. 22. The Emperor is, however, Frederick and the Pope
Alexander (Wattenbach, "Iter," p. 51); there is no accompanying
theoretical treatise.

5. HUGH, canon and master of Bologna, *Rationes dictandi prosaice*,
ca. 1119–24. Of this work the following manuscripts are known:

    A. Salzburg, St. Peter's, MS. V. 13.

    B. Wolfenbüttel, MS. 5620, ff. 1–4 v, incomplete (in the name ot
       Bishop Benno of Meissen).

    C. Pommersfelden, MS. 2750, ff. 56 v–68 v.

    D. Graz, MS. 1515, ff. 20 v–45 (cf. *Neues Archiv*, xxii. 299).

It was printed from B by B. Pez, *Thesaurus anecdotorum*, vi, 1,
coll. 264–278; from A, B, and C by Rockinger, *Q. E.*, ix. 49–94. Cf.
Bütow, pp. 44–46.

The treatise is dedicated to D. of Ferrara, imperial judge. The
author declares himself a follower of Alberic and criticizes Aginolf
and Albert of Samaria, but he draws freely from Albert, and a letter
in Albert's name appears among the forms.[2] The doctrine resembles
that of Henricus Francigena, but the forms centre about Bologna
and include a student letter which emphasizes philosophy and *dictamen* instead of law. In another letter, not published by Rockinger,
the student's literary interests are indicated by a request for a
Priscian and an *Argentea lingua*.[3]

6. WILLELMUS, *Aurea gemma*, ca. 1126. MS. from Weissenau, now
in private hands, from which seven letters are printed by K. Höfler,

---

[1] 'Cum iuxta philosophorum sententiam mundus iste ex quatuor elementis
constat, creator ipse mundi providit ut mundus sibi similia in se contineret.
Continet enim hominem qui microcosmus dicitur et minor mundus, qui ex
quatuor elementis nihilominus constat nec solum ex illis elementis sed etiam
ex iiii[or] humoribus qui similes proprietates sortiti sunt' (f. 190 v).

[2] *Q. E.*, ix. 84. Contemporary with Hugh of Bologna is a fragment in Vienna,
MS. 861, ff. 82 v–84 (saec. xii), apparently the work of a canon of Faenza
('suo preceptori carissimo Dei nutu sancte Faventine ecclesie canonico'). The
salutations are of the time of Calixtus II (1119–24) and Henry V (1106–25),
with mention of Faenza, Ravenna, Aquileia, Milan, and Venice; they are
followed by *exordia* in the name of Innocent II (1130–43) and Conrad III
(1138–52).   [3] *Neues Archiv*, xxii. 300 (1897).

"Böhmische Studien," *Archiv für Kunde österreichischer Geschichts-Quellen*, xii. 314–316 (1854); also cited by Wattenbach, "Iter," p. 38. Very little is known of the contents of this collection or of its affinities.[1] Of the letters published by Höfler, four relate to Bologna and three to Milan.

7. A Lombard collection of *ca.* 1132. Vienna, MS. 2507, ff. 27–63; analysed by Wattenbach, "Iter," pp. 39–51. The letters touch upon imperial relations and local affairs in Lombardy and the Romagna. Some of them are closely related to the *Aurea gemma* of Willelmus ("Iter," pp. 47–49).

Curious light on Franco-Italian relations is thrown by a letter from a student to his father (ff. 43 v–44 v), which shows that the young man is studying at Chartres under Master Bernard, where he hopes to receive a remittance at the hands of pilgrims to Compostela:

Miserere itaque pater, miserere, porrige manum egenti filio, subeat tibi paternus animus, non te deserat pietatis affectus, et per oratores qui veniunt ad Sanctum Iacobum saltim .iiii. marcas argenti Carnotum ubi ego sub disciplina domini magistri Bernhardi dego mihi mittere studeas. In proxima vero Resurrectione sentenciis illis pleniter instructis repatriare studebo.

The father answers:

Tribus namque vicibus per peregrinos qui ad Sanctum Iacobum ibant pecuniam misi. Quarto fratrem tuum Grandulfum ad te direxi, cui querenti et diligenter de te investiganti a multis relatum et confirmatum est te obiisse. Post quod tempora in merore [2] et luctu erumpnosam vitam duxi et nullam consolationem accepi. Sed nuper tuis litteris consolatus et quasi ab inferis resuscitatus et ante divinam faciem deportatus pecuniam quam postulasti per Stephanum fidelissimum vernaculum nostre domus integram tibi mandare curavi. Quam cicius igitur potest expedire te cura, et si meam faciem ulterius videre desideras cum eo reddere matura.

8. Anonymous *Rationes dictandi*, *ca.* 1135. Munich, Cod. Lat. 14784, whence the first book was printed by Rockinger, *Q. E.*, ix. 9–28, as a work of Alberic of Monte Cassino. The proper names, however, point to a later date, and to the region of Bologna; later also is the more fully developed doctrine, in which first appear the five parts of a letter: *salutatio, captatio benevolentie, narratio, petitio, conclusio*. Thus crystallized, this division passes into the manual of

---

[1] The *Aurea gemma* at Admont, mentioned in *Archiv*, x. 644 (1851), seems to be a later production: cf. Wattenbach, "Iter," p. 38, note 1.

[2] MS. *memerore*.

Bernard of Bologna (below, no. 10). See Bütow, pp. 58–59; Bresslau, pp. 251 ff.

9. HERMANNUS (?). A reference of Bernard of Bologna to a teacher 'Her.' leads Kalbfuss (*Quellen und Forschungen*, xvi, 2, p. 11) to identify this master with one mentioned in the Vienna MS. 2507, f. 85 v: 'Incipiunt alię pulcrę posiciones magistri Heremanni.' Indeed the word 'alię' might imply his authorship of the *Flores dictaminis* of the same type which precede and are chiefly taken from the Fathers (see below, no. 12). Many of the *posiciones* are from the letters of Ivo of Chartres.

10. BERNARD OF BOLOGNA, *Introductiones prosaici dictaminis*, ca. 1145. The following manuscripts are known:

A. University of Graz, MS. 1515, ff. 46–127 (saec. xii).

B. Vatican, MS. Pal. lat. 1801, ff. 1–51 (saec. xii).

C. Savignano di Romagna, MS. 45 (*ca.* 1200).

D. Mantua, MS. A. II. 1, ff. 73–122 (saec. xii).

E. Poitiers, MS. 213, ff. 1–32 (*ca.* 1200).

F. Bruges, MS. 549, ff. 57–105 v (early thirteenth century).

G. Brussels, MS. 2070, ff. 92–104 (saec. xii).

H. Vatican, MS. Vat. lat. 9991, ff. 97–104 v (late twelfth century).

I. Vienna, MS. 246, ff. 51–57 v (saec. xiii).

K. Anonymous fragment at Copenhagen, MS. Gl. kgl. S. 1905, f. 123 and verso.

L. Bodleian, MS. Laud Misc. 569, ff. 190 v–191 v, 195 v–196 v. Brief anonymous extracts adapted to the use of Cistercians.

See H. Kalbfuss, "Eine Bologneser Ars dictandi des XII. Jahrhunderts," in *Quellen und Forschungen aus italienischen Archiven und Bibliotheken*, xvi, 2, pp. 1–35 (1914), based on MS. D, from which he prints numerous letters; and Haskins, "An Italian Master Bernard," in *Essays in History Presented to R. L. Poole* (Oxford, 1927), pp. 211–226, where the manuscripts are analysed and from which the following description is summarized.

These manuscripts show various redactions of a treatise on prose *dictamen* composed by a teacher named Bernard in the Romagna in 1144–45 (MSS. A and B). This was revised in the same region and probably by the author himself between 1145 and 1152 (MSS. C, D, E, F, and G). As early at least as the second redaction the models were provided which meet us in the manuscripts of Savignano (C, ff. 87 v–112) and Mantua (D). The name Bernard indicates that this collection was the work of the author of the treatise, and the place-names point to the same region, with emphasis upon Bologna in the student letters which are usual in such collections. Before long a copy of the first redaction (MS. B) has taken on elements from the Eastern Alps, and the second redaction early crosses the Alps. By the time of Adrian IV (1154–59) and probably by 1152 this has reached France (MSS. E and F); and by 1159–67, perhaps after passing through France, it has been localized at Cologne (MS. G). Bernard's influence persists as late as MS. I, a greatly modified version made in France in the time of Innocent III. Bernard calls himself *dictaminum professionis minister* and *clericus et Tullianus imitator*, but says nothing of his training unless it be in a reference to Master Hermann (*ante*, no. 9); the *exordia* are dedicated to a certain Henry in a passage which shows that Bernard was attached in some way to the cathedral of Faenza, while other passages connect him with Arezzo. The body of Bernard's manual is based on the *Rationes dictandi* (no. 8), but with further developments and an elaborate treatment of *exordia*.

This treatise in one of its forms, or perhaps the treatise of another Bernard which has been confused with it, also discusses poetical *dictamen*, a topic generally passed over by the writers of the Bolognese school. The similarity of names has caused further confusion with the Bernards who wrote on *dictamen* in France.[1]

11. A collection of models relating to Tuscany in the time of Adrian IV (1154–59). Savignano di Romagna, MS. 45, ff. 115–134: 'Mirę commoditatis epistolę a pluribus sapientibus editę incipiunt quę secundum dictatoris industriam multis negotiis accommodantur.'

12. GUIDO OF BOLOGNA, *ca.* 1160. MS. 2507 of the National-bibliothek at Vienna (saec. xii) contains, ff. 1–7 v, a brief anonymous *Ars dictandi*, beginning 'Introducendis in arte dictandi dicendum est primo quid sit dictare . . .' Wattenbach pointed out ("Iter Austriacum," p. 39) the mention of Frederick Barbarossa and the anti-Pope Victor on f. 4 v, which fixes the date between 1159 and 1164; but he did not note that Wido is the regular name for the writer in the ordinary salutations. The manuscript of Bernard of Bologna at Savignano, MS. 45 (*ante*, no. 10), has a section which begins (f. 134) 'Incipiunt epistolę secundum rectum et naturalem ordinem a Guidone non inutiliter composite,' from the time of Frederick Barbarossa and the region of Bologna.

---

[1] Cf. Langlois, "Maître Bernard," *B. E. C.*, liv. 225–250, 792–795 (1893); Haskins, "An Italian Master Bernard," pp. 211–213.

The succeeding treatise in MS. 2507, ff. 7 v–13, is very similar and also anonymous: 'Alius tractatus de dictamine. Epistola grecum nomen est . . .' The example of the master to his pupils runs in the name of 'G. Bononiensis ecclesię canonicus et sacerdos humillimus solo nomine magister' (f. 11 v), and Bologna is mentioned on the following page.

The volume contains other anonymous treatises and collections of the same type and still of the twelfth century, besides the Lombard collection of letters analysed by Wattenbach (ff. 27–63; see *ante*, no. 7) and the *Posiciones* of Master Hermann (f. 85 v; see *ante*, no. 9). Thus, ff. 13–14 v, 'Tractatus qualiter materia debeat ordinari in dictamine. Primum autem omnium . . .' Ff. 14 v–27, *Exordia*, resembling those of Bernard of Bologna. F. 68, 'Qualiter verba venuste ponantur.' F. 68 v, *Flores dictaminis*, chiefly from the Fathers, but with a Bolognese touch in the *Liber Pandectarum* (f. 72).

13. ALBERT OF SAN MARTINO, canon and master of Asti, *Flores dictandi*, *ca.* 1150. MS. lat. n.a. 610, ff. 1–25 v (saec. xii), where it precedes Henricus Francigena. Dedicated to L., canon of Geneva:

Incipiunt flores dictandi quos Albertus Astensis de Sancto Martino ex multis locis collegit et nonnullis insertis in unum redegit. Venerabili domino et amico suo L. Dei gratia Gebenensi canonico ceterisque sociis eius Al. de Sancto Martino sancti Astensis ecclesię eadem gratia qualiscumque canonicus salutem et Tullianam eloquentiam. Inter cetera Latine ęloquentię precipua summum utile arbitror. . . .

Albert is frequently mentioned in the salutations (f. 8 v, 'suis scolaribus') and the models, in which the Pope is Eugene III (1145–53) and the Emperor Conrad III (1138–52). The other proper names (ff. 6 and 7) relate to the region of Asti, namely An[selm], bishop of Asti (1148–67), Ar., bishop 'Saonensis' (of Savona?), Al[fonso], bishop of Pavia (1132–*ca.* 1145), O., bishop of Alba, M., abbot of Fruttuaria, also (f. 23) the church of Tortona and (f. 24) 'Astenses Albensibus.' Most space is given (ff. 13–20 v) to the twenty-six *modi epistolarum*. The examples of letters (ff. 22–25 v) are comparatively few; the manuscript breaks off abruptly.

14. Anonymous *Precepta prosaici dictaminis secundum Tullium*, *ca.* 1138–52. B.M., Add. MS. 21173 (saec. xii), ff. 61–73, with an appendix of documents, ff. 74–82, which appears to be distinct. The treatise begins:

Tulliane florem eloquencię prosaici scilicet dictaminis industriam verumne an falsum constet sub leporis volubilitate congrua debere tractari mecum multotiens cogitavi sollicitus, atque aliquotiens sic meditando reperi plures contextionum series tali super [1] modulo promtula verbositate formatas potius repulsum iri nichilque proprie dignitatis habentes quam ob id pedulcum commovere auditorem. Ceterum cum earum dignitates commodas Tulliana constitutas modestia considero, non modo de omni de quo agitur negotio placabilis et mansuetus redditur auditor, verum etiam ad cuncta petita seu petenda mellifluę rationis eloquio plane tractabilis invenitur. . . .

In the salutations the bishop of Asti appears occasionally, 'A. Astensis servus ecclesie,' so that there is some apparent connexion with Albert's treatise (no. 13, above); but the proper names have a somewhat wider range, and apparently centre about Bologna. The Emperor is still C[onrad] (1138–52), but the initials of ecclesiastical dignitaries cannot be identified in their present form; G., also B., prepositus of Lucca; P., also G., archbishop of Milan; R., archbishop of Pisa; V., also C., bishop of Vicenza; D., bishop of Piacenza. On f. 71 v P., bishop of Vercelli, is addressed in a student letter from Bologna.[2]

15. MASTER A. (?), anonymous Italian treatise, *ca.* 1138–52, with an appendix of French models of the early thirteenth century. Valenciennes, MS. 483, ff. 90–97 v (early thirteenth century); M. Henry Omont called my attention to the fact that there is a copy of the late thirteenth century made from this manuscript in MS. lat. 8566A, ff. 106–125. The treatise begins, with no heading, as follows:

Ad plenam scientiam dictaminum habendam et si quis expeditus esse voluerit in scientia versificandi, optimum est prenosse quid faciat sermonem gravem, quid prolixum, quid levem, quid ornatum et iocundum reddat sermonem. Ad gravitatem orationis valent emphasis et translatio . . .

There are numerous definitions of rhetorical terms, and a quotation from Cicero, followed by examples of salutations but with little of the usual analysis of letters. There may be a hint of the author's name in the initial A. of the address of pupils to their master, e. g., "A. Dei gratia Tulliani leporis industria prefulgenti." The Emperor is Conrad; there is mention of C., archbishop of Pisa; and under *captatio benivolentie* (f. 92) the text reproduces a portion of the *Rationes dictandi* (*ante*, no. 8) including the passage concerning the alliance of Roger of Apulia with Ancona against Benevento.[3]

---

[1] MS. *sup.*

[2] See Chapter I, p. 18, note 5. Bologna also appears on f. 65 v.

[3] *Q. E.,* ix. 25.

To this Italian treatise there is appended a collection of letters relating to Northern France in the time of Innocent III and Philip Augustus, and evidently centring around Orleans. The following example concerning Flemish students of the classics at Orleans is of some general interest: [1]

(F. 96 v, no. 34) Venerabili et discreto viro tali magistro tales scolares salutem et debitam magistro reverentiam. Arbitrari debet cum diligentia vir fidelis et providus qui pro contentionibus sopiendis arbiter est electus. De Flandria provincia recedentes scolas Aurelianas elegimus expetendas ut actores [2] nobis cum attenta sollicitudine legerentur. Sed quia magistri graves erant et minus instructos minus sollicite quam expediret singulis instruebant, frequentare scolas eorum sumus reveriti, semiplenam nostram scientiam attendentes non posse lectionum sufficere gravitati. Talis vero scolaris Ovidianos sub certo precio repromisit nobis secundum possibilitatis exigentiam se lecturum, sed quia promissionem suam non est efficaciter prosecutus, inter nos et dictum scolarem contentio pullulavit propter quod in discretione vestra hic inde nostra sedulitas compromisit. Nos igitur de vestre discretionis abundantia confidentes dilectionem vestram dulciter imploramus quatinus utriusque partis diligenter rationibus intellectis sine dilatione rectum arbitrium proferatis. Questionem debet vero iudicio decidere qui super dubiis electus fuerit iudicare. In commissum ius debet arbiter caute procedere: ne iuris transgressio possit ipsum aliquatenus excusare.

Doubtless this list of Italian manuals and collections of models down to *ca.* 1160 is far from complete. Several teachers of *dictamen* are known, such as Aginolfus, Anselm, Peter, and perhaps Hermann, of whom no writings have been identified, while very likely there were others of whom we lack even the names. Certain of the treatises which have reached us are incomplete, while others cite works which have been lost. In the nature of the case biographical details are exceedingly meagre. The general course of development is, however, fairly clear. The new rhetoric starts, apparently, at Monte Cassino with Alberic; but no other Cassinese master is known, and the next writer who can be identified, Albert of Samaria (1111–18), is associated with Bologna. An effort is made to draw Albert to Cremona, and his younger contemporary, Henricus Francigena, teaches and writes at Pavia; but from the time of Albert and

---

[1] Cf. Chapter I, p. 26, note 4.   [2] MS. *astores.*

Hugh (1119–24) there is an unbroken series of Bolognese masters and almost every manual or collection has some relation with Bologna. These treatises are closely connected in content as well as in time and place, for there is much borrowing from predecessors and from contemporaries. Thus Alberic and Albert furnish material to Henricus and Hugh, who in turn have other portions in common, while the *Rationes* (no. 8) influences no. 15 and Bernard, from whom nos. 12 and 14 seem to draw. There is an obvious attempt to keep the several manuals up to date by changing proper names and initials, seen most clearly in the case of Bernard, but this rarely carries beyond 1200, nearly all our manuscripts of this series of treatises being of the twelfth century.

The rhetorical doctrine of these manuals need not long detain us, as it has been analysed at length by Bütow[1] on the basis of nos. 1–5 and 8. The author usually begins by distinguishing three species of *dictamen*, prose, metrical, and rhythmical, and announces that he will confine himself to prose, and especially to epistolary composition. The letter is then defined with its several parts, in accordance with a division which obviously goes back to the sixfold division of *inventio* by the Auctor ad Herennium[2] but is modified to suit mediaeval practice. After some uncertainties a fivefold classification meets us in the *Rationes dictandi* and persists throughout the Middle Ages: *salutatio, captatio benivolentie* (or *exordium*), *narratio, petitio, conclusio*. The salutation receives most attention down to the time of Bernard, who treats the *exordium* with especial fullness. Abundant examples of each part of a letter are characteristic of all these early writers. The older rhetorical tradition persists till the middle of the century in *Flores dictandi* and citations of Cicero and the Latin Fathers, while on the other hand detached collections of letters and documents become more common as the century advances. Whereas these collections contain many invented letters, they are lacking in those pieces of pure fancy —correspondence between Pyramus and Thisbe, Soul and Body, letters from Venus and the Devil, etc.—which abound in the

---

[1] *Op. cit.*, pp. 47–73.   [2] i. 3.

writings of the Orleanese school and the Italian *dictatores* of the thirteenth century.[1]

So far as one may judge from the available evidence, the generation following 1160 in Italy was not fruitful in treatises on the *ars dictaminis*. Men were apparently satisfied with copying earlier treatises, like Bernard's, and keeping their collections of models up to date.[2] At Bologna the gap is noticeable until the turn of the century, when a new school begins there with the more individual and entertaining writings of Buoncompagno and his successors.[3] Meanwhile the Beneventan Albert de Mora, vice-chancellor of the Roman curia as early as 1157 and chancellor from 1178 to 1187, when he became Pope as Gregory VIII, had formulated the rules of the papal *cursus*, while his notary, Master Transmundus, also composed a *summa dictaminis*;[4] and the reorganization of the chancery by Innocent III forms the starting-point of an important series of papal formularies.[5]

In Germany the Italian rhetoric spread but slowly in the course of the twelfth century, indeed we cannot be certain that the Germany of this period produced any distinct *artes dictaminis*. The needs of German *dictatores* were satisfied by collections of letters without any theoretical introduction, such as have been preserved from Tegernsee and Hildesheim, or as at Reinhardsbrunn accompanied by copies of certain of the Italian treatises.[6] Some of the early manuscripts of Henricus Francigena and Hugh of Bologna may well have been the work of German

---

[1] *Supra*, pp. 3–4, 137–139; Haskins, *The Renaissance of the Twelfth Century*, pp. 142–145; Cartellieri, *Ein Donaueschinger Briefsteller*, nos. 62, 65, 216, 227, 228.

[2] A different type is represented by a Camaldolese monk, Paul, whose treatise is preserved in a manuscript of the twelfth century at Paris, MS. lat. 7517. Here the *ars dictaminis* appears as an adjunct to grammar and versification. Cf. C. Thurot, in *Notices et extraits*, xxii, 2, pp. 24–25.

[3] On whom see above, Chapter I, p. 6, note 2.

[4] N. Valois, "Étude sur le rythme des bulles pontificales," in *B. E. C.*, xlii. 161–198, 257–272 (1881); Delisle, "Notice sur une 'summa dictaminis,'" in *Notices et extraits*, xxxvi, 1, pp. 181–184 (1899); Poole, *Lectures on the History of the Papal Chancery*, ch. iv; Gustav Kleeman, *Papst Gregor VIII*. (Jena diss., 1912).

[5] Bresslau, ii, 1, pp. 264 ff.; Haskins, "Two Roman Formularies in Philadelphia," in *Miscellanea Francesco Ehrle*, iv. 275–286 (1924).

[6] Bresslau, pp. 253–254; Bütow, pp. 24–27.

scribes; but the proper names remain Italian, except in the somewhat puzzling instance where letters have been put in the name of Bishop Benno of Meissen (d. 1106).[1] Early in the reign of Frederick Barbarossa, however, two manuscripts of the Italian Bernard (no. 10) contain German names, viz., MS. Pal. 1801 of the Vatican, where in the redaction of 1144–45 we find Regensburg substituted for Milan, and E[berhard] archbishop of Salzburg (1147–64); and MS. 2070 at Brussels, which shows a text of 1145–52 brought to Cologne in the time of Archbishop Reinald (1159–67). An early example of the transplantation of the Italian rhetoric to the Eastern Alps is found in the treatise of a certain Baldwin preserved at Graz (MS. 1515,[2] ff. 1–20), in which Conrad (1138–52) is Emperor and Eugene (1145–53) Pope, while we find Eberhard archbishop of Salzburg[3] (1147–64) and Romanus bishop of Gurk (1131–67). The treatise, which shows Bolognese influence but lacks general interest, is designed for monks and begins as follows:

Incipit prologus Baldwini in librum dictaminum. [D]ilectis in Christo fratribus suis M. et A. tam docentium quam discentium minimus B. cum omnibus sarcinulis suis se ipsum. Amicorum peticio pretendit que equitati non repugnant amicum retundere non decet si tamen obsequendi facultas amico est. Quare cum vestram peticionem considero me quod petitis estimo debere, sed item in me reversus ac ipsius mei propius ruditatem intuitus et de promisso fere penitentia teneor et suscepte rei diffidentia confundor. At certe quoniam nobis semel promisso defixus [!] tenere licet, difficile id mee fuerit incurie, si non pro velle tamen pro posse, amicorum peticioni cum ne satis saltem aliquid temptabo facere, ut cum fecero quod potero et de negligentia erga tam desiderabiles amicos excuser et illud sapientis elogium in promissores stultos prolatum declinem, Est qui pre confusione promittit amico et lucratus est eum inimicum gratis.[4] Quia igitur vestra peticio est ut aliquam per me dictandi noticiam habeatis, eam vobis quam brevius ac lucidius potero tradere curabo. Pretermissis itaque illis dictandis speciebus que claustralem curiositatem minus spectare videntur, rithmo videlicet et metro, de ea tantum specie que prosa dicitur, quod etiam vestra videtur querere peticio, dicamus. Explicit prologus.

---

[1] No. 5, MS. B; cf. Bütow, pp. 44 f.; also no. 4, MS. E.

[2] Saec. xii; cf. Loserth, in *Neues Archiv*, xxii. 299.

[3] For Salzburg letters of Eberhard's time, see *M.I.O.G.*, xlii. 313–342 (1927).

[4] Ecclesiasticus, xx. 25.

France, on the other hand, developed a school of her own, or rather two schools, in the course of the twelfth century,[1] and by the following century French influence is felt in Italy and French treatises and models penetrate into Germany.[2] We have seen that letters of Albert of Samaria reached France soon after 1130,[3] and that one of the manuscripts of Henricus Francigena bears signs of having been retouched in the neighbourhood of Rheims,[4] although Henry's French origin, as seen in his name, cannot be taken as showing any French influence upon the doctrine of his Pavian treatise. Soon after 1150 the treatise of Bernard of Bologna (MSS. E and F) has been fitted out with French proper names.[5] About the same time we hear, albeit vaguely, of a school of *dictamen* at Tours,[6] associated in some

[1] L. Delisle, "Les Écoles d'Orléans au douzième et au treizième siècle," in *Annuaire-Bulletin de la Société de l'Histoire de France*, 1869, pp. 139-154, and "Notice sur une 'Summa dictaminis' jadis conservée à Beauvais," in *Notices et extraits*, xxxvi, 1, pp. 171-205 (1899); L. Auvray, "Documents Orléanais du XIIᵉ et du XIIIᵉ siècle," in Société Archéologique et Historique de l'Orléanais, *Mémoires*, xxiii. 393-413 (1892); N. Valois, *De arte scribendi epistolas apud Gallicos medii aevi scriptores rhetoresve* (Paris, 1880); Langlois, "Maître Bernard," in *B. E. C.*, liv. 225-250, 792-795 (1893), and "Formulaires de lettres du XIIᵉ, du XIIIᵉ, et du XIVᵉ siècle," in *Notices et extraits*, xxxiv, pt. 1, pp. 1-32, 305-322 (1891); pt. 2, pp. 1-29 (1895); xxxv, pt. 2, pp. 409-434, 793-830 (1897); A. Luchaire, *Études sur quelques manuscrits de Rome et de Paris* (Paris, 1899), and "Une correspondance inédite des abbés de Saint-Victor sous Louis VII," in *Séances et travaux* of the Académie des Sciences Morales et Politiques, clii. 547-569 (1899).

[2] Bruno Stehle, *Über ein Hildesheimer Formelbuch* (Sigmaringen, 1878); A. Cartellieri, *Ein Donaueschinger Briefsteller* (Innsbruck, 1898); H. Simonsfeld, "Ueber die Formelsammlung des Rudolf von Tours," Munich *S. B.*, 1898, i. 402-486. Cf. also a group of letters of Frederick I in a manuscript of French origin, now in Prague, described by A. Brackmann, "Dictamina zur Geschichte Friedrich Barbarossas," Berlin *S. B.*, 1927, pp. 379-392.

[3] No. 3, p. 176.   [4] No. 4, MS. D., p. 179.   [5] No. 10, p. 183.

[6] The nature and growth of one of these early French collections is illustrated in a manuscript at Bruges, MS. 549, ff. 4 v-32 v, beginning: 'Duplici maceratur gravamine qui nec parentum presidio nec diviciarum suffragio solidatur. . . .' The collection has no accompanying theoretical treatise, and breaks off abruptly in the manuscript, which is of the end of the twelfth century; it contains numerous forms of letters and many drafts of official documents of ecclesiastical interest. The letters are almost destitute of proper names, the principal exception (f. 9 v) being Jocius, archbishop of Tours (1156-74). The formal documents, several of which are dated 1166, concern St. Martin's of Tours, and also Orleans, Chartres, Paris, and Meaux: Alexander is Pope, Louis king of France, and Henry king of England. In three instances the name is given of

way with Bernard Silvester, and toward the close of the century another school appears in the region of Orleans and more particularly at Meung-sur-Loire. To the Orléanais in the time of Philip Augustus can be traced several treatises and groups of letters; the chief treatise bears the name of Bernard of Meung, and the many letters both real and imaginary are closely associated with the studies of Latin literature which flourished at Orleans and Fleury. In the treatises of this period, the *cursus* now has an assured place.

No manual of the new epistolography yet appears in England, unless England be credited with Peter of Blois, whose brief treatise on *dictamen* (1185–89) seeks to replace both Master Bernard and the school of Tours. Peter also has a brief section on the *cursus*.[1] The treatise of Gervase of Melkley, *De arte versificandi et modo dictandi*,[2] written in the reign of King John, is concerned almost exclusively with poetical composition, following in the steps of Matthew of Vendôme, Geoffrey of Vinsauf, and especially Bernard Silvester, "a parrot in prose, but in verse a very nightingale."[3] Only a brief concluding chapter deals with prose *dictamen*.

In all this the influence of Italy upon France is in general quite clear, but the specific connexions escape us, especially in the second half of the century. Moreover the intellectual currents

the *dictator* from whom the draft has been taken over: 'negotium de libertate secundum Magistrum Hilarium Aurelianensem' (f. 27 v); 'scriptum de ordine diaconi vel presbiteri secundum M. R.' (f. 28 v); 'secundum Magistrum Theobaldum' (f. 31 v).

This collection is preceded in the manuscript (ff. 1–4 v) by a curious 'Tractatus primus Iohannis de dictamine,' beginning 'Cum omnis scientia rudis sit et inculta . . .,' in which the author's devotion to Cicero leads him to throw his treatise into the form of a dialogue between Cicero and his son, but cannot keep him at the end from discussing the proper form of salutation to be observed between Frederick Barbarossa and Henry II of England.

[1] Langlois, in *Notices et extraits des manuscrits*, xxxiv, pt. 2, pp. 23–29.

[2] Balliol College, MS. 263, ff. 153 v–176; MS. 276, ff. 127–153 v. On Gervase cf. F. M. Powicke, *Stephen Langton* (Oxford, 1928), pp. 102 f.

[3] 'Scripserunt autem hanc artem Mattheus Vidocinensis plene, Galfridus Vinesa [*sic*] plenius, plenissime vero Bernardus Silvestris, in prosaico psitacus, in metrico philomena.' Balliol MS. 263, f. 153 v. On such treatises see E. Faral, *Les arts poétiques du XIIe et XIIIe siècle* (Paris, 1924); W. B. Sedgwick, "The Style and Vocabulary of the Latin Arts of Poetry of the Twelfth and Thirteenth Centuries," in *Speculum*, iii. 349–381 (1928).

between the two countries flowed in both directions. Law and *dictamen* spread from Italy to the North, while theology, particularly in the form which it received at the hands of Anselm and Abaelard, affected the canonists as well as the theologians of Italy. Now and then the *dictatores* give us glimpses of this intellectual interchange. Thus in the letters of Albert of Samaria a Bolognese student asks for the loan of a collection of theological sentences recently brought from France, *divinarum sententiarum excerptum quod nuper de Francia detulisti*—interesting evidence of the early spread of the new sentence literature as worked out in the schools of Laon and Paris.[1] In a Lombard collection of *ca.* 1132 we found an Italian student studying at Chartres under Master Bernard, with whose sentences he hopes to become fully imbued by the coming Easter.[2] In the earliest redaction of the treatise of Bernard of Bologna, *ca.* 1145, a student, apparently of rhetoric, has come from France to Bologna.[3] On the other hand, an early letter-book from Chartres shows Pisans studying at Laon under Anselm, who died in 1117.[4] Such evidence is rare and fragmentary at best; but other material of the sort may reward further investigation.

[1] No. 3, above, letter 3. On the influence of the new sentence literature in Italy, cf. the works of Grabmann and de Ghellinck cited above, no. 3, p. 177, note 4.

[2] No. 7, *ante*.

[3] 'Ex quo divina vos comitante gratia de Gallie partibus Bononiam venistis, quo dilectionis affectu vos viderim et qualiter vobis prompta devotione paruerim ipsis rerum effectibus evidenter, ut arbitror, agnoscitur.' Graz, MS. 1515, f. 97 v; Vatican, MS. Pal. lat. 1801, f. 43.

[4] *B. E. C.*, 1855, pp. 465-466.

CHAPTER X

ROBERT LE BOUGRE AND THE BEGINNINGS OF THE INQUISITION IN NORTHERN FRANCE [1]

In few fields of historical investigation has greater advance been made in recent years than in the study of the mediaeval Inquisition. Long a favourite battle-ground of passion and prejudice, occupied chiefly by the controversialist and the pamphleteer, the history of the Inquisition has begun to yield to the methods and spirit of modern historical science; and while the issues which it involved are not always easily separable from those of our own day, there has been a noticeable gain, not only in the critical accumulation of knowledge which reveals the real workings of the Inquisition, but also in the application to it of the historical spirit, which seeks neither to approve nor condemn an institution as such, but only to understand it in the light of its own age. Scholars of many lands have contributed to this result, and it is a source of pride to American students that the work of one of their countrymen, Henry Charles Lea,[2] still remains, in spite of the active investigations

---

[1] Revised from the *American Historical Review*, vii. 437–457, 631–652 (1902). I have gone through the subsequent publications on the mediaeval Inquisition without finding reason to modify the conclusions reached in 1902. The intervening years have produced a number of works, particularly by Roman Catholic writers; see Paul Fredericq, "Les récents historiens catholiques de l'Inquisition en France," in *Revue historique*, cix. 307–334 (1912). Of these the most important are the defence of the Inquisition by Mgr. C. Douais, *L'Inquisition: ses origines—sa procédure* (Paris, 1906), and by Jean Guiraud, article "Inquisition," in A. d'Alès, *Dictionnaire apologétique*, 4th ed., ii. 823–890 (Paris, 1915); the excellent brief account by the Abbé E. Vacandard, *L'Inquisition* (Paris, 1906; 5th ed., 1914; English translation by B. L. Conway, New York and London, 1908); Vacandard's article "Inquisition" in A. Vacant and E. Mangenot, *Dictionnaire de théologie catholique*, vii. 2016–68 (1922); J. M. Vidal, *Bullaire de l'Inquisition française au XIVᵉ siècle* (Paris, 1913); and the elaborate treatise, with a portentous bibliography, of T. de Cauzons, *Histoire de l'Inquisition en France* (Paris, 1909–12, 2 vols.). A. L. Maycock, *The Inquisition* (New York and London, 1927), is a compilation at second hand. Of non-Catholic works, see especially the keen analysis of Ch.-V. Langlois, *L'Inquisition d'après des travaux récents* (Paris, 1902); and the convenient sketch of A. S. Turberville, *Mediaeval Heresy and the Inquisition* (London, 1920).

[2] *A History of the Inquisition of the Middle Ages* (New York, 1887, 3 vols.).

of the forty-two years which have elapsed since its publication, "the most extensive, the most profound, and the most thorough history of the Inquisition which we possess."[1] At the same time no one would have been slower than its author to claim finality for a work which, with all its enormous research, could not utilize many of the sources now accessible, or profit by the monographic studies upon the Inquisition which in 1887 had scarcely begun to appear; and no one was more ready to welcome the numerous contributions to the history of the Holy Office. Of these more recent studies, some have dealt with the more general aspects of the Inquisition, such as the organization and procedure of its tribunals or their relation to such matters as witchcraft and magic, others have been content to examine more closely its vicissitudes in the various countries of Europe and America.

These general and local investigations can never be wholly independent, and their connexion is peculiarly close in the case of an institution like the Inquisition, which developed slowly and to a certain degree as the result of experiments carried on in different places at the same time, and which it is consequently impossible to understand as a whole without examining the varying conditions which affected it in different countries. This is particularly true of the formative period of the thirteenth century, and it is with this period and with the comparatively

French translation, *Histoire de l'Inquisition au moyen-âge*, ouvrage traduit sur l'exemplaire revu et corrigé de l'auteur par Salomon Reinach (Paris, 1900–02, 3 vols.). German translation by Heinz Wieck and Max Rachel, edited by Joseph Hansen, *Geschichte der Inquisition im Mittelalter* (Bonn, 1905–13, 3 vols.). Italian translation of vol. i by Pia Cremonini, *Storia dell'Inquisizione: fondazione e procedura* (Turin, 1910).

[1] Quoted from F. H. Reusch by Paul Fredericq, in his essay on the "Historiographie de l'Inquisition," prefixed to the French and German translations of Lea's *History of the Inquisition of the Middle Ages* (cf. *Revue historique*, cix. 309 (1912)); repeated by Vacandard, p. vii, who, however, denies finality to Lea's work. Lord Acton declared that the central portions of Lea's work "constitute a sound and solid structure that will survive the censure of all critics." *E.H.R.*, iii. 788 (1888); *The History of Freedom and other Essays* (London, 1907), p. 574. For less favourable Roman Catholic judgements, see Paul Fournier, in *Revue d'histoire ecclésiastique*, iii. 709 (1902); Charles Moeller, *ibid.*, xiv. 721 (1913); Baumgarten's volume cited on p. 261 below; and *Catholic Encyclopedia*, article "Inquisition." On Lea's work in general, see Chapter XII.

neglected field of Northern France that the present chapter is concerned. The necessity for the Inquisition in the North was at all times small, when compared with the grave situation which confronted the church in Languedoc, and its history is naturally of far less importance. Still, the wide prevalence of heresy in the South and the drastic measures which were found necessary for its extermination were to a certain extent abnormal, and are apt to create a false impression of the conditions which called the papal Inquisition into existence. The naturalness, one may almost say the inevitableness, of the rise of the papal Inquisition appears much more clearly if it is studied under more normal conditions, in a field which presented no exceptional difficulties to the operation of the older system. Some account of the early history of the Inquisition in the North will be found in the general work of Lea, in Tanon's useful study of inquisitorial procedure in France,[1] and in Fredericq's admirable history of the Inquisition in the Netherlands.[2] It is hard gleaning after such scholars as these, yet their somewhat incidental treatment of Northern France and the additional material that is now available upon the subject may perhaps justify a more special study. I shall deal briefly with the period preceding the introduction of the papal Inquisition, and shall then treat more at length the general history and the procedure of the Inquisition under the first papal inquisitor, the Dominican friar Robert le Petit, better known by his popular name of Robert le Bougre.[3]

[1] L. Tanon, *Histoire des Tribunaux de l'Inquisition en France* (Paris, 1893).

[2] *Corpus documentorum Inquisitionis Haereticae Pravitatis Neerlandicae.* Ghent and the Hague, 1889–1906, 5 vols. *Geschiedenis der Inquisitie in de Nederlanden. Ibid.*, 1892–97, 2 vols. Many of the documents in the *Corpus* were already in print, but I shall frequently refer to this collection because of its convenience.

[3] The only special study of Friar Robert is the monograph of Jules Frede-richs, a pupil of Paul Fredericq, entitled *Robert le Bougre, premier Inquisiteur Général en France*, and published as the sixth fascicle of the *Recueil de travaux* of the Faculty of Philosophy of the University of Ghent (32 pp., Ghent, 1892). So far as it goes, this is a very creditable piece of work, being particularly useful for events in Flanders and the adjacent regions, but its author overlooked several important sources of information. The accounts in Fredericq (*Geschiedenis*, i. 42–59) and Tanon (pp. 113–117) accept Frederichs' results. Other brief accounts are in Lea, ii. 113–117 (with some corrections and additions in the French and German translations); E. Berger, *Blanche de Castille* (Paris,

The sources for the history of the Inquisition in Northern France, when compared with the materials available for Langue-doc, are disappointingly meagre. There was here far less to record than in the South and far less system in the records, and even the material that once existed has largely disappeared in the destruction of one kind and another which has wrought such sad havoc with the French archives of the thirteenth century. There is for the North no Collection Doat, with its rich mass of copies from ecclesiastical archives; there are no registers of pro-ceedings like those of the tribunals of Carcassonne and Pamiers or of the inquisitor Bernard de Caux; there are no manuals of procedure like the famous *Practica* of Bernard Gui.[1] The most that careful search can collect for the North consists of some scattered local charters, a fair number of papal bulls, a few edifying examples garnered into the pious collections of Caesar of Heisterbach,[2] Étienne de Bourbon,[3] and Thomas de Cantim-pré,[4] and the narratives of contemporary chroniclers, whose accounts of local matters are often of considerable value. Of

1895), pp. 294–296; Tillemont, *Vie de Saint-Louis*, ii. 289–293 (remarkably good for its time); and M. D. Chapotin, *Histoire des Dominicains de la province de France* (Rouen, 1898), pp. 216–226. Chapotin's recital is incomplete and careless and contains little that is new. The account in Paul Beuzart, *Les hérésies pendant le moyen âge et la réforme dans la région de Douai, d'Arras, et au pays de l'Alleu* (Paris, 1912), does not go beyond the material in Frederichs. My articles in the *A. H. R.* were also overlooked by E. Chénon, "L'hérésie à La Charité-sur-Loire et les débuts de l'Inquisition monastique dans la France du nord au XIIIᵉ siècle," in *Nouvelle revue historique de droit*, xli. 299–345 (1917). See Fredericq, *Corpus*, iii, p. xviii (1906).

¹ On these see Charles Molinier, *L'Inquisition dans le Midi de la France* (Paris, 1880), and *Études sur quelques manuscrits des bibliothèques d'Italie con-cernant l'Inquisition et les croyances hérétiques* (Paris, 1888: reprinted from *Archives des missions scientifiques et littéraires*, 3d series, xiv) ; C. Douais, "Les sources de l'histoire de l'Inquisition dans le Midi de la France," in the *Revue des questions historiques*, xxx. 383–459 (1881), and *Documents pour servir à l'histoire de l'Inquisition dans le Languedoc* (Paris, 1900, 2 vols.).

² *Caesarii Heisterbacensis . . . Dialogus miraculorum*, ed. Strange (Cologne, 1851); *Die Fragmente der Libri VIII Miraculorum*, ed. A. Meister (Rome, 1901).

³ *Anecdotes historiques, légendes, et apologues tirés du recueil inédit d'Étienne de Bourbon*, ed. Lecoy de la Marche (Paris, 1877). Étienne was himself an inquisitor. On such collections of *exempla*, see *supra*, Chapter II.

⁴ *Bonum universale de apibus* (Douai, 1627). Cf. E. Berger, *Thomae Canti-pratensis Bonum universale de apibus quid illustrandis saeculi decimi tertii moribus conferat* (Paris, 1895), and A. Kaufmann, *Thomas von Chantimpré* (Cologne, 1899).

the records of the royal administration under St. Louis, which must once have contained important information regarding the persecution of heresy, nothing remains touching the Inquisition save some scattered notices in the royal accounts; the administrative correspondence is gone, even the general ordinance issued by St. Louis for the punishment of heresy in the North has disappeared.[1] Fortunately the papal documents of the thirteenth century are better preserved, thanks to the numerous originals in local depositories and to the registers so carefully kept by the papal chancery from the accession of Innocent III; and it is from these more than from any other single source that we derive the greater part of our knowledge of the early history of the papal Inquisition and—so scarce are local documents relating to heresy—much of our knowledge of the later history of the episcopal Inquisition as well. Still the registers, whose publication in recent years has been of the greatest assistance to all students of the thirteenth century,[2] sometimes fail us when we most need their aid; all bulls were not registered, and many important acts of the papal administration were issued through legates or subordinate bureaus whose records have for the most part disappeared.[3]

[1] Fredericq, *Corpus*, ii, nos. 20, 55; *Geschiedenis*, i. 111–113.

[2] The registers of Innocent III have been in print since the seventeenth century, those of Honorius III have been edited by Pressutti, while the publication of the registers of the other Popes of the thirteenth century is due to the French School at Rome. For the years from 1198 to 1276 practically the entire series of registers is in print, the most important for the present purpose being *Les registres de Grégoire IX*, edited by L. Auvray (Paris, 1896–1910, 2 vols. and 2 fascicles; the index has not yet appeared). Of the older collections of papal bulls the most important for the study of the Inquisition is of course the *Bullarium Ordinis FF. Praedicatorum* edited by Thomas Ripoll (Rome, 1729–40); the *Analecta sacri Ordinis Fratrum Praedicatorum* (Rome, 1893 ff.) contains supplementary material.

[3] From one of these bureaus valuable documents, some of them relating to the Inquisition, have been preserved in a collection of forms of the papal penitentiary discovered and published by Lea in his *Formulary of the Papal Penitentiary* (Philadelphia, 1892). There is no evidence that any of the documents contained in the formulary are subsequent to 1243, and so far as they can be dated they fall within the pontificate of Gregory IX. The collection is ascribed in the title to a cardinal priest 'magister Thomasius,' whom Lea (p. xxxviii) identifies with Jacobus Thomasius Gaetanus, cardinal priest of St. Clement from 1295 to 1300. It is much more probable that the compiler was the famous

The existence of heresy in the North of France can be traced back as far as the early part of the eleventh century, when heretics were discovered and punished at Orleans, Arras, and Châlons-sur-Marne, and as time goes on heretics are found in most parts of the North, even in regions as remote as Brittany.[1] These heretics were Manicheans who had passed westward and northward from Italy and Provence along the great lines of trade, just as their predecessors may have followed the routes of Balkan commerce into Italy,[2] and they were most numerous in the classes that travelled most, the merchants and artisans of the towns. Their chief centres in the North were in French Burgundy and the Nivernais, in Champagne, whose fairs constituted the great international market of the twelfth and thirteenth centuries and brought together large numbers of traders from Italy and the North,[3] and in Flanders, where the

Thomas of Capua, who is mentioned in certain of the forms. See Martin Souchon, in *Historische Zeitschrift*, lxxiii. 87 (1894); and my papers on "The Sources for the History of the Papal Penitentiary," in *American Journal of Theology*, ix. 421–450 (1905), and "Two Roman Formularies in Philadelphia," in *Miscellanea Francesco Ehrle* (1924), iv. 275–286.

Most of the forms concerning heretics in Lea's *Formulary* were taken over into the new edition of the formulary under Benedict XII, of which I have collated the manuscript at Tours (MS. 594, ff. 2–73).

[1] On the early history of heresy in Northern France see the excellent pioneer work of Charles Schmidt, *Histoire et doctrine de la secte des Cathares ou Albigeois* (Paris, 1849), i. 24–50, 86–94; Havet in the *B. E. C.*, xli. 498 ff.; Lea, i, chs. 2 and 3; H. Theloe, *Die Ketzerverfolgungen im 11. und 12. Jahrhundert* (Freiburg diss., 1913); T. de Cauzons, *Histoire de l'Inquisition en France*, i. 235 ff.

[2] Cf. Karl Müller, *Kirchengeschichte* (Freiburg, 1892–1919), i. 495; and on the predominance of the Catharan form of heresy in the North see Charles Molinier in the *Revue historique*, xliii. 167. Most of the places mentioned in the eleventh and twelfth centuries as seats of heresy in the North lie directly on the great trade routes, as may be seen by examining the map of overland trade routes at the end of Schulte's *Geschichte des mittelalterlichen Handels und Verkehrs zwischen Westdeutschland und Italien* (Leipzig, 1900). That the Albigensian Crusades also scattered heretics northward is altogether likely (Lea, ii. 113).

For instances of the close connexion between the heretics of Northern France and those of Italy see Fredericq, *Corpus*, i, no. 2; Albericus in *SS.*, xxiii. 940, 944; Mousket, *Chronique rimée*, verses 28873, 28996; H. F., xviii. 726; and the papal bulls in Auvray, no. 1044, and Chapotin, *Histoire des Dominicains de la province de France*, p. 224.

[3] C. Alengry, *Les foires de Champagne* (Paris, 1915). On the central position of the fairs of Champagne at this time see Schulte, i. 156, 160. On Flemish

development of manufactures attracted considerable bodies of workmen from a distance and crowded them in towns for whose religious welfare the older ecclesiastical organization made no adequate provision.[1] So popular did the dualistic doctrines become among the weavers that the name *textor* became a synonym for heretic,[2] while suspicion easily fell upon the Flemish merchants by reason of their intercourse with the South and of the popular association of heresy with usury.[3] The Waldensian element in the North of France was of later origin than the Manichean and of much less importance. Adherents of this sect are found in several neighbouring cities of the Empire, such as Metz, Toul, Strasbourg, and Besançon,[4] and a later writer states that it was possible for a Waldensian journeying from Antwerp to Rome to spend every night with people of his faith,[5] but exceedingly little is known of them in France. The clearest case is that of a baker of Rheims, named Echard, who was burnt in 1230 or 1231 after condemnation by a provincial council which at the same time felt it necessary to forbid the circulation of Romance versions of the Scriptures.[6]

The discovery and punishment of heresy in the earlier Middle

merchants at the fairs see F. Bourquelot, *Études sur les foires de Champagne*, i. 139–141, 191 ff.; Pirenne, *Histoire de Belgique*, i, 2d ed. (1902), p. 254. Among the various discussions of the intercourse of Italian merchants with Champagne, see particularly C. Paoli, *Siena alle fiere di Sciampagna* (Siena, 1898), and A. Schaube, *Handelsgeschichte der romanischen Völker des Mittelmeergebiets bis zum Ende der Kreuzzüge* (Munich, 1906), pp. 374–391. Champagne was also of great importance in the woollen industry (Schulte, i. 127).

[1] Karl Müller, *Kirchengeschichte*, i. 493, 557; Pirenne, *Histoire de Belgique*, i. 333.

[2] Pirenne, *l. c.*; Schmidt, i. 43, 47; ii. 281; Du Cange under 'Textores'; Bernard of Clairvaux, *Sermones in Cantica*, lxv, in Migne, *P. L.*, clxxxiii, col. 1092.

[3] Persecution of merchants for heresy at Lille and Arras in Mousket, v. 28988; Fredericq, *Corpus*, i, no. 121. The association of heresy with usury is illustrated by Matthew Paris, *Chronica majora*, iii. 520, where he is speaking of Flanders. On the prevalence of usury in Flanders see *SS.*, xxiv. 309; xxviii. 442; Auvray, no. 392.

[4] H. Haupt, "Waldenserthum und Inquisition," in *Deutsche Zeitschrift für Geschichtswissenschaft*, i. 285 ff. (1889).

[5] Trithemius, *Annales Hirsaugienses, ad an.* 1230 (edition of 1690, i. 543). The source of the statement is unknown. K. E. Müller, *Quellen welche der Abt Tritheim im ersten Theile seiner Hirsauer Annalen benutzt hat* (Leipzig, 1871), p. 30.   [6] See Chapter XI, *infra*.

Ages was the duty of the bishop, assisted in the exercise of this, as of other judicial functions, by the archdeacon and later the official.[1] In securing information the bishop might avail himself of the machinery of local inquest, inherited from the Carolingian government, which placed at his disposal in every parish a body, usually seven, of *testes synodales*, sworn to reveal whatever they might know or hear of any offence coming within the bishop's jurisdiction. That among such offences heresy should have a prominent place was in itself natural, and was moreover particularly commanded by various councils, notably the great Lateran council of 1215. After an accusation of heresy had been brought to the bishop, by public presentment or private information— and the vagueness of the chroniclers on this point rarely permits us to determine the method employed in a particular case— there was still chance for considerable perplexity regarding the subsequent procedure. Cases of heresy were not of common occurrence, and while the canon law contained principles which were capable of application to such cases, the local prelate had few precedents to guide him as to the procedure to be followed or the penalty to be inflicted—indeed the preliminary question as to what constituted heresy might often puzzle any one but a theological expert. It is therefore not surprising to find the French bishops seeking the advice of their fellow prelates,[2] turning to a papal legate, if one happened to be near, or even consulting the Pope himself.[3] The procedure was deliberate— at times too deliberate for the patience of the people, who in some instances lynched those whom the bishops sought to protect[4]—and apparently an effort was made to give the accused a fair trial as that was then understood. The examina-

---

[1] On the organization and procedure of the episcopal inquisition see particularly Lea, i. 305–315; Tanon, pp. 255–325; P. Hinschius, *Kirchenrecht*, v. 337 ff., 425 ff.; de Cauzons, i. 316 ff., 386 ff.; Theloe, *Die Ketzerverfolgungen im 11. und 12. Jahrhundert*. What is given below is of course only a very brief outline, and no attempt is made to treat the various legal questions involved.

[2] Examples in Fredericq, *Corpus*, i, nos. 3, 46, 48; *H. F.* xii. 266.

[3] As at Liége in 1145 (Fredericq, *Corpus*, i, no. 30), Arras in 1153 (*ibid.*, no. 32), and Rheims in 1162 (*ibid.*, no. 36).

[4] The instances will be found in the *B. E. C.*, xli. 507, 515; or in Tanon, p. 15. Cf. H. Maillet, *L'Église et la répression sanglante de l'hérésie* (Liége, 1909), pp. 33 ff., who cites such instances in order to relieve the clergy of responsibility.

tion was often conducted in the presence of a number of bishops,[1] or even an organized church council,[2] and mention is sometimes made of the presence of skilled jurists or masters in theology as well.[3]

When the matter of checking the spread of heresy was first taken up by the Popes, no fundamental change was made in the system just described. The legislation of Lucius III and Innocent III, besides defining heresy more sharply and requiring active assistance on the part of the secular power, was directed primarily toward increasing the responsibility of the bishop and empowering him to proceed against suspected persons on his own initiative, by virtue of his official authority, without waiting for formal accusations.[4] Ultimately the legislation establishing this new inquisitorial procedure proved of the greatest importance in relation both to the pursuit of heretics and to the criminal process of the lay courts, but it created no new tribunals

---

[1] As at Vézelay in 1167 (H. F., xii. 343) and in the persecutions at La Charité.

[2] Examples are: Liége, 1135 (Fredericq, Corpus, i, no. 25); Sens, 1198 (H. F., xviii. 262); Dijon, 1199 (Hefele-Knöpfler, Conciliengeschichte, v. 798; French tr. by Leclercq, v. 1226); Paris, 1201 and 1210 (ibid., v. 801, 861); Trier, 1231 (Fredericq, Corpus, i, no. 82); Rheims, 1230 or 1231 (Chapter XI, infra).

[3] Potthast, nos. 693, 4197; SS., xxvi. 275. On the evidence used in the earlier French cases see Tanon, pp. 275, 303 ff., 324. Another example of the use of witnesses in Hauréau, i. 178. The application of canonical purgation was more common than Tanon states; see the instances of its employment for laymen at La Charité in Auvray, nos. 1044, 2825; Potthast, no. 10044. In the best known case, that of the dean of Nevers in 1199 and 1200 (Potthast, nos. 693, 1124, 1577), it appears that the accused was restored to office; his signature as dean is found in a charter of the year 1200, according to Parmentier, Histoire sommaire de nosseigneurs les évêques de Nevers (MS. in the Archives de la Nièvre), i. 102.

[4] On the episcopal inquisition and the Popes see, besides the works cited above, the chapter in Fredericq's Geschiedenis (i, ch. 2); and on the obligations of the bishop, Henner, Beiträge zur Organisation und Competenz der päpstlichen Ketzergerichte (Leipzig, 1890), p. 47. The canons of the council of Verona and the Lateran council of 1215 which relate to heresy will be found in Fredericq, Corpus, i, nos. 56, 68. For the development of the so-called official procedure on the part of the bishop, which was by no means limited to cases of heresy, the eighth canon of the Lateran council (Corpus Juris Canonici, ed. Friedberg, ii. 745) is also important. Cf. Hinschius, Kirchenrecht, v. 349 ff.; Paul Fournier, Les officialités au moyen âge (Paris, 1880), pp. 91, 270–281; and A. Esmein, Histoire de la procédure criminelle en France et spécialement de la procédure inquisitoire (Paris, 1882), pp. 66 ff.

and for the time being affected only the episcopal authorities. Under Innocent III there was a significant growth in the number of appeals from bishops' sentences, and occasionally, in Languedoc, papal legates were sent out to supplement the local authorities, but no new organization was introduced, and the episcopal Inquisition remained until the time of Gregory IX the only regular machinery for the repression and punishment of heresy.

The practical workings of the episcopal Inquisition were frequently tested in the later twelfth and earlier thirteenth centuries in Northern France.[1] In the ecclesiastical province of Rheims, within whose borders were to be found the principal industrial and commercial centres of the North, a council met as early as 1157 to legislate against the Manichean weavers, "men of the lowest class who move frequently from place to place and change their names as they go,"[2] and within the next half-century numerous adherents of this sect were condemned in this region, particularly in Flanders, whence heretics fled to Cologne and even as far as England.[3] Archbishop Guillaume I, who was also cardinal legate, and Count Philip of Flanders particularly distinguished themselves in these persecutions, yet heretics appear again at Soissons in 1204, at Arras in 1208, and at Cambrai in 1217,[4] while in 1230–31 it was found necessary to convene a council of the province in order to forbid the circulation of Romance versions of the Scriptures and condemn the Waldensian errors of the baker Echard.[5] At Paris in 1210 the bishop took the initiative in the proceedings against the followers of Amauri de Bène, who were then examined and condemned

---

[1] Many of the instances cited below will be found, often narrated at greater length, in Schmidt, i. 86–94, 362–365; Havet, *B. E. C.*, xli. 511 ff.; Lea, i. 130, 131, 307 ff.; Fredericq, *Geschiedenis*, i. 21 ff.

[2] Fredericq, *Corpus*, i, no. 34.

[3] Fredericq, *Corpus*, i, nos. 36–38, 40–44, 46, 48–55; ii, nos. 9, 10, 17; Ralph of Coggeshall, ed. Stevenson, pp. 121 ff.; Frederichs, "De Kettervervolgingen van Philips van den Elzas," in the *Nederlandsch Museum* for 1890, pp. 233–245. Frederichs places in 1160 the council at Oxford which condemned the Flemish heretics, evidently failing to observe the evidence on this point contained in the Assize of Clarendon of 1166.

[4] *H. F.*, xviii. 713; Fredericq, *Corpus*, i, nos. 64, 69.

[5] See below, Chapter XI.

by a provincial council, and burnt by authority of Philip Augustus.[1] The same council pronounced against the doctrines of Amauri and others, a precedent which was followed some years later by a council of the same province,[2] and early in the reign of St. Louis a Franciscan who preached heresy at Paris was condemned by a papal legate.[3] No ecclesiastical authority is mentioned in the accounts of the heretics who were burnt at Troyes in 1200 and 1220[4] and at Orleans about the same time;[5] those who appeared in 1206 in Brittany were reported by the parish priest directly to the Pope, who referred the matter to the archdeacon of St. Malo and two abbots.[6]

In the East, in the dioceses of Auxerre and Nevers and the adjoining portions of the dioceses of Langres and Autun, cases of heresy were of more frequent occurrence, and called for constant watchfulness on the part of the bishops. Appearing in this region first in 1167 at Vézelay, where several were condemned at the instance of the abbot of the monastery,[7] the heretics soon spread their teachings in the neighbouring lands of French Burgundy and the Nivernais, where they numbered among their converts knights and wealthy bourgeois as well as men and women of the lower classes, and even brought suspicion, at Nevers, upon the abbot of St. Martin's, the dean, and one of the canons of the cathedral. The whole machinery of the episcopal Inquisition was turned against them—the preaching of Foulques de Neuilly, the active efforts of the archbishop of Sens and the

---

[1] See in particular the *Chartularium Universitatis Parisiensis*, i, nos. 11, 12; Caesar of Heisterbach, ed. Strange, i. 304 ff.; *H. F.*, xvii. 83; xix. 250; *SS.*, xxvi. 275; G. Théry, *Autour du décret de 1210* (Kain, 1925–26: *Bibliothèque Thomiste*, vi, vii); M. De Wulf, *Histoire de la philosophie médiévale*, 5th ed. (Louvain and Paris, 1924–25), i. 235. References to the numerous modern discussions concerning the doctrines condemned in 1210 will be found in Mandonnet, *Siger de Brabant* (2d ed., i. 17–19, Louvain, 1911).

[2] Hefele-Knöpfler, v. 933; *Chartularium Universitatis Parisiensis*, i, no. 50.

[3] *H. F.*, xviii. 319; xxi. 598.

[4] *SS.*, xxiii. 878 ; Caesar of Heisterbach, i. 307.

[5] *Enquête* of the time of St. Louis concerning the king's justice at Orleans: 'Hugo de Fossatis iuratus dixit quod vidit in tempore Manasseri episcopi quendam hominem dampnatum pro incredulitate de quo dominus rex fecit iusticiam secularem per ignem.' Archives Nationales, JJ. 26 (the so-called 'Register E of Philip Augustus'), f. 277. The bishop was probably Manasses de Seignelay (1207–21). [6] Potthast, no. 2941. [7] *H. F.*, xii. 343, 345.

bishops of the region, the authority of provincial councils, the
aid of the secular arm[1]—and the zeal of Bishop Hugues of
Auxerre gained for him the title of 'hammer of heretics,'[2] yet
in spite of conversions and penances and sentences of death the
infection remained.[3] For a time it seemed as if some impression
had been made upon the chief stronghold of the movement, the
town of La Charité-sur-Loire, yet after the death of Bishop
Hugues in 1206[4] the fugitives returned and many of the
converts relapsed into their old ways, so that within two years
the Pope was obliged to send the new bishop of Auxerre and
the bishop of Troyes against them.[5] The new inquisitors did
diligent service, among other things promulgating a set of
statutes "to confound the abuses of heresy and strengthen the
state of the faith,"[6] and for several years nothing is heard from
the scene of their labours. In 1231, however, Gregory IX discovered that heresy had again lifted its head at La Charité,
under the protection of certain nobles of the region, who were
at open feud with the prior and temporal lord of the town,[7] and
this time the archbishop of Bourges, who had some reputation
as a successful persecutor, was commissioned to act with the
bishop of the diocese.[8] Traces of the activity of these inquisitors

[1] Hervé, count of Nevers, who died in 1222, is called 'hereticorum precipuus
persecutor.' *Histoire littéraire*, xxxii. 530; Vincent de Beauvais, *Speculum
historiale* (Douai, 1624), iv. 1275.
[2] See his biography in *H. F.*, xviii. 726, and L. M. Duru, *Bibliothèque historique de l'Yonne*, i. 433; and cf. Robert d'Auxerre in *H. F.*, xviii. 273, or *SS.*,
xxvi. 270.
[3] On the heretics of the Nivernais see the other passages in the chroniclers
just cited (*H. F.*, xviii. 262, 264, 729; *SS.*, xxvi. 258, 260); also *H. F.*, xix. 7;
Potthast, nos. 693, 745, 1124, 1577, 1678, 1909, 2131; and the bulls cited in the
following notes. The *Cartulaire du prieuré de La Charité-sur-Loire* published by
Lespinasse (Nevers, 1887) and the charters from La Charité in the Bibliothèque
Nationale (MSS. Lat. n. a. 2274, 2275) do not appear to contain anything on
the subject. The persecutions for heresy at La Charité have now been narrated
by E. Chénon, in *Nouvelle revue historique de droit*, xli. 299-345 (1917).
For cases in the diocese of Langres see Potthast, nos. 4197, 4700; Auvray,
no. 1078.   [4] For a case in this year see Potthast, no. 2787.
[5] Potthast, no. 3271.   [6] Auvray, no. 637.
[7] The prior of La Charité had possessed temporal jurisdiction over the town
since 1174. Lespinasse, *Cartulaire*, p. 160.
[8] Auvray, no. 637. The archbishop died in 1232. Cf. his epitaph in P. Labbé,
Nova bibliotheca manuscript. librorum (ii. 109), beginning 'Exuperans hereses.'

are found in various documents in the papal registers,[1] yet in January, 1233, the Pope found it necessary to arouse the local authorities to action against a knight of La Charité who had fallen under suspicion because of the heresy of his brothers and his supposed connexion with the attacks of the count of Nevers on the neighbouring monasteries,[2] and some weeks later he appealed to the French king on behalf of the prior in his valiant struggle to maintain the faith in the face of the hostility of neighbouring lords.[3] Near the end of February Gregory IX, notwithstanding his earlier laudations of the French church as the "unshaken foundation of the faith,"[4] was obliged to confess that heresy was spreading "in a certain part of the circumference of the kingdom,"[5] and in April of the same year (1233), the reports of Friar Robert indicating an even worse state of affairs at La Charité than had been supposed, the papal Inquisition was introduced into the North.

In spite of repeated effort the episcopal Inquisition had plainly failed to accomplish the suppression of heresy at La Charité, and while we cannot be sure that it was given an equally fair trial in Champagne and Flanders, it is clear from the numerous convictions secured by the first papal inquisitor sent to those regions that the bishops had had no greater success in the other infected areas of the North. That the indifference of the bishops and their absorption in secular affairs may have had some share in this result, it would be idle to deny. But when a man of the energy and persistence of Hugues de Noyers was unable to eradicate the new beliefs from his diocese, it would seem that we must, in part at least, look elsewhere for an explanation. For one thing the duties of the episcopal office were so manifold

---

[1] Sentence of exile and confiscation (Auvray, no. 997); canonical purgation of a citizen of Souvigny (Auvray, no. 2825; Potthast, no. 10044); acquittal of a woman of La Charité (B.N., Coll. Moreau, 1191, f. 25). The examination of a canon of Chablis by the bishops of Auxerre and Nevers and the abbot and dean of Vézelay (Auvray, no. 1078) belongs to the same period.

[2] Auvray, no. 1044. The bishop's act of summons to the suspected knight, Colin Morand, is cited by J. Lebeuf, *Mémoires concernant l'histoire civile et ecclésiastique d'Auxerre* (ed. Challe and Quantin), i. 411.

[3] Bull of 28 February, 1233: Auvray, no. 1145. Cf. no. 1144.

[4] Bull of 18 July, 1227: Auvray, no. 133.

[5] Bull of 27 February, 1233: Auvray, no. 1152.

that no bishop could give more than intermittent attention to the investigation of heresy.[1] Then, if one bishop began a persecution, it was easy, in the absence of concerted action, to find at least temporary safety in another diocese,[2] while if heretical doctrine were entirely driven out of a district, it might immediately be reintroduced by some wanderer from Lombardy or Languedoc. The fact is that heresy had become more than a local problem, and by the thirteenth century something more than local means was necessary if it was to be suppressed. The system of procedure, too, was slow and cumbrous, having been for the most part taken over from the practice in dealing with offences where the rights of the accused were more carefully regarded, and satisfactory proof of heresy was particularly difficult to obtain by ordinary means, while the growing tendency to appeal to Rome or consult the Pope introduced a further element of delay. The disadvantages of the current procedure —and the evident desire of Innocent III to do justice—are illustrated by the case of certain inhabitants of La Charité. Excommunicated as suspects by the bishop of Auxerre, they succeeded, in 1199, in maintaining their orthodoxy before the papal legate, Peter of Capua, who proclaimed their release from excommunication in a council at Dijon and assigned them a penance which evidently included pilgrimage to Rome. Some, however, were too old or too feeble to undertake this journey, and Innocent III directed the bishops of Autun and Mâcon and the abbot of Cluny to pass upon their case and to protect from further molestation those who had satisfactorily performed the penance. The bishop of Auxerre still continued his accusations, carrying the matter to two other sets of judges and finally bringing the archbishop of Sens and certain of his suffragans to La Charité to conduct the examination. When the accused remained away on this occasion, as they had at the time of the

---

[1] On this point cf. Fredericq, *Corpus*, i, nos. 75, 89.

[2] Gregory IX says of the heretics of La Charité: 'Si quis vulpes incipiat prosequi, ut iurisdictionem eius effugiant vel evitent, ad aliam se transferunt regionem.' Bull *Gaudemus*: Fredericq, *Corpus*, i, no. 90. So in the time of Innocent III residents of the diocese of Auxerre would declare that they belonged in the diocese of Bourges or that of Nevers. Potthast, no. 3271.

bishop's previous visits to the town, and failed to appear at a hearing set for them at Auxerre, the archbishop condemned them as heretics. The case was then carried to the Pope, who referred it to the archbishop of Bourges, the bishop of Nevers, and the abbot of Cluny, with instructions to publish the men in question as heretics and hand them over to the secular power unless they made public confession of their error and gave security for their future orthodoxy.[1] After some months the archbishop and abbot—the bishop of Nevers having died—reported their findings to the Pope, at the same time sending to Rome three of the accused whom the archbishop had adjudged orthodox, and in May, 1203, four years after the proceedings had begun, the Pope sent back the parties with instructions to the judges delegate to prescribe penance for them and continue the examination of the other cases.[2] This affair may have run on longer than was usual,[3] but where such delays could occur, it is obvious that, if the mediaeval view of the enormity of the crime of heresy and the absolute necessity of its extermination were to continue to prevail, some more effective agency for the purpose must be devised. What was evidently needed was a set of inquisitors who could give their whole time and energy to the detection and punishment of heresy, inquisitors able to act promptly and without regard to diocesan boundaries, locally powerful, yet independent of local control, the willing instruments of the papal policy, yet not hampered by the delay of frequent appeals to Rome—in short just such an institution as the Popes ultimately organized in the Dominican Inquisition.

We cannot too often remind ourselves that the papal Inquisition "was not an institution definitely projected and founded, but was moulded step by step out of the materials which lay nearest to hand fitted for the object to be attained." A Pope

[1] Bull *Accedentes* of 12 May, 1202: Potthast, no. 1678.
[2] Bull *Qualiter* of 21 May, 1203: Potthast, no. 1909.
[3] An equally convincing illustration of the delays of the procedure under Innocent III is afforded by the case of a certain canon of Langres and priest of Mussy who appears in the papal registers in 1211 and 1213. Potthast, nos. 4197, 4700; Lea, i. 307. If this person is the same as the heretical priest of 'Musciac' mentioned in a papal bull of 1233 (Auvray, no. 1044) he had great success in eluding the Inquisition.

who had the extermination of heresy very much at heart found the old methods ineffective; "the preaching friars were the readiest instrument within reach for the accomplishment of his object;" he tried them, and the success of the experiment "led to an extended and permanent organization."[1] The episcopal Inquisition was not thereby abolished, indeed the Dominicans were instructed to act in conjunction with the bishops, and it was only considerably later that a new set of tribunals for the trial of heresy came into existence, with their own distinct organization and rules of procedure.[2] How this development came about and how it was related to the centralizing tendencies within the church, it is no part of our present purpose to examine; our only immediate interest is to observe the events which led up to the introduction of the Dominican Inquisition into Northern France. The first definite move toward the establishment of a distinctively papal Inquisition was made in the territory of the Empire, in June, 1227, when Gregory IX commissioned the fanatical Conrad of Marburg to proceed against the heretics of Germany with the assistance of such associates as he might select,[3] and placed the case of certain heretics of Florence in the hand of the local members of the Dominican order.[4] It was not, however, until early in 1231 that Gregory IX seriously took up the task of unifying and defining more sharply the ecclesiastical and secular legislation against heresy and, with the support of the Emperor, compelling its general enforcement throughout Roman Christendom.[5]

[1] Lea, i. 328. Douais, L'Inquisition, pt. 1, ch. 5, tries without success to shift the responsibility from Gregory IX to Frederick II; cf. Turberville, pp. 151 ff.

[2] Cf. Hinschius, Kirchenrecht, v. 450. It is at the same time true, as Tanon points out (pp. 36, 291), that much of the exceptional character of the penalties and the procedure was in germ before the organization of the Dominican Inquisition.

[3] Potthast, no. 7931; Auvray, no. 109. Conrad had been engaged in the persecution of German heretics in 1224, in connexion with the bishop of Hildesheim, and perhaps earlier. For his remarkable career see Emil Michael in his Geschichte des deutschen Volkes (Freiburg, 1897–1916), ii. 318 ff.; A. Hauck, Kirchengeschichte Deutschlands, iv (1903), pp. 879 ff.   [4] Lea, i. 326.

[5] On the legislation of 1231 see J. Ficker, "Die gesetzliche Einführung der Todesstrafe für Ketzerei," in M. I. O. G., i. 177–226 (1880); Winkelmann, Kaiser Friedrich II. (Leipzig, 1889–97), ii. 296 ff.; H. Köhler, Die Ketzerpolitik

The immediate occasion which decided the Pope to action seems to have come then, as at other critical moments in the history of the church, from the city of Rome. Returning after an absence of some months, Gregory found the city infested with a considerable body of heretics, and in order to facilitate the proceedings against them he had the various provisions of the canon law with reference to the punishment of heresy collected and consolidated, with some modifications, into the so-called 'new statutes' of 1231, and at the same time gave his sanction to a series of constitutions drawn up by the senator and people of Rome which made the secular penalties against heresy more severe. In the course of the following summer copies of the new code were sent to the archbishops and bishops throughout the church with instructions to have the papal statutes read in public once a month and the secular constitutions transcribed into the local books of law. In November of the same year the execution of the new statutes at Friesach, in Carinthia, was entrusted to the Dominicans,[1] and early in 1232 the Preaching Friars engaged in the work of the Inquisition were especially commended to the protection of the German princes by both Pope and Emperor.[2] In this year the Pope also recommends the employment of the Dominicans to the archbishop of Tarragona,[3] and Dominican inquisitors are found acting under papal commissions in Lombardy[4] and Burgundy.[5] In France, while some inquisitorial authority had previously been exercised in the South by members of the order,[6] the definite establishment

---

der deutschen Kaiser und Könige in den Jahren 1152–1254 (Bonn, 1913). The statutes of Gregory and the accompanying Roman legislation will be found in Fredericq, *Corpus*, i, nos. 79, 80; Auvray, nos. 539, 540. Havet, *B. E. C.*, xli. 602, ascribes a decisive influence to Bishop Guala of Brescia, a Dominican, while Acton, *History of Freedom*, p. 557, suggests the importance of Raymond of Peñafort.

[1] E. Winkelmann, *Acta Imperii inedita*, i. 499, where similar documents of the following year for Mainz and Strasbourg are cited.

[2] Potthast, nos. 8859, 8866; *M. G. H., Constitutiones et acta publica*, ii. 196.

[3] Potthast, no. 8932.   [4] Potthast, no. 9041.

[5] The bull appointing inquisitors in Burgundy is lost, but its contents are known from a citation in the bull *Gaudemus* of 19 April, 1233, and it evidently belongs to 1232. Potthast, no. 9152; see below.

[6] Potthast, no. 9153.

of the Dominican Inquisition dates from April, 1233, when Gregory IX informed the French bishops that in view of their overwhelming cares and anxieties he had decided to reduce their burdens by sending the Preaching Friars against the heretics of the kingdom,[1] and, at the same time that he ordered the Dominican provincial prior to designate preachers against heresy in Provence,[2] he commissioned Friar Robert and his fellow inquisitors at Besançon to proceed against the heretics of La Charité.[3]

Concerning the early life of the Dominican friar whom Gregory IX selected as the first papal inquisitor in Northern France, our only knowledge is derived from the incidental statements of those who treat of his later career. That he had once been a heretic (*bougre*) is clear from the name, Robert le Bougre, by which he was generally known, and is confirmed by the general agreement of the chroniclers; but beyond this point the accounts are somewhat conflicting,[4] and it is not certain how much of

[1] Bull of 20 April, 1233, copied in the Collection Doat (xxxi. 21) of the Bibliothèque Nationale from the Archives of the Inquisition at Carcassonne. Part of it, with date of 13 April, was published by Percin, *Monumenta conventus Tolosani*, iii. 92, whence it is reproduced by Fredericq, *Corpus*, i, no. 89 (Potthast, no. 9143; not in Auvray).   [2] Potthast, no. 9155.

[3] Bull *Gaudemus*, of 19 April, 1233. Auvray, no. 1253; Potthast, no. 9152; Fredericq, *Corpus*, i, no. 90.

[4] Most of the contemporary chroniclers treat only of particular episodes in Friar Robert's history. Those of special importance as general authorities for his career are:

Matthew Paris, in his *Chronica majora* (edited by H. R. Luard, iii. 361, 520; v. 247; by F. Liebermann in the *SS.*, xxviii. 133, 146, 326); his *Historia Anglorum* (edited by Madden, ii. 388, 415; and by Liebermann, *SS.*, xxviii. 411); and the *Abbreviatio chronicorum Anglie*, attributed to him (edited by Madden as part of the *Historia Anglorum*, iii. 278; and by Liebermann, *SS.*, xxviii. 448). Liebermann's edition is preferable; Frederichs missed important passages by relying upon the edition of 1640.

Albericus Trium Fontium, ed. P. Scheffer-Boichorst, *SS.*, xxiii. 936, 937, 940, 945; also in *H. F.*, xxi. 614, 615, 618, 623. On the composition of this work see Scheffer's masterly introduction to his edition. Albericus was a monk of Trois-Fontaines, in the diocese of Châlons-sur-Marne, and had special opportunities of knowledge regarding Robert's doings in Champagne; some portions of the chronicle in its present form were added by a monk of Huy.

Philippe Mousket, *Chronique rimée*, verses 28871–29025. Best edited, but with important omissions, by Tobler in *SS.*, xxvi. 804–806: also ed. de Reiffenberg (Brussels, 1836–38); *H. F.*, xxii. 55–56; Fredericq, *Corpus*, ii, no. 23

these stories is fact and how much is the product of aetiological imagination playing about his name. His real name, it has recently been discovered, was Robert le Petit,[1] so that he would seem to have been a Frenchman, but we know nothing of the time or place of his birth. A work attributed to Matthew Paris makes him the son of a heretic,[2] but according to Albericus he left the orthodox faith about the time of the Lateran council of 1215 and followed a Manichean woman to Milan, then famous as one of the principal breeding-grounds of false doctrine. He is said to have remained a member of this sect[3] for several years —the chroniclers give the round numbers ten and twenty—and to have risen to the rank of 'apostle' among them. Certain it is that he acquired in his earlier years a familiarity with heretics and their ways which, combined with his fiery zeal and ambition, made him particularly terrible as an inquisitor and gained for

Mousket lived at Tournai, where he is mentioned in certain leases of the years 1236 or 1237. On his life and family see B. C. Du Mortier in the *Compte-Rendu* of the Commission Royale d'Histoire, ix. 112–145 (Brussels, 1845); and Pirenne in the *Biographie nationale*, xv. 329.

With these we may for convenience mention a less trustworthy writer who characterizes Robert briefly, Richer de Senones. His *Chronicon* has been edited by Waitz, SS., xxv. 307; this passage is omitted in the older edition of d'Achery.

[1] 'Quondam frater Robertus dictus Lepetit.' Bull *Constitutus* of Urban IV, 25 October, 1263, published from the papal registers by Chapotin, *Histoire des Dominicains de la province de France*, pp. 224–225; J. Guiraud, *Les registres d'Urbain IV*, no. 1180.

[2] *Historia Anglorum*, iii. 278; SS., xxviii. 448. Richer says that as inquisitor he condemned his father and mother to death. SS., xxv. 308.

Finke, in the *Historisches Jahrbuch*, xiv. 335, points out that in the case of Robert it would have been better if the Pope had followed the later rule of appointing as inquisitors only those of orthodox family and unblemished orthodoxy.

[3] 'Circa tempus magni concilii apostatavit, secutusque mulierculam manicheam Mediolanum abiit, et factus est de secta illa pessima per annos 20, ita quod inter eos fuit perfectissimus.' Albericus, SS., xxiii. 940. Mousket, vv.· 28873–28876:

> Et dist quil ot mes a Melans,
> Et si eut este par dis ans
> En la loi de mescreandise
> Pour conoistre et aus et lor guise.

The passage of Albericus is perfectly plain, but Chapotin (*Histoire des Dominicains*, p. 216, note) makes it say that Robert was a Dominican before his apostasy, and then became a Waldensian.

him the name of the Hammer of Heretics.[1] He was supposed to
be able to tell unbelievers by their speech and gestures alone,[2]
and Gregory IX declared that God had given him "such special
grace that every hunter feared his horn."[3] It would also seem
that he had acquired something of the learning of his day, for
Matthew Paris declares him well educated and a ready and
effective preacher,[4] and Richer calls him *magister* and speaks of
his learning and eloquence.[5] Of the personal character of Friar
Robert we have only unfriendly judgements, formed after his
fall. Matthew Paris, certainly no admirer of the Mendicant
Orders at their best,[6] finds him false and corrupt, a deceiver and
seducer of men worthy of being compared to the leader of the
Pastoureaux—a man whose crimes it were better not to mention
and who was "turned aside like a deceitful bow" at the last.[7]
He was a man who seemed to have much religion but had it
not, says Albericus.[8] To Richer he was the incarnation of
hypocrisy, a wolf in sheep's clothing, wholly given over to un-
cleanness and the glory of this world, who did not hesitate to
avail himself of magic arts in order to bend people to his will.[9]

The first definite point in Friar Robert's biography appears in
or about the year 1232, when we find him, already a member of
the order of Preaching Friars, appointed on a commission with
the Dominican prior at Besançon and a certain Friar William,

[1] Matthew Paris, *Chronica majora*, iii. 361, 520; *SS.*, xxviii. 133, 147.

[2] 'Per solam loquelam et per solos gestus, quos habent heretici, deprehendebat
eos.' Albericus, *SS.*, xxiii. 940.

[3] Bull *Quo inter ceteras* of 22 August, 1235. Auvray, no. 2737; Potthast, no.
9994; Fredericq, *Corpus*, ii, no. 28.

[4] 'Vir quidem competenter literatus et in officio predicationis efficax et
expeditus.' *Chronica majora*, iii. 520; *SS.*, xxviii. 146.

[5] 'Vir doctissimus et eloquio clarus . . . qui tantam habuit gratiam ut nullus
ei tunc secundus haberetur.' *SS.*, xxv. 307.

[6] Cf. H. Plehn, *Der politische Charakter von Matheus Parisiensis*, p. 45 (in
Staats- und socialwissenschaftliche Forschungen, ed. G. Schmoller, xiv, 3 (Leipzig, 1897).

[7] *Chronica majora*, iii. 520; v. 247; *Historia Anglorum*, ii. 388; *SS.*, xxviii.
147, 326, 411.   [8] *SS.*, xxiii. 940.

[9] *SS.*, xxv. 307. One is tempted to see an allusion to our inquisitor in the
' Frere Robert' whom Rutebeuf mentions together with five other friars in one
of his satires on the hypocrisy of the Mendicants (ed. Jubinal, 1874, i, p. 246;
ed. Kressner, p. 72); but I agree with Jubinal that the names are probably
fanciful.

or Walter, to investigate heresy in Burgundy.[1] It is no longer possible, with the materials at our command, to follow the course of the Inquisition in Franche-Comté.[2] This part of the Empire never became notorious as a centre of heretical activity, and while his authority under the papal bull was limited to the Burgundian lands, we are not surprised to find Friar Robert, early in 1233, seeking a more promising field of labour at La Charité in the Nivernais. Acting here as the representative of his official superior at Besançon, Robert began to preach the true faith with such success, so he reported to the Pope, that many of the erring came to him of their own will, presenting themselves for punishment with chains about their necks and offering to give evidence against their associates and even against members of their own families. He found the town a 'foul nest' of heresy, even fouler than was generally supposed, and discovered that its inhabitants had scattered their dire poison through the whole of Northern France, particularly in the neighbouring provinces and in Flanders; and he adds, what was undoubtedly one of the serious difficulties in any merely local attempt to suppress heresy, that when pursued the heretics fled to another jurisdiction.[3]

[1] The bull is lost but is known to us from a citation in the bull *Gaudemus* of 19 April, 1233: 'Cum enim nos dudum dilectis filiis .. priori Bisuntino et fratri Willelmo (Ripoll has Wallerio), de ordine fratrum predicatorum, ac tibi nostris dedissemus litteris in mandatis, quod in Burgundia super crimine prenotato sub certa forma cum ipsis perquireres diligenti sollicitudine veritatem' (Auvray, no. 1253; Potthast, no. 9152; Fredericq, *Corpus*, i, no. 90). This appointment of inquisitors for Burgundy is evidently subsequent to the decrees of February, 1231, and probably belongs to 1232. The name of the prior at Besançon is not given in the bull; in an act of April, 1233, he appears as 'frater W. prior ordinis predicatorum Bisuntinensium' (B.N., Coll. Moreau, MS. 863, f. 539 v).

[2] Cf. Lea, ii. 119. There are two bulls on this subject from the year 1233, one of 27 May to the suffragans of the archbishop of Besançon (published by Lea, i. 567, from the Collection Doat, where it is classified under Gregory X) repeating the instructions recently given to the German prelates for the imprisonment of relapsed heretics (Rodenberg, *Epistolae*, i, no. 514), the other of 17 June answering certain questions of the Dominicans of Besançon (Auvray, no. 1416; Potthast, no. 9235). I have looked in vain for documents at Besançon, where the Dominicans had been established since 1224 (Richard, *Histoire des diocèses de Besançon et de Saint-Claude*, i. 473; Chapotin, *Histoire des Dominicains de la province de France*, p. 53).

[3] Our knowledge of Robert's experiences at La Charité rests upon his own

La Charité not being within the limits of his commission, Robert was obliged to confine his efforts to preaching, and his report to the Pope was evidently made with a view to having his jurisdiction as inquisitor extended to France. Gregory IX was not averse to more vigorous measures, and in a bull of 19 April, 1233, he ordered Robert and his fellow inquisitors of Burgundy to undertake, with the advice of the bishops and in accordance with their previous instructions, "the extirpation of heresy from the aforesaid town and the adjoining regions," invoking if necessary the aid of the secular arm. They were empowered to proceed against harbourers of heretics in accordance with the statutes of 1231, and were cautioned against feigned conversions.[1] Having written to the same effect to the provincial prior of the Dominicans in France,[2] the Pope informed the archbishops and bishops of that kingdom that he had decided to send the Friars Preachers against the heretics of France and adjacent provinces and would expect the clergy to render them all necessary assistance.[3]

By these bulls the papal Inquisition was regularly set to work in Northern France, and the fires of orthodoxy soon began to blaze at La Charité.[4] We do not know how many were put to death at this time, but that Friar Robert went aggressively to work is evident from the reaction which followed and also from such appeals from his sentences as have come down to us. One of these may serve to illustrate his methods. A certain Pierre Vogrin, of Souvigny, in the diocese of Clermont, who had been at La Charité at the time of the episcopal Inquisition of 1231 and 1232, had cleared himself before the inquisitors by the

statement as reproduced in the bull *Gaudemus* of 19 April, 1233 (Auvray, no. 1253; Potthast, no. 9152; Fredericq, *Corpus*, i, no. 90). Doubtless he informed the Pope promptly of his labours there, so that they must have fallen in the early months of 1233. The *Circa mundi vesperam* of 28 February (Auvray, no. 1145) mentions the efforts of the prior of La Charité, but says nothing of Robert. See further E. Chénon, "L'hérésie à La Charité-sur-Loire," in *Nouvelle revue historique de droit*, xli (1917).

[1] Bull *Gaudemus*, as above.

[2] This bull has been lost but is referred to in the bull *Quo inter ceteras*, of 22 August, 1235 (Auvray, no. 2737; Potthast, no. 9994; Fredericq, *Corpus*, ii, no. 28).   [3] Fredericq, *Corpus*, i, no. 89; Potthast, no. 9143.

[4] Mousket, vv. 28877 ff.

canonical purgation. Accused again by certain of his enemies, he had satisfied the bishop of Clermont and other prelates of his innocence. A third summons came to him from Friar Robert after his appointment, and when Pierre appeared before them and agreed to submit to their jurisdiction, the friar and the bishop of Clermont promised him that he would not be compelled to appear before either of them separately and that the legal procedure would be observed. Notwithstanding this, Robert, without waiting for his colleague, cited him to a dangerous place before the appointed time, publicly threatening to take him and bringing an armed band to the spot, whereupon Pierre prudently stayed away and took an appeal to the Pope, sending his nephew to represent him and notify Robert of his appeal. The inquisitor then excommunicated the nephew and suspended him from his benefice—he was a priest—until he should renounce his uncle's defence. Pierre then started for Rome, but in spite of his appeal was excommunicated by Robert and a certain Franciscan who had been pressed into service in place of the bishop of Clermont.[1]

Such open disregard of a bishop and contempt for the findings of predecessors would naturally irritate the higher clergy, already jealous of the growing privileges and influence of the Mendicant Orders. It appears further that Robert did not limit his efforts to the region of La Charité. We find him also in company with another friar, Jacques, on the lands of the count of Champagne, where he is in conflict with the chapter of Saint-Quiriace of Provins, in the diocese of Sens, over a certain Gile, nicknamed ' the abbess,'[2] whom he had put in prison as a heretic. They style themselves "judges delegated by the Pope against heretics in the kingdom of France,"[3] and it is evident from what followed

---

[1] Bull of 8 November, 1235, to the bishop of Nevers, the Dominican provincial prior, and the archdeacon of Paris, published by Sbaralea in his *Bullarium Franciscanum*, i. 177, and by Auvray, no. 2825 (Potthast, no. 10044).

[2] On Gile ' the abbess,' compare Albericus, *SS.*, xxiii. 945.

[3] 'Frater Robertus iudex contra hereticos mandat regi ut deliberet decano et capitulo Sancti Quiriaci Gilam abbatissam suam, ut dicunt, si ita est.

'Nobili viro Theobaldo comiti Campanie et Brie fratres Robertus et Iacobus de ordine Predicatorum, iudices a domino papa contra hereticos in regno Francie delegati, salutem in Domino. Quoniam ex precepto nostro Gilam

that victims were sought in still other dioceses less notorious than that of Auxerre as centres of heresy. 'Pernicious activity' of this sort was a direct reflection on the zeal and efficiency of the French bishops, and it is not strange that some of them soon protested to the Pope, declaring that there were no heretics in their dioceses. The documents are lost, but their general tenor is clear from some pointed allusions in later letters of the Pope.[1] These objections must have been urged with considerable force, for in February, 1234, the Pope, declaring in the midst of an extraordinary mixture of metaphors that he had never intended to authorize their proceedings in regions that were free from taint of heresy, ordered the Dominicans to suspend their functions as inquisitors entirely, except where the archbishop and his suffragans called them in, a course which he warmly recommended to the several archbishops.[2]

dictam abbatissam detinetis in carcere, quam venerabiles viri decanus et capitulum Sancti Quiriaci de Pruvino suam asserunt esse mulierem, auctoritate [MS. actum] nobis commissa vobis mandamus quatinus, si est ita sicut dicunt, eam absque contradictione aliqua tradatis eisdem ad custodiendum, et custodes a rebus et domibus dicte G. removeatis, si forte aliquos posuistis.

'Datum anno Domini MoCCoXXXoIIIo, die martis ante cathedram sancti Petri [21 February, 1234].' B.N., MS. lat. 5993A (Cartulary of Champagne known as *Liber pontificum*), f. 412. Cf. F. Bourquelot, *Histoire de Provins*, i. 182. There is an incorrect analysis in H. d'Arbois de Jubainville, *Catalogue des actes des comtes de Champagne*, no. 2293 (*Histoire des comtes de Champagne*, v. 332). This is the only document issued by Friar Robert that I have found.

Cf. also the following document relating to the same subject:

'Item compromiserunt in bonos super immuratione Gile abbatisse et magna iusticia hominum ecclesie sue.

'Omnibus presentes litteras inspecturis Gaufridus decanus totumque capitulum ecclesie Beati Quiriaci Pruvinensis salutem in Domino. Noverit universitas vestra quod cum illustris dominus Th., Dei gratia rex Navarre et comes Campanie et Brie palatinus, moveret contra nos questionem super inmur-⟨mur⟩atione Gile dicte abbatisse et rebus eiusdem et super magna iusticia hominum nostrorum de Pruvino pro sceleribus suis ad mutilationem membrorum vel ad mur⟨mur⟩ationem vel ad mortem dampnandorum et super rebus eorum, tandem in venerabiles viros dominum Petrum de Ianicuria et dominum Anssellum de Cremonia compromittimus, ratum et firmum habituri quidquid super predictis dicti arbitri pace vel iuditio duxerint statuendum. Datum anno Domini MoCCo trecesimo quarto, mense Ianuario [1235].' MS. lat. 5993A, f. 436; analysis in d'Arbois, *Catalogue*, no. 2319.

[1] Bulls *Dudum* and *Quo inter ceteras* of August, 1235 (Auvray, nos. 2735, 2736, 2737; Potthast, nos. 9993, 9994, 9995).

[2] Bull *Olim intellecto* to the prior provincial of the Dominicans, 15 February, 1234 (Auvray, no. 1764—limited in this form to the province of Sens). The

Accordingly, early in 1234, Robert was obliged to cease his pursuit of heretics. People whom he had imprisoned were still maintained at public expense,[1] but there is no evidence that any bishop followed the Pope's advice to the extent of employing the terrible inquisitor.[2] How the friar occupied himself during this enforced vacation, it is impossible to say. We know that early in 1234 a royal messenger was sent to him "for the bailli of Bourges,"[3] and that in November of the same year Gregory IX addressed him at Paris. Evidently Robert remained in full favour with the Pope and with St. Louis, for the Pope appealed to him to use his influence to secure peace between the kings of

same, 4 February, 1234, to the archbishop of Sens and his suffragans (Auvray, no. 1763; Potthast, no. 9388). The same, 4 February, 1234, to the archbishop of Rheims and his suffragans (Potthast, no. 9386; Fredericq, *Corpus*, i, no. 93; not in Auvray). The same, without date, to the dean and chapter of Bourges—the see was vacant—and the bishops of the province, in the cartulary of the chapter of Bourges (B.N., MS. lat. n.a. 1274), p. 42. This copy, which is headed 'De revocatione iurisdictionis fratris Roberti,' differs from the other bulls in revoking the authority of Robert alone, not of the Dominican inquisitors generally. The explanation would seem to be that while the diocese of Bourges itself was in the North, adjoining that of Auxerre, the other dioceses of the province were in the South, where the Dominicans were working under different commissions. The copy in the cartulary breaks off about the middle, just before the word 'oculis.' On the authorship of this cartulary see Delisle, in the *B. E. C.*, lx. 7–44.

[1] At Saint-Pierre-le-Moutier, not far from La Charité. Prévôt's account, Ascension term, 1234, in *H. F.*, xxii. 570J. From the documents published above it appears that Gile 'the abbess' was likewise in prison at this time. Heretics are also mentioned in the royal accounts of All Saints' term, 1234 (Sens), and Candlemas term, 1235 (Paris), in the *B. E. C.*, xxviii. 621 (cf. Tillemont, *Histoire de St. Louis*, ii. 292); and in the account of the King's household, Ascension term, 1234, in *H. F.*, xxi. 227F, 237B. Du Cange, under 'Bulgari,' interprets the words 'bougri' and 'bogrii' in such passages as meaning usurers. It is often difficult to determine in a given case whether the word refers to heresy, usury, or unnatural vice; one of these crimes was frequently supposed to involve the others.

[2] Albericus, *SS.*, xxiii. 936, speaks of Robert's activity as inquisitor 'throughout France' in 1234. But this is very doubtful, unless it applies to the beginning of the year. Chronological exactness is not always the strong point of this chronicler.

[3] 'Simon de Sancto Germano, ad fratrem Robertum, pro baillivo Bithuricensi, xx. s.' Account of the King's household, Ascension term, 1234, *H. F.*, xxi. 233E. The date of the entry is 24 March or thereabouts, but there is no indication when the service was performed or just what its purpose was. The King had been at Bourges late in February and perhaps into March (*H. F.*, xxii, p. xxxv).

France and England,[1] and wrote to him on behalf of Florentine merchants who had been accused of heresy;[2] and in the following year he was restored to more active service.

With the exception of an episcopal admonition which has been preserved from the diocese of Thérouanne,[3] existing records do not permit us to say whether the withdrawal of the Dominicans served as a stimulus to the episcopal Inquisition. Certainly whatever local efforts may have been made were insufficient to satisfy Gregory IX, and on 21 August, 1235, he re-established the Dominican Inquisition throughout France. With scarcely suppressed indignation at those who in certain provinces, where they alleged there were no heretics, had murmured against the conduct of the inquisitors, he declared that in every part of the kingdom the poisonous reptiles of heresy swarmed in such numbers that they could no longer be endured or concealed. Against their deceits he commands Robert, like a veteran soldier of the cross, prepared to meet even death in this great cause, to loose the reins of the Inquisition "throughout the provinces of Sens, Rheims, and the other provinces of the kingdom of France generally," proceeding with the advice of the bishops, his fellow Dominicans, and other experts (sapientes) so that the innocent should not perish or the guilty remain unpunished. The provincial prior was directed to appoint other friars to assist him, and the archbishop of Sens—and doubtless other archbishops—was ordered to co-operate actively with them and such others as might be selected for the purpose.[4] Thus the papal

[1] Bull of 6 November: Auvray, no. 2185.

[2] Bull Accurri of 23 November, 'priori et fratri Roberto de ordine Predicatorum Parisiensibus': Auvray, no. 2221 (Potthast, no. 9772, following Ripoll, has 'fratri Raynerio'). There is also a bull of 20 November, 1234 (Relatum est auribus), relating to Florentine merchants, which is addressed 'Fratri R.' in the text of Ripoll (Bullarium Ordinis Praedicatorum, i. 71, no. 115; Potthast, no. 9766, and Auvray, no. 2216), as well as in the manuscript of the register, which I have collated at the Vatican; but reads 'Fratri Roberto ordinis Predicatorum Parisius' in the Analecta Ordinis Fratrum Praedicatorum, iv. 383.

[3] Letter of 7 June, 1235, to the provost of St. Martin's at Ypres, with vidimus of the archbishop of Rheims: Fredericq, Corpus, i, no. 99. Perhaps the proceedings of the bishop of Noyon against Michel de Cerizy (see bull of 5 December, 1235, in Auvray, no. 2854) belong to this period.

[4] Bull Dudum ad aliquorum murmur, to the provincial prior of the Friars

Inquisition was re-established in Northern France. Robert was made general inquisitor, he was particularly commended by the Pope, and the bishops were forced to act as his assistants. Under the new commission there were no limitations of place; it covered the whole of France and clothed the inquisitor with full power to proceed under the decrees of the Lateran council and the statutes of 1231.

Armed with his new authority, Friar Robert began a vigorous campaign against heresy among high and low. According to one chronicle his efforts extended over "various cities and towns of France, Flanders, Champagne, Burgundy, and the other provinces."[1] Besides La Charité,[2] our more specific information relates to Châlons-sur-Marne, where a number of heretics were burnt, notably a certain barber Arnolinus, "entirely devoted to the devil and offensive beyond measure,"[3] and to the region of the North, where the persecution seems to have raged most violently.[4] Apparently Robert began his work in this region by establishing his headquarters at Cambrai, which was not in

Preachers in France, 21 August, 1235 (Auvray, no. 2736; Potthast, no. 9993; Fredericq, *Corpus*, i, no. 100). Bull *Dudum*, to Friar Robert, 23 August (Auvray, no. 2735; Potthast, no. 9995; Fredericq, i, no. 101; also in abbreviated form, without date, copied from a MS. in the Ottoboni collection at Rome, in the B.N., Collection Moreau, 1193, f. 229). Bull *Quo inter ceteras* to the archbishop of Sens, 22 August (Auvray, no. 2737; Potthast, no. 9994; Fredericq, ii, no. 28).

[1] *Annales Sancti Medardi Suessionensis, SS.*, xxvi. 522; Fredericq, *Corpus*, ii, no. 26. Delisle (*Histoire littéraire*, xxxii. 235 ff.) has shown that these annals are the work of Gobert de Coinci, from 1233 to 1254 prior of Vic-sur-Aisne. Their account of Robert's persecutions, though brief, is sober and accurate.

[2] The bull of 1263 in Guiraud, *Registres*, no. 1180, refers back to events of 1235.   [3] Albericus, in *SS.*, xxiii. 937; Fredericq, *Corpus*, ii, no. 24.

[4] The fullest account of events in the North is contained in the chronicle of Mousket, who was a resident of Tournai, and unless otherwise indicated the narrative in the text is based upon his statements, vv. 28887 ff. Albericus (*l. c.*), and Matthew Paris (*Chronica majora*, iii. 361; *SS.*, xxviii. 133) dismiss the subject very briefly, as do the continuators of André de Marchiennes (*SS.*, xxvi. 215; *H. F.*, xviii. 559; Fredericq, *Corpus*, ii, no. 25) and Sigebert de Gembloux (*SS.*, vi. 440), who give the same account, derived perhaps from a common source (cf. Waitz, in *SS.*, xxvi. 204). The chronicle of Hainaut attributed to Baudoin d'Avesnes (*H. F.*, xxi. 166; *SS.*, xxv. 455) has also a brief mention.

Two writers of the fourteenth century, Gilles de Muisit (de Smet, *Corpus chronicorum Flandriae*, ii. 150) and Jean d'Outremeuse (ed. Borgnet, v. 231)

France at all, but in the territory of the Empire.[1] We are told that he had with him an armed band from the king and that the bishop of Cambrai, Godefroi, who accompanied him also had an armed escort. Their progress through this region began at Péronne, where Pieron Malkasin and Matthieu de Lauvin, their wives, and Robert de Lauvin were burnt. Matthieu's pregnant daughter was also taken, but by the intercession of the French queen her life was spared on profession of orthodoxy.[2] Pieron's son fled to Valenciennes, but was caught and taken on to Cambrai. On the way back to Cambrai four seigneurs were burnt at Heudicourt.[3] At Cambrai Robert had with him the archbishop of Rheims and the bishops of Arras, Cambrai, Tournai, and Noyon, and on the first Sunday in Lent[4] a famous sorceress named Alice and some twenty others were burnt— "men of good cheer and in all manner courteous," says Mousket, "except for the fact that they did not believe in God."[5] Among the notable victims were three who had been chosen échevins of the city. Eighteen others were left there in prison, three who recanted were condemned to wear the sign of the cross, and still others were taken on to Douai, where a number of heretics had

record the persecution of heretics in this period, but their statements have no particular value, as may be seen from the way in which Jean confuses Friar Robert with the more famous Dominican, Albertus Magnus. The extract from Dynter's *Chronica* given by Fredericq (*Corpus*, i, no. 104; Dynter, ed. de Ram, i. 564, 625) is merely a reproduction of the passage in the continuations of André and Sigebert. Frederichs' treatment of the Northern episode is particularly good.   [1] Cf. Baudoin d'Avesnes, *H. F.*, xxi. 166.

[2] Later in the reign of St. Louis it was the law that a pregnant woman condemned to death should not be executed before the birth of the child. *Livre de jostice et de plet*, p. 55.

[3] 'Heldincourt.' There are various places in the vicinity of Cambrai with which this may be identified (cf. *H. F.*, xxii. 55). Holder-Egger, Frederichs, and Tanon incline to Élincourt (Nord, arrondissement Cambrai). I prefer Heudicourt (Somme, arrondissement Péronne, canton Roisel) which is directly between Péronne and Cambrai, and was anciently known as Heldincourt (cf. Paul de Cagny, *Histoire de l'arrondissement de Péronne*, ii. 723).

[4] 17 February, 1236. As Frederichs has pointed out, both Waitz and Holder-Egger have confused the chronology of these events by forgetting that in this region the year began at Easter.

[5] Vv. 28944 ff. On the number compare Albericus, *SS.*, xxiii. 937. The story of a heretic of Cambrai, recounted by Thomas of Cantimpré, *Bonum universale de apibus*, ii. 57, no. 68 (ed. Douai, 1627, p. 592; cf. Fredericq, *Corpus*, i, nos. 106, 107) may relate to this persecution.

been collected to await the inquisitors' arrival. The proceedings at Douai were not unduly prolonged, for on the second of March, the second Sunday after the executions at Cambrai, ten heretics, old men and women, were led "out of the gate of Olivet, on the Road of the Lepers, which leads to Lambres" and there burnt in the presence of the countess of Flanders, the archbishop of Rheims, and the bishops of Arras, Cambrai, and Tournai.[1] Some, who professed themselves converted, had their heads shaved and were condemned to wear the cross, others were imprisoned "to repent and to stay."[2] At Lille and in the neighbouring villages of Ascq, Lers, and Toufflers,[3] a number of heretics, amounting perhaps to a score,[4] were burnt and others imprisoned. The persecution at Lille seems to have been particularly aimed at merchants and also at a certain Robert de la Galie, against whom Friar Robert was said to have a grudge because of a woman of Milan.[5] In all, during a period of two or three months, about fifty had been burnt or buried alive.[6]

For the persecutions of the two following years our evidence is very scanty. In October, 1237, the Pope declared that heretics were rising more boldly against the vineyard of the Lord,[7] but

[1] This specific account is given by a contemporary chronicle of the town, the *Notae Sancti Amati Duacenses* (*SS.*, xxiv. 30; Fredericq, *Corpus*, i, nos. 98, 106). Cf. J. Buzelinus, *Gallo-Flandria* (Douai, 1625), i. 256, 279. Mousket is more general, vv. 28980–87, but likewise gives the number as ten. The persecution at Douai and Cambrai is also mentioned in the annals of Lobbes (Martène and Durand, *Thesaurus*, iii. 1427; *SS.*, iv. 26; Fredericq, *Corpus*, i, no. 94); and in a local notice from Douai, published in Fredericq, *Corpus*, iii, no. 1.

[2] Mousket, v. 28987.

[3] Nord, arrondissement of Lille. Cf. Frederichs, p. 19.

[4] If we accept the statement of Albericus that a good thirty were burnt at Douai and thereabouts, and deduct the ten executed at Douai. Mousket, with whom Albericus agrees in the case of Cambrai, gives no figures for Lille. Cf. Fredericq, *Corpus*, iii, no. 3.

[5] Mousket, vv. 28988–29005. Part of the passage, especially line 29000, is obscure and has perplexed all the editors. I cannot pretend to have any new light upon it.

[6] Matthew Paris, *l. c.* This total agrees very well with the more detailed statements of Mousket and Albericus.

[7] Bull of 6 October to the archbishops and bishops of France (Potthast, no. 10460). The allusion is to the "little foxes that spoil the vines" (Canticles, ii. 15), which in the Middle Ages, even by the Waldenses themselves, was interpreted to mean the heretics. Cf. Lea, i. 78, note.

no record of a condemnation appears in this year.[1] The royal accounts of this year, were they in existence, might tell us more. In 1238 these useful sources show us, in the roll for the Ascension term, that heretics had been convicted at Miraumont, near Péronne, and their goods to the value of eighty livres confiscated to the royal treasury.[2] Matthew Paris mentions under this year a general persecution by Robert, but this may very well be a confusion with the similar entry of two years before.[3] Toward the close of the summer we find Robert at Paris, examining a witness in the case of the prior of Mazille, in the Nivernais, who was under charge of fautorship of heretics.[4] A writer of the seventeenth century asserts that the Inquisition was established at Arras in this year, in the Dominican convent.[5] Certain it is that at some time before 1244 Robert exercised his inquisitorial functions at Arras against Henri Hukedieu, a well-to-do wool merchant of the city.[6]

The climax of Friar Robert's career as an inquisitor was reached in May, 1239, at Mont-Aimé,[7] an ancient seat of heresy

[1] In the "Annals of La Trinité de Vendôme" in the *E. H. R.*, xiii. 698, the 'combustio Bugrorum' ascribed to Blois under the year 1237 is apparently an error for 'combustio burgorum.'

[2] *H. F.*, xxi. 252 D.   [3] *Chronica majora*, iii. 520 (*SS.*, xxviii. 146).

[4] 'Per idem tempus erat in Francia inquisitor hereticorum frater Robertus de ordine Predicatorum, qui fratrem Iodoinum priorem de Masiliis prosequebatur asserens eum esse fautorem hereticorum, ob quam causam dictus abbas [Regnaudus] accessit Parisius, ubi dictus frater Robertus morabatur, inde vero rediens apud Villam Novam Givardi obiit anno Domini MCCXXXVIII. nonis Septembris.' *Gesta Abbatum Autissiodorensium*, in Labbé, *Nova bibliotheca manuscriptorum*, i. 581. Cf. *Gallia Christiana*, xii. 387.

[5] Fredericq, *Corpus*, ii, no. 29. See also Proville, *Histoire du couvent des Dominicains d'Arras* (B.N., MS. fr. 11620), pp. 387, 683, citing a modern MS. of the convent.

[6] Letter patent of Asson, bishop of Arras, April, 1244 (or possibly 1245, since Easter in 1245 fell on 16 April), recognizing that Hukedieu had been excommunicated by Robert. Original, with traces of seal, in the Archives du Pas-de-Calais, A. 105. Published by Fredericq, *Corpus*, i, no. 121, from a cartulary at Lille.

On Henri Hukedieu see A. Jeanroy and H. Guy, *Chansons et dits Artésiens du XIII*^e *siècle* (Bordeaux, 1898), pp. 80, 121, 132; and A. Guesnon in the *Bulletin historique et philologique* of the Comité des travaux historiques et scientifiques, 1898, p. 192, and in the *Moyen âge*, new series, iv. 31.

[7] Marne, arrondissement of Châlons, commune of Bergères-lez-Vertus. Cf. A. Longnon, *Dictionnaire topographique de la Marne*, p. 171, where the numerous

in Champagne where a crowd of suspected Manicheans, some of them probably merchants from the great May fair at Provins,[1] had been collected from all parts of the country. Their examination lasted the better part of a week, being attended by the archbishop of Rheims and ten of his suffragans, as well as by the bishops of Orleans, Troyes, Meaux, Verdun, and Langres, and "many abbots, priors, and deans,"[2] and ended on Friday, 13 May, in a "holocaust, very great and pleasing to God," in which more than a hundred and eighty Cathari were burnt, after receiving the sacrament of the *consolamentum* from their 'archbishop.'[3] "And so," concludes Albericus, "as the story

variants of the name are given. The different mediaeval forms of this name have caused some confusion, and have even given one writer a lame excuse for doubting the fact of the great burning (*Histoire littéraire*, xviii. 249). On the early history of heresy at Mont-Aimé see Schmidt, *Histoire des Cathares*, i. 33, 411; F. Vernet, article "Cathares," in Vacant and Mangenot, *Dictionnaire de théologie catholique*, ii. 1990-91 (1905).

For the great *auto da fé* of 1239 we have the brief report of an eyewitness, the Dominican Étienne de Bourbon, in his *Anecdotes historiques*, ed. Lecoy de la Marche, pp. 150, 415 ('Cui sentencie ego interfui'). The fullest account is given by Albericus (*SS.*, xxiii. 944-945; *H. F.*, xxi. 623), who lived in the same diocese. Mousket mentions the affair (vv. 30525 ff., omitted in the extracts in the *SS.*), as do also the Dominican annals of Erfurt (*Monumenta Erphurtensia*, ed. Holder-Egger, pp. 96, 235; Böhmer, *Fontes rerum Germanicarum*, ii. 400; *SS.*, xvi. 33). It is also noted by two writers of a somewhat later date: Jean de Saint-Victor, in his *Memoriale historiarum* (B.N., MS. lat. 14626, f. 339 v; Quétif and Échard, *Scriptores Ordinis Praedicatorum*, i. 190); and Geoffroy de Courlon, *Chronique de l'abbaye de S. Pierre-le-Vif de Sens*, ed. Julliot (Sens, 1876), p. 518 (*H. F.*, xxii. 3; omitted in the extracts printed in the *SS.*). Through the kindness of Professor Grant Showerman, I have seen collations of the two MSS. of Geoffroy in the Vatican (Reg. lat. 455 and 480) which have not been used by the editors. The MS. of Sens on which the published text is based places the execution of heretics 'apud Moimerillonem,' which the editors of the *H. F.* identified with Montmorillon in the department of the Vienne. The Vatican MS. Reg. lat. 480, f. 117, has 'Moimer,' a common form of the name of Mont-Aimé.

[1] We know at least that Robert on one occasion summoned a merchant of Arras to appear before him 'in quibusdam nundinis de Campania' (Archives du Pas-de-Calais, A. 105; Fredericq, *Corpus*, i, no. 121), and the Erfurt annals mention expressly the nearness of Mont-Aimé to Provins. The May fair regularly began the Tuesday before Ascension (Bourquelot, *Les foires de Champagne*, i. 81; Alengry, *Les foires de Champagne*, p. 95), which in 1239 would bring it on 3 May, just before the trial of the heretics began.

[2] Albericus, who mentions the bishops by name.

[3] On the *consolamentum* see Lea, i. 96, with the additional note in the French translation; and J. Guiraud, "Le *Consolamentum* ou initiation cathare," in his

runs that dogs once came from all directions and tore themselves to pieces in a battle at this same place, as a sort of prophecy of what was to be, so these Bougri, worse than dogs, were there exterminated in one day to the triumph of holy church." Not all of the ecclesiastical dignitaries remained for the end, but the count of Champagne and king of Navarre, Thibaut IV, was there with his barons, and the crowd present, of both sexes and all ages and classes, was estimated by Albericus, with characteristically mediaeval looseness in dealing with large numbers, at seven hundred thousand.[1]

After the great *auto da fé* of 1239 comparatively little is known of Friar Robert's acts as an inquisitor. Like his contemporary pioneer of the papal Inquisition in Germany, Conrad of Marburg, Robert seems to have pursued his victims with a fury which bordered upon mania,[2] and it is not strange that a reaction occurred against the friar and his methods. It does not appear that this arose from any feeling of pity for the terrible end of those who persisted in their heretical beliefs; worse than dogs, their destruction was pleasing to God, declared the monk of Trois-Fontaines, and he had the thirteenth century with him.[3] If the persecutions had been confined to those who were clearly guilty, it is not likely that serious protests would have been

Questions d'histoire et d'archéologie chrétienne (Paris, 1906), pp. 93–149. The different accounts are in strikingly close agreement as to the number. Albericus has 183, Mousket 187, the Annals of Erfurt 184. Étienne de Bourbon in one passage gives "about 180," in the other "more than 80"—the latter with an evident omission of the hundred. Jean de S. Victor has 180; Geoffroy de Courlon gives no number.

[1] Bourquelot in his *Histoire de Provins* (i. 183) says that the local antiquary Grillon speaks of similar executions at Troyes and Provins, but I have found no contemporary evidence.

[2] 'Un homicide maniaque' he is called by Langlois, in the *Histoire de France* of Lavisse, iii, 2, p. 73.

[3] Albericus in *SS.*, xxiii. 944. Still there were some who pitied the fate of heretics, as we learn from a general of the Dominicans, Humbert de Romans, in a work written for the instruction of preachers: 'In condemnatione hereticorum quando sententia fertur contra eos, solent publice homines convocari, et quia sunt multi qui quadam falsa pietate moventur circa eos et iudicant ecclesiam de nimia crudelitate circa illos, expedit in sermone publice ostendere quare ecclesia de hereticis plusquam de aliis peccatoribus diligentius inquirit, et quare gravius istos punit, et quare eos difficilius ad penitentiam recipit.' *Maxima bibliotheca patrum*, xxv. 555.

made. According to Matthew Paris, however, Robert passed the bounds of moderation and justice, and in the pride of his power and of the terror that he inspired punished the simple and innocent along with the wicked. "Great numbers of innocent people were infatuated by him and then handed over to their death,"[1] until at length he was peremptorily removed from office by the Pope, and "when his crimes—which it were better not to mention—became known, he was condemned to perpetual imprisonment." What the dark deeds were which the monk of St. Albans prefers to pass over in silence our other sources do not enable us to say with much definiteness. The rare appeals from Robert's sentences relate only to the earlier stages of the inquisitorial procedure; they show his persistence in the pursuit of those upon whom suspicion of heresy had once rested, his arbitrariness and impatience of interference, but they tell us no more than this. One story, however, has come down to us unnoticed in the pages of a gossiping chronicler of the time, and the new light that it may serve to throw on the friar's methods justifies its quotation at some length.[2] In substance it runs as follows:

Robert had by magic art made a bit of writing (cartula) which when placed on any one's head compelled him to say whatever the friar desired. One day while preaching he was smitten with the beauty of a woman in the crowd, and when she refused to yield to him he threatened to have her burnt as a heretic. So approaching her in public he seized her and said, "Are you not a heretic?" She answered, "I am indeed." "Will you return to the Catholic faith?" "No." "Would you rather be burnt than recant?" "Yes." Whereupon he said, "You have all

---

[1] 'Tandem abutens potestate sibi concessa, et fines modestiae transgrediens et justitiae, elatus, potens, et formidabilis, bonos cum malis confundens involvit, et insontes et simplices punivit. Auctoritate igitur papali jussus est praecise ne amplius in illo officio fulminando desaeviret. Qui postea, manifestius clarescentibus culpis suis, quas melius aestimo reticere quam explicare, adjudicatus est perpetuo carceri mancipari.' Chronica majora, ed. Luard, iii. 520; SS., xxviii. 147. 'Dicebatur . . . infinitos infatuasse et infatuatos innocuos incendio tradidisse.' Ibid., v. 247; xxviii. 326. Cf. the Historia Anglorum, ed. Madden, ii. 415; SS., xxviii. 411.

[2] Richer de Senones, Chronicon, in SS., xxv. 307–308 (omitted in the edition of d'Achery): 'De magistro Roberto Parisiensi ordinis Predicatorum et fallaciis eius . . .' On Richer as an historian see Wattenbach, Deutschlands Geschichtsquellen, 6th ed., ii. 399.

heard how this woman has confessed her baseness." The bystanders were surprised and said they had never heard such a thing of her, and she was put in prison. The woman had a son, a well disposed youth and a clerk, who was much disturbed over his mother's dangerous position and went about among his neighbours and relatives seeking advice as to how he might get her free. A certain man who knew the friar well was moved by sympathy for the young man and said to him: "Go tomorrow to the public meeting where your mother will have her second examination. Stand near her, and when Master Robert places his hand on her and begins to question her on her belief, seize his hand, for you are stronger, and take away the writing which you will find in it. Keep it yourself, and ask him in a loud voice to examine your mother again." This was done, and when the clerk had taken the writing out of the friar's hand and his mother was questioned as before, she swore that she had never been examined by Master Robert concerning her faith and had never given him any answers at all, nor had she even heard what heresy was. Then the young man showed the writing to all and explained how by means of it Robert deceived whom he would and delivered them to death. When the people heard this, they tried to kill the friar, but he was carried off by the clergy and put in a stone prison perpetually closed. And because, in order to conceal his own iniquity, he had by such devices caused his father and mother and many other innocent people to be burnt, God imposed such a penalty on him in this life, if perchance he should turn from his evil ways while yet alive.

Whether Richer has here given us the real occasion of Friar Robert's downfall it is impossible to say, but if we substitute hypnotic suggestion for the *cartula*, there is nothing impossible in the story, and it agrees in a general way with the statement of Matthew Paris respecting the 'infatuation' of the innocent. With regard to the friar's imprisonment and subsequent fate two other accounts have been preserved, and while they form no part of the history of the Inquisition, their neglect by later writers [1] warrants their insertion here. In a chronicle attributed to Matthew Paris we read that Robert, after procuring the burning of many thousands in Flanders, was "at length, by the judgement of the members of his order—who condemn no one

---

[1] The passage attributed to Matthew Paris does not seem to have been used. That from Gérard de Frachet was printed in an out-of-the-way part of the *Scriptores Ordinis Praedicatorum* of Quétif and Échard (ii. 543), where it was noticed by Proville, *Histoire du couvent des Dominicains d'Arras* (B.N., MS. fr. 11620, pp. 420 ff.) and by Chapotin, *Histoire des Dominicains de la province de France*, p. 224.

to death—put in prison to do perpetual penance for his horrible crimes; but ultimately, by means of a large sum of money he succeeded in securing a papal dispensation which, to prevent further scandal, permitted him to be received as a canon of St. Victor." [1] This is confirmed and supplemented by a collection of biographies of Dominicans compiled toward 1260 for circulation among members of the order, where Robert figures as a terrible example of the "evil end of apostates:"

There was a certain other man in France who had the office of inquisitor and was in such renown that almost the whole of France trembled before him and even the great held him in the highest reverence. Relying on his popularity, he became insolent and unwilling to govern himself by the advice of his elders, so that the friars at Paris kept him for a long time in bonds until his friends finally succeeded in inducing the Pope to have him released and received into another order. He joined first the brothers of the Trinity and then those of St. Victor, but having been expelled from each of these orders because of his evil deeds, he at last entered Clairvaux. Here he began with great honour, but when his wickedness—which God did not allow to remain hidden long— was discovered, he was reduced to a vile position in that monastery. And so, having been confounded before many, he died not long afterward in great shame and sorrow.[2]

---

[1] *Abbreviatio chronicorum Angliae*, in Madden's edition of the *Historia Anglorum*, iii. 278; *SS.*, xxviii. 448. On the authority of the Dominicans to imprison erring brothers see the *acta* of the general chapters of 1238 and 1240, *Acta capitulorum generalium Ordinis Praedicatorum*, ed. B. M. Reichert, i. 10, 16; and Potthast, no. 11089.

[2] Gerardus de Fracheto, *Vitae fratrum Ordinis Praedicatorum*, ed. Reichert (Rome and Stuttgart, 1897), p. 292. The author entered the order in 1225 and lived mostly at Limoges; the work was composed between 1256 and 1260, but touched up afterward. Cf. the introduction, p. xvi, and pp. 4 and 5 of the text. Although the passage plainly refers to Robert, his name does not appear in the MSS. given by Reichert; but Échard (ii. 543) states that the name appears in his own contemporary MS. One of the MSS. collated by Reichert adds that the friar began to sow discord at Clairvaux.

In view of this passage it is curious to see the efforts of certain modern Dominicans to clear Friar Robert's memory. Bremond in his notes to Ripoll (*Bullarium Ordinis FF. Praedicatorum*, i. 81) scolds Spondanus for accepting the statements of so untrustworthy a writer as Matthew Paris, whose works were interpolated by an heretical hand. Instead of being imprisoned later, Robert died at Saint-Jacques in 1235—' ut liquet ex priscis monimentis ejusdem conventus' ! Choquet claims for him the glorious crown of martyrdom as the friar Robert who was killed at Avignonnet in 1242 (Fredericq, *Corpus*, i, p. 111). Proville (*l. c.*) thinks it unlikely that such a man as Robert could become suddenly perverted, believes him too old to have gone through so many religious

In the present state of our information it is not possible to determine accurately the date at which Robert le Bougre ceased to exercise his functions as inquisitor. If his commission was revoked by the Pope, the bull is not recorded in the papal registers, and if he was removed from office by a legate or by the general of the Dominican order,[1] the chances for the preservation of a documentary record are still less. As there is no notice of any condemnations made by Robert after the great burning of 1239, Lea[2] and Tanon[3] assume that he fell from power in that year, while Frederichs[4] places the date "about 1241." On the whole I am inclined to believe that he remained in office at least as late as 1244 or 1245. A careful contemporary chronicle states that the persecutions of heretics went on until 1241 and later.[5] In the summer of 1242 a Preaching Friar Robert, of Saint-Jacques, appears as one of the executors of a will in

orders, and finally takes refuge behind the absence of his name from the MSS. of Gérard. A. Danzas (*Études sur les temps primitifs de l'Ordre de S. Dominique,* iv. 470 ff.) gives extracts from the very chapter of Gérard, but does not mention Robert. Chapotin (*l.c.,* p. 224) concludes that if Robert passed the bounds of justice and humanity, the Pope and the Dominican order did not fail to punish him. Échard alone, best scholar of them all, faces the facts squarely, declaring Robert 'hominem ab ordine extorrem, nec iam ex ordine memorandum' (*Scriptores Ordinis Praedicatorum,* ii. 543).

   [1] The general of the Dominicans was authorized by a bull of 7 July, 1246, to remove inquisitors, even when they had been appointed by the Pope, and appoint others in their stead. Douais, *Documents pour servir à l'histoire de l'Inquisition en Languedoc,* p. xiv. A similar bull for the Franciscans had been issued in January of the same year (Potthast, no. 11993).

   [2] *History of the Inquisition,* ii. 116; *Formulary of the Papal Penitentiary,* p. 53, note.

   [3] *Tribunaux de l'Inquisition,* p. 116.   [4] *Robert le Bougre,* pp. 27, 32.

   [5] 'Non solum istud factum est in isto anno [1236] sed ante per tres continuos annos et post per quinque continuos annos et plus.' *Annals of St. Médard of Soissons,* SS., xxvi. 522.

   In Lea's *Formulary of the Papal Penitentiary,* pp. 52 f., there is a letter addressed to "the archbishop of Sens and Friar R." concerning the penance of a follower of Simon de Montfort, who was to accompany Simon on his crusade. If we were to follow Bémont (*Simon de Montfort,* p. 12) in the statement that Simon took the cross after hearing of the defeat at Gaza, which occurred 13 November, 1239, the document would belong to the year 1240, before the month of June, when Simon set forth for the East (R. Röhricht, *Geschichte des Königreichs Jerusalem,* p. 850). However, a bull of 25 February, 1238 (W. H. Bliss, *Calendar of Papal Letters,* i. 167), shows that the crusade had been vowed as early as 1238.

Flanders,[1] and the following January we find mention, in a Paris document, of a "clerk of Friar Robert of the order of the Preachers."[2] Robert's fall is not referred to by Mousket, who died in 1244 or 1245,[3] and indeed in April of one of these years the bishop of Arras gives notice of Robert's excommunication of Hukedieu.[4] On the other hand it is known that the friar died before 1263,[5] and from the account given of the various other orders through which he passed it is plain that he must have left the Dominicans several years before.

In tracing the career of Friar Robert as an inquisitor we have had little occasion to speak of those engaged with him in the task of hunting out and punishing heresy. By the Pope's commission he had been directed to proceed, "with the advice of prelates, other Dominicans, and experts,"[6] and as a matter of fact he does not often appear as acting alone. There is, it is true, but scant mention of other Dominican inquisitors, acting either independently or as his associates,[7] and the only known

[1] Testament of Arnoul d'Audenarde, June and August, 1242, in *Inventaire des archives de la Chambre des Comptes de Lille* (Lille, 1865), i. 307, nos. 740, 741.

[2] Brièle and Coyécque, *Les archives de l'Hôtel-Dieu de Paris*, p. 225, no. 466.

[3] Pirenne, in the *Biographie nationale de Belgique*, xv. 329.

[4] The date is April, 1244, but as Easter fell on 3 April in 1244, and on 16 April in 1245, the document may belong to either of these years. Archives du Pas-de-Calais, A. 105; Fredericq, *Corpus*, i, no. 121.

[5] 'Quondam frater Robertus dictus Lepetit, tunc ordinis fratrum Predicatorum, in illis partibus inquisitor pravitatis huiusmodi.' Bull *Constitutus* of Urban IV, 29 October, 1263, in Chapotin, p. 224; Guiraud, no. 1180.

[6] 'Cum prelatorum et fratrum tuorum religiosorum sapientumque consilio.' Bull *Dudum*, in Fredericq, *Corpus*, i, no. 101; Potthast, no. 9995; Auvray, no. 2735. On the advisers of inquisitors in general see C. Henner, *Beiträge zur Organisation und Competenz der päpstlichen Ketzergerichte* (Leipzig, 1890), pp. 138 ff.; de Cauzons, ii. 111–119.

[7] A Dominican friar Jacques was with Robert in Champagne early in 1234 (see the document printed above, p. 215), and a Franciscan acted with him in one instance at La Charité (Auvray, no. 2825, Potthast, no. 10044). Robert and the Paris prior also receive a joint commission of inquiry in one case (Auvray, no. 2221; Potthast, no. 9772). The only examples of independent action I have found are at Troyes, where the Dominican prior and a Franciscan of the same city appear as assigning penance (bull of 11 March, 1236, Auvray, no. 3006; Potthast, no. 10114), and at Arras, where a modern history of the Dominican convent mentions Pierre Danvin, or Darvin, as inquisitor in 1238 (Proville, *Histoire du couvent des Dominicains d'Arras*, B.N., MS. fr. 11620, pp. 387, 683). The case at Troyes must have been subsequent to 1232, when the

instance of the employment of an 'expert' is the presence at
Châlons of the chancellor of the University of Paris, Philip, an
eminent theologian and a staunch upholder of orthodoxy;[1] but
there is abundant evidence that the bishops of Northern France
were actively associated in the work of the Inquisition. At
Cambrai, besides the bishop of the diocese, Robert had with him
the archbishop of Rheims and the bishops of Arras, Tournai,
and Noyon,[2] and all of these, except the last-named, were likewise present at Douai.[3] At Mont-Aimé the number of prelates
was so great that Albericus enumerates sixteen and an eyewitness speaks of the presence of "almost all of the bishops of
France."[4] Furthermore, it is plain from the words of the
chroniclers that the presence of the bishops was not merely
formal, but that they conducted the examination of the accused.
We have specific statements to this effect relative to the persecutions at Cambrai and Mont-Aimé,[5] and the annals of Saint-
Médard sum up the whole matter accurately when they say that
"by the instrumentality of a certain preaching friar Robert,
a great multitude of heretics was taken, examined, and convicted by archbishops, bishops, and prelates of the other ecclesiastical degrees."[6] Whatever may have been the practice in less
celebrated cases, it is clear that the responsibility for the great
burning of heretics in the North and in Champagne rests with
the leaders of the French clergy quite as much as with the
terrible friar.

Of the independent action of the bishops in the pursuit of
heresy, the episcopal Inquisition proper, we hear very little in

Dominicans were established there (Chapotin, *Histoire des Dominicains de la
Province de France*, p. 179).

[1] Albericus in *SS.*, xxiii. 937. Cf. Chapters II and XI.

[2] Mousket, vv. 28915, 28958–61.   [3] *SS.*, xxiv. 30.

[4] 'Fere omnes episcopi Francie.' Étienne de Bourbon, *Anecdotes historiques*,
p. 150, and cf. p. 415. See further Albericus in *SS.*, xxiii. 944, and Mousket, vv.
30535, 30536. Other examples of bishops associated with Robert are those of
Clermont (Auvray, no. 2825; Potthast, no. 10044), Cahors (probably; Lea,
Formulary of the Papal Penitentiary, no. 35, 1), and Arras (Fredericq, *Corpus*,
i, no. 121, and note), the archbishop of Sens (Lea, no. 35, 2), and the archbishop
of Sens and the bishop of Troyes (Potthast, no. 10114; Auvray, no. 3006).

[5] Mousket, v. 28885; Étienne de Bourbon, p. 415. Cf. Albericus in *SS.*,
xxiii. 945.   [6] *SS.*, xxvi. 522.

Northern France, either in the time of Friar Robert or later.[1] The absence of records is probably due in the first instance to the lack of any noteworthy proceedings to record, at least at a time when the papal inquisitor was taking the initiative so vigorously and the bishops were so busily occupied in considering the cases which he brought before them; and yet, if the sources permitted a study of the relations of the papal Inquisition to the local ecclesiastical authorities, we should probably hear more of the local jealousies of Dominican interference whose faint echoes reach us in the papal documents of the period.[2] The duties of the bishops in the suppression of heresy did not cease with the establishment of the Dominican Inquisition, and some effort was certainly made to put new energy into the episcopal machinery for the detection and punishment of misbelief. In 1239 the provincial council of Tours sought to revive the old institution of the synodal witnesses by prescribing the appointment in each parish of three persons sworn to reveal all offences concerning the faith.[3] Somewhat later, councils of the province of Sens decided to coerce obstinate excommunicates by bringing them before the council as heretics.[4] From the diocese of Tournai there has been preserved a proclamation against heresy, written in the Romance tongue, which was to be read in the parish churches every other Sunday,[5] and in the

---

[1] The material for the episcopal inquisition in the Netherlands in this period has been collected by Fredericq, *Geschiedenis*, i, ch. 6. Cf. de Cauzons, ii. 121–124.

[2] Bulls *Dudum ad aliquorum murmur* and *Quo inter ceteras* of 1235. Auvray, nos. 2735–37; Potthast, nos. 9993–95; Fredericq, *Corpus*, i, nos. 100, 101; ii, no. 28. For the late thirteenth century see Fredericq, *Geschiedenis*, i. 68–71.

There were also differences among the secular clergy, so that in a controversy with his suffragans the archbishop of Rheims even went so far as to assert that some of them were tainted with heresy (P. Varin, *Archives administratives de Reims*, i. 675; Potthast, no. 12062), but there is no evidence that the charge was substantiated.

[3] Mansi, *Conciliorum collectio*, xxiii. 497; Hefele-Knöpfler, v. 1083. Cf. also the council of Trier in 1238, in Fredericq, *Corpus*, i, no. 115, and for the South the councils cited in Hinschius, *Kirchenrecht*, v. 449, note 4.

[4] Concilium Parisiense, 1248, c. 20; Concilium Pruvinense, 1251. Mansi, xxiii. 768, 793; Hefele-Knöpfler, v. 1151; vi. 45.

[5] Fredericq, *Corpus*, i, no. 158 (undated, but evidently of the thirteenth century).

adjoining diocese of Thérouanne we find the bishop instructing
the parish priests to see that the people do not fall under
suspicion of heresy by remaining away from church.[1] Some
actual cases of the pursuit of heretics by the bishop are
also found, in the diocese of Troyes [2] and in the diocese of
Noyon, where in 1235 a priest was kept in close confinement in
spite of his vigorous assertions of orthodoxy and proffers of
proof,[3] while a few years later the bishops of Cambrai, just over
the northern frontier, showed their zeal for the suppression of
heresy and social discontent at Antwerp.[4] At Paris, too, the
bishops and the masters of theology kept a careful watch against
theological error,[5] and the bishop's prison awaited those who
persisted in upholding forbidden doctrines,[6] while the time was
coming when the University of Paris would virtually supplant
the Inquisition as an agency for the maintenance of orthodoxy
in France.[7] Still, when all known instances of such sporadic
local activity are enumerated, they make a small showing in
comparison with the persistent labours of the papal inquisitors.

When we turn from the external history of the persecutions
of heretics by Friar Robert and his associates to an examination
of their procedure and the penalties which they inflicted, we
are embarrassed by the scarcity of evidence and its one-sided
character. An occasional summons, a few appeals from sentences
in which appellants state their version of the case to the Pope,
some forms of the papal penitentiary, and the incidental state-

[1] Fredericq, *Corpus*, i, no. 99 (1235).

[2] Lea, *Formulary of the Papal Penitentiary*, no. 37, 2.

[3] The case of Michel de Cerizy: Auvray, no. 2854.

[4] Fredericq, *Corpus*, i, nos. 125, 126, 133; *Geschiedenis*, i. 84.

[5] See the notices of errors condemned in 1241, *Chartularium Universitatis Parisiensis*, i, no. 128; in 1247, *ibid.*, no. 176; in 1270, *ibid.*, no. 432; and in 1277, *ibid.*, no. 473. Cf. also no. 522 and the documents relating to the condemnation of the Talmud, especially no. 178. On the condemnations of 1270 and 1277 see Mandonnet, *Siger de Brabant*, and L. Thorndike, *History of Magic and Experimental Science* (New York, 1923), ii. 707–712, 869. Cf. M. Grabmann, Munich *S.B.*, 1924, no. 2.

[6] *Chartularium*, i, no. 176. It is worth noting that the papal legate who acted when Master Raymond was condemned the second time uses the phrase 'de bonorum consilio,' so common in the inquisitorial documents of the South.

[7] Lea, ii. 135 ff.

ments of the chroniclers constitute our only sources.[1] This
material is too fragmentary to serve as the basis of a special
study of the methods of the Inquisition, yet it is valuable so
far as it goes and has been little used by the general writers on
the subject;[2] and, for the sake of comparison with the course
of the papal Inquisition elsewhere and with the earlier practice
in Northern France, it may be worth while to bring together
what may be learned of the procedure of the Inquisition in the
North in the time of Gregory IX.

On his first visit to La Charité Friar Robert began with the
usual preliminary sermon[3] exhorting heretics to return to the
faith, with the result, so he tells us, that not only those who
were specially summoned, but many who did not wait for his
summons and some who were not even suspected, came forward

[1] The only cases in which we have any extended account of Robert's method
of procedure are: At La Charité, the appeals of Pierre Vogrin (Sbaralea, *Bullarium Franciscanum*, i. 177; Auvray, no. 2825; Potthast, no. 10044) and
Petronilla (Auvray, no. 3106) and the petition of Jean Chevalier (Chapotin,
Histoire des Dominicains de la province de France, p. 224), all of them statements by the accused (cf. also the appeal of a certain M. of the diocese of
Cahors in Lea, *Formulary of the Papal Penitentiary*, no. 38, 2). At Arras the
excommunication of Hukedieu (Archives du Pas-de-Calais, A. 105; Fredericq,
Corpus, i, no. 121), where Robert's proceedings are described by the excom-
municating bishop. At Paris (?) Richer's story of the woman who was compelled by magic to make a false confession (*SS.*, xxv. 307). For the procedure
of the episcopal Inquisition in the same period we have only the case of the
bishop of Noyon and Michel de Cerizy (Auvray, no. 2854); the earlier cases at
La Charité should of course be compared.

[2] On the procedure of the Inquisition in general see Lea, i. 399 ff.; Tanon,
pp. 326 ff.; Hinschius, v. 481 ff.; Douais, *L'Inquisition*, pt. 2; de Cauzons,
Histoire de l'Inquisition en France, ii. Important information on the early procedure of the papal Inquisition is afforded by certain consultations of the papal
penitentiary, Raymond de Peñafort, relative to the treatment of heretics in
the province of Tarragona. See the *Moyen âge*, 2d series, iii. 305–325; and
Raymundiana (*Monumenta Ordinis Praedicatorum*, vi), ii. 41, 73. For Languedoc, in the years 1250–67, see the elaborate study of the workings of the Inquisition at Carcassonne in Molinier, *L'Inquisition dans le Midi de la France*,
pp. 273–451; the register of the *greffier*, upon which Molinier's account is based,
and the important *Sentences* of Bernard de Caux and Jean de S. Pierre (1244–
48) have since been published by Douais in his *Documents pour servir à l'histoire de l'Inquisition dans le Languedoc*.

[3] On which see Tanon, p. 329; Hinschius, v. 458, note 3, 481. Forms of
citation to such a sermon may be seen in Martène and Durand, *Thesaurus*, v.
1810; and in the *Nouvelle revue historique de droit*, 1883, p. 671.

to confess their error and undergo penance. Information was freely offered against others, parents even "denouncing their children and children their parents, husbands their wives and wives their husbands." Robert had as yet no special authority in France, but in the commission which he soon received from the Pope indulgence was promised to all who attended his preaching and assisted him in his work.[1] Prompt confession, where no accusation had been made, relieved the heretic from further pursuit, only a moderate penance being exacted;[2] and information against others was so much desired that, even after sentence of death had been pronounced, a reprieve might be granted on promise of producing other victims.[3] From all accounts, Robert lent a ready ear to all accusations, and when his suspicions had once fastened on any one it was difficult to secure release. At La Charité we have already seen his relentless pursuit of Pierre Vogrin, who had been twice acquitted by the episcopal Inquisition,[4] and the same unwillingness to accept the findings of his predecessors was shown in the case of a certain Petronilla of the same town who also offered canonical purgation without success.[5] Particularly in the case of merchants, whose wandering life and close relations with Italy and Southern France made them natural objects of suspicion, did the papal Inquisition exercise unusual watchfulness. Thus a Florentine merchant, after talking with certain heretics whom he supposed to be orthodox and giving their servants ten sous, first confessed to a Dominican and a Franciscan at Troyes, who assigned him penance; he then consulted the Pope, who after referring the matter to the bishop of Florence and receiving his report, approved by a cardinal, respecting the merchant's unblemished reputation in Italy for purity of faith, still found it necessary, after imposing penance, to have his orthodoxy further

[1] Bull *Gaudemus*: Fredericq, *Corpus*, i, no. 90.

[2] 'Si predictus G. non accusatus nec convictus sed sponte confessus est et suum confitetur errorem et ea que exiguntur in talibus, abiurata prorsus heretica pravitate, de absolutionis beneficio iuxta formam ecclesie provideatis eidem, iniungentes ei penitentiam salutarem et alia prout in similibus censure debite modus et ordo deposcunt.' Lea, *Formulary*, no. 35, 1; Tours, MS. 594, f. 29 v, no. 141.   [3] Albericus, in *SS.*, xxiii. 945.

[4] Potthast, no. 10044; Auvray, no. 2825.   [5] Auvray, no. 3106.

investigated in France by Friar Robert, the archbishop of Sens, and the bishop of Troyes.[1] A man from the diocese of Cahors who had once consorted with heretics and listened to their preaching confessed his error to the local authorities and was admitted to penance, but on coming north he was accused of heresy by his enemies and put in prison by Robert in spite of the letter of security which he carried.[2] Another case is that of Jean Chevalier, of La Charité, who had consorted with a woman suspected of heresy; though he established his own soundness in the faith upon examination, he was nevertheless condemned to an elaborate public penance, with the further threat that if he ever took usury or visited Lombardy he would be considered as a heretic and treated accordingly.[3]

The manner of citation before the inquisitors is illustrated most fully in a case from the later years of Friar Robert's activity, the facts being related by the bishop of Arras on the testimony of parish priests of his diocese, who constituted the usual intermediary between the inquisitor and the suspected party.[4] Robert proclaimed several times that the accused, a wool merchant named Henri Hukedieu, should appear before him at a place which he was ready to designate and should there answer the questions which the friar desired to propound; then in a public sermon a certain fair in Champagne was set as the time for the merchant to appear and establish his innocence, and after the time had elapsed without his coming, Robert excommunicated him as a heretic in a public sermon at Arras.[5]

That a formal examination preceded conviction is often stated

---

[1] Bull *Ildebrandiscus* of 11 March, 1236, printed in Sbaralea, *Bullarium Franciscanum,* i. 188; *Raymundiana,* ii. 49; Potthast, no. 10114; Auvray, no. 3006. Similar bull of 23 November, 1234 (*Accurri ...*) in *Raymundiana,* ii. 27; Auvray, no. 2221; Potthast, no. 9772. There are a number of papal bulls of this period for the protection of Italian merchants in Northern France, e.g., Auvray, nos. 2842, 2843, 2857, 2764.

[2] Lea, *Formulary,* no. 38, 2; Tours, MS. 594, f. 30 v, no. 148.

[3] Bull *Constitutus,* in Chapotin, p. 224, and Guiraud, no. 1180.

[4] Cf. Tanon, p. 340; Henner, *Ketzergerichte,* p. 292. An order from the bishop of Auxerre to a priest of La Charité to summon a suspected person (1233) is cited in Lebeuf, *Mémoires concernant l'histoire d'Auxerre* (ed. Challe and Quantin), i. 411.

[5] Fredericq, *Corpus,* i, no. 121.

by the chroniclers,[1] who sometimes describe the beliefs to which the heretics confessed,[2] but leave us very much in the dark as regards the nature of the proceedings. Usually, as we have seen, bishops were present and took an active part in the examination, but in two cases of which we know Robert appears to have conducted the trial alone. The woman of La Charité, Petronilla, was required to prove her assertion of innocence by the oath of three compurgators, but when she appeared for this purpose the friar declared that she had failed and put her in prison, along with her son-in-law, whose purgation had formerly been accepted.[3] In Richer's story of the proceedings in the case of the woman under the influence of the *cartula* we have a case of enforced confession. Robert approaches her suddenly in public with the questions: "Are you not a heretic?" "Will you return to the Catholic faith?" "Would you rather be burnt than recant?" She admits the charges, whereupon he calls the bystanders to witness her statements and puts her in prison. The same questions are repeated at a second examination, which is likewise public.[4] With the exception of these instances and the general statement of Matthew Paris that Robert punished the innocent as well as the guilty,[5] we know nothing of the rigour of the examination or the frequency of acquittal. It is at this stage in the proceedings, between accusation and conviction, that such appeals as have come down to us were lodged with the Pope. From an inquisitorial condemnation for heresy no such appeal was possible,[6] but in three of the cases we have been considering an appeal to the Pope was taken before sentence was pronounced, and in all three the Pope orders further investigation. In each instance, in addition to the innocence of the accused, some irregularity in the proceedings was alleged—either imprisonment in spite of a letter of protection,[7] or refusal to accept compurgation, followed by arbitrary im-

---

[1] See the passages cited above, apropos of the participation of the bishops.
[2] Étienne de Bourbon, *Anecdotes historiques*, p. 149; Albericus, in *SS.*, xxiii. 945.
[3] Auvray, no. 3106.
[4] *SS.*, xxv. 307.
[5] *Ibid.*, xxviii. 147, 326.
[6] Tanon, p. 435; Hinschius, v. 467.
[7] Lea, *Formulary*, no. 38, 2.

prisonment,[1] or in one case the violation of an agreement which had been made to guarantee a fair hearing, and excommunication after appeal had been taken.[2]

Impenitent heretics, after they had been condemned by the church, were regularly handed over to the secular power to suffer their 'due punishment' of death by burning. Whatever the origin of capital punishment for heresy in the Middle Ages, whether it was inherited from the legislation of the Roman emperors or was introduced from the popular practice of the Germanic nations,[3] by the middle of the thirteenth century the stake had become the regular penalty in Northern Europe, a penalty which prefigured, it was declared, the unquenchable fire of the world to come.[4]

Those who repented of their heresy were admitted by the church to undergo penance.[5] The most severe form, reserved

[1] Auvray, no. 3106.   Pierre Vogrin: Potthast, no. 10044.

[3] The theory of the Germanic origin of the laws for the execution of heretics is worked out in the classical monographs of Ficker, "Die gesetzliche Einführung der Todesstrafe für Ketzerei," in *M. I. O. G.*, i. 177–226, 430, and Havet, *L'Hérésie et le bras séculier au Moyen-Âge*, in the *B. E. C.*, xli. 488–517, 570–607 (and in his *Oeuvres*, ii. 117–180). Their results have been accepted by Lea (i. 222), Fredericq (*Geschiedenis*, i, chs. 7–9), Hinschius (*Kirchenrecht*, v. 379), and Joseph Hansen (*Zauberwahn, Inquisition, und Hexenprozess*, pp. 220 ff.). The Roman origin of the penalty is upheld by Tanon, pp. 441 ff. (Cf. also P. Viollet, *Établissements de S. Louis*, i. 253; and P. Guilhiermoz in *B. E. C.*, lv. 383.) For further discussion see Maillet, *L'Église et la répression sanglante de l'hérésie* (Liége, 1909); de Cauzons, i. 279–315; Charles Moeller, "Les bûchers et les auto-da-fé de l'Inquisition depuis le moyen âge," in *Revue d'histoire ecclésiastique*, xiv. 720–751 (1913).

[4] Philip, chancellor of the University of Paris, says of the baker Echard of Rheims burnt in 1230: 'Translatus est ad furnum temporalis pene et deinde ad furnum gehenne' (Hauréau, vi. 241; cf. Chapter XI, *infra*). Caesar of Heisterbach (ed. Strange, i. 298) and Guillaume le Breton (*Philippis*, i. 418 ff.) use similar phrases. So also John of Garland, *De triumphis ecclesiae*, ed. Wright, p. 79:

> De morte hereticorum mala.

> Excrescit fatua ficus, ficulnea mundi
> Quam paris, hanc urit flamma, gehenna cremat.
> Latrantes et aves direpta cadavera rostris
> Asportant, animas nigra caterva legit.

So the chancellor of Paris, Eudes de Châteauroux, says (Arras, MS. 137, pp. 305 f.): 'Consummatio hereticorum et in presenti et in futuro ignis est. In presenti ignis corporalis, quia comburuntur ad ostendendum magnitudinem peccati . . . In futuro consummatio eorum erit ignis gehennalis qui non extinguetur.'

[5] On the penances of the Inquisition see Lea, i, ch. 12; Tanon, pp. 479 ff.;

for those who repented from fear of death, consisted of perpetual imprisonment, either in the milder form of detention within the prison walls (*murus largus*) or in the harsh solitary confinement of a narrow cell (*murus strictus*), where in many cases the prisoner was also chained to the wall.[1] A less severe but exceedingly humiliating form of punishment, often substituted for imprisonment, was the *poena confusibilis* of wearing some conspicuous sign of infamy, such as a yellow cross on the breast and back. For lesser degrees of guilt the ordinary penances of pilgrimages and pious observances could be prescribed in the discretion of the judge. In the case of priests the more serious punishments for heresy were preceded by degradation from orders, but so great was the difficulty of getting together the number of bishops canonically required to perform this act that it was early found necessary to simplify and expedite the procedure so that the diocesan might act alone with the advice of such as he might summon from his diocese.[2]

These general principles of inquisitorial practice Friar Robert seems to have observed. "Many he consumed with avenging flames, many he handed over to perpetual prison," says one chronicler.[3] Another states the distinction more exactly: "Some were shut up in prison to do penance, others who refused to renounce their heresies were consumed by fire."[4] Burial alive

de Cauzons, ii. 288 ff. Besides the texts there cited see Lea, *Formulary of the Papal Penitentiary*, pp. 50-60; and the manual of procedure prepared by the archbishop of Tarragona in consultation with the papal penitentiary, Raymond de Peñafort, published by Douais in the *Moyen âge*, 2d series, iii. 305-325.

[1] For an early instance of close confinement see the bull of Gregory IX to the abbot of La Cava, 4 March, 1231: Auvray, no. 562; Potthast, no. 8672.

[2] The undated bull of Gregory IX to this effect which was inserted in the canon law (c. i in Sexto, v. 2) was probably called forth by some case in Northern France in this period, since it is addressed to the archbishop of Rheims and his suffragans and since its omission from the *Decretals* indicates that it was issued after their publication in September, 1234. There are earlier bulls to the same effect addressed to the bishop of Strasbourg, 19 October, 1232 (Auvray, no. 933; Rodenberg, *Epistolae*, i, no. 485), to the archbishop of Bremen, 12 November, 1232 (Potthast, no. 9042), to the archbishop of Salzburg, 22 November, 1232 (Winkelmann, *Acta imperii inedita*, i. 504; Potthast, no. 9046), and to the prelates of Southern France, 19 April, 1233 (MS. Doat xxxi. 19; Potthast, no. 9356). Cf. also Hinschius, *Kirchenrecht*, v. 61, note 1.

[3] *SS.*, vi. 440; xxvi. 215.   [4] *SS.*, xxvi. 522.

is mentioned by one chronicler,[1] but in the account of the persecutions in the North, where fifty met their death, at Châlons, and at Mont-Aimé, it is expressly stated that the heretics were burnt. We have specific mention of the use of imprisonment as a penalty at Douai, in the region of Lille,[2] and at Cambrai, where the number left in prison, variously stated at eighteen and twenty-one, was almost exactly equal to the number burnt.[3] The *poena confusibilis* also appears at Cambrai, where three women were 'marked,' and at Douai, where the penitents were shaved and sentenced to wear crosses.[4] At La Charité one of the first results of Robert's preaching was the great number of people who appeared voluntarily before him for penance, having already placed wooden collars or chains about their necks.[5] Of the less rigorous forms of penance few examples have been preserved. There is an instance of exile to Constantinople,[6] and one man who had made voluntary confession was ordered to take the cross and accompany Simon de Montfort to the East, as well as to attend divine service whenever opportunity offered and to lay aside linen and fast every Friday for the rest of his life.[7] At La Charité Robert, besides prescribing religious observances of this character, publicly forbade penitents to carry arms or take usury or go into Lombardy, under pain of being condemned as heretics.[8]

The practice of the Inquisition in Northern France also illustrates certain of the secondary consequences of conviction for heresy—civil and ecclesiastical disabilities, destruction of

[1] *SS.*, xxviii. 133. Frederichs seeks to interpret the words 'vivos sepeliri' as merely a slightly exaggerated way of describing the close imprisonment of heretics, but Tanon has shown that burying alive was not an unknown form of punishment in the thirteenth century. *Tribunaux de l'Inquisition*, p. 117; *Histoire des justices des anciennes églises de Paris*, pp. 29–33 (for an instance of its employment to punish unnatural vice see Lea, *Formulary*, no. 16). It should be observed that the totals would be far too small if the imprisoned were reckoned in. [2] Mousket, vv. 28986, 29006.

[3] *Ibid.*, v. 28966; Albericus, in *SS.*, xxiii. 937.

[4] Mousket, vv. 28964, 28984, 28985.

[5] Fredericq, *Corpus*, i, no. 90. [6] Mousket, vv. 29002, 29003.

[7] Lea, *Formulary*, no. 35, 2; Tours, MS. 594, f. 29 v, no. 142. For a similar penance imposed by the bishop of Troyes, see Lea, no. 37, 2 (where the rubric should read 'crimine' instead of 'elemosine'): Tours, MS. 594, f. 30, no. 146.

[8] Bull *Constitutus*, in Chapotin, p. 224; Guiraud, no. 1180.

houses, and confiscation of property. The papal statutes of 1231 excluded the sons and grandsons of heretics from holding ecclesiastical offices or benefices,[1] but in a case from the diocese of Tournai it was held that this provision was not retroactive,[2] and dispensations from the disability might be granted.[3] It was a further principle of the legislation against heresy that the houses of heretics should be destroyed and their sites remain deserted, but as this seriously diminished the profits arising from the confiscation of heretics' property, it was not rigidly enforced.[4] The forfeiture of the property of heretics, inherited from the Roman law of lese-majesty, had been accepted as a principle by the church as early as the time of Innocent III. Conviction of heresy regularly carried with it confiscation, the property becoming at once subject to seizure by the secular power.[5] The various applications of this principle, which presented a constant temptation to the cupidity of princes and was ultimately made to furnish the means for the support of the Inquisition itself, it is not necessary to follow out here. In France confiscation is decreed against the heretics of the South by the legislation of Louis VIII and Louis IX,[6] and while no similar ordinance has been preserved for the northern portion of the kingdom, the customary law of this region explicitly states that the pro-

---

[1] Fredericq, Corpus, i, no. 79. The statutes mention other disabilities as well.

[2] Lea, Formulary, no. 41; Tours, MS. 594, f. 31, no. 151. On the date cf. Fredericq, Corpus, ii, no. 21.

[3] Case of a monk of La Charité in Lea, Formulary, no. 40, where the address should begin, 'De Caritate priori'; Tours, MS. 594, f. 31, no. 150.

[4] See in general Lea, i. 481–483; Tanon, pp. 519+523; de Cauzons, ii. 336–340. Douais, in the Revue des questions historiques for October, 1881, p. 411, cites an order of 1329 for the destruction of houses at Carcassonne (Cabinet historique, xi. 163) as "the first, and perhaps the only, sentence of the sort"; but as early as 1255 Alexander IV had permitted the prior and convent of La Charité, as temporal lords of the town, to rebuild houses which had been destroyed by order of papal inquisitors. C. de La Roncière, Registres d'Alexandre IV, no. 817. Indeed, the destruction of houses is ordained against receivers of heretics in the Assize of Clarendon, 1166 (Stubbs, Select Charters, 9th ed., 1921, p. 173); and the Pipe Roll of the following year (13 Henry II) has various references de domibus fractis super assisam.

[5] On confiscation see Lea, i, ch. xiii.; Tanon, pp. 523 ff.; and the references in Henner, Ketzergerichte, p. 232.

[6] Ordonnances des rois, xii. 319; i. 50.

perty of the condemned heretic goes to his lord.[1] The heirs of
the heretic lost all share in his estate, but both king and Pope
sought to protect the dower rights of orthodox wives,[2] and
there exists, from Friar Robert's time, a decision of the king's
court regulating the respective rights of wife and lord.[3] That
the king derived pecuniary profit from the property of heretics
in Northern France is shown by entries in the royal accounts of
the period,[4] but the sums there collected were paltry enough
in comparison with the proceeds of confiscation in Languedoc.[5]

Any consideration of the relation of the secular power to
the Inquisition in Northern France must necessarily be brief

[1] *Livre de jostice et de plet*, p. 12; *Établissements de Saint-Louis*, ed. Viollet, ii.
147; iii. 50; Beaumanoir, ed. Salmon, § 833.

[2] Ordinance of 1259 in the *Histoire générale de Languedoc*, viii. 1441, and
Ordonnances des rois, i. 63. Bull of Gregory IX of 1238 cited in Tanon, p. 532;
Innocent IV in c. 14 in Sexto, v. 2. In 1269 the dower of the widow of a certain
'Henricus Bougrius' was charged against the royal treasury (roll of the *bailliage*
of Amiens, *B. E. C.*, xxviii. 621). For definition of the conditions under which
the wife might claim, see *Livre de jostice et de plet*, p. 13, and cf. A. Beugnot,
Olim, i. 579.

[3] '*Li jugement des Bougres qui furent ars au tans frere Robert*. Si fu teus fais
en le cort le Roy Loeys de France que tout li Aretage ki viennent naissant de
par le Bougre qui est jugé a ardoir vif doivent demourer quitement au Seigneur
dont il muet, sauf cou que li feme de ce Bougre si a sen douaire tant quele vit,
et après se mort revient au Seigneur dont il muet ⟨sauf cou que li feme de ce
bougre si a sen douaire tant quele vit, et apres se mort revient au Seigneur⟩
perpetuellement; et en tous les aquests kil ont acquis ensanle li feme et si oirs
en ont la moitié, et li sires lautre moitié, et en cele moitié doit li feme avoir sen
Douaire tant quele vit, et après sen décès doit venir au Seigneur dont li iretages
muet.' *Livre Rouge de Saint-Vaast*, f. 157 of the modern copy in the Archives
du Pas-de-Calais at Arras (H. 2); now in Fredericq, *Corpus*, iii, no. 2.

[4] *H. F.*, xxi. 237, 252. Cf. the *Annals of S. Médard*, *SS.*, xxvi. 522.
Among the others who benefited by confiscations in the North we find the
count of Champagne (see the documents on Gile printed on p. 216, where the
count's right is disputed by the collegiate church of Saint-Quiriace at Provins),
and the prior of La Charité as temporal lord of the town (La Roncière, *Registres
d'Alexandre IV*, no. 817). On the practice in the case of condemned ecclesiastics
there is little evidence in the early period; the only case I have found in the
North is in the diocese of Noyon, where the bishop took the horse and perhaps
other personal effects of the accused (Auvray, no. 2854).

[5] See Douais, *Documents*, pp. ccxv, ccxxvii. An example of the sums which
confiscation might yield is afforded by the inventory of the property of certain
heretics of the south in 1261, which gave a net return of 1413 livres 9s. 10d. to
the treasury. 'Bona Petri Bermundi,' Archives Nationales, J.306,85, published
in part in the fourth volume of the *Layettes du Trésor des Chartes* (Paris, 1902),
pp. 62–63.

because of the scarcity of information. Louis IX, as would be expected in the case of a sovereign of such piety and zeal for the Christian faith, was a declared enemy of heretics, considering it a king's duty to expel them from his kingdom,[1] and even declaring that a knight ought to kill with his own sword any one whom he knew to be an unbeliever.[2] He was, moreover, a staunch friend of the Mendicant Orders, by whom he had been educated,[3] and not only showed special favour to the inquisitors who came to him on the business of their office,[4] but gave to the Inquisition the firm support of the royal administration. If we may judge from the ordinances issued for the southern portions of his kingdom, the king's officials were ordered to give active assistance by hunting out heretics and bringing them before the proper ecclesiastical authorities, and by executing promptly the sentences pronounced against them, while a reward was promised to any who assisted in the capture of heretics, and those who attempted to shield or harbour them were threatened with confiscation of goods and civil disabilities.[5] In 1233 the cause of the Inquisition at La Charité was especially commended to the favour of St. Louis by the Pope,[6] and the labours of Friar Robert there and elsewhere were performed with the king's aid and under his authority.[7] The king's

[1] Instructions to his son, edited by Delaborde, *B. E. C.*, lxxiii. 261 (1912), c. 28; Guillaume de S. Pathus (ed. Delaborde), p. 26.

[2] Joinville, p. 19; Guillaume de S. Pathus, p. 25.

[3] See the biographies of St. Louis and the royal accounts, *passim*, and cf. Danzas, *Études sur les temps primitifs de l'Ordre de S. Dominique*, iii. 408 ff.; and Chapotin, *Dominicains de la Province de France*, pp. 494 ff.

[4] Guillaume de Chartres, in *H. F.*, xx. 33.

[5] Ordinance for the South, beginning 'Cupientes in primis aetatis,' *Ordonnances des rois*, i. 50. A lost ordinance of St. Louis, 'Cupientes in favorem,' which probably related to the North, is cited by Philip VI. *Ordonnances des rois*, ii. 41; cf. Fredericq, *Corpus*, ii, nos. 20, 55; *Geschiedenis*, i. 112. Ordinances of St. Louis concerning heresy and a letter patent directing the "dukes, counts, etc., to aid the inquisitors of heretical pravity," are mentioned in the contents of a lost formulary of the royal chancery. Langlois, *Formulaires de lettres*, vi. 3, 14, nos. 1, 318.   [6] Auvray, no. 1145.

[7] Mousket, vv. 28881, 28882:

> Et par la volente dou roi
> De France, ki len fist otroi.

Matthew Paris (*Chronica majora*, iii. 520; *SS.*, xxviii. 146): 'Adjutus brachio saeculari et domino rege Francorum impendente subsidium.'

officers carry out the friar's sentences, the king's soldiers accompany him as a guard,[1] the king and queen themselves take a personal, and it must be said a merciful, interest in his proceedings and the fate of his victims.[2] There is no record that the sovereign attended in person any of the executions for heresy, but there is mention of the presence of certain of the great feudatories, Countess Jeanne of Flanders at Douai, and Thibaut IV of Champagne at Mont-Aimé.[3] After Friar Robert's fall the same policy seems to have continued. In the accounts of the year 1248 the expenses of friars inquisitors are charged against the royal treasury at several places in the North,[4] and at various times we find the cost of the imprisonment and execution of heretics defrayed by the king's agents;[5] while it was at the king's special request that Alexander IV gave more effective organization to the French Inquisition in 1255.[6]

It is not the purpose of this study to follow the vicissitudes of the Inquisition under the successors of Gregory IX. The legislation of Innocent IV was of great importance in the firm establishment of the Inquisition and the development of its procedure, but it is directed primarily against the heretics of Languedoc and Italy, and touches only in the most general way upon conditions in Northern France.[7] Alexander IV devoted more attention to affairs in the North, and to his pontificate belongs the definite organization of the French Inquisition

[1] Mousket, vv. 28912-14:
> Cil Robiers, o lui siergans vint;
> Quar li rois le faisoit conduire,
> Pour cou con ne li vosist nuire.

Matthew Paris, *Historia Anglorum*, ii. 388: 'Qui eidem Roberto auxilium praestitit militare.' Sbaralea, *Bullarium Franciscanum*, i. 178: 'Ad locum ipsum manu veniebat armata.'

[2] Mousket, vv. 28899 ff. Cf. Berger, *Blanche de Castille*, p. 295.

[3] *SS.*, xxiv. 30; xxiii. 944.

[4] *H. F.*, xxi. 262, 264, 268, 269, 273, 274, 276, 280, 281. Cf. also the account of Paris for the Ascension term, 1255, *B. E. C.*, xxviii. 618.

[5] *H. F.*, xxi. 262, 274; xxii. 570, 745; *B. E. C.*, xxviii. 621. Cf. *H. F.*, xxi. 227, 237; Tillemont, *Histoire de S. Louis*, ii. 292.

[6] Bull *Prae cunctis mentis* of 13 December, 1255. Potthast, no. 16132; Fredericq, *Corpus*, i, no. 132.

[7] See for Languedoc, Douais, *Documents*, pp. xiii-xxii; for Italy, the bulls of 1254 in Berger, *Registres d'Innocent IV*, nos. 7790-7802, 8310-13.

under the direction of the Dominican prior provincial at Paris, who finally came to exercise control over the South as well.[1] "Little remains to us of the organization thus perfected over the wide territory stretching from the Bay of Biscay to the Rhine." [2] In 1248 the almost universal silence of the contemporary records is broken by the royal accounts, which reveal heretics in prison at Paris, Sens, and Corbeil, and inquisitors supported by the king in a dozen different districts of Northern France.[3] Three inquisitors are mentioned by name at Paris in 1255; [4] in 1277 and 1278 Simon du Val, "inquisitor in the kingdom of France," was at work at Orleans, at St. Quentin, and in Normandy; [5] and in 1285 Friar Guillaume d'Auxerre appears as inquisitor in Champagne and Brie.[6] The record of their condemnations has disappeared even more completely than the names of the inquisitors. A woman burnt at Pontoise in 1261, presumably for heresy,[7] a payment of dower to a heretic's widow in 1269,[8] a conflict of jurisdiction in 1272 between the bishop of Auxerre and the prior of La Charité[9]—such are the scattered notices of the victims of the French Inquisition in the later thirteenth century. "The laborers were vigorous, and labored according to the light which was in them," concludes Lea, "but the men and their acts are buried beneath the dust of the forgotten past. That they did their duty is visible in the fact that heresy makes so little figure in France, and that the slow but remorseless extermination of Catharism in Languedoc was not accompanied by its perpetuation in the North." [10]

[1] Fredericq, Corpus, i, nos. 130 ff.; Douais, Documents, pp. xxii–xxv; Lea, ii. 119; and particularly the excellent account in Fredericq, Geschiedenis, i, ch. 5, where the papal legislation affecting the Inquisition in the North is followed through to the time of Boniface VIII.

[2] Lea, ii. 120.

[3] H. F., xxi. 262, 264, 268, 269, 273, 274, 276, 280, 281.

[4] Royal account, in B. E. C., xxviii. 618.

[5] Martène and Durand, Thesaurus, v. 1810–13; Lea, ii. 120; Fredericq, Geschiedenis, i. 60–63; Mandonnet, Siger de Brabant, i (1911), pp. 254–255.

[6] Lea, ii. 121, citing MS. Doat, xxxii. 127.

[7] H. F., xxii. 745 A.   [8] B. E. C., xxviii. 621.

[9] Gallia Christiana, xii, instrumenta, col. 173.   [10] Lea, ii. 120.

CHAPTER XI

THE HERESY OF ECHARD THE BAKER OF RHEIMS

OF the two principal groups of heretics in Western Europe in the Middle Ages, Dualists and Waldenses, the Waldenses are decidedly the more obscure. Being both less numerous and less conspicuous, they appear more rarely in the documents and theological writings of the period; indeed their teaching seems to have spread chiefly among the lower classes, and they rarely rise to the surface in such a way as to leave a record of their doctrines or their geographical distribution. Particularly little is known of the Waldenses in the North of France; in Fredericq's great collection of documents relating to heresy in the Low Countries and adjacent French lands the cases reported are almost exclusively Manichean.[1] It is accordingly not without interest to note a well defined instance of Waldensianism at Rheims about 1230, especially as it shows us an example of the pursuit of heretics just before the introduction of the papal Inquisition and brings to light a noteworthy provincial council otherwise unknown. Moreover, the chief heretic, Echard, was a baker by trade and thus gives us a glimpse of a social class not often mentioned in this period.[2]

In a communication to the Académie des Inscriptions et Belles-Lettres in April, 1889, Barthélemy Hauréau called attention to a sermon of Philip, the chancellor of the University of Paris from 1218 to 1236, in which he speaks at some length of a certain Echard, a baker of Rheims who had been condemned for heresy by a provincial council and burnt.[3] Having been delivered on Holy Thursday,[4] the anniversary of the Last Supper, the sermon takes as its subject bread: there are two

[1] Fredericq, *Corpus*, i, ii; cf. on this point Charles Molinier's review in the *Revue historique*, xliii. 167 (1890).

[2] Cf. the condemnation of the barber Arnolinus at Châlons in 1235, at which Philip was also present. Albericus Trium Fontium, in *SS.*, xxiii. 937.

[3] Académie des Inscriptions et Belles-Lettres, *Comptes rendus*, 1889, pp. 107–108; *Revue critique d'histoire et de littérature*, 1889, i. 340; Hauréau, "Un concile et un hérétique inconnus," in *Journal des savants*, 1889, pp. 505–507; idem, vi. 239–242 (1893). See my note in *A. H. R.*, vii. 442 (1902).

[4] This was also the day of the great annual sacrament of the French Waldenses: Karl Müller, *Die Waldenser* (Gotha, 1886), pp. 81–84.

kinds of bread, good and bad, and three kinds of ovens for each. For the good bread there are the ovens of the study of the Scriptures, of penance, and of the altar; and the bakers are respectively the doctors of the sacred page, confessors, and priests. "But, alas, over against these the Devil has in our day built his ovens in the Albigeois, the Roman territories, at Milan, and in these parts. His first oven is the secret haunt of suspected doctrine, the bakers are false preachers, the bread is secret error. . . . Echard[1] the baker, who was condemned in the synod of Rheims, was a baker of this sort, and those who preach in secret imitate him." St. Bernard teaches us that, although rustics are ignorant, they must not be dealt with carelessly; "whence it was decreed in the council of Rheims that the books of Holy Scripture should not be translated, as heretofore, into the Gallic tongue." "The second oven is that of misleading confession; the bakers are those who despise the keys of the church." Some of these entirely destroy confession; others would merely restrict its efficacy, denying the validity of indulgences to Crusaders; while still others extend its scope by declaring that it is lawful for any one to confess to whomsoever he wishes. "The third oven of the Devil is the congregation of those who form a pernicious union; its bakers are the sowers of schism. Such was Echard the baker of Rheims and such are his imitators. . . . This baker of Rheims was taken from the threefold oven of false doctrine, misleading confession, and pernicious congregation, and was handed over to the oven of temporal punishment and then to the oven of Hell."

Primi panis furnus est studium sive gymnasium sacre Scripture; huius furni furnarii sunt doctores sacre Scripture. Secundi panis est furnus penitentie; huius furni furnarii sunt confessores. Tertii panis furnus est sacrosanctum altare; huius furni furnarii sunt sacerdotes.

Sed ve nobis hodie, quia contra hos furnos edificavit diabolus suos furnos in Albigensi, in Romanis, in Medulanis et in partibus istis. Primus furnus diaboli est latibulum suspecte doctrine; huius furni furnarii sunt pseudo-predicatores; panis huius furni est falsa doctrina abscon-

1 The manuscript has Hyechardus, which Hauréau renders Guichard, but in the further mention of the case to which we shall come below the Troyes MS. 1099 has Ethardus (ff. 167, 173 v) and the Avranches MS. 132 has Ezhardus (f. 4 v) and Hezhardus (f. 12).

dita; Prov.: Aque furtive dulces sunt, panis absconditus suavior.[1] De istis furnariis erat Hyechardus furnarius, in Remensi synodo condemnatus. Huius imitatores sunt illi qui in abscondito predicant, sicut predixerat Dominus in Matth., 24: Multi pseudo-prophete surgent, et seducent multos; et cet.: Si quis vobis dixerit: Ecce hic est Christus aut illic, nolite credere; et cet. usque ibi: Si ergo dixerit vobis: Ecce in deserto est, nolite exire; Ecce in penetralibus, nolite credere; sicut enim fulgur, et cet. . . . . Suspecti sunt qui querunt solitudines; et propter hoc dicit Dominus in Evangelio: Attendite vos a fermento Phariseorum, quod est hypocrisis.[2] Hos docet reprehendere beatus Bernardus, dicens: Rusticales homines sunt idiote; non tamen negligendi sunt, neque cum eis negligenter agendum est; sermo enim eorum serpit ut cancer; et cet. Propter hoc preceptum est in Remensi concilio ne transferantur sicut hactenus libri sacre Scripture in gallicum idioma. [In Actibus, Multi autem curiosa sectati contulerunt libros suos, etc.][3]

Secundus furnus est furnus confessionis seductorie. Huius furni sunt furnarii clavium ecclesie contemptores, quorum quidam ex toto confessionem destruunt. . . . Item alii sunt qui confessionis virtutem diminuunt, dicentes quod nihil valent indulgentie crucesignatis. . . . Item alii sunt qui confessionem non diminuunt, sed confessionis potestatem extendunt, dicentes quod licet unicuique cuilibet confiteri, [non intelligentes illud verbum Iac.:[4] Confitemini alterutrum peccata vestra.] Horum imitatores sunt quidam sacerdotes qui nimis potestatem suam extendunt, mittentes falcem in messem alienam. Tales sunt illi qui mulierum que sunt de parochia aliena audiunt confessiones; qui potius querunt corruptionem earum quam correptionem. . . . In hoc ergo maximum est periculum illis qui se ingerunt confessionibus, quod mulieres, proprios sacerdotes relinquentes, querunt alienos, quia sic proprii sacerdotes non possunt suas mulieres cognoscere, cum tamen eis dicatur: Diligenter inquire vultum pecoris tui.[5]

Tertius furnus diaboli est congregatio unitatis perniciose. Huius furni sunt furnarii schismatum seminatores. Talis erat Hyechardus, Remensis furnarius, et eius imitatores tales. Hec est congregatio de qua dicitur in Psalmo: Odivi ecclesiam malignantium.[6] Iste furnarius Remensis de triplici furno, scilicet doctrine corrupte, confessionis seductorie, et congregationis unitatis perniciose, translatus est ad furnum temporalis pene et deinde ad furnum gehenne.[7]

From this characteristic bit of sermonizing, certain facts stand out definitely. A baker of Rheims, Echard, had secretly

---

[1] Proverbs, ix. 17. The same text is applied to heretics by Philip in a sermon on St. Bartholomew. Avranches, MS. 132, ff. 23 v–26.

[2] Luke, xii. 1.   [3] Acts, xix. 19.   [4] James, v. 16.

[5] Proverbs, xxvii. 23.   [6] Psalms, xxvi. 5.

[7] Hauréau, vi. 240–241, collated with MS. lat. n. a. 338, f. 152, from which the two clauses in square brackets have been added.

preached heretical doctrines in which he especially attacked the system of confession, and had gathered about him a body of heretics. He was condemned by a local council and burnt, and at the same time the council forbade translation of the Bible into French. "We know," concludes Hauréau, "of no other evidence concerning this Guichard and this council; it is quite extraordinary that none of the chroniclers mention so important a fact." [1] "It is to be regretted that Philip de Grève does not tell us what were the doctrines whose impiety shocked the Church and brought Guichard to the stake." [2]

As the heretic and council here mentioned were unknown to previous historians, it becomes a problem of some interest to discover the doctrines which the humble preacher professed and the date of the council by which he was condemned. It is certainly an excellent illustration of the value of sermons as an historical source that such further information as I have been able to collect on both these problems is contained in two other sermons of the same chancellor of Paris, Philip. These belong to a group of his sermons to which none of the earlier writers on the chancellor called attention. Hauréau, whose remarkable knowledge of mediaeval sermons was almost wholly confined to Paris manuscripts, knew but three series of sermons by Philip, namely the *Festivales*, the *Dominicales*, and those *De Psalterio*.[3] The sermons of what we may call a fourth series are of a more miscellaneous sort and were prepared not only for the ordinary Sundays and holy days of the ecclesiastical year but for various special occasions, as appears from some of the titles: "Sermon to scholars between Epiphany and Purification at the time when King Louis took the cross against the Albigenses" (1226); "at the feast of St. Martin in his church at Paris in council"; "in council at Bourges to the Crusaders in the King's presence"; "on Passion Sunday at Chambéry (?) in the presence of the Countess of Flanders"; "on Easter eve at Orleans to the students concerning the departure of the students from Paris"; "before the Pope and cardinals at Rome"; "in the chapter of Laon at

[1] Hauréau, vi. 241.   [2] *Journal des savants*, 1889, p. 507.
[3] On Philip's sermons and their authorship, see Chapter II, p. 43, note.

the time of the dissension between the bishop and the citizens";
etc.[1] As these sermons do not constitute a regular series, they
do not seem to have been brought together in any single collection. The most numerous body of these appears to be the
ninety-four *Sermones Ph. Cancellarii Parisiensis* of MS. 1099
at Troyes. In MS. 132 of Avranches, a manuscript from Mont-
Saint-Michel, which contains the most complete collection of
the chancellor's sermons to be found in a single volume with
which I am acquainted, several of these are scattered among the
Dominicales and *Festivales*. Some are also to be found in the
Omelie et Sermones Magistri Philippi Cancellarii Parisiensis of
MS. 69 of Vitry-le-François, and two are in the manuscript of
the Bibliothèque Nationale, MS. lat. n.a. 338, which was used
by Hauréau (ff. 152, 256). Two copies of *Sermones Cancellarii
Parisiensis* having the same *incipits* as the Troyes MS. were in
the Papal Library in 1295.[2]

[1] 'Sermo scolaribus inter epiphaniam et purificationem tempore quo rex
Ludovicus assumpsit crucem in Albigenses' (Avranches, MS. 132, f. 248 v;
also in Troyes, MS. 1099, f. 15 v, and Vitry, MS. 69, f. 107, where the heading
is 'In dissensione clericorum Parisius'). 'In festo Sancti Martini in ecclesia
eius apud Parisius in concilio' (Vitry, MS. 69, f. 101). 'In concilio Bituricensi
ad crucesignatos presente rege' (Vitry, MS. 69, f. 139). 'In passione apud
Camberon presente comitissa Flandrie' (Vitry, MS. 69, f. 133 v). 'Sermo cancellarii Parisiensis quem fecit Aurelianis ad scolares de recessu scolarium a
Parisius, quem fecit in vigilia Pasche' (Avranches, MS. 132, f. 340; Troyes, MS.
1099, f. 160 v). 'Coram domino papa et cardinalibus Rome' (Troyes, MS. 1099,
ff. 152, 154; Vitry, MS. 69, f. 119 v). 'In capitulo Laudunensi tempore dissen-
sionis episcopi et civium' (Avranches, MS. 132, f. 1; Troyes, MS. 1099, f. 160).
'Sermo in institucione prelati. Pro abbate Dunensi . . .' (Troyes, MS. 1099,
f. 176). 'Pro archiepiscopo Remensi H.' (*ibid.*). 'Sermo in capitulo sancti Vedasti
aput Atrebatum in festo beati Bernardi' (Avranches, MS. 132, f. 16 v), etc.

[2] *Archiv für Litteratur- und Kirchengeschichte des Mittelalters*, i. 29–30 (1885).
Scattered references to heresy occur in other sermons of Philip. Thus, in a
MS. of Peterhouse, Cambridge, I. 3. 9 (James, no. 135), in a sermon for the ninth
Sunday after Pentecost, we read of heretics who forbid marriage, and 'alii ita
circa Resurrectionem vacillant . . . inter quos nonunquam mulieres et laici
evangelizare audent.' In MS. Alencon 153, f. 89 v, he says: 'Hoc est subtilitas
diaboli, ut sicut in exercitu Albigensi machine et ingenia comburantur.'
Another reference to the Albigensian Crusades appears at Vitry, MS. 69, f. 71 v
(=Troyes, MS. 1099, f. 30): 'Que est ista affectio quod hic plangimus pereuntes
propter duas vel tres prebendas vel cetera minora peccata, ibi autem non
plangimus hereses, periculum fidei? Pudeat omnes quod comes Montis Fortis
invenit milites stipendiarios, clerici autem nec stipendiis possunt allici ut
defendant et propagant [*sic*] fidem Dei.'

In a sermon on the duties of the priesthood, delivered before a synod held at Laon on the Tuesday following Trinity Sunday, Philip exhorts the priests to imitate Moses, who led the flock of Jethro to the backside of the desert (Exodus, iii. 1), by leading their people to the inner meanings of Scripture. "The Jew," he continues, "or the heretic does not lead his flock to the interior of the desert, but regards superficially only the externals of Scripture, of whom it is said in the third of Second Corinthians [iii. 6], 'The letter killeth.' Whence some by adhering to externals have fallen from the faith, such as the Poor Men of Lyons, following whom the baker Echard, a citizen of Rheims who was recently condemned, presumed to say that under no circumstances is it lawful to swear, superficially adducing the words of our Lord, Matthew, v. [34], 'I say unto you, Swear not at all.' Likewise he asserted that it is not lawful under any circumstances to kill, because of the passage in Matthew, xiii. [29], 'Gather not up the tares, lest ye root up also the wheat with them.' He also declared it is lawful to confess to whomsoever one wishes, following the last chapter of the Epistle of James [v. 16], 'Confess your faults one to another.' Concerning such it is said in Job, xxx. [4], 'They cut up mallows by the bushes, and juniper roots for their meat.'..."

Interiora ergo deserti sunt spirituales sensus sacre scripture. Iudeus vel hereticus non ducit oves suas ad interiora deserti, exteriora solummodo scripture superficialiter attendentes, circa quod dicitur .ii. ad Cor. iii., Littera occidit etc. Unde quidam exterioribus adherentes exciderunt a fide, sicut Pauperes a Lugduno quos sequens Ethardus fornarius, Remensis civis nuper dampnatus, dicere presumebat quod in nullo casu iurare licet, superficialiter inducens verbum Domini, Mat. v., Ego dico vobis non iurare omnino, etc. Asserebat etiam quod in nullo casu licet occidere, propter illud Mat. xiii., Non colligatis zizania ne simul eradicetis cum eis et triticum. Dicebat etiam quod licet cuilibet confiteri, iuxta illud Iacobi ultimi, Confitemini alterutrum peccata vestra. Circa quos dicitur, Iob xxx., Mandebant herbas et harborum cortices, radix iuniperorum erat cibus eorum. Pastores autem boni catholici non dant ad esum arborum cortices sed medullas et fructus dulces, id est sensus spirituales, ut Augustinus, Ambrosius, Gregorius, Ieronimus, et alii, et hoc est oves ducere ad interiora deserti.[1]

[1] 'Sermo in synodo Laudunensi. Symon Iohannis, diligis me.... Multa casu plerumque videntur fieri....' Troyes, MS. 1099, f. 167. The same sermon

Evidently the chancellor feared that the false doctrines of the baker had spread and needed to be met, for on the day after the synod he addressed the people at Bruyères [1] upon the seven sacraments as the pillars of the church, and took occasion to refute in detail the errors of heretics regarding them. He mentions the usurpation of preaching and confession by heretics,[2] their ridicule of the Eucharist, their denial of marriage and of the virtue of extreme unction, and their belief that the rite of baptism and the administration of the Eucharist can be better performed by a good priest than by a bad. None of the heretics are mentioned by name until the close of the sermon, where, speaking of the sacrament of penance and the power of the priest to give absolution, he says, "Those heretics sin who, like Echard, the baker of Rheims, hold wrong opinions concerning the power of the keys."

Sermo de .vii. sacramentis in episcopatu Laudunensi apud Brueres in crastino post sinodum. Sapientia edificavit sibi domum, excidit columnas .vii. [Proverbs, ix. 1]. Hec domus ecclesia, cuius .vii. columpne .vii. sacramenta. Heretici qui sacramenta impugnant ecclesiam subvertere moliuntur. . . . Cum ergo hec tria sint necessaria predicanti, scilicet scientia, devotionis affectus, et bona opera, oportet autem quod in hiis non sit neophytus . . . Quid est ergo quod videmus magis neophitos in hiis sese intrudere ? . . . Contra mortem nonne necessarium fuit matrimonium ut decedentes per legitimam generationem restituerentur ?

with a slightly different *incipit*, at Avranches, MS. 132, f. 4, the passage quoted being found at the end of f. 4 v and the beginning of f. 5. Also, with still a different *incipit* and with the mention of Echard omitted, at Vitry-le-François, MS. 69, f. 153 v.

In the course of the sermon the date of the synod is given: 'Considerans quidem tempus videbit quod ad sinodum celebrandum post festum Sancte Trinitatis tertia feria prefigitur. Attendens sinodi negocium intelliget quod ipsi negocio tale tempus convenienter aptatur.' Troyes, MS. 1099, f. 166 v. So at Vitry, MS. 69, f. 153 v, the date is given as 'tertia feria post Trinitatem.'

[1] Probably Bruyères-et-Montbérault (' Brueres-en-Laonnois '), in the canton of Laon, eight kilometres from Laon. A. Matton, *Dictionnaire topographique de l'Aisne* (Paris, 1871), p. 42.

[2] On the usurpation of confession there is also a passage in the sermon just cited: 'Fures sunt confessionis usurpatores presumptuosi . . .: Psalmi, lxvii. [31]: Congregatio taurorum, id est hereticorum, in vaccis populorum, id est in mulierculis coniugatis, ut excludant eos, id est eminere faciant, qui probati sunt argento, id est eloquio divino. . . . Qui ergo ingerunt se confessionibus audiendo pocius suspecti sunt de furto quam presumant de eorum zelo.' Troyes, MS. 1099, f. 168; Avranches, MS. 132, f. 5 v.

Unde Dominus dixit, Gen. [i. 22], Crescite et multiplicamini, etc., qui
tamen ad ecclesiam non pertinent, quicquid dicant heretici, nisi renati
spiritualiter, unde Ioh. iii. [3] (f. 171). . . . Peccant heretici [i.e., contra
baptismum] qui vim habere non credunt vel qui melius esse credunt
datum ab uno sacerdote quam ab alio. Primi peccant contra potestatem
Christi quam auferunt; secundi quia alii quam debent conferunt . . .
Sciant igitur quod quanto enormius mentiuntur de hoc heretici, tanto
efficacius capit tinctura (f. 172). . . . Peccant heretici qui dicunt melius
esse sacramentum a digno sacerdote quam indigno. Alii nichil reputant
et hii destruunt potissimum ecclesie remedium et medicamentum, et
irridendo dicunt, Si esset mons, totus consumptus esset (f. 173). . . .
Peccant heretici quorum aliqui nupcias destruunt quas Deus in paradiso
constituit sacramentum primum. . . . Peccant contra extremam unc-
tionem . . . heretici qui nullam inesse virtutem credunt (f. 173 v). . . .
Peccant heretici qui de potestate clavium male sive perperam senciunt,
ut Ethardus Remensis civis fornarius (f. 173 v).[1]

Echard, then, it is expressly declared, was one of the Poor
Men of Lyons, otherwise known as the Waldenses, and evidently
one of the body of preachers who constituted the organized
hierarchy of the sect.[2] This statement is abundantly confirmed
by what is said of his beliefs and practices. Secret preaching by
men of humble station and limited education, the possession
of vernacular versions of the Scriptures and an uncompromis-
ingly literal interpretation of the biblical prohibitions of oaths
and the taking of human life, and denial of the power of the
keys as seen in the practice of lay confession and in the rejection
of the validity of priestly absolution—all these are familiar
manifestations of Waldensian beliefs. Whether Echard and his
followers belonged to the French or the Lombard group of the
Waldenses, it is impossible to determine. Broadly speaking, the

[1] Troyes, MS. 1099, ff. 169–174; Avranches, MS. 132, ff. 6 v–12 (where the
title reads, 'Sermo apud Laudunum ad populum de .vii. sacramentis').
[2] That the earlier organization of the Waldenses comprised only a body of
itinerant preachers, *perfecti*, without organized local communities of *credentes*,
was first established by Karl Müller in his monograph cited on p. 245, above, and
is now generally accepted. Cf. H. Haupt, "Neue Beiträge zur Geschichte des
mittelalterlichen Waldenserthums," in *Historische Zeitschrift*, lxi. 45 (1889);
A. Hauck, *Kirchengeschichte Deutschlands*, iv. 863 (1903); and H. Böhmer,
article "Waldenser," in the Herzog-Hauck *Realencyclopädie für protestantische
Theologie und Kirche*, 3d ed., xx. 812 (1908). Wilhelm Preger still adhered to
the view of universal priesthood in his monograph "Ueber die Verfassung der
französischen Waldesier in der älteren Zeit," Munich Academy, *Abhandlungen*,
hist. Classe, xix. 639–711 (1890).

matters which divided them concerned internal organization and relation to the Roman church rather than belief,[1] and the meagre statements regarding Echard tell us nothing of these subjects. The geographical position of Rheims in relation to the routes of trade was such that the new doctrines might have come either from Italy or from the valley of the Rhone, but the French propaganda spread southward rather than toward the north, whereas the Lombard influence made itself felt throughout Southern Germany and in the valley of the Rhine. The presence of Waldenses at neighbouring centres like Metz, Toul, Strasbourg,[2] and the close parallelism with the heresies discovered at Trier in 1231,[3] would render more probable a connexion between the heretics of Rheims and the German branch of the Lombard movement.

The date of Echard's condemnation would seem to have been 1230 or early in 1231. The extreme limits are 1222, the year of the death of Stephen, bishop of Noyon, who is called "of blessed memory" in the sermon delivered at Bruyères,[4] and the death of Chancellor Philip in December, 1236. Now Lecoy de la Marche long since pointed out,[5] on the basis of the concordance of fixed and movable feasts which any one can verify, that the group of sermons in MS. lat. n.a. 338 in which Hauréau first discovered Echard forms a series for the ecclesiastical year from 8 Septem-

[1] See Müller, pp. 3–65; Alanus, *Contra hereticos*, lib. ii, in Migne, *P. L.*, ccx. 377–400. Besides the authorities cited by Müller, reference should also be made to the treatise *Supra stella*, printed by Döllinger in his *Beiträge zur Sektengeschichte des Mittelalters* (Munich, 1890), ii. 62–84; and to the Vatican MS. Lat. 2648, *De Pauperibus de Lugduno*, printed *ibid.*, pp. 92–97, and also by Preger, *loc. cit.*, pp. 708–711. A convenient English summary of the contemporary Roman Catholic accounts of Waldensian teaching is given by H. C. Vedder, "Origin and Early Teachings of the Waldenses, according to the Roman Catholic Writers of the Thirteenth Century," in *American Journal of Theology*, iv. 465–489 (1900). Böhmer's article "Waldenser" (p. 252, note 2, *supra*) is quite full.

[2] Hauck, *Kirchengeschichte Deutschlands*, iv. 866 ff.; H. Haupt, "Waldenserthum und Inquisition im südöstlichen Deutschland bis zur Mitte des 14. Jahrhunderts," in *Deutsche Zeitschrift für Geschichtswissenschaft*, i. 285–286 (1889).

[3] *Gesta Treverorum*, a. 1231, in *SS.*, xxiv. 400–402; Fredericq, *Corpus*, i. 76–78, 80–82; ii. 39–41.

[4] Troyes, MS. 1099, fol. 170 v; Avranches, MS. 132, fol. 8 v.

[5] *La chaire française au moyen âge*, 2d ed. (Paris, 1886), pp. 327, 525, 540.

ber 1230 to 29 August 1231. Holy Thursday in 1231 fell
20 March, and the condemnation by the council of Rheims is
referred to as something fresh in the hearers' minds; the sermon at Laon in which Echard is *nuper damnatus* was delivered
on the Tuesday after Trinity and that at Bruyères a few days
later, so that these can be placed on and shortly after 20 May,
1231.

The council in which the condemnation took place is otherwise unknown. The phrase "in Remensi synodo" may refer to
a council held at Rheims, or perhaps only to a council of the
ecclesiastical province of Rheims; [1] but no such gathering is
known which exactly fits the date at which we have arrived.
It cannot well have been the synod of Laon, at which the sermon refers to the condemnation as something past, nor is there
any special reason for identifying it with the council of Noyon
at which Philip preached a sermon.[2] Councils of this province
were numerous between 1233 and 1235, but all of these fall too
late for our purpose.[3]

That a heretic who persisted in his heresy should be burnt, as
a fitting preparation for his fate in the world to come, was to
be expected in the thirteenth century,[4] and in 1230 it was
altogether natural that the sentence should be pronounced by
a provincial council. Cases of heresy were not so frequent in
Northern France at this time that there should exist any general
understanding as to what constituted false doctrine, and few
bishops were ready to decide so important a matter without
consulting their fellows. It is not strange that the official accounts of this council should have disappeared in the losses of
the French archives of the period; indeed there are many serious
gaps in the acts of councils throughout the thirteenth century.[5]

[1] For an example of this usage see P. Varin, *Archives administratives de la
ville de Reims* (Paris, 1839), i. 593.
[2] Avranches, MS. 132, fol. 342 v: 'Sermo cancellarii quem fecit in concilio
Noviomensi coram archiepiscopo Remensi et suis suffraganeis.'
[3] See particularly the councils concerned with the bishop of Beauvais, in
Varin, i. 548 ff.; and cf. Finke, *Konzilienstudien*, pp. 64–66.
[4] See Chapter X.
[5] The incompleteness of the collections of Labbé and Mansi is well known;
see particularly the additional material in H. Finke, *Konzilienstudien zur*

It is, however, curious that no other record is left of a matter of such permanent importance as the council's prohibition of Romance versions of the Scriptures. Vernacular translations of portions of the Bible are mentioned in connexion with the Waldensian troubles at Metz in 1199 [1] and appear also at Liége in 1202 [2] and at Trier in 1231,[3] as well as at Rheims;[4] but while they are forbidden by the council of Toulouse in 1229 [5] and by an act of the king of Aragon and his bishops in 1234,[6] no other record of such action has been found in the North of France.[7]

Geschichte des 13. Jahrhunderts (Münster, 1891), and cf. P. Glorieux, "Un synode provincial inconnu, Reims, 1267," in *Revue des sciences religieuses*, viii. 230–256 (1928).

[1] S. Berger, *La Bible française au moyen âge* (Paris, 1884), pp. 38 ff.; H. Suchier, in *Zeitschrift für romanische Philologie*, viii. 418 ff. (1884); G. Voigt, "Bischof Bertram von Metz," in *Jahr-Buch der Gesellschaft für lothringische Geschichte und Altertumskunde*, v, 1, pp. 51–54 (1893); cf. the notice of the Lorraine version, B.N., MS. fr. 24728, given by Paul Meyer in Société des Anciens Textes Français, *Bulletin*, xxxi. 38–48 (1905).

[2] Suchier, *loc. cit.*, p. 422; Fredericq, *Corpus*, i. 63.

[3] Fredericq, *Corpus*, ii. 41; *Gesta Treverorum*, a. 1231, in *SS.*, xxiv. 401.

[4] A portion of a translation of the Bible made in the second quarter of the thirteenth century and formerly preserved at Strasbourg seems to have been written in the dialect of Rheims. Berger, *La Bible française*, p. 116.

[5] J. D. Mansi, *Sacrorum conciliorum collectio* (Florence, 1759–98), xxiii. 197, ch. 14; C. J. von Hefele and A. Knöpfler, *Conciliengeschichte*, 2d ed. (Freiburg, 1873–90), v. 982; Hefele, French tr. by H. Leclercq, v, 2, p. 1498 (1913).

[6] Issued at Tarragona. E. Martène and U. Durand, *Veterum scriptorum amplissima collectio* (Paris, 1724–33), vii. 123, art. 2; Hefele-Knöpfler, *op. cit.*, v. 1037; Hefele-Leclercq, v, 2, p. 1559.

[7] On the Waldensian translations and their possible influence, see Berger, *La Bible française*, with the review thereof by Paul Meyer in *Romania*, xvii. 121–141 (1888); H. Suchier, "Zu den altfranzösischen Bibelübersetzungen," in *Zeitschrift für romanische Philologie*, viii. 413–429 (1884); Berger, "Les Bibles provençales et vaudoises," in *Romania*, xviii. 353–422 (1889); H. Haupt, *Die deutsche Bibelübersetzung der mittelalterlichen Waldenser* (Würzburg, 1885) and *Der waldensische Ursprung des Codex Teplensis* (Würzburg, 1886), with the reviews by Berger in the *Revue historique*, xxx. 164–169; xxxii. 184–190 (1886). Cf. "Bibelübersetzungen, romanische," article by E. Reuss revised by S. Berger, in Herzog-Hauck, *Realencyklopädie*, 3d ed., iii. 126–128 (1897).

CHAPTER XII

TWO AMERICAN MEDIAEVALISTS

Henry Charles Lea [1]

The death of Henry Charles Lea removes from this Society's roll of Honorary Members the name of one who, for more than forty years, has brought honour to American historical scholarship. Born in 1825, the son of Isaac Lea and the grandson of Mathew Carey, Mr. Lea represented the best intellectual traditions of Philadelphia and showed his early bent toward the things of the mind by publishing an article on conchology in the *American Journal of Science* at the age of fifteen; but his health as a youth was not strong and he never had a formal academic education. In 1851 he became a partner in the publishing house of Lea Brothers, with which he retained his connexion until 1880, the greater part of this time as the active manager of the business. During the Civil War he was an efficient member of the military committee of the Union League and served as bounty commissioner; on the organization, in 1871, of the first association for the reform of municipal government in Philadelphia he was made its president; and throughout his life his influence was steadily exerted toward better political conditions in city, state, and nation.

Mr. Lea's first publications in the field of history were certain essays on early law which began to appear in the *North American Review* in 1859, and were expanded into a volume in 1866 under the title of *Superstition and Force*. This was followed the next year by a *History of Sacerdotal Celibacy in the Christian Church*, enlarged in a subsequent edition (1907) to two volumes, and in 1869 by a collection of *Studies in Church History*. The direction of Mr. Lea's studies was now defined, but eighteen years elapsed before the appearance of his next book, a period

[1] Reprinted from Massachusetts Historical Society, *Proceedings*, xliii. 183–188 (December, 1909). For a fuller account of Mr. Lea's life and work, see the memoir by Professor E. P. Cheyney in volume 50 of the *Proceedings* of the American Philosophical Society (1911), and the preliminary memoir privately printed by his family, *Henry Charles Lea, 1825–1909* (Philadelphia, 1910).

occupied partly with the responsibilities of business, and partly with laying broad and deep the scholarly foundations of the works upon which his reputation as an historian chiefly rests. These are: *A History of the Inquisition of the Middle Ages* (1887); *Chapters from the Religious History of Spain connected with the Inquisition* (1890); *A Formulary of the Papal Penitentiary* (1892); *A History of Auricular Confession and Indulgences in the Latin Church* (1896); *The Moriscos of Spain* (1901); *A History of the Inquisition of Spain* (1906–07); and *The Inquisition in the Spanish Dependencies* (1908). In all, not counting new editions, Mr. Lea's published work fills eighteen substantial volumes, beside a number of monographic articles and a small volume of *Translations and other Rhymes* privately printed in 1882.

Looked at broadly, the central theme of Mr. Lea's histories is the Latin Church, which was to him "the great fact which dominates the history of modern civilization," and within the church the development of those institutions which have established and maintained its power over the intellect and conscience of men. These institutions interested him, not as legal or theological abstractions, but as actual working forces, reflected, it is true, in the jurisprudence of the church, which offers "the surest basis of investigation for a given period," but really understood only when studied in the concrete detail of daily life. This detail, the real warp and woof of history, does not lie on the surface, but must be sought beyond code and statute in scattered chronicles and charters and fugitive publications, and in the dusty records of tribunals. In other words, any treatment of these subjects which was to be anything but superficial and temporary involved years of labour in the great folio collections of law and theology, in out-of-the-way tracts and pamphlets, and in the libraries and archives of every part of Europe. From this life of patient toil Mr. Lea never shrank. Remote from the original materials, with none of the formal training of the historian, this self-made scholar set himself to attack some of the hardest problems of the world's history, whose difficulties were to prove the measure of his success. From the outset he formed the habit of going directly to the original sources, and while he never left Philadelphia for purposes of research, his large fortune enabled him to bring together an exceedingly valuable library of printed works and to maintain searchers and copyists in the collections of manuscripts which were most important for his purpose.[1] Dealing with matters which have long been the subject of bitter polemic, he deliberately abstained from reading modern writers lest they should obscure or distort his vision of the past, and he carried this practice so far as to neglect even the non-controversial writings of contemporary historians. This disregard of modern material proved a disadvantage, not only in such matters as his awkward mode of citing authorities and his failure to use recent editions of texts, but especially in his treatment of the early church, where the original records cannot be properly studied without constant reference to the results of critical scholarship; but the fault was the defect of an admirable quality, and few are in danger of repeating it. Frederic William Maitland, the greatest writer on the history of law that the English-speaking world has produced, once said, "It is Dr. Lea's glory that he is one of the very few English-speaking men who have had the courage to grapple with the law and the legal documents of continental Europe. He has looked at them with the naked eye instead of seeing them—a much easier task—through German spectacles. We trust him thoroughly because he keeps his gaze fixed on the middle ages, and never looks round for opinions to be refuted or quarrels to be picked. This is not exactly the policy that we could recommend to any but a strong man. Dr. Lea, however, is strong, and sober, and wary." [2]

[1] Mr. Lea's books and manuscripts are now in the Library of the University of Pennsylvania, where a chair of history bears his name. He is also commemorated by the Henry Charles Lea Professorship of Mediaeval History at Harvard University, endowed by the bequest of his daughter, Miss Nina Lea.

The volume of Monsignore Baumgarten mentioned in a subsequent note affords a curious example of *a priori* criticism. He says (p. 11): "From his works it is apparent that Lea must have a card index of extraordinary dimensions, which afforded him ready, though sometimes misleading, answers to most of his questions. Whenever he crossed the ocean he has brought back with him considerable additions to his book treasures." Mr. Lea did not have a card index, and he did not build up his library by journeys to Europe.

[2] *E. H. R.*, viii. 755.

Mr. Lea's style is clear and at times forcible, and his matter does not lack interest, but his books are read by scholars and by thoughtful readers rather than by the general public. His theme is naturally better suited to interest a European than an American audience, and it is not generally realized among us that probably no American writer of history is so widely known and read on the Continent of Europe. Even in his native city he was better known as a man of affairs than as a man of learning, and Philadelphians of some reading were likely to be surprised when they were told that the excellent judge of city real estate who lived at Twentieth and Walnut Streets was one of the greatest scholars of his time. While, however, Mr. Lea's fame was mainly European and his erudition of the kind more commonly found in Europe, his career as a man of affairs who trained himself to be an historian was characteristically American; and there can be little doubt that his business experience helped to give him a sense of reality, an ability to see straight amid a mass of complicated detail, and a solidity of judgement which are often lacking in writers of a more academic type.[1]

In America his best-known book is probably his *Superstition and Force*, which is familiar to a large number of lawyers who have more than a practitioner's interest in their profession. This has passed through four editions and still remains, in spite of all that others have done to illuminate the early history of legal procedure, the best comprehensive account in any language of the methods of trial embodied in the ordeal, compurgation, judicial combat, and torture. In Europe his best-known work is the *History of the Inquisition of the Middle Ages*. Appearing at a time when the most distinguished French student of the Inquisition had pronounced such an undertaking chimerical, this was speedily recognized as the standard authority on the subject, and while it needs to be corrected from time to time with the progress of monographic investigation, there is no prospect of its being superseded. It has been translated into French, a German edition is in process of publication, and it is

[1] Cf. my address on "European History and American Scholarship," *A.H.R.*, xxviii. 215–227 (1923).

understood that arrangements have been made for an Italian version.[1] Mr. Lea's most mature work is the *History of the Inquisition of Spain*,[2] toward which all the efforts of his later years were directed. The subject is intricate and thorny; the materials were for the most part unprinted and uncalendared; and, except for certain publications of the author, scarcely anything had been done in the way of preliminary exploration or monographic investigation. Under such conditions the historian was obliged to be quarry-man as well as architect, and the four solid volumes which he produced were fashioned out of the living rock of original documents. It was characteristic of the author that when he found the first draft of the work too long for purposes of publication, he took up calmly the task of rewriting the whole at the age of nearly eighty. Rarely has so significant an institution been so sanely and comprehensively studied, and rarely has the reader been placed in so good a position to observe its workings and draw his own conclusions from the evidence presented. There is no striving for dramatic effect; the nature of the Holy Office is manifested in its normal operations rather than in the sensational episodes of its history, and its significance is shown to lie "not so much in the awful solemnities of the auto de fe, or in the cases of a few celebrated victims, as in the silent influence exercised by its incessant and secret labours among the mass of the people and in the limitations which it placed upon the Spanish intellect." The narrative is sober and self-contained and there is little moralizing, but the general tendencies of the system are impressively pointed out, and the great lesson taught by the history of the Inquisition is declared to be "that the attempt of man to control the conscience of his fellows reacts upon himself," and that "the unity of faith which was the ideal of statesmen and churchmen alike in the sixteenth century is fatal to the healthful spirit of competition through which progress, material and moral, is fostered." Such a conclusion will not command universal assent, and

[1] Written in 1909. See now Chapter X, p. 194, note.

[2] Cf. my reviews of the successive volumes of this work in *The Nation* (New York), lxxxii. 385–387 (1906); lxxxiv. 455–457 (1907); and lxxxvi. 262–263 (1908).

much of Mr. Lea's work has been sharply attacked from the side of the Roman Catholic church. Such institutions as the Inquisition, the confessional, and the celibacy of the clergy have long been the subject of acute controversy, and their history touches issues of living moment. Mr. Lea might assert his lack of polemic purpose and declare his ideal of history to be "a serious attempt to ascertain the severest truth as to the past and to set it forth without fear or favour"; he might mitigate the conventional horrors of the Spanish Inquisition, and even contrast its enlightened treatment of the witch-delusion with the witch-burnings of Protestant Europe; but the deductions from his investigations were generally unfavourable to the ecclesiastical system, and it is not surprising that Roman Catholic writers have impugned his accuracy, and even his good faith.[1] Still, fair-minded Catholics acknowledge his merits, and in course of time his works will be recognized as having added materially to the body of fact, considerable even now, upon which both Protestant and Catholic historians are in funda-mental agreement. Lord Acton not only pronounced the *History of the Inquisition of the Middle Ages* to be "the most important contribution of the new world to the religious history of the old," but declared that its essential parts "constitute a sound and solid structure that will survive the censure of all critics." [2] The Abbé Vacandard, author of the best volume on the Inquisition written from the Catholic point of view, while he denies the finality of the work, accepts Reusch's characterization of it as "l'histoire de l'Inquisition la plus étendue, la plus profonde et la plus fouillée que nous possédions." [3] Even Mr. Lea's latest assailant, Monsignore Baumgarten, cannot close without expressing "esteem and admiration for his industry, his endurance and undisputed results." [4]

---

[1] Beside numerous articles in reviews, see particularly P. H. Casey, *Notes on A History of Auricular Confession: H. C. Lea's Account of the Power of the Keys in the Early Church* (Philadelphia, 1899); and P. M. Baumgarten, *Henry Charles Lea's Historical Writings: a Critical Inquiry into their Method and Merit* (New York, 1909); and cf. the other judgements noted, Chapter X, p. 194, note 1.

[2] *The History of Freedom and other Essays*, pp. 551, 574.

[3] *L'Inquisition* (Paris, 1907), p. vii.

[4] *Henry Charles Lea's Historical Writings*, p. 143.

Personally Mr. Lea had the modesty, the candour, the serenity, and the unselfish devotion of the truly great scholar. He was generous of his time and his learning to others, as I can personally testify, and many beginners in difficult tasks of research look back with gratitude to his advice and encouragement. Recalling his own intellectual isolation in the early years of his studies, he watched with pleasure the growing circle of well trained scholars in the United States, and looked forward with assurance to the future of the American school of history. Such optimism was characteristic of the man, but it also belonged to a view of history which held that the study of the past in the scientific spirit would render us not only more tolerant of outgrown ethical standards, but also "more impatient of the present and yet more hopeful of the future." [1]

CHARLES GROSS [2]

Charles Gross was born in Troy, New York, 10 February, 1857, the son of Louis and Lottie (Wolf) Gross, and died in Cambridge, 3 December, 1909. He was prepared for college at the Troy High School, where he led his class, and he maintained the same rank at Williams College, from which he graduated in 1878. After a short period of teaching in Troy he went abroad for travel and study, first at the universities of Leipzig, Berlin, Paris, and Göttingen, later in the libraries and archives of England. He received the degree of Ph.D. from Göttingen in 1883, the honorary degrees of A.M. from Harvard in 1901 and LL.D. from Williams in 1904. In 1888 he came to Harvard as instructor in history, and was advanced to an assistant professorship in 1892 and in 1901 to a professorship of history—after 1908 with the title of Gurney professor of history and political science. He became a Member of the Massachusetts Historical Society in 1901; he also served as vice-president of the American Jewish Historical Society and was a corresponding member of the Royal Historical Society.

[1] See his presidential address on "Ethical Values in History," in the *American Historical Review*, ix. 233–246.
[2] Reprinted from Massachusetts Historical Society, *Proceedings*, xlix. 161–166 (December, 1915).

Throughout his life Gross was a tireless seeker after knowledge. He had a remarkable power of intense and sustained work, and he never spared himself. His love of study for its own sake appeared in his college years, when his room-mate regularly left him at his desk at night and found him there in the morning. His interest in history likewise declared itself at college, and after he had laid his foundations under such European masters as Pauli, Bresslau, and Monod, he devoted himself single-heartedly to the advancement of historical learning by research and teaching. As the field of his special interests he early selected the history of English institutions in the Middle Ages, and like his friend Liebermann, also a pupil of Pauli, he brought the critical and systematic methods of Continental scholarship to bear upon the vast and comparatively unexplored resources of the English records. He had the advantage of some years of work in the British Museum and Public Record Office before he took up academic duties in America, and he used every subsequent opportunity to return to these hunting-grounds, as well as to utilize the valuable collection of books which he gathered about himself in the Harvard library. He avoided no subject because of its difficulty or obscurity, and shrank from no labour which his investigations might demand, so that his works are models of thoroughness and accuracy; but he also brought to his studies qualities of insight, balance, and perfect lucidity of thought and statement which made him an acknowledged master in his profession. Among English historians he chiefly admired Maitland, most of all for the flashes of intuition and inspiration which he found wanting in himself; but if he lacked something of Maitland's brilliancy, he was not inferior in the sureness of his judgement or the solidity of his learning.

The promise of noteworthy achievement was shown in Gross's first piece of historical work, his doctoral dissertation entitled *Gilda Mercatoria*, which riddled prevailing theories and placed the history of English gilds upon a new foundation of established fact. After prolonged research in local records this was enlarged into his *Gild Merchant*, published in 1890, and still the standard authority upon the subject. A *Bibliography of British Municipal History* followed in 1897, preliminary to a comprehensive work on English municipal institutions, which never advanced beyond a series of articles on special aspects of the subject. Although not a lawyer and modestly disclaiming acquaintance with the law, Gross contributed two important volumes to the legal records published by the Selden Society— *Select Cases from the Coroners' Rolls* (1896) and *Select Cases concerning the Law Merchant* (1908)—both accompanied by historical introductions of much value. Significant brief contributions dealt with such topics as the Exchequer of the Jews, the jurisdiction of the Court of Exchequer, the law of intestacy, and the early history of the ballot. His best-known work is *The Sources and Literature of English History from the Earliest Times to about 1485*, which appeared in 1900, and at once took rank as an indispensable instrument of investigation and an unsurpassed example of bibliographical workmanship. It became the model of the bibliography of the modern period undertaken co-operatively by the Royal Historical Society and the American Historical Association, which are attempting by the joint efforts of several scholars what Gross accomplished for his field unaided and alone. It was entirely characteristic of its author that he should have devoted to lightening the labours of others long years which he was free to give to his own more special studies; and only those who followed the progress of his work can appreciate the thorough preparation that went into its brief and meaty comments, and the months of drudgery spent in verification and in going through masses of material in which he had no personal interest. A labour which sometimes taxed the patience of the administration of the British Museum never exceeded his powers. The later months of his life were occupied with the preparation of a new edition, which has been completed and published (1915), with the co-operation of his family, under the direction of a committee of his Harvard colleagues.

As a teacher Gross showed the same qualities of clearness, thoroughness, and sanity which appeared in his books. He lectured in a high voice with much emphatic repetition, and his manner and the subjects of his courses appealed rather to the advanced than to the elementary student, but he attracted undergraduates who looked forward to law as well as those who were to continue the study of history. While he also gave instruction in the history of France and of municipal institutions in the Middle Ages, his favourite course was History 9, the constitutional history of England to the sixteenth century. Expounding with great care the *Select Charters* of Stubbs, he summed up with admirable judgement and precision the chief problems of early English institutions in a way that made a profound impression upon his students and held before them the highest ideals of historical scholarship. His methods of work were instilled even more completely into the small number of those whom he directed in special problems of investigation, which he selected with much skill and discernment and which generally led the young investigators to follow up their researches in England. To these he gave of his time and learning with the greatest freedom, and his weekly conferences were occasions for searching yet kindly criticism. He can hardly be said to have founded a school, yet by their teaching and publications in European history his pupils have made perhaps the largest contribution of any single group of American scholars to that field, as may be seen from such names as Colby of McGill, Cross of Michigan, Gray of Bryn Mawr, Hemmeon of Nova Scotia, Lapsley of Trinity College, Cambridge, Lunt of Cornell, McIlwain of Harvard, Morris of California, Perkins of Ohio State University, Sullivan and Wolfson of New York, Trenholme of Missouri, and Wells, formerly of the University of Minnesota. His influence also extended beyond his classroom to men like Baldwin of Vassar, whose elaborate work on the king's council owed its inception to Gross. Though he never taught modern history, men like H. Nelson Gay and the late William Garrott Brown freely acknowledged their indebtedness to his instruction. His mind was concrete rather than philosophic, and he had little interest in the history of ideas or of civilization, limitations which showed themselves less in the content of his instruction than in his obvious lack of real interest in subjects, such as Gothic architecture, which he explained with clearness and skill. The enthusiasm which students caught from him came partly from his deep interest in the history of institutions, partly from his obvious candour and love of truth and thoroughness. One of those who studied longest with him—Lapsley—writes:

> From this distance one looks back on Gross's training as primarily moral. I think it would have horrified him to hear it put so, for he took good care that one acquired certain information and certain indispensable proficiencies. But all that could have been obtained in other quarters, and one remembers him chiefly as letting in upon one with increasing intensity and explicitness the pressure of certain moral necessities. He required of himself and of others truth in the inward parts and was unmindful of praise or reputation. What he cared for was that the work would be done, not who should have the credit of doing it.

Save for his constant attendance at college baseball games, Gross did not evince interest in the ordinary forms of undergraduate activity, but he had a deep and abiding affection for the university of his adoption. He took an active part in the administrative work of Harvard, serving on the administrative board of the College and on numerous committees, and acting for nine years as chairman of the department of history and government. He was active in the establishment of the *American Historical Review* and of the *Harvard Historical Studies*, assisting in the publication of the first fourteen volumes of the Harvard series and giving the last hours of his working life to revising the proofs of the book of his pupil Morris on "The Frankpledge." In the Harvard Library,[1] where so much of his time was spent, he is commemorated by a special fund for the purchase of books concerning English history.

Outside of academic walls Gross's life was the patient, uneventful life of the scholar. He cared little for general travel, and did not return to the Continent till shortly before his death, when he visited Normandy and spent some weeks in Spain and

---

[1] Since this was written, the Harvard Menorah Society has placed a tablet in the Historical Seminary Room in the Widener Library, commemorating "Charles Gross, 1857–1909, for twenty-one years a teacher of history in this University, guide, friend, seeker after knowledge, a great scholar."

Sicily. So far as possible he gave his vacations to work in London, where he also passed two sabbatical years. He regularly took lodgings in the neighbourhood of the Public Record Office or the British Museum, and his long sojourns made him a familiar figure in Bloomsbury. To many of his friends he is associated most closely with the precincts of the Museum. W. J. Ashley, who had known him in the Göttingen days and was for many years his colleague at Harvard, wrote of their last meeting: "It is not of American sunshine, but of a gray day in London that I think when I recall that steady, quiet, unemotional, solitary, purposeful worker—*ohne Hast, ohne Rast.*" Gross knew his London as do few Americans, and delighted to show its historic spots to friends or pupils. He had few distractions beyond a dinner at some quiet restaurant, coffee at intervals in the day somewhere near his work, and long walks about the streets after hours. His professional associations, too, were with the scholars of London and those who frequented its libraries and archives rather than with Oxford or Cambridge dons. Hubert Hall, who was probably closer to Gross than was any one else in London, writes of their friendship:

I do not remember exactly how this bond of sympathy was shaped or when it was perfected, but since the year 1892, or thereabouts, I have been accustomed to rely upon his knowledge of certain aspects of medieval history very much as I would rely upon the Records themselves. Further than this, I have been accustomed to rely upon his judgment of historical values as I would rely upon that of my own banker or broker in mundane affairs. But it was not the play of human emotion nor the display of intellectual strength that gave to myself and, I am sure, to many others, this feeling of security in his historical cooperation. I think that it was rather the perception of strength reserved and the consciousness that it could be applied when necessary with the force and precision of hydraulic power! This impression accords with my experience of Gross as a correspondent and as a companion. His letters were for the most part extremely brief and laconic; but every sentence was weighed and every sentiment was measured. Equally characteristic was his conversation. He would sit unmoved, smoking sedately, while men talked at random on subjects that he alone, perhaps, knew how to deal with adequately. When appealed to, he would deliver himself, in a matter-of-fact style, of the true solution of the difficulty without the slightest show of impatience or dogmatism. So when you were alone with him, he would ask questions at short intervals in the manner of one who thinks aloud, and indeed at such times as he was not absorbed in work his mind was actively pursuing some train of learned thought.

Naturally modest and retiring, Gross mixed little in the general society of his academic community, and the distressing and long-continued illness of his wife isolated him still further from the world. He was, however, no recluse, and he delighted in the companionship of colleagues and pupils, both in Cambridge and in London. His former students in particular could always count on the helpfulness and friendship which were characteristic of a singularly unselfish and loyal nature. In every activity of his life he carried more than his share of work and responsibility, and under the most trying circumstances he neither held back nor complained. The only things that taxed his patience were superficiality, sham, and attempts at deception. A great scholar, he brought into every task the scholar's devotion and a certain large simplicity of purpose, and his historical work was merely one expression of a deep sincerity of life and character.

INDEXES

INDEX OF MANUSCRIPTS AND LIBRARIES

Unless otherwise indicated, the library is in each case the public library of the town.

GENERAL INDEX

Michel de Cerizy, 218, 232, 233.
Microcosmus, 180.
Milan, 75, 180, 181, 189, 221, 246.
Mileto, 95.
Milo de Châtillon-Nanteuil, bishop of Beauvais, 254.
Minorites, 65. See Franciscans.
Miraumont, 222.
Moamyn, writer on falconry, 111, 117, 129.
Modena, 75, 174.
Moeller, C., 194, 237.
'Moimer,' 223.
Molin, H., 130.
Molinier, A., 45.
Molinier, C., 196, 198, 233, 245.
Monaci, E., 140, 142.
Monasteries as intellectual centres, 94 ff.
Money, requests for, 7–15.
Monod, G., 263.
Montagnone, G. di, 142.
Mont-Aimé, 222, 230, 239, 243.
Monte Cassino, 186.
Monte Santangelo, 95.
Montfaucon, B. de, 166.
Montmorillon, 223.
Montpellier, 5, 9, 23, 26, 27, 50.
Mont-Saint-Michel, 95.
Moore, C. H., 83.
Moralities, 120 f.
Morandi, L., 140.
Moravia, 16.
Morelli, C., 171.
Morris, W. A., 265, 266.
Mortet, V., 42.
Moses of Bergamo, 99.
Mosher, J. A., 40.
Mount Cenis, 95.
Mousket, P., 198, 199, 210 f., 219 f., 221, 223, 224, 229, 230, 239, 243.
Müller, K., 198, 199, 245, 252, 253.
Müller, K. E., 199.
Munich, 6, 12.
Munro, D. C., 40.
Muratori, L. A., 128, 129, 143.
Murray, H. J. R., 120, 121.
Murus largus, 238.

Murus strictus, 238.
'Musciac,' 207.
Music, Arabic, 100; *cantus Uticensis*, 95; *filie carminis*, 69; instrumental, 15, 28, 33, 62; vocal, 28, 62, 70; singing-lessons, 88.

Naples, 5, 7, 26, 30, 75, 129, 136, 138, 139, 140.
Narbonne, 33.
Narratio, 3, 9, 171, 181, 187.
'National hands,' 95 f.
Nebuchadnezzar, 169.
Necromancy, 68.
Neilson, G., 110.
Nemesianus, 107.
Netherlands, 98, 231.
Nevers, 201, 203, 206; diocese of, 203.
Nicholas of Breslau, 21.
'Nicholas the Fish,' 118.
Nicholas of Iamsilla, 128.
Nicholas, St., 34, 63; feast of, 34, 69; miracles of, 95.
Nicola della Rocca, 133, 134 f.
Nicolaitanes, 69.
Nicolas de Brie, bishop of Troyes, 223, 230, 235, 239.
Nicolas de Nonancourt, 45, 55, 60, 69.
Nicolas de Roie, bishop of Noyon, 218, 220, 230, 233.
Niemann, G., 84.
Niese, H., 125, 127, 134, 140.
Nietzsche, F., 124.
Nieules, 66.
Nigel Wireker, 73.
Nivernais, 198, 203, 204, 222.
Nominalism, 85, 86.
Non-residence, 48 f.
Norman Conquest, 161.
Normandy, 95, 244, 266.
Norway, 111.
Notae Sancti Amati Duacenses, 221.
Note-taking, 56.
Notre Dame, 42, 58.
Novalese, 95.
Novati, F., 79.
Noyon, council of, 254; diocese of, 232, 241.